1969

❦

Milton's
Epic
Characters

❦

❦ ❦ ❦

Milton's Epic Characters

❦ ❦ ❦

Image and Idol

by
John M. Steadman

The University of North Carolina Press
Chapel Hill

Manufactured in the United States of America
Library of Congress Catalog Card Number 68–14363

TO

John Marcellus Steadman, Jr.

(1889–1945)

AND

Medora Rice Rembert Steadman

(1890–1938)

Foreword

❦ This volume explores the intellectual background of *Paradise Lost* and *Paradise Regain'd*, with particular emphasis on problems of characterization. Though its end is literary criticism, its method is primarily that of the history of ideas.

Like all "secondary" epics, and indeed far more than most, Milton's heroic poems build on buried foundations. They rise (like Schliemann's Troy) on the glories and detritus of the past, substructures that we may regard alternatively as the work of "giants old"—or of dwarfs. But the groundwork is important for the later edifice, and the task of uncovering it belongs to the literary historian no less than to the archaeologist.

The following chapters are, therefore, "exploratory diggings" into the strata of ideas and motifs beneath Milton's Renaissance architecture, the older foundations that underlie and support his "vast design." Though one cannot hope to uncover them *in toto* (whether medieval or Renaissance, classical or Hebraic, they are far too extensive for that), one can, nevertheless, sink a few tentative shafts, lay a cross-trench or two at selected sites—and endeavor thereby to throw additional light on the intricacy of the problems involved. So complex, so varied a poem as *Paradise Lost* or its sequel requires a corresponding variety and complexity in methodology. A strictly unilateral approach can be not only severely limited but seriously misleading. Hence I have attempted to approach Milton's major poetry from different angles and through distinct, though interrelated, disciplines. Rhetoric and logic, ethics and poetics, theology and iconology—all of these arts or sciences contributed to the fabric of his poems, influencing their matter as well as their form. With equal propriety they may become the concern of the literary critic and scholar.

Though originally conceived as components of a single study, most of the chapters in this volume have been published separately in American and European journals. In assembling them here for the first time, I have made various revisions, enlarging some, curtailing others, translating most of the foreign-language quotations in the text, reducing documentation, and adding a few necessary appendixes.

For Heraclitus, "Character is Fate." For Milton, it is (in a very special sense) this and much more. Character is inseparable from ethical decision. It reveals itself not only in external action but also in the internal choice (proairesis) that precedes the course of action. Though the latter may be overruled by a "higher power"—directed and governed not by Heraclitean Fate but by Christian Providence—the act itself, insofar as it is voluntary, is both the index and result of Character, the consequence of moral intent. In the Miltonic epic, accordingly, Character and Plot are closely interinvolved; the type of choice made by the principal *personae* plays a determining role in the epic action. The texture of the poetic Fable thus becomes a complex skein of conflicting wills—conflicting, but woven nevertheless into a single coherent pattern by the unified vision of Providence. Milton's ethics and theology are, consequently, of vital significance for his poetics. To analyze the chief actors in his epics one must place them in their proper moral and religious context, reviewing them in the light of Renaissance conceptions of the heroic *Ethos* and comparing them with Milton's own practice elsewhere, notably in *Samson Agonistes*.

In this study I shall not reopen the issue of the "hero" of *Paradise Lost*. As Waldock observed some years ago, this is largely a matter of phrasing. It is enough to say that in the language of Renaissance criticism, Adam—the central figure of the poem—is clearly the "epic person" or "primary hero."[1] It is he who receives first mention in the proposition; it is his action that constitutes the nominal argument of *Paradise Lost*.

The problem of the appropriate moral formula (fortitude, wisdom, magnanimity, etc.) for an epic hero has been explored in my book

1. Cf. A. J. A. Waldock, *Paradise Lost and Its Critics* (Cambridge, 1947), pp. 1–2; Bernardo de Balbuena, *El Bernardo*, in *Biblioteca de Autores Españoles . . . Poemas Epicas*, ed. Cayetano Rosell (Madrid, 1851), I, 140; Malatesta Porta, "Il Rossi," in Torquato Tasso, *Opere* (Florence, 1724), VI, 264.

Milton and the Renaissance Hero (Oxford, 1967). The relationship between characterization and rhetorical discourse in Milton's epics has received attention in my essay "*Ethos* and *Dianoia*: Rhetoric and Character in *Paradise Lost*," included in *Language and Style in Milton* (ed. Ronald David Emma and John T. Shawcross [New York, 1967]). The reader should bear in mind Aristotle's basic distinction between Fable, Character, and Thought; his requirement that Character be "good," "appropriate," "like the reality," and "consistent"; and his insistence that both Character and Fable should meet the requirements of necessity and probability.[2]

Renaissance theory brought to poetics the same studied gravity it imposed on the plastic arts. Just as it tended to approach the heroic poem in terms of Aristotle's *Poetics*, so it usually interpreted the *Poetics* in terms of the *Nicomachean Ethics* and *Politics*. The result was to emphasize the intellectual element in poetry, to rationalize the relationship between Character and Action, to underline the importance of probability and necessity in Plot and Character alike, and to stress the logical or rhetorical method of the speeches by the various *personae*. *Mythos*, *Ethos*, *Dianoia* (Fable, Character, and Thought)—Aristotle had rationalized all three; and in theory, if not always in practice, Renaissance poets found it difficult to escape the limitations of this philosophical attitude towards the problems of literary composition. The tight logical structure of Milton's epic and the prominence he assigns to the analysis of the causes and effects of the central action reflect this rationalistic approach to the epic plot.[3] Equally significant is his apparently disproportionate emphasis on Character and Thought in relation to the Fable. "Apparently"—for, though he seems to differ considerably from Aristotle on this point, his orientation remains strikingly similar. Indeed it is his predominantly logical approach to these problems (the relationships between Fable, Character, and Thought) that has carried him a step or two beyond the Stagyrite.

2. See Aristotle, *On the Art of Poetry*, trans. Ingram Bywater (Oxford, 1951), pp. 36, 38, 66: "The Fable . . . is simply . . . the combination of the incidents . . . in the story. . . . Character is what makes us ascribe certain moral qualities to the agents; and Thought is shown in all they say when proving a particular point or . . . enunciating a general truth." Thought, in other words, is simply "the power of saying whatever can be said, or what is appropriate to the occasion," and the critic must not confuse it with Character. In the speeches of tragedy (and in epic dialogue as well) the element of Thought belongs properly to Politics and Rhetoric. "The older poets make their personages discourse like statesmen"; the "moderns" make them speak "like rhetoricians." Finally, "the Thought of the [dramatic] personages is shown in everything to be effected by their language—in every effort to prove or disprove, to arouse emotion (pity, fear, anger, and the like), or to maximize or minimize things."

3. Cf. Dennis H. Burden, *The Logical Epic: A Study of the Argument of Paradise Lost* (London, 1967); Ernest Sirluck, *Paradise Lost, A Deliberate Epic* (Cambridge, 1967); G. A. Wilkes, *The Thesis of Paradise Lost* (Melbourne, 1961).

The striking fact about *Paradise Lost* is how closely Milton has articulated these three elements. Structurally the Fable hinges on the temptation-scene, and the core of this scene is an act of moral choice. The plot is so organized as to give maximum emphasis to Character. (This is also true of *Paradise Regain'd* and *Samson Agonistes*, and is partly responsible for some of the difficulties that critics have experienced in interpreting these poems.) The techniques that precipitate this crisis, however, are rhetorical and belong accordingly to *Dianoia*, the primary instrument whereby the crucial spiritual battle of the poem is waged. In Fable, Character, and Thought alike, Milton conforms, on the whole, to neo-Aristotelian principles; it is chiefly in their relative importance that he seems to diverge. His basic orientation is decidedly in the direction of Aristotelian rationalism, and the result is a poem more logical, more tightly conceived and articulated, than any of the epics or tragedies lauded in the *Poetics*.

For permission to reprint material published elsewhere, I am indebted to the editors of the *Journal of the Warburg and Courtauld Institutes, Harvard Theological Review, Anglia, Studies in Philology, Journal of the History of Ideas, University of Toronto Quarterly, Modern Philology, Review of English Studies, Modern Language Review, Modern Language Notes, Philological Quarterly, Emory University Quarterly, Neophilologus, Modern Language Quarterly, Archiv für das Studium der neueren Sprachen und Literaturen*, and *Journal of English and Germanic Philology*.

I am grateful to Dr. A. L. Rowse, of All Souls College and the Huntington Library, for reading the manuscript and suggesting revisions. I should also like to express my appreciation to my colleagues of the Henry E. Huntington Library, to the staffs of the Bodleian Library, British Museum, and Taylorian Institute, and to the scholars with whom it has been my privilege to read Milton—Professor Thomas H. English, Professor Robert R. Cawley, Professor Maurice Kelley, and Miss K. M. Lea. To their advice and inspiration I owe an incalculable debt.

John M. Steadman
The Henry E. Huntington Library
San Marino, California

Contents

List of Abbreviations

ELH	*English Literary History*
JEGP	*Journal of English and Germanic Philology*
MLN	*Modern Language Notes*
MLQ	*Modern Language Quarterly*
MP	*Modern Philology*
N & Q	*Notes and Queries*
PMLA	*Publications of the Modern Language Association of America*
PQ	*Philological Quarterly*
RES	*Review of English Studies*
SP	*Studies in Philology*
TLS	*The Times Literary Supplement*
UTQ	*University of Toronto Quarterly*

Milton's
Epic
Characters

1. *Introduction*

Mimesis and Idea

❦ *Paradise Lost*, as its apologists and detractors alike remind us, is often dismissed as a "monument to dead ideas." This sepulchral verdict falls short of justice and accuracy, but it does reflect a certain half-truth. Milton's world is no longer our world. The realities of the seventeenth century have become the myths, the "superstitions and traditions," of the twentieth.

The most striking feature of this charge, however, is not its limited validity but its virtually unique application to *Paradise Lost*. Both temporally and spiritually the worlds of Homer and Virgil are even more remote from us, yet critics do not pronounce the *Odyssey* or the *Aeneid* intellectually dead or hold coroner's inquests to determine the causes of decease. Lucretius' philosophical epic *On the Nature of Things* would be valid only for the school of Epicurus, but scholars rarely conduct post mortems over its corpse. If Milton's theology seems primitive to some observers, surely that of Homer and Virgil is much more archaic. If Milton's cosmology seems antiquated, Lucretius' is even more old-fashioned. Yet our contemporaries rarely condemn any of these classical poems on such grounds. The criterion of intellectual modernity is a yardstick they reserve to measure—and berate—the author of *Paradise Lost*.

First published, in somewhat different form, in *The Emory University Quarterly*, XX, No. 2 (1964), 67–80.

Nor has the aesthetic relevance of this criterion been adequately established. If *Paradise Lost* is a monument to dead ideas, so is a Greek temple. So are the statues of the Hellenic and Roman pantheons. Yet how absurd it would be to dismiss the ruins at Delphi and Phygalia on the grounds that one no longer believes in the cult of Apollo! How irrelevant to reject the Elgin marbles as mere vestiges of ancient superstitions! If Milton's ideas are "dead," so are many of the ideas of Shakespeare and Marlowe and Donne. If we carried this charge against Milton to its logical conclusions, we should be left not with a literary tradition, but with a literary necropolis. Instead of the "lifeblood of a masterspirit," we should possess merely a stately mausoleum enshrining "death in a handful of dust." Our literature would be infinitely the poorer for such sophisticated naïveté, such critical impertinence.

But is not this accusation actually a tacit recognition of the nature and character of *Paradise Lost*? a paradoxical tribute to its very excellence? Milton's poem has been called a "cosmic epic"—but the cosmos it represents is the universe of the seventeenth century. It has also been termed a "Biblical epic" and a "theological epic"—but both Biblical scholarship and theological study have changed radically since Milton's day. In raising the charge of intellectual obsolescence, the critic is indirectly acknowledging the poet's claim to be taken seriously. If Milton had not committed himself to delineating a seventeenth-century world-view or if his expression of this view had been less profound, less comprehensive, and less compelling, this accusation would have been superfluous. Ironically the charge of retailing "dead ideas" stems from his very success in embodying the intellectual outlook of his age.

Nevertheless, the problems raised by this accusation are neither minor nor secondary. They lie at the very core of Renaissance poetics. From the Italian theorists of "that sublime art which . . . teaches what the laws are of a true epic poem," Milton had learned to think of his art as essentially mimetic. Its value for society resided primarily in the truths it depicted and in the vitality of its imitation. *Paradise Lost* was, accordingly, both "an imitation of an action"—man's fall and expulsion from Eden—and an imitation of a system of ideas, the moral and physical universe of seventeenth-century Puritanism. Its argument and larger intellectual content were alike based on solid truth, and in the poet's own eyes the poem's value derived largely from this fact. Today, however, both Milton's subject and his *Weltanschauung* have lost much of their reality, and the status of the poem itself has undergone a significant change. For the modern reader, *Paradise Lost* is no longer an imitation of eternal truth, but an imitation of seventeenth-century opinion. The epic has changed with the reality it sought to express. The relationship between the poem and the poet's world—between *mimesis* and *idea*—has altered, and critic and scholar alike must face the implications of this change.

I

The Renaissance poet was a "committed" artist. Aristotle had taught him that poetics is a branch of ethics and politics and that poetry is more philosophical than history because it imitates the "idea." From Horace he had learned that poetry should "profit or delight" and that Homer was a better moralist than such philosophers as Chrysippus and Crantor. Most literary theorists shared Milton's belief in the poet's ability to teach over "the whole book of sanctity through all the instances of example" and his power "to inbreed and cherish in a great people the seeds of virtue and public civility." Most would have approved, in principle at least, of his verdict on Spenser as "a better teacher than Scotus or Aquinas." The question of the moral, political, and theological validity of *Paradise Lost* would have been a crucial issue for Milton and for most Renaissance theorists.

Nevertheless, the poet's didactic office was not restricted to ethics and the related disciplines of politics and theology. Like their classical predecessors, Renaissance critics laid heavy stress on the ideal of the learned poet—the *poeta doctus*—who took all knowledge as his province and who gave poetic expression to the basic principles of all arts and sciences. The apologists for poetry extolled their art as the fountainhead of all branches of learning. Commentators discovered in Homer, Virgil, and Dante a veritable encyclopaedia of erudition. The authors of the *Odyssey*, the *Aeneid*, and the *Divina Commedia* were (it appeared) not merely moralists and theologians, but also astronomers, physicists, logicians, and mathematicians. Milton conceived his own role in terms of this tradition. He rivals Dante as the supreme exemplar of the *poeta doctus* in Western vernacular literature, and his epic ranks with Dante's in the breadth and universality of its learning. If the greater part of this erudition has lost its original value, then *Paradise Lost* has suffered an analogous loss. Its scope and nature have been altered, and its original relationship to reality—or to reality as Milton and his age conceived it —has been radically changed.

This disparity between the reality which Milton sought to portray and the reality in which his modern reader believes is further complicated by the altered historical status of his argument. For Milton, the "whole Subject" of his epic—"*Mans disobedience, and the loss thereupon of Paradise*"—was historical fact. Founded as it was on divine testimony, it possessed an authenticity and intrinsic value denied to most heroic poetry. The romantic epics of Ariosto and Boiardo centered upon the fictitious exploits of heroes largely legendary or entirely fabulous.

Though Homer and Virgil had received praise for basing their arguments on fact, both had long been charged with historical inaccuracies. Milton's condemnation of his predecessors for celebrating "fabl'd Knights in Battels feign'd" ranged him with Tasso on the side of truth. For both poets, the historical validity of the epic argument represented a principle of major aesthetic importance. Tasso devoted considerable space to this point in his *Discorsi del Poema Eroico*, and Milton's early plans for an epic centered on some "King or knight before the Conquest" indicated his intention to base his subject on national history.

Tasso's principles underlie Milton's heroic poem as well as his own *Gerusalemme Liberata*. Beginning with a sharp dichotomy between fiction and history ("The matter, which can also be called the argument, . . . is either feigned . . . or is taken from histories"), the *Discorsi* argued that verisimilitude required the poet to base his argument on historical fact, for it was not "*verisimile*" that "an illustrious action, like those he is treating, should not have been written down and transmitted to posterity by the pen of some historian. . . ." Moreover, a purely fictitious subject would have much less authority for the audience and less power to arouse its emotions. "Esteeming such actions false, the readers do not lightly yield consent to what the author has written—to those things which ought to move them alternately to wrath, pity, sorrow, vain joy, suspense, or rapture. In short, they do not await the outcome of events with the eagerness they feel when they deem these actions wholly or partially true. For where faith is wanting, the capacity to arouse passion and pleasure in the reader is also missing." Accordingly, the "argument of the most excellent epic ought to be based on history"—and, more specifically, on the history of a true religion. By drawing his argument from Christian history, the poet could reconcile the conflicting claims of verisimilitude and the epic marvelous.

In both of his epics one finds Milton's practice conforming to Tasso's theory. The chief point of difference is the type of Christian history the two poets preferred. Whereas Milton took his subject from the Bible itself, Tasso based the argument of his *Gerusalemme Liberata* on accounts of the First Crusade. Though less authoritative and less sacrosanct than Holy Writ, such secular sources possessed, in his opinion, one distinct advantage; they allowed the poet greater scope for his own invention and greater freedom in organizing his material. In the case of *Paradise Lost* and Tasso's *Il Mondo Creato*, however, the limitations imposed by a scriptural subject were less apparent. The summary nature of the early chapters of Genesis left both poets free to embellish, amplify, and reorganize the story of the creation without distorting Biblical truth.

For the modern reader, Milton's argument no longer represents historical fact, and as a result it has lost much of its original authority.

The aesthetic values Tasso finds in a subject based on historical truth no longer seem relevant to *Paradise Lost.* For the seventeenth-century reader, Milton's epic was the imitation of an historical action. For the twentieth-century reader, on the other hand, it is merely the imitation of a myth. Biblical scholarship and anthropology have rendered its interpretation of Genesis obsolete. Though a reader may still find Adam's story symbolically significant, Milton would undoubtedly have found a purely symbolic reading altogether inadequate. For him, the narrative of the Fall was literally, as well as allegorically, true.

Even more drastic in its effect on Milton's poem has been the disintegration of Milton's world—the progressive dismemberment of the seventeenth-century universe by modern science. For a seventeenth-century reader, *Paradise Lost* was a miniature cosmos, a compendium of encyclopaedic range and breadth. Not only did it represent "Heav'n, Hell, Earth, Chaos, All." It also represented a systematic, coherent, and universally accepted world-view. It represented the basic principles of many of the traditional arts and sciences—theology, metaphysics, ethics, politics, psychology, astronomy, and natural history. It embodied the very structure of truth.

Since Milton's day, however, science has usurped much of his domain. Biology contradicts his account of the origin of species. Chemistry has multiplied his four elements to upwards of ninety. Physics has severed the links in his chain of being and smashed his "scale of Nature." Astronomy has shattered his cosmos—not only the compact Ptolemaic world, constructed like a Chinese toy, sphere within sphere and orb within orb, but also its Copernican alternative. The dimensions of the twentieth-century universe would have staggered the angelic intellect of Milton's Raphael. For a world barely six millennia old, geology substitutes an earth whose years are reckoned in millions.

The "little world of man" has altered with the greater. The microcosm has changed with the macrocosm. Physiology has banished the ancient analogies between the structure of the universe and that of the human body. A more complex psychology has superseded the simpler "faculty psychology" which divided the human psyche into three distinct souls and pictured Reason as a charioteer guiding the unruly passions of Wrath and Desire. Archaeological discoveries have altered our views of chronology; Michael's survey of world history in the final books of *Paradise Lost* has lost conviction. Anthropology and comparative religion have modified our attitudes towards other faiths; we no longer regard the myths of the Gentiles as fabulous corruptions of Biblical truth or the pagan deities as masks of the devil. The structure of truth has changed, and in the light of the new learning much of Milton's erudition appears obsolescent and invalid.

The "New Philosophy calls all in doubt." Donne's observation was prophetic. Even as Milton wrote, the intellectual forces which would ultimately destroy his world were at work. The genesis of modern science has been as disastrous as that of the goddess Athene—or that of Milton's Sin. It has shattered the older wisdom which gave it birth.

Milton and his age seem separated from us by an impassable gulf. The flood of new ideas, the currents of modern thought, have swept away the world he knew and believed in, just as the first deluge swept away the earthly Paradise. What is left for us is the structure of his poetry, the edifice of his poetic imagination—still afloat, like Noah's ark, still stemming the tides of intellectual change, still steering between a "world destroy'd and world restor'd."

Let us pursue the architectural metaphor with which we began. *Paradise Lost* is not merely a monument *to* ideas; it is also a monument *of* ideas. In other words, it possesses two sorts of structure—a poetic structure (and this provides its basic form) and an intellectual structure, a structure of ideas (and this provides its basic content). The first is, to a very considerable extent, an "imitation" of the second, an attempt to realize it in poetic form. The two structures are not identical, but they are nevertheless closely interrelated. They do not coincide, but they overlap. And to understand the one, the reader must also understand the other.

The gulf that separates our world from Milton's world has tended to distort both types of structure. The intellectual structure no longer carries complete conviction. The "new Philosophy" has shattered it. And because it has been shattered, the poetic structure has also been warped. The modern reader no longer sees the poem "steadily" or "sees it whole." Instead he perceives it dimly, at a distance, and "through a glass darkly." Because Milton conceived poetry as an imitation of ideas, his poetry began to lose definition once his ideas had lost their original significance. *Paradise Lost* and the world-view that inspired it are interdependent. When Milton's universe began to crumble, his poem began to suffer a similar disintegration.

A large proportion of the problems that confront the Miltonist today stem from this dual disintegration. The changed relation of poetry to belief—of *mimesis* to *idea*—presents a formidable stumbling-block to the modern reader. Even a near-contemporary of Milton's, like John Dryden, could radically misinterpret his poem. For the twentieth-century critic, still further estranged in time, in belief, and in sensibility, the hazards are much greater. Unable to accept the reality Milton believed in, the reader tends to ignore it and to emphasize alternative realities in its stead. He may (like Miss Bodkin or Mr. Broadbent) substitute for Milton's ideas the concepts of twentieth-century psychology and reinterpret *Paradise Lost* in terms of Freudian symbols and Jungian archetypes. Or, like Mr. Empson, he may find a point of departure in a temperamental hostility to Milton's God. Or he may, with Mr. Waldock and Mr. Peter, discover inherent contradictions between the poem and the poet's intent—contradictions, that is, between the poetic structure and the structure of ideas. Or else, like Mr. Leavis and Mr. Eliot, he may cull out a few isolated passages of genuine poetry and dismiss the poem as a whole.

Most of these critical viewpoints are rooted in the disintegration of Milton's universe and the consequent disintegration of his epic. Unable to react to the poem in its entirety or to see it through seventeenth-century eyes, the modern sensibility reacts to it sporadically and in parts. The very fact that many of its ideas shine only by the reflected light of its poetry constitutes a further hazard to clear vision. The highlights and shadows our contemporaries see are not necessarily those that would have struck Milton's contemporaries most forcefully. Because he feels certain passages of poetry more intensely than others, the modern reader is prone to accept the ideas they express—vicariously quickened as they are by the vitality of the verse—as more alive than the rest, and consequently more fundamental to the poem. In this way he distorts the intellectual and poetic structures alike.

Much of the traditional misinterpretation of *Paradise Lost*—and of its author as well—stems from this tendency to neglect the total structure and focus attention instead on isolated verses or isolated ideas. Let us consider one example out of many—the Satanist fallacy. For many readers, Milton's devil is a much stronger character than his God, and his image of Hell far more forceful than his picture of Heaven. From such subjective impressions as these they infer (wrongly) that the Hell-scenes must be more "sincere" than the descriptions of Heaven. They conclude, with Dryden, that Satan must be the real "hero" of *Paradise Lost*, and they endorse Blake's opinion that Milton must have been "of the Devil's party without knowing it." The same readers have found it equally hard to take the central episode—"Man's First Disobedience"—very seriously. Adam and Eve retain the audience's sympathy even at the moment of their fall. She sins so charmingly, and he so gallantly, that the reader finds it hard to reconcile the massive retribution they incur with the triviality—indeed, the graciousness—of the sin itself. It seems like crushing a gnat with a sledge-hammer. Thus the poem designed to "assert eternal Providence" seems, on the contrary, to demonstrate eternal Negligence. The epic intended to "justifie the wayes of God to men" seems, instead, to affirm divine injustice. Conversely, the crucial scenes which present the other side of the picture—the true side—generally fail to convince; the reader disregards them because they neither engage his sympathy nor stir his imagination. The survey of world-history, culminating in the prophecy of redemption, strikes him as flaccid and dull. The divine councils, which predict man's fall but counter it with the scheme of salvation, impress him as frigid pedantry. The angelic war, which provides a celestial archetype of the future warfare between the church and its enemies, looks like a mud-battle between seraphic punsters. He accepts Pope's verdict,

> *In quibbles, angels and archangels join,*
> *And God the Father turns a school-divine.*

For the twentieth-century reader, Milton has given his strongest support to the case *against* Providence. He has thrown the full weight of his poetry on the side of the prosecution. Whatever arguments the defense may muster seem inadequate against the full power of his verse, summoned not so much in the cause of God as on the side of the fallen creature—the side of Satan and Adam and Eve.

To many a contemporary critic, *Paradise Lost* has become a patchwork quilt rather than a poem, a mélange of velvet and sackcloth, purple passages and dreary fustian. It has ceased to be an organic whole and has instead become simply an assemblage of unequal and ill-coordinated parts. Instead of the integrated structure of a single poem, one is left with no more than a miscellany, a mere anthology.

This approach is sheer Jack Hornerism. It picks out a few isolated sugar-plums and throws away the rest of the pudding. It is also literary vandalism. It differs little from the medieval vice of looting classical temples for column-drums and capitals to embellish a barbarian's palace or to stoke a lime-kiln. But it is also aesthetic murder. The form and content of a truly great work are as intimately fused as soul and body; to separate them is to inflict literary death.

Nevertheless the time-gap which divides us from Milton's age has its fortunate aspects as well as its bad. Though it is a primary reason why contemporary critics so often misread his epic, it possesses compensating advantages.

In the first place, it gives us detachment. Regarding his epic across the chasm of three centuries, we can see it in perspective. No longer embroiled in the quarrels and controversies of his hectic age, we can approach his poem more objectively and dispassionately than his contemporaries could. The very fact that the political, religious, and literary dissensions of the seventeenth century no longer engage our loyalties or our passions is itself an aid to understanding. It enables us to contemplate *Paradise Lost* with the same tranquillity with which we might regard a Greek temple. The poem has acquired aesthetic distance.

Secondly, the very simplicity and clarity of Milton's world-view are poetic assets. The fact that his universe was so much less complicated than ours enabled him to accomplish what no modern poet can hope to achieve. It permitted him to compress into a single poem a complete system of belief. In our own day the increasing complexity and specialization of the arts and sciences have made a similar poetic achievement impossible. If art is indeed a "vision of reality," then we must recognize in Milton's art a more complete vision of the realities his age believed in than any later poet can attain. If poetry does indeed "imitate the idea," then *Paradise Lost* comes closer than any subsequent poem to imitating a completely integrated world-view, a comprehensive and coherent structure of ideas.

In a work of art one requires both an extension of experience and an imposition of order on the details of experience. *Paradise Lost* gives us both. The relative simplicity of Milton's universe enabled him to cover virtually the entire range of beings, from inert matter up to God. Firmly centered on the principle of the "great chain of being"—

> *. . . the scale of Nature set*
> *From center to circumference, whereon*
> *In contemplation of created things*
> *By steps we may ascend to God—*

such a world already exhibited the essential qualities of a work of art—the attributes of harmony, order, significance, and hierarchy. Underlying the poetic structure of *Paradise Lost* was an intellectual structure whose organization and coherence gave it an intrinsic aesthetic value. The world-view of the seventeenth century possessed an artistic potential unparalleled in our time. Milton's triumph as an artist consisted precisely in realizing this potential in poetic form.

Thirdly, even though we shall never be able to see *Paradise Lost* exactly as Milton and his contemporaries saw it, we do possess certain compensatory insights largely denied to them. We are able to set his work in a larger context than they and to detect meanings and values which only a deeper and broader historical perspective can confer. It is not simply an "harmonious vision" that one seeks in a work of art. "The Beautiful" is not the only aesthetic category that matters; "the Characteristic" and "the Significant" are also important, and besides order and harmony the spectator also requires meaning. *Paradise Lost* has been enriched by the additional significance that time has conferred upon it. The conscientious observer who brings to bear the insights of historical and biographical research will find the poem representative both of the poet himself and of the larger intellectual and spiritual currents of his time. If there is a partial truth in Croce's conception of "art as expression," we must, in Milton's case at least, extend this definition. The art of *Paradise Lost* is more than an expression of the poet's own sensibility; it is also the expression of his age.

Finally, the decay of Milton's world has paradoxically heightened the poetic element in his epic. The changes which have undermined its scientific and historical authority have broadened and deepened its status as a poem. What it has lost as a statement of solid fact it has gained as imaginative vision.

What Milton regarded as history the contemporary critic sees as myth. What he accepted as literal truth, the modern reader regards as symbol. But, in fact, myth may be more poetic than history, and symbol itself may be an instrument of truth. The myths that underlie the poem are, in a sense, a symbolic means of apprehending realities that defy conceptualization. Besides the poetic structure of *Paradise Lost* and its structure of ideas, there is (perhaps) a third structure—a structure of myth and symbol—which transcends both. In the long run this may prove the most permanently vital aspect of the poem.

We began with a particular problem—the changed relationship between *Paradise Lost* and the universe it sought to depict. Unless we are to dissociate the poem entirely from the author's intent (and there is more than one fallacy in current denunciations of "the intentional fallacy"), the altered ratio between *mimesis* and *idea* has profoundly affected the character and status of the poem itself. For its author it was essentially an "imitation" of reality. It was, as he conceived it, less an object in itself than a reference to an object. Far from existing in and for itself, it pointed to an ideal order outside and beyond itself. Implicit in its very nature was its epistemological character, its reference to external—and eternal—truth.

One is not concerned here with how and why our conception of truth has changed, but with the implications of this change for *Paradise Lost*. Neither the literary critic nor the historian of ideas can afford to ignore the essentially mimetic character of Milton's epic, its status as an imitation of nature as the seventeenth-century mind conceived it, and its orientation toward a reality that has largely ceased to be real.

The poem is, of course, one of the casualties of our Hundred Years War between science and religion—a conflict that, like Milton's own daemonomachia, has altered the topography of Heaven and destroyed Paradisal innocence. The garden of sapience remains, but a changed intellectual climate has transformed its vegetation; with more scientific techniques of cultivation the tree of knowledge bears subtler and more variegated fruits.

Alas how simple, to these Cates compar'd
Was that crude Apple that diverted Eve!

Milton conceived his epic as an imitation of reality—of ideas that were permanently valid and events that were historically true. For the modern reader, both the events and the ideas are myths; he can accept them not as revealed truth but as poetic fiction, not through religious but through poetic faith. The relationship between imitation and reality is no longer the same.

Paradise Lost will never be merely a "monument to dead ideas." Milton's own poetry will always give even the most moribund concepts a vicarious, if shadowy, life. But the poem does run the risk of becoming a ruined monument. Its integrity has been threatened again and again by critics and scholars who disregard its seventeenth-century context and substitute twentieth-century ideas for those of Milton's age. In actuality, the poetic structure and the intellectual structure are inseparable, and the poem's integrity depends largely on this "hypostatic union" of two different orders. The imitation presupposes a reality beyond itself. To dissociate *Paradise Lost* from the structure of ideas is to violate the very nature of poetry, as Milton and his generation conceived it.[1]

II

For a heroic poet no idea was more crucial than the concept of heroic virtue. This was the *raison d'être* of the epic; and if this form rivaled tragedy as the highest and foremost of literary genres, one reason was the superlative *Ethos* of its protagonist. The epic poet did not merely imitate an action; he also imitated Character. He did not simply portray "highest deeds"; he also portrayed the "godlike virtues" from which they sprang. Action itself proved and demonstrated character; and character, in turn, exhibited a moral ideal. Whatever "profit" or "delight" the poet imparted through imitation derived its value primarily from the concepts behind the poetic image. The concrete example hinged on the abstract idea, the particular on the universal. In his "epic person," he laid the "pattern" of an ideal hero; in his heroic image he embodied the Platonic archetype.

Unfortunately, *virtus heroica* is another of the ideas that separate us from the Renaissance intellectual milieu. In the age of Prufrock and the "anti-hero," it has lost its philosophical significance along with its relevance for poetry. Where it still survives, it haunts the remote frontiers of polite letters, the near-wildernesses of popular fiction. Banished from the more sophisticated Parnassus with its archaic vehicle—the heroic poem—it lingers on in the Limbos of outer space, the deserts

1. For fuller discussion of problems raised in this chapter, see Douglas Bush, *Paradise Lost in Our Time* (London, 1945); B. Rajan, *Paradise Lost and the Seventeenth Century Reader* (London, 1947); I. G. MacCaffrey, *Paradise Lost as Myth* (Cambridge, Mass., 1959); Stanley E. Fish, *Surprised by Sin: the Reader in Paradise Lost* (London and New York, 1967).

of the American West, and the shadows of the metropolitan underworld. Stripped of his Mycenaean armor, the *theios anēr*—the "godlike man"—dons the badge of a deputy sheriff or the space-helmet of an astral voyager. The blurbs of the comic strip have replaced the classical hexameter; the heroes of Troy have shrunk to the dimensions of a Dick Tracy, a Red Ryder, or a Superman.

Nevertheless, heroic virtue was a keynote of the Renaissance—the theme of demonstrative oratory, the argument of epic and romance, the topic of panegyric and encomium. It served as the *Leitmotif* of private masque and public triumph, the subject of painting and sculpture and monumental art. It became the common concern of history and myth, of hagiology and moral philosophy. It provided the *topos* from which the poet or painter glorified his patron or extolled church and state. It was inseparable from the humanist's emphasis on "teaching by example" and the warrior's or poet's quest for an immortality of fame.

A characteristic feature of the Renaissance attitude toward heroism was its eclecticism—its composite character and, at times, its contradictions. The writers of the age had at their command the heroic traditions of Greece and Rome, Christian Europe and heathen Asia, Moslem Africa and pagan America. They might draw at will on learned and popular traditions, on sacred and profane sources. From Aristotle and his scholastic successors they learned that, unlike other virtues, *virtus heroica* lies in an excess rather than a mean. From the Platonists they discovered that the hero is a "purified" soul who has not only conquered, but also annihilated his sensual appetites. From the Pythagoreans they inherited the conception of heroes as an order of aerial spirits, superior to man but inferior to the gods. In Greek myth they found heroes portrayed as demigods, notable for their prowess in battle, their superhuman strength or wisdom, and their mixed parentage, divine and human. In patristic tradition they saw the hero metamorphosed into the martyr and the saint. History—secular or Biblical, ancient or modern—contained exploits that compared favorably with those of epic heroes, yet possessed the additional advantage of being true. The legendary deeds of national and regional heroes rivaled those of classical myth. Finally, the allegorical tradition and its close allies—the emblem literature and mythography—helped to bridge the gap between mythology and moral philosophy and between painting and poetry, the sister arts.

The task that confronted the Renaissance in this area was one of criticism and synthesis. The very range and complexity of the heroic tradition necessitated reassessment and revaluation. In this field, as in so many others, the wealth of materials posed its own peculiar problem.

Here, as elsewhere, the crucial difficulty for the Renaissance artist was to reorder, reappraise, and reconcile the traditions he had inherited.

It is customary to praise the "medieval synthesis" and to overlook Renaissance efforts to achieve a compromise. The problem was more complex in the latter age, but both societies attempted to reconcile diverse—and sometimes contradictory—heroic traditions. Thus, in the late Middle Ages, the convention of the Nine Worthies achieves a synthesis of legendary and historical, sacred and profane traditions by carefully balancing three heroic triads against one another: classical (Hector, Alexander, Julius Caesar); Biblical and Judaic (Joshua, David, Judas Maccabaeus); Christian and "modern" (Arthur, Charlemagne, Godfrey of Bouillon).

The dream-vision and the supernatural journey offered further opportunities for synthesis. In adapting the *Somnium Scipionis* to the epic framework of his *Africa*, Petrarch peopled the heavens with classical heroes, but through the device of prophecy he also managed to introduce Christian worthies as well—including himself. Though Dante assigned a wide variety of classical or Christian heroes to different levels of Hell or Heaven in accordance with his moral and eschatological scheme (Ulysses in Inferno among the fraudulent, Justinian and Constantine in Paradise), his castle of the virtuous pagans includes both ancients and moderns, military and intellectual heroes. Among the classical poets, warriors, and philosophers are such Moslem worthies as Saladin, Avicenna, and Averroes. In the *Hous of Fame* Chaucer includes not only the poets of Troy, Thebes, and Rome but also the historians who had recorded the exploits of Hebrew worthies.

For both medieval and Renaissance poets, the romance tradition provided yet another opportunity for fusing disparate heroic motifs. In Chaucer's Knight's Tale and *Troilus and Criseyde* the setting is classical, but the primary emphasis falls not on the conventional epic theme of wars but on the romantic motif of love. In the *Orlando*s of Boiardo and Ariosto the immediate context is the warfare of a medieval "Worthy"—Charlemagne—but the chief interest of both poets is rather "amours" than "arms." Though Ariosto models Rogero on Achilles, he remains (like Orlando) essentially a romantic hero. It is as the lover of Bradamante that one remembers him.

The epics of several later Italians—Trissino, Alamanni, Tasso—are closely modeled on the *Iliad*, but all three poets adapt their narratives to romantic and Christian conceptions of heroism. Alamanni carefully divests his hero of the savagery and cupidity of his Homeric prototype. (When he slays his foe—an Irish Hector—the protagonist treats the corpse with highest respect, and from his commander he asks nothing more costly than the spurs of knighthood.) The wars of Trissino and

Tasso are holy wars, crusades against Arian heretics or Saracen infidels. Despite its classical structure, the setting of Alamanni's poem is romantic (King Arthur's siege of Bourges), and his Achilles is no less a person than Lancelot. Trissino's plot turns on the love of Corsamonte (a Christian Achilles) for an Italian princess. Tasso's fable hinges on the love-affair of Rinaldo (an Achilles turned crusader) for a beautiful witch allied with the Saracens and the devil.

Finally, for all its conscious medievalism, Spenser's *Faerie Queene* celebrates the worthies of Tudor England in terms of the Britain of Prince Arthur. Here the loves and wars of romance acquire a dual orientation--toward the realm of Elizabeth and the realm of Ideas. Shadows of both time and eternity, they figure historical events, but they also embody moral archetypes. They are symbols not only of the poet's contemporaries, but also of Christian virtues. Through these heroes and heroines of romance, he celebrates the national heroism of his own age, the glories of the British past, and a Christian heroism that is timeless.

Yet another facet of Renaissance syncretism appears in the emblems of Cesare Ripa. The four images of Heroic Virtue in the *Iconologia*[2] transform myth into moral philosophy. All four are unequivocally classical in inspiration, and all four display strong affinities with classical and Renaissance art. Three are based on medals of Roman

2. *Della più che novissima iconologia di Cesare Ripa Perugino* (Padova, 1630), pp. 178–80. This interpretation of Hercules and the apples of the Hesperides is strongly influenced by the section on "Tres Herculis Virtutes" in the *Hieroglyphica* of Joannes Pierius Valerianus (Lugduni, 1626), p. 576: "Quòd verò ad Herculem pertinet, initio diximus statuam eius esse in Capitolio egregiè factam ex aere, Leonino insignem spolio, & clava, quaeque tria laeva manu poma contineat: ea significare tres in Heroë virtutes insigniores, quarum una esset excandescentiae moderatio, altera avaritiae temperamentum, tertia generosus voluptatum contemptus. Verùm quòd fabulantur illum, quò mala haec ab hortis Hesperidum auferret, draconem extinxisse, qui pervigli custodia hortos eos tuebatur, significat illum concupiscentiae modum imposuisse, ut alibi per Draconem voluptuosam libidinis mollitudinem intelligi declaravimus ex Philone. Spolium verò Leonis dubio procul generosum animi robur, mentisque praestantiam ostendit. Quid verò clava sibi velit, alibi explicuimus, cùm illam & rationem & disciplinam significare contenderemus, quoque praestantiùs haec in Hercule vigescunt, eò illi ex firmiori validiorique trunco, quippe ex quercu materia incorrupta clavam attribuunt. Firmitatem enim & vires indicari ex quercu superiùs ostensum. Nodosa verò fingitur clava, propter scrupulos & difficultates, quae virtutem indagantibus, qua duce veram virtutem agnoscere possumus, sese contrà magno errorum agmine contracto frequenter obiiciunt, ac omnibus occursant locis." Cf. p. 147 on Hercules "quem vetustas illa pro virtutem omnium tam animi, quàm corporis idea proposuit. . . ." The same emblem and interpretation reappear in Henry Peacham's *Minerva Britanna* (London, 1612), p. 36, under the heading "Virtus Romana et antiqua." Here again Hercules represents "The image of th' Heroicque virtuous mind," while the apples symbolize the same "three Heroique vertues old."—"Moderation of anger," "Contempt of pleasure," and "Abstinence from covetousness." For other interpretations of the Hercules-myth in the Renaissance, see Douglas Bush, *Mythology and the Renaissance Tradition in Poetry* (new rev. ed.; New York, 1963), and Eugene M. Waith, *The Herculean Hero in Marlowe, Chapman, Shakespeare, and Dryden* (New York, 1962).

emperors, while the fourth is derived from a Roman statue. All four "lay the pattern" of heroic virtue in the image of Hercules.

In the first emblem the hero holds three apples of the Hesperides, which signify "the three heroic virtues attributed to Hercules"—the "moderation of anger," the "tempering of avarice," and a "noble contempt for delights and pleasures." As Ripa explains, heroic virtue subdues the sensuous affections by reason and transcends all moderate virtues. It is so "pure and illustrious" that it surpasses "human excellence" and approximates that of the angels.

The second emblem interprets Hercules' lion-skin and club as symbols of constancy. His nakedness signifies the rejection of "riches" in pursuing "immortality, glory, and honor." His heroism is a rational heroism, for (as the commentary explains) "virtue . . . is reason itself."

Though the third emblem depicts one of the Twelve Labors without allegorical comment, the fourth shows Hercules slaying a dragon coiled about an apple-tree. This motif (as Ripa observes) symbolizes the victory of virtue over concupiscence. Whereas the dragon represents the "pleasant appetite of lust," the lion-skin signifies "nobility and strength of mind," while the club denotes "reason, which rules and masters the appetite." Since the latter is made of oak—a "firm, strong tree"—it is an appropriate sign of "firmness and force." Its knots, in turn, symbolize the "difficulties" that attend the pursuit of virtue. This detail provides a link with the tradition of Hercules' Choice. As Ripa points out, the youthful hero had rejected the easy "path of pleasures" for the arduous and more difficult way.

A fifth emblem, portraying Hercules as an image of "Virtue of Mind and Body," follows these representations of Heroic Virtue. This too derives its inspiration from the medal of a Roman emperor. It shows the hero guiding a lion and a boar which have been linked together and symbolize the conjunction of physical and mental strength. Hercules himself represents "the Idea of all the virtues," while the two beasts signify "corporal virtue" and "magnanimity and strength of mind."

These are visual images, but they can illuminate another type of image—the poetic *icon*. Poetry is a speaking picture (or so it seemed to the Renaissance), and like the painted image the poetic image could be a vehicle of ethical truth, a picture of the "Idea of all the virtues." The same conceptions of heroic virtue that Ripa embodies in a graphic Hercules could also find expression in a poetic Hercules—in the Ercole of Giraldi's epic or in Milton's Hebrew Alcides—Samson and Christ.

The commonplaces of Ripa's exegesis are those of Renaissance ethics in general and Milton's verse in particular. "To scorn delights and live laborious days" typifies Milton's idea of heroic virtue as well as Ripa's. The rejection of riches characterizes the Christ of *Paradise*

Regain'd as well as the Hercules of the *Iconologia.* If the latter slays the dragon and wins the apples of Hesperides, so does the Messiah. He too conquers sensual appetite through reason. He too rejects the way of ease and pleasure for the path of labor and difficulty. If Hercules faces a choice between virtue and vice in the desert, so does Milton's hero.

Nor are these Renaissance commonplaces irrelevant to *Samson Agonistes.* When Samson laments his "impotence of mind, in body strong," he is invoking the same theme as Ripa's emblem of Hercules guiding the linked beasts. Only the situation is reversed. Instead of coupling "virtue of mind and body," Samson has dissociated them, and "These two proportion'd ill drove [him] transverse." Without "strength of mind," physical might is not heroic virtue.

But if the Renaissance was forced to synthesize, it was also compelled to discriminate. The wide range of traditions on which he might draw and authorities to which he might appeal gave the poet ample scope for originality, but it also taxed his critical judgment. It compelled him to choose among variant traditions, to reassess his predecessors and contemporaries, and to work out his own poetic theory and practical compromise. Trissino, Giraldi, and Tasso wrote treatises to justify their poetry or guide them in composing it. Milton's theory of heroic verse changed and developed with his plans for a heroic poem. *Paradise Lost* is an altogether different sort of epic from the "Arthuriad" of his youthful ambitions; and the difference springs partly from a maturer theory of heroic poetry. The literary controversies that attended virtually every major innovation in epic and drama provide striking testimony of the diverse tastes and principles of the age. Critics and poets contended over the question of subject matter—ancient or modern, secular or Biblical. They fought over the issue of epic machinery—classical or Christian, angelic or magical. They debated the nature of epic heroism—piety or valor, philosophic or poetic virtue.

It is against this background—of variety and conflict, of complexity and contradiction, with its dual imperative to synthesize and to discriminate—that we must examine Milton's heroic image.

III

When Milton's Christ rejects the poetry of Greece, he condemns it on aesthetic as well as moral grounds. Since it contains little of "profit" or "delight," it misses the ends of the poetic art. Since it is "ill-imitated," it violates the nature of poetry. Since it celebrates the "vices" of gods and men, it is hopelessly inferior to "*Sion's* songs,"

> *Where God is prais'd aright, and Godlike men,*
> *The Holiest of Holies, and his Saints*; . . .

However questionable this verdict may be as literary criticism, it throws considerable light on the principles that governed Milton's verse. In particular, it illuminates the crisis that confronted him in celebrating Christian virtues in a genre whose most notable exemplars were pagan. Substituting the sacred muse of Biblical inspiration for Calliope entailed a sweeping reappraisal of epic tradition. Within a literary framework derived from Homer and Virgil, he must delineate an altogether different heroism—a heroism based on Scriptural revelation. Athens must yield to Jerusalem, Helicon to Sinai, Achilles and Odysseus to Christ.

Though the basis of this reappraisal was moral and theological, it held profound implications for Milton's *ars poetica*. Ethical condemnation of the ancients necessarily meant revaluing their literary achievement. It meant reconsidering the ends of poetry and re-examining the nature of poetic imitation. In one sense, the crisis sprang from a conflict in the basic principles of heroic poetry—a tension between its formal, material, and final causes. If the *form* of his heroic poem must be classical—based on the example of Homer and Virgil and the "rules of Aristotle"—its *matter* and *ends* must be Christian. He must choose a Biblical argument, celebrate Biblical heroic virtues, and orient his epics toward the Biblical idea of felicity.

Yet the crisis could be restated in other terms. In another sense, it consisted in a clash between different ideals of imitation, to which the heroic poet was *a priori* committed. He must imitate classical models. He must imitate Nature. He must imitate an action. He must imitate an Idea. He must imitate a perfect hero. Moreover, as a "moral teacher," he must attempt to "move" his readers to imitate the very actions and virtues he had celebrated. As a Christian, he must persuade them to imitate the example of a more "perfect Hero"; he must aim at the imitation of Christ. Finally, since heroic virtue and the hero himself were by definition "godlike," the poet could only imitate them adequately by recognizing that they were themselves essentially "imitations." They were "divine resemblances"; and to portray them faithfully, he must imitate them in their relationship to the divine.[3]

As a heroic poet, Milton could escape neither the literary principles of the Renaissance nor the religious convictions of the Reformation. If the former worshiped the ancients, the latter dismissed them as Ethnics. However brightly they seemed to shine, they were nevertheless overshadowed by Gentile darkness. Just as their virtues were

3. On art as imitating nature, see Allan H. Gilbert (ed.), *Literary Criticism, Plato to Dryden* (New York, 1940), pp. 174, 285–86, 497; on the imitation of the classics as a means of imitating nature, see Joel E. Spingarn, *A History of Literary Criticism in the Renaissance* (New York, 1899), pp. 131 ff. For Milton, classical art was not an adequate guide for imitating nature, since it was ignorant of the Fall and of the true nature of God and man.

splendid vices, their arts were ingenious folly. For Milton the conflict between classical taste and Protestant sensibility was never completely reconciled, but the tensions between them proved, in the long run, to be creative assets. They shaped his attitude toward his poetry, and they molded his art. On one level, the primary tension was one of form and end; on another level, it reduced itself to moral and poetic imitation—the problem of *mimesis*.

Part I

❦

The Heroic Image

❦

2. *The "Godlike Man"*

Heroic Virtue and the Divine Image

> "*Vous m'ordonnez a célébrer les saints.*
> *Ma voix est faible et même un peu profane.*"

"You command me to celebrate the saints," descanted Voltaire, "but my voice is feeble and even a trifle prophane!" Feeble it may have been. Prophane it certainly was; for these lines are the exordium to a travesty of sacred epic—a burlesque of Chapelain's heroic poem on Jeanne d'Arc. When Voltaire turned his own hand to serious heroic poetry, he chose an altogether different kind of subject—the warrior-king Henry IV, Huguenot by birth, Catholic by expediency, libertine by temperament; a tolerant man who embraced a Medici as his destiny and sired an interminable line of reactionary Bourbons.

Both the *Henriade* and Chapelain's *Pucelle* are national epics, though spiritually poles apart—one the product of the Enlightenment, the other of the Counter-Reformation. Yet, for all their diversity, they belonged to a common tradition; and this was itself far more varied and diverse than either or both of these poems might seem to suggest. The polarity

First published, in somewhat different form, in *The Journal of the Warburg and Courtauld Institutes*, XXII (1959), 88–105.

between continuity and diversity, tradition and innovation had indeed been one of the salient features of European epic since antiquity, and the paradox is of vital significance for assessing Milton's contribution to this genre. It is in terms of this polarity that one must approach the characters of his heroic poetry.

I

Though critics have long debated the identity of the "hero" of *Paradise Lost*, they have devoted less attention to the definition of heroic virtue.[1] The ambiguity of the word "heroic" and the failure to ascertain what it meant to Milton himself have made it a sort of semantic no-man's-land, over which contending scholars have skirmished without establishing possession. In the absence of a clear-cut definition they have wittingly or unwittingly substituted their own conceptions, assigning different degrees of heroism to Adam, Satan, or the Messiah in accordance with this subjective bias.

As a result, they have obscured Milton's intent as well as his artistry. Certainly one purpose underlying his treatment of the three principal characters was to define clearly the essence of true heroism by contrasting it with spurious norms. To achieve this end he relied on the method of antithesis. In Adam, Satan, and Messiah he deliberately portrayed contrasting patterns of heroic virtue, contrary versions of the heroic enterprise. Through his extended comparison of these figures in virtues, merits, and rewards, he emphasized the distinction between divine and secular ideas of the hero, between sacred and profane ideals of heroic poetry. By this juxtaposition of conflicting criteria—letting "truth and falsehood grapple"—he sought to resolve the confusion (long inherent in the epic tradition) between genuine and counterfeit virtue, true and false standards of praise.

If Renaissance and late medieval moralists possessed a *locus classicus* for the definition of heroic virtue, it was the opening section of Book VII of Aristotle's *Nicomachean Ethics*. Though other interpretations[2] were also current, this had the advantage of frequent citation by

1. For recent studies of the heroic concept in *Paradise Lost* and *Paradise Regain'd* see Merritt Y. Hughes, "The Christ of *Paradise Regained* and the Renaissance Heroic Tradition," *SP*, XXXV (1938), 254–77; E. M. W. Tillyard, "The Christ of *Paradise Regained* and the Renaissance Heroic Tradition," *SP*, XXXVI (1939), 247–52; Merritt Y. Hughes, "Milton and the Sense of Glory," *PQ*, XXVIII (1949), 107–24; Milton Miller, "*Paradise Lost:* The Double Standard," *The University of Toronto Quarterly*, XX (1951), 183–99; Frank Kermode, "Milton's Hero," *RES*, N.S. IV (1953), 317–30; Burton O. Kurth, *Milton and Christian Heroism: Biblical Epic Themes and Forms in Seventeenth-Century England* (Berkeley and Los Angeles, 1959); Barbara K. Lewalski, *Milton's Brief Epic: The Genre, Meaning, and Art of Paradise Regained* (Providence and London, 1966).

2. See, for example, Francesco Piccolomini, *Universa Philosophia de Moribus* (Venice, 1583), pp. 328–29.

scholastic theologians and in Renaissance ethical treatises.[3] It constituted, on the whole, the standard definition of the term.

In Aristotle's opinion, heroic virtue is superhuman, godlike, and divine. It consists in an excess of virtue, just as its logical contrary—brutishness—entails an excess of vice.

> ... to brutishness [τὴν θηριότητα] it would be most fitting to oppose superhuman virtue [τὴν ὑπὲρ ἡμᾶς ἀρετήν], a heroic and divine [ἡρωικήν τινα καὶ θείαν] kind of virtue, as Homer has represented Priam saying of Hector that he was very good,
>
> *For he seemed not, he*
> *The child of mortal man, but as one that of God's seed came.*
>
> Therefore, if as they say, men become gods by excess of virtue [ἀρετῆς ὑπερβολήν], of this kind must be the state opposed to the brutish state. . . .
> Now, since it is rarely that a godlike man is found—to use the epithet of the Spartans, who when they admire anyone highly call him a "godlike man" [θεῖος ἀνήρ]—so too the brutish type is rarely found among men. . . .
> . . . we also call by this evil name [brutishness] those men who go beyond all ordinary standards by reason of vice.[4]

Four aspects of this definition are relevant to the argument and major characters of *Paradise Lost*:

(1) Like its logical contrary—brutishness (ἡ θηριότης)—heroic virtue lies in an excess (ἡ ὑπερβολή) rather than in a mean.

(2) Heroic virtue is superhuman, godlike, and divine (θεῖα).

(3) In the strictest sense of the term, the hero is human rather than entirely supernatural. He is either a "godlike man" or a man "of God's seed."

(4) An excess of vice renders a man similar to beasts.

II

Renaissance moralists laid heavy stress on the superlative quality of heroic virtue. Developing Aristotle's definition (which he regarded as far too fragmentary), Tasso defined it as an excess and perfection of virtue, comprehending in itself all other virtues. Just as the hero excels other men but does not equal the gods, so heroic virtue surpasses ordinary human virtues but does not equal the divine.[5]

3. Cf. Joachim Camerarius, *Ethicorum Aristotelis Nicomachiorum Explicatio* (Frankfurt, 1578), pp. 311–13; Joannes Bernardus Felicianus, *Aristotelis . . . Ethicorum . . . Nicomachiorum libri decem . . ., una cum Eustratii, Aspasii, Michaelis Ephesii . . . Explanationibus* (Basle, 1542), pp. 291–92; Joannes Magirus, *Corona Virtutum Moralium* (Frankfurt, 1628), pp. 639–41; Antonius Riccobonus, *Aristotelis Ethicorum ad Nicomachum libri decem* (Hanover, 1610), pp. 675–79; Petrus Victorius, *Commentarii in X libros Aristotelis de Moribus ad Nicomachum* (Florence, 1584), pp. 367–69.

4. Aristotle, *The Nicomachean Ethics*, ed. Sir David Ross (London, 1954), p. 159.

5. Torquato Tasso, *Della Virtù Eroica e della Carità*, in *Opere* (Florence, 1724), III, 314–15: "ch' ella sia dell' altre tutte più nobile, il suo nome medesimo cel manifesta; perciocchè tal'

In their highest perfection the various virtues are also called heroic, deriving this title from heroic virtue. They are essential in the heroic poem, for they constitute one of the distinguishing features between epic and tragedy. "The epic genre . . . requires in its persons the highest pitch of the virtues, which are called heroic from Heroic Virtue. In Aeneas one finds the excellence of piety, in Achilles of military fortitude, in Ulysses of prudence, and (to come to our own poets) of loyalty in Amadis of Gaul, of constancy in Bradamante. Indeed, in some of these characters one discovers the sum of all these virtues."[6]

Francesco Piccolomini also derived the definition of heroic virtue from the nature of the hero. Since the essence of the hero consists in his elevation above the ordinary human condition, heroic virtue involves an eminence and splendor of the moral virtues. Though any moral virtue is potentially heroic, the heroic dignity especially appears in universal justice, or righteousness.[7]

è ella in rispetto delle altre virtù, quale in rispetto degli altri uomini è l'Eroe, e siccome Eroi coloro son detti, che trapassano l'umana condizione, e che mezzi sono tra gl'Iddij e gli uomini, così le virtù eroiche, la nobiltà dell' umane virtù trapassando, tra loro, e tra le divine quasi mezzo son poste." "Molto debile [*sic*] nondimeno è quella cognizione, che da Aristotile averemo della virtù Eroica. . . . Ma forse in un altro luogo, che ne i libri delle Morali, ci dà della virtù Eroica alcuna luce Aristotile? ci la dà senz' alcun dubbio nella Politica, ove dice, che Eroe per natura, ed Eroi son quelli, fra' quali, e i soggetti non è alcuna proporzione di virtù; ma ivi ancora altro non c'insegna, se non che la virtù Eroica è un eccesso [per così dire] della virtù. Questo dunque prima porremo per cosa costante, ch' ella non sia mediocrità, come son le virtù morali: ma che sia piuttosto eccesso, e perfezione di bene. . . . Ma ha ella alcun soggetto determinato, come la temperanza ha i piaceri, e la fortezza i pericoli, e la magnificenza le grandi spese? o piuttosto senz' alcun fermo subietto . . . ? credero io piuttosto, ch' ella termine non abbia, nè subietto particolare, ma che suo soggetto sia tutto ciò, che può cadere sotto le altre virtù . . . la virtù Eroica comprehende in se ciascun' altra virtù. . . ."

6. Torquato Tasso, *Dell' Arte Poetica*, in *Opere* (Florence, 1724), IV, 16. Cf. *Discorsi dell' Poema Eroico*, in *Prose*, ed. Francesco Flora (Milan and Rome, 1935), p. 368.

7. Piccolomini, pp. 328–32: "In virtutum genere ea maximè fulget, eximiamque in animis ingenuis parit admirationem; quae Heroica dicitur, & hominem supra hominis conditionem elevare nata est: de qua ego verba facturus, a nomine ordiar . . . de hoc consentiunt omnes, Herois nomen denotare gradum & conditionem supra hominem collocatam." "Colligamus itaque, ex Poetarum commentis Heroem esse Semideum, ex Deo & homine ortum: Ex opinione Platonis esse animam hominis illustri vita functam, solutam a crasso corpore; vel hominem flagranti Virtutis amore supra humanam conditionem elevatum." "Sed quoniam haec commenta sunt Poetarum; propterea, quid veri (ex sententia Aristotelis) sub his fabularum involucris claudatur, explicandum ac evolvendum occurrit. Heroes sunt illustres homines, qui per eximiam aliquam Virtutem conditionem sunt adepti super humanam refulgentem [*sic*]; per quam vel praeclaram ducunt Vitam, vel vita functi per ora hominum celeberrimè circunferuntur. Hi dicuntur supra hominis conditionem elevari, quia (ut homini licet) se Diis similes praestiterunt." "Constat itaque, quid herois . . . nomine significetur . . . ; Ex quo constat heroem consensione omnium solam denotare praestantiam, & eminentem quandam hominis conditionem." "At cum Heroica Virtus sit splendor quidam & eminentia, quaenam ea eminentia sit, considerandum occurrit . . ." "Si propriè loqui volumus, Heroica Virtus est splendor Moralium Virtutum; & earum praesertim, in quibus refulgere est difficilius; magis supra hominis vires collocatum, magisque Divinam quandam facultatem exposcit." "Nam Heroes ex humana &

Milton's references to superhuman eminence and excess seem obviously intended to evoke the heroic concept, to invest his characters with heroic stature. However evil, superficial, and false the heroic virtues of the fallen angels may be, he has nevertheless gilded them with at least the reflection of heroic splendor. They shine with a false glory, but it is a shadow of the glory which is real; by juxtaposing shadow and substance, illusion and reality, the poet makes it easier to discriminate between truth and falsehood. These allusions, moreover, should have possessed definite significance for an audience familiar with Aristotle's discussion of heroic virtue. Echoing the standard definition of the term, they reinforce Milton's explicit evocations of the heroic concept. He describes the loyal angels, for example, as marching to harmony

> ... *that breath'd*
> *Heroic Ardor to advent'rous deeds* ...;
> (*P.L.*, VI, 65–66)

the rebels are similarly inspired by music

> ... *such as rais'd*
> *To highth of noblest temper Hero's old*
> *Arming to Battel*. ... (*P.L.*, I, 551–53)

His references to superhuman excellence serve essentially the same purpose as these more direct statements; they are consciously designed to suggest the idea of heroic virtue.

The nature of his subject permitted Milton to fill his stage entirely with characters of a superhuman grade or condition. God and Messiah are divine. In their native perfection Adam and Eve surpass their posterity:

> Adam *the goodliest man of men since born*
> *His Sons, the fairest of her Daughters* Eve.
> (*P.L.*, IV, 323–24)

Divina natura sive conditione dicuntur orti; tales autem sunt illustres mores, qui ex recta ratione divinitatem praeseferente, humanaque appetitione ei obtemperante, ortum ducunt: Propterea quicunque dicti sunt Heroes, vel eminenti Fortitudine, vel Magnanimitate, vel Temperantia refulserunt. ... Hinc finxit antiquitas Heroas, cum viventes, tum vita functos, semper versari inter homines; non alia ratione, nisi quia Moralibus & Civilibus Virtutibus refulserunt, ob quas per ora hominum splendidè circunferuntur. In re igitur dictum est Heroicam Eminentiam ad morales Virtutes pertinere." "Cum itaque Heroica Virtus sit splendor Civilium & Moralium virtutum; non iniuria Carmina illa, quibus praeclara facinora illustrium virorum celebrari consueverunt, Heroica nuncupabantur. Et quoniam in omni morali Virtute eminentia & fulgor locum habere potest, propterea in omni Virtute Morali Heroica dignitas valet refulgere; Praesertim tamen in virtute Universa, quae eadem est cum universa Iustitia. ..."

Faithful and unfaithful angels are spirits, and even after their fall the latter retain vestiges of their superior nature. They are

> . . . *Godlike shapes and forms*
> *Excelling human* . . . . (*P.L.*, I, 358–59)

In number and strength, they surpass the heroes of epic and romance:

> . . . *For never since created man*
> *Met such imbodied force, as nam'd with these*
> *Could merit more then that small infantry*
> *Warr'd on by Cranes.* . . . *Thus far these beyond*
> *Compare of mortal prowess.* . . . (*P.L.*, I, 573–88)

Satan excels these, as they excel human heroes. He stands

> . . . *above the rest*
> *In shape and gesture proudly eminent.* . . .
> (*P.L.*, I, 589–90)

His own "merit" exalts him to a "bad eminence" above the infernal peers.

All three of the major characters of *Paradise Lost* exhibit various moral qualities in excess. Eve hails Adam's decision to partake of the apple as a

> . . . *glorious trial of exceeding Love,*
> *Illustrious evidence, example high!*
> *Engaging me to emulate.* . . . (*P.L.*, IX, 961–63)

Satan excels his fellows in fortitude:

> . . . *none among the choice and prime*
> *Of those Heav'n-warring Champions could be found*
> *So hardie as to proffer or accept*
> *Alone the dreadful voyage; till at last*
> Satan, *whom now transcendent glory rais'd*
> *Above his fellows, with Monarchal pride*
> *Conscious of highest worth, unmov'd thus spake.*
> (*P.L.*, II, 423–29)

In the parallel scene in Heaven, Messiah's analogous decision to undergo death on man's behalf manifests his superiority over the angels in fortitude and in love. Milton repeatedly emphasizes the excess of charity:

> . . . *in him all his Father shon*
> *Substantially express'd, and in his face*
> *Divine compassion visibly appeerd,*
> *Love without end, and without measure Grace.* . . .
> (*P.L.*, III, 139–42)

> *. . . the Son of God*
> *In whom the fulness dwels of love divine. . . .*
> (*P.L.*, III, 224–25)

> *O unexampl'd love,*
> *Love no where to be found less then Divine!*
> (*P.L.*, III, 410–11)

Messiah's charity is exceeded by his obedience:

> *. . . his meek aspect*
> *Silent yet spake, and breath'd immortal love*
> *To mortal men, above which only shon*
> *Filial obedience. . . .* (*P.L.*, III, 266–69)

Similarly, in the angelic war, he exhibits the excess (though not the plenitude) of divine might and wrath:

> *Into thee such Vertue and Grace*
> *Immense I have transfus'd, that all may know*
> *In Heav'n and Hell thy Power above compare. . . .*
> (*P.L.*, VI, 703–5)

In the ensuing conflict

> *. . . to trie with mee*
> *In Battel which the stronger proves, they all,*
> *Or I alone against them,* (*P.L.*, VI, 818–20)

his effortless victory over the rebels leaves him supreme in heroic eminence.

Milton thus invests his three major characters with superhuman eminence, but contrasts them to manifest the supreme excellence of Messiah. The Son exceeds the rebel angels in might. His decision to die for man surpasses in merit Satan's parallel resolution to risk extinction for the public good. It also excels Adam's analogous resolution to perish with Eve; in these contrasting trials of "exceeding love" Messiah exhibits the fullness of divine charity, whereas Adam, "overcome with Female charm," is not heroically charitable, but humanly incontinent.

Milton also enhances Messiah's excellence by establishing a hierarchy of ethical values; eminence in certain virtues is nobler than in others. Patience and martyrdom are superior to military fortitude, and Messiah himself censures the rebel angels for holding too narrow a conception of heroic virtue, for seeking heroic excellence in strength alone:

> *. . . by strength*
> *They measure all, of other excellence*

Not emulous, nor care who them excells;
Nor other strife with them do I voutsafe
(*P.L.*, VI, 820–23)

This opinion is expressed elsewhere in *Paradise Lost* and *Paradise Regain'd.*

Consistent with this broader and loftier conception of heroic virtue is the hymn with which the angels greet Messiah after the creation of the world. This is hailed as a nobler exercise of divine power than the expulsion of his enemies:

Great are thy works, Jehovah, *infinite*
Thy power; what thought can measure thee or tongue
Relate thee; greater now in thy return
Then from the Giant Angels; thee that day
Thy Thunders magnifi'd; but to create
Is greater than created to destroy. (*P.L.*, VII, 602–7)

Creation thus exalts Messiah to a further pinnacle of heroic excellence, and this in turn is surpassed by his voluntary sacrifice—an act which displays the fullness of divine love, filial obedience, and

. . . . *the better fortitude*
Of Patience and Heroic Martyrdom. . . .
(*P.L.*, IX, 31–32)

Messiah alone of the three major characters of *Paradise Lost* is heroically—i.e., superlatively—obedient. His obedience outshines even his charity. Adam's act of "exceeding Love," on the other hand, openly flouts the divine command. Satan's seemingly heroic qualities—his superhuman courage, ingenuity, and strength—are all exercised in direct opposition to God. His enterprise is founded on the resolve to seek "the contrary of his high will" and to

. . . *disturb*
His inmost counsels from their destind aim.
(*P.L.*, I, 167–68)

Satan's eminence, like Adam's "exceeding Love," is ultimately robbed of the quality of true virtue—and consequently of true heroism—because it is manifested in disobedience to the divine will, violation of divine law, and disregard of the supreme good.[8] Though it certainly involves excess, this is not the excellence of virtue, but the excess of vice. Dedicated to evil, his excellence itself becomes evil—becomes, paradoxically, excellence *in* evil. His eminence is essentially what Milton calls it—a "bad" eminence, a supremacy in misery. It cannot, therefore,

8. See B. Rajan, *Paradise Lost & the Seventeenth Century Reader* (London, 1947), p. 95.

be genuinely heroic. It is as diametrically opposed to true heroic virtue as virtue is to vice. An excess of vice, an eminence in evil, it is (properly speaking) brutishness, or θηριότης.

That disobedience should inevitably deprive Adam and Satan of heroic status is a logical corollary of current ethical doctrines. For Suessanus, as for Piccolomini, heroic virtue constitutes the essence of the hero. Both moralists insist that a virtue misdirected to a wrong end is essentially a vice. For Suessanus either a false religion or a false good may make an apparently virtuous action vicious.[9] Similarly, Piccolomini observes that "Multi vitiosi inter Heroes celebrantur" and warns that vice may be mistaken for heroic virtue.[10]

According to this view, any virtues which Adam or Satan display in disobeying the divine command are made vicious through their disregard for their ultimate ends. Their apparent heroism is manifestly false; only to Eve or to the devils in Pandaemonium do their sins seem heroically virtuous.

Similar conclusions follow under the Aristotelian ethical system. According to the *Nicomachean Ethics*, right reason and universal justice are essential to virtue:

Now that we must act according to the right rule is a common principle and must be assumed . . .

. . . even now all men, when they define virtue, after naming the state of character and its objects add "that [state] which is in accordance with the right rule"; now the right rule is that which is in accordance with practical wisdom [prudence].

This form of justice, then, is complete virtue . . . ; and proverbially "in justice is every virtue comprehended". And it is complete virtue in its fullest sense because it is the actual exercise of complete virtue. . . . Justice in this sense, then,

9. Augustinus Niphus Suessanus, "De Sanctitate," in *Opuscula Moralia et Politica* (Paris, 1645), pp. 158–60: ". . . quare veluti feritate homines evadunt belluae ferae, atque immanes, sic virtute heroica homines evadunt dij, hoc est sancti, atque heroës: Est enim heroica ipsa virtus, supra humanam virtutem virtus, & homo igitur qui hac virtute pollet supra homines heros." "Quo ratione fit ut virtus heroica, & sanctitas, & deitas idem sit, nam cùm habet ad eam perfectionem vehitur, quae excedit humanam virtutem, evadit heros, hoc est semideus, sanctus. . . ." "At si virtus qua agimus ordinetur in Deum sub ratione qua est obiectum infidelitatis, modo videlicet, quo Mahumetis sectatores dirigunt, aut alij qui de Deo veram agnitionem non habuerunt, hoc pacto omnis actio erit peccatum cùm non ordinetur in ultimum finem, ea videlicet ratione qua est obiectum verae fidei. & si virtus qua agimus ordinetur in particularem finem non qui est re ipsa bonum sed apparens, etiam vitium erit: sicuti non est vera virtus avarorum prudentia . . ., avarorum iustitia . . ., avarorum temperantia . . ., & avarorum fortitudo. . . ."

10. Piccolomini, pp. 341–42: "At cavendum summopere est, ne vice virtutis Heroicae vitium commendemus, ac pro fulgore Heroico vitium populari voce formosum amplectamur. Et quoniam ordinata in finem per solam finis rectam constitutionem rectè formantur; propterea, qui in decernendo, ac statuendo fine aberrant, ut etiam in ordinatis ad illum delinquant necesse est."

is not part of virtue but virtue entire, nor is the contrary injustice a part of vice but vice entire.

Inasmuch as Adam and Satan choose lesser goods in preference to the supreme good, they violate right reason. Inasmuch as they break divine laws, they are unjust, for "the lawless man was seen to be unjust and the law-abiding man just. . . ."[11] Thus their disobedience is "vice entire"; neither has a legitimate claim to heroism.

Though Milton invests all three characters with superhuman eminence and excess, only Messiah meets the ethical requirements of heroic virtue. He alone, therefore, is truly heroic—"Found worthiest to be so by being Good. . . ."

III

In so far as it is godlike and divine, heroic virtue is practically synonymous with the divine image. Previous scholarship, however, has largely ignored the similarity of these concepts and its bearing on the arguments of both of Milton's epics.

If heroic virtue is by definition godlike, then the loss of the divine image through Adam's transgression and its recovery through Christ's satisfaction are of cardinal importance for the heroic poet; they concern the very essence of heroic virtue. Since the divine image has been largely (though not entirely) obscured by the Fall, true heroism can be found only in Christ and the regenerate, in whom the divine image has been renewed. Thus the arguments of *Paradise Lost* and *Paradise Regain'd* directly concern the basic problems of human heroism. They depict its theological limitations—the conditions under which heroic virtue is or is not possible.

In both epics the adjective "godlike" occurs frequently as a virtual synonym for "heroic." The fallen angels are "Godlike shapes and forms," with "visages and stature as of Gods." The celestial legions move under "Godlike Leaders." Christ's victory over Satan in his crucifixion and resurrection is "this God-like act." In *Paradise Regain'd* Satan comes to behold Christ's "Godlike deeds" and wonders why he conceals "These God-like Vertues." Christ is endowed "with Godlike force" against Satan. His praise of Hebrew poetry,

> *Where God is prais'd aright, and Godlike men,*
> *The Holiest of Holies, and his Saints; . . .*
> (*P.R.*, IV, 348–49)

11. Aristotle, p. 30, 107–9, 157. Cf. also pp. 39, 55, 65, 139, 142–43.

restates the true function of heroic poetry and the true identity of the hero: the hero—the godlike man—is the saint.[12]

Beyond its theological significance, the phrase "Son of God" recalls the Aristotelian definition of the hero as one "of God's seed." In both epics the Son proves his divine Sonship through manifesting his superior virtue, his heroic excellence. In *Paradise Lost* he is found

> *By Merit more then Birthright Son of God,*
> *Found worthiest to be so by being Good,*
> *Far more then Great or High. . . .*
> (*P.L.*, III, 309–11)

Paradise Regain'd appropriately begins with divine testimony of Christ's Sonship at his baptism; then follows his proof of his divine origin under temptation:

> *That all . . . may discern,*
> *From what consummate vertue I have chose*
> *This perfect Man, by merit call'd my Son,*
> *To earn Salvation. . . .* (*P.R.*, I, 163–67)

> *True Image of the Father whether thron'd*
> *In the bosom of bliss, and light of light*
> *Conceiving, or remote from Heaven, enshrin'd*
> *In fleshly Tabernacle, and human form,*
> *Wandring the Wilderness, whatever place,*
> *Habit, or state, or motion, still expressing*
> *The Son of God. . . .* (*P.R.*, IV, 596–602)

IV

Paradise Lost and *Paradise Regain'd* appear to be unique among epic poems in their full appreciation of the significance of the Adam-Christ parallel for the heroic concept. This parallel is explicit in the opening lines of either poem and integral to the argument of each. In the former

12. The relationship of sanctity to heroism has interested theologians from Augustine to Benedict XIV. Suessanus, p. 148, finds the two concepts virtually identical and also equates their logical contraries: "Quoniam de sanctitate atque prophanitate pertractare proposuimus, de quibus Plato in Euthiphrone, & Aristoteles septimo Ethicorum sub nomine heroicae virtutis, atque immanitatis disseruerunt. . . ." Scacchus, *De cultu, et veneratione servorum Dei* (Rome, 1639), p. 16, observes that sanctity requires "non solum animam sine culpa, ac labe peccati, sed etiam ut sit virtutum omnium exercitijs, habitibus, atque actibus in gradu heroico condecorato." Castellinus, *De Certitudine Gloriae Sanctorum Canonizatorum* (Rome, 1628), p. 262, declares that "inter sacros, qui eminent fide, humilitate, vel alia virtute, charitate informata Heroes meritò appellantur. Hinc est, quod . . . Sanctus Augustinus libro 10. de Civitate Dei dicebat. *Martyres nostri* (hoc est, ij, qui pro Christo patiuntur) *Heroes nuncupantur; si usu Ecclesiastici sermonis id permitteret.*" See also Benedict XIV, *On the Beatification and Canonization of the Servants of God* (3 vols; London, 1850–52).

work Milton delineates the divine image as originally manifested in the first man, recounts its subsequent loss in Adam and his descendants, and outlines the conditions of its recovery through spiritual regeneration. In the latter epic he depicts its restoration in Christ. In both works the divine image is the norm—the "essential form"—of heroic virtue.

The roots of the Adam-Christ parallel—the idea of the divine image forfeited by the first Adam and regained by the second—occur in the epistles of St. Paul:

Wherefore, as by one man sin entered into the world, and death by sin. . . . Therefore as by the offence of one judgment came upon all men to condemnation; even so by the righteousness of one the free gift came upon all men unto justification of life. For as by one man's disobedience many were made sinners, so by the obedience of one shall many be made righteous.[13]

The first man is of the earth, earthy: the second man is the Lord from heaven. . . . And as we have borne the image of the earthy, we shall also bear the image of the heavenly.[14]

The Pauline doctrine of the two Adams was subsequently elaborated into Irenaeus' "recapitulation" theory of redemption. According to this view, Christ "recapitulates" or "sums up" man or Adam or human life.[15] God became man so that "*what we had lost in Adam*, that is, being after the image and likeness of God, we might recover in Christ Jesus."[16]

According to Athanasius, "the renewal of creation has been wrought by the Self-same Word who made it in the beginning"[17] and who alone could recreate mankind after the divine image which it had forfeited.[18] For Gregory of Nyssa, resemblance to God is the end of the virtuous life. Just as enslavement to the passions is participation in the

13. Romans 5:12–19.

14. 1 Corinthians 15: 47–49. Cf. Colossians 3:9–10 and Ephesians 4:22–24.

15. Norman Powell Williams, *The Ideas of the Fall and of Original Sin* (London, 1927), pp. 197–98. See also Northrop Frye, "The Typology of *Paradise Regained*," *MP*, LIII (1956), 227–38.

16. Williams, p. 197. For a summary of Irenaeus' doctrine, see *ibid.*, pp. 198–99: "Adam, being in his paradisal state coextensive with humanity, possessed the 'image and likeness' of God, and then lost it by the Fall: the subsequent multiplication of the human race is nothing other than the proliferation and subdivision of this original Adam into myriads of individual men, each, in consequence of the Fall, destitute of the divine image. Christ then came as the Logos, who is the perfect divine image, and as the second Adam, the Ideal Man or Son of Man, who sums up in Himself all the splendours which man's unfallen state had potentially possessed, and purposes to gather into Himself, by sacramental incorporation into His Mystical Body, the countless individuals into which the ancient protoplast has split up, thereby re-uniting humanity into one single organism, endowed with the image and likeness of God, as at the beginning."

17. St. Athanasius, *On the Incarnation* (London, 1953), p. 26.

18. *Ibid.*, pp. 41–42: "What, then, was God to do? What else could He possibly do, being God, but renew His Image in mankind, so that through it men might once more come to know Him? And how could this be done save by the coming of the very Image

sin of Adam and Eve, so restoration to the primitive state of perfection is participation in the restoration of Christ. In Him the divine image is restored for all humanity.[19]

In Gregory's opinion, the characteristics of the divine image were purity, liberty, beatitude, dominion, justice, virtue, moral perfection, and the like.[20] For Calvin, similarly, it involved perfection, purity, righteousness, and holiness.

[Though] the image of God was not utterly defaced and destroyed in him [Adam], it was, however, so corrupted, that any thing which remains is fearful deformity; and, therefore, our deliverance begins with that renovation which we obtain from Christ, who is, therefore, called the second Adam, because he restores us to true and substantial integrity.

... the end of regeneration is to form us anew in the image of God.[21]

These conventional attributes of the divine image recur in Milton's[22] first description of Adam and Eve:

> *Two of far nobler shape erect and tall,*
> *Godlike erect, with native Honour clad*

Himself, our Saviour Jesus Christ? Men could not have done it, for they are only made after the Image; nor could angels have done it, for they are not the image of God. The Word of God came in His own Person, because it was He alone, the Image of the Father, Who could recreate man after the Image." "You know what happens when a portrait that has been painted on a panel becomes obliterated through external stains. The artist does not throw away the panel, but the subject of the portrait has to come and sit for it again, and then the likeness is re-drawn on the same material. Even so was it with the All-holy Son of God. He, the Image of the Father, came and dwelt in our midst, in order that He might renew mankind made after Himself. ... This also explains His saying to the Jews: 'Except a man be born anew ...' He was not referring to a man's natural birth from his mother ..., but to the re-birth and recreation of the soul in the Image of God." Cf. *Paradise Lost*, III, 281, "Thou therefore whom thou only canst redeeme. ..."

19. Gregory of Nyssa, *Contemplation sur la Vie de Moïse ou Traité de la Perfection en Matière de Vertu*, ed. Jean Daniélou (Paris, 1941), p. 36.

20. *Idem, La Création de l'Homme*, ed. Jean Laplace (Paris, 1943), pp, 95–97.

21. John Calvin, *Institutes of the Christian Religion*, ed. Henry Beveridge (Edinburgh, 1863), I, 164. Cf. *ibid.*, pp. 164–65: "To this corresponds another passage, 'Put ye on the new man, who after God is created' (Eph. iv. 24). We must now see what particulars Paul comprehends under this renovation. In the first place, he mentions knowledge; and, in the second, true righteousness and holiness. Hence we infer, that at the beginning the image of God was manifested by the light of intellect, rectitude of heart, and the soundness of every part. For ... this principle cannot be overthrown—viz. that the leading feature in the renovation of the divine image must also have held the highest place in its creation. To the same effect Paul elsewhere says that, beholding the glory of Christ with unveiled face, we are transformed into the same image. We now see how Christ is the most perfect image of God, into which we are so renewed as to bear the image of God in knowledge, purity, righteousness, and true holiness." See also Calvin's *Commentaries on ... Genesis*, ed. John King (Edinburgh, 1947), I, 94–95.

22. In the *Christian Doctrine*, Book I, Chapter 7 (*Prose Works* [Bohn's Standard Library; London, 1872], IV, 195), Milton declares that since man was "formed after the image of God, it followed as a necessary consequence that he should be endued with natural wisdom, holiness, and righteousness."

In naked Majestie seemd Lords of all,
And worthie seemd, for in thir looks Divine
The image of thir glorious Maker shon,
Truth, Wisdome, Sanctitude severe and pure,
Severe, but in true filial freedom plac't. . . .
(*P.L.*, IV, 288–94)

Sharing with his contemporaries an interpretation of the divine image, inherited from scriptural, patristic, and Reformation sources, Milton made it the basis of his treatment of heroic virtue and the godlike man in *Paradise Lost* and *Paradise Regain'd*. Messiah is, of course, the perfect image of God—the divine "archetype" (to echo Gregory) of the divine image in man, and hence the absolute norm of heroic virtue. The perfect exemplar of what is "godlike" and "divine," the Son of God is himself the archetypal pattern of the human hero, and Milton portrays him as such in either epic. In his image Adam was first created and the regenerate are renewed.[23]

The scope of *Paradise Lost* enables Milton not merely to contrast the "earthy" man and the "heavenly" man in Adam and Christ, but also to portray three phases of the divine image in Adam himself—its original splendor, its obscuration through sin, and its gradual restoration through spiritual regeneration. The final books of the epic, showing Adam's repentance and revived knowledge and trust in God, portray the gradual emergence of the "new man, which is renewed in knowledge after the image of him that created him."

Paradise Lost emphasizes one element of the Adam-Christ parallel, *Paradise Regain'd* the other. Both poems, however, concern the nature and significance of the divine image manifested in Adam and Christ respectively, and in either work this divine similitude constitutes the essence of heroic virtue.

V

By definition the hero is a godlike *man*—a human being of superlative virtue or (metaphorically at least) of divine seed. Hence Adam alone of the major characters of *Paradise Lost* can be properly designated a "hero." Messiah and Satan are divine and angelic figures respectively. For the same reason Michael, Gabriel, Uriel, Abdiel, Zephon, Ithuriel, and their colleagues cannot be styled "heroes" in the strictest sense of the term. Adam himself, moreover, is heroic only so long as he retains

23. In the *Christian Doctrine* (I, 18) Milton defines regeneration as "*that change operated by the Word and the Spirit, whereby the old man being destroyed, the inward man is regenerated by God after his own image, in all the faculties of his mind. . . .*" In the same work (I, 16) he states that the "effect and design of the whole ministry of mediation is, the satisfaction of divine justice on behalf of all men, and the conformation of the faithful to the image of Christ."

the divine image. His transgression (as we have noted) robs him of his virtue and consequently of his heroic excellence. After the Fall, when he and his wife awake

> *. . . destitute and bare*
> *Of all their vertue:* (*P.L.*, IX, 1062–63)

he is no longer godlike, and to recover divine resemblance he must await regeneration through "one greater Man."

The Christ of *Paradise Regain'd*, on the other hand, is a hero *par excellence*. As a "perfect Man" of "consummate vertue" he meets the requirement that the hero be a man of superlative virtue. As "True Image of the Father" he is the highest exemplar of what is godlike and divine. Moreover, he is Son of God—"one that of God's seed came"—and the frequent references to his divine Sonship in this poem seem to be more than conventional reiterations of theological dogma. They also serve to emphasize his just title to supreme heroic eminence. The encounter which reveals him

> *By proof the undoubted Son of God*

demonstrates how far his virtue surpasses that of other heroes.

As the norm to which the regenerate must be conformed, he is, furthermore, the ideal pattern of the Christian hero. It is from his example that Adam, in the final book of *Paradise Lost*, learns the virtue of obedience and the nature of true fortitude:

> *Henceforth I learne, that to obey is best,*
> *And love with feare the onely God, to walk*
> *As in his presence, ever to observe*
> *His providence, and on him sole depend . . .;*
> *. . . that suffering for Truths sake*
> *Is fortitude to highest victorie . . .;*
> *Taught this by his example whom I now*
> *Acknowledge my Redeemer ever blest.*
> (*P.L.*, XII, 561–73)

VI

Though Messiah and Satan are not, in the strictest sense of the word, "heroes," they play, notwithstanding, a significant part in Milton's delineation of the idea of heroic virtue. Inasmuch as Messiah is the perfect image of the Father and Satan pretends to divinity, both figures are to some extent norms of the godlike and divine; both are spiritual archetypes of the human hero. In the case of Satan, who is merely an "Idol of Majestie Divine," the pretensions to divinity are, of course, false. The heroic virtue of which he is the archetype is likewise spurious.

In juxtaposing Messiah and Satan as contrasting exemplars of true and false heroism, Milton profoundly modified the conventional epic machinery, but deepened its moral significance. By confronting an apparent hero with the real, a counterfeit virtue with the true, he succeeded in throwing both into sharper relief. Whereas Satan embodies a pattern of heroism which is ultimately "of true Virtue void," Messiah manifests the godlike virtue which "justly gives Heroic name to Person or to Poem."

The ethical antithesis between genuine and spurious heroism is intensified by the parallels between the divine and infernal strategies. The council scenes in Books II and III isolate Messiah and Satan from their fellows and emphasize their unique status as the champions of either cause—antagonists in a Holy War. Gabriel's account of how Satan's initial rebellion was prompted by envy of Messiah's preeminence and ultimately quelled by Messiah's power, Michael's prophecy of Christ's future victories over Satan, and Messiah's own judgment of Satan in Book X heighten the pattern of spiritual antagonism.

Satan is, then, in large measure a foil for Messiah. He is an idol—a spurious imitation—of the divine image. His primary function is to throw into bolder relief the perfect image of divine virtue manifested by the Son. By the ethical contrast between them Milton brought into clearer focus the essential distinction between true heroic virtue and its counterfeit.

As the perfect manifestation of the divine image, Messiah serves at least two purposes in *Paradise Lost*. First, he embodies the essential form of heroic virtue, the ideal pattern of the Christian hero. Secondly, through his mediation he renews and restores the divine image obscured in Adam and his descendants. He is thus the norm and the agent of human heroism. Both of these functions are vital to Milton's delineation of heroic virtue and thus to the very *raison d'être* of the heroic poem. Both are based on familiar theological doctrines—the line of reasoning developed from St. Paul by Irenaeus, Athanasius, Calvin, and others. A seventeenth-century reader should have found little startling or extraordinarily difficult in either.

Satan's significance as the exemplar of a spurious heroism, on the other hand, has been frequently misunderstood and requires a more detailed explanation.

Unfortunately, critics have tended to approach this character in terms of a clear-cut dichotomy—he must be either hero or fool.[24]

24. See Rajan's discussion of this point, pp. 93–94.

Actually, he is both; he represents an ideal heroic in the eyes of the world, but foolish in the eyes of God. Milton consciously invests him with a concept of heroism relatively conventional in heroic poetry, but also deliberately repudiates this concept as false.

The "problem" of Satan resolves itself essentially into why Milton chose to deck absolute vice in the conventional trappings of superlative virtue, why he chose to make the devil himself appear heroic. The answers seem fairly obvious. First, this is an excellent device for discrediting a popular, but inadequate, conception of heroic virtue. Secondly, it serves, by contrast, to emphasize the nature of true heroism as exemplified in Messiah.

In supplying Satan with many of the conventional attributes of the epic hero, Milton indirectly censures the epic tradition for celebrating vice as heroic virtue.[25] As a "godlike" devil is clearly a logical absurdity—a contradiction in terms—the portrait of the "heroic" Arch-fiend is self-refuting.[26] Milton relies on a *reductio ad absurdum* to discredit a spurious conception of heroism.

A similar intent underlies his account of Satan's metamorphosis in Book X. This is not only a divinely-ordained punishment for transgression; it also represents the divine (and therefore the *true*) judgment of Satan's character and acts—a definitive repudiation of the ideal of heroism he embodies. Unmasked, its true nature manifested, this pattern is not heroic virtue, but its logical contrary. The essence of Satan's apparent heroism is brutishness, and Milton expresses this fact allegorically through the physical obscuration of the divine image. Satan and his companions forfeit their "Godlike shapes" and "resemblance to the Highest" for the image of a beast. This physical contrast highlights the spiritual antithesis of heroic virtue and θηριότης.[27]

In thus delineating the excess of vice in addition to that of virtue—brutishness as well as heroic virtue—Milton obeys the rules of the epic genre, as Tasso conceived them:

Epic poems do not only portray the highest pitch of virtue in the persons they describe, but also the highest degree of vice ("l'eccellenza del vizio"). This they are able to portray with less peril than can the tragic poet. Such characters are Mezentius, Busiris, Procrustes, Diomedes, Thersites, and similar persons. Such too (or at least not very different) are the Cyclopes and Laestrygonians,

25. See C. M. Bowra, *From Virgil to Milton* (London, 1945), pp. 228–30.

26. C. S. Lewis, *A Preface to Paradise Lost* (London, 1942), p. 95, regards Satan as "a personified self-contradiction." Bowra, p. 224, observes "an apparent contradiction between his [Satan's] heroic spirit and his corrupt motives, between his courageous acts and the end to which they are directed."

27. In George Sandys' translation of Ovid's *Metamorphoses* (Oxford, 1632) the contrast between divine and bestial shapes symbolizes the antithesis of heroic virtue and brutishness.

in whom brutishness (*ferità*) takes the place of vice. This is, however, far more terrifying than vice, and more fearful.[28]

VII

The logical basis of Milton's portrait of Satan is a "dissentany argument" as to the true nature of the hero. As brutishness and heroic virtue are "adverses"[29] ("affirming contraries"), both concepts are thrown into clearer relief by their juxtaposition. Milton's *Art of Logic* offers a detailed account of this type of argument:

But dissentany arguments are equally manifested with relation to each other; each is equally argued by the other; yet by their dissent they more evidently appear.

... yet from their dissent, or as others put it, their juxtaposition, they more evidently appear. Thus the conveniences of good health are made more manifest by the inconvenience of bad health; praises of the virtues are elucidated by censure of the contrary vices.[30]

Milton also refers to the utility of contraries in *Areopagitica* and *Of True Religion, Heresie, Schism, and Toleration*:

... triall is by what is contrary.

... the knowledge and survay of vice is in this world so necessary to the constituting of human vertue, and the scanning of error to the confirmation of truth....

... of contraries the definitions must needs be contrary.

In *Logic* they teach, that contraries laid together more evidently appear.[31]

Since the whole force of dissentany arguments resides in their ability "*to appear more evidently*" by their dissent, the logical value of Milton's portraits of Satan and Messiah lies in manifesting the nature of true heroic virtue by contrasting it with brutishness. The example of Satan

28. Tasso, *Prose*, pp. 368–69.

29. John Milton, *Works* (New York, 1935), XI, 131. Adverses are "*affirming contraries, which are absolutely diagonally adverse to each other*," like black and white, heat and cold, justice and injustice, liberty and servitude, good and evil, virtue and vice (*ibid.*, pp. 130, 132). Contraries, in turn, are opposites, of which one is opposed to one (*ibid.*, p. 116). Opposites, finally, are dissentanies, which dissent in reason and in thing (*ibid.*, p. 108).

30. *Ibid.*, pp. 99, 101. Cf. *ibid.*, pp. 101, 103: "So these places of dissentanies, as Aristotle (*Topics* 3.4) says, are useful not merely for arguing and explaining, but also for persuading and refuting, for as the places of the consentanies are valuable chiefly for arguing, proving, and confirming, thus the heads of the dissentanies are useful in contradicting, overthrowing, and refuting, so that he who does not wish to be taught by the consentany argument is led to it by the absurd result of a dissentany argument, so that even an unwilling man is unable not to assent to the truth. Hence Aristotle (*Rhetoric* 3.17) places *refuting* before *demonstrative arguments*."

31. *Ibid.* (New York, 1931), IV, 311; (New York, 1932), VI, 167, 178.

demonstrates "the absurd result of a dissentany argument." By censuring the contrary vice, Milton enhances his praise of heroic virtue.

The ethical contrast between such adverses as good and evil, virtue and vice, heroism and brutishness is also symbolized by the very structure of Milton's universe, where Heaven and Hell are diametrically opposed, and by the military antagonism of the two realms. This moral antithesis, furthermore, is brought into still sharper focus through the consistent allocation of contrary rewards.

Since "*whenever one opposite is affirmed the other is thereby denied,*"[32] the inherent absurdity of a "godlike" devil should, moreover, have been apparent to any reader familiar with Aristotelian, Ciceronian, or Ramist logic. Inasmuch as "godlike" and "diabolical" are logical contraries, Satan's seemingly heroic qualities can only be superficial and illusory; his "resemblance to the Highest" is merely external. Critics have, on the whole, misinterpreted the contrast between the apparently "heroic" Archangel of Books I and II and the "degraded" devil of Book X. There is no inconsistency here in Milton's concept of Satan, no disparity between the poet's conscious and unconscious intent. In the early books he deliberately creates a figure which appears to be a logical contradiction—a "godlike" devil—but the concept is too patently absurd to be taken seriously; as Satan merely *seems* heroic, there is no inconsistency in the fact that he is ultimately exposed as bestial.

VIII

Milton's descriptions of Messiah and Satan are actually imperfect definitions of heroic virtue and brutishness. According to the *Art of Logic,* there are two types of definition—perfect and imperfect. The former is properly called a definition, the latter a description.

A perfect definition comprehends the essence of a thing and designates its genus and form. Thus man is defined as a "rational animal"—the term "animal" specifying his genus and the adjective "rational" indicating his form.

Nevertheless, a perfect definition may consist of form alone.

For genus and form . . . constitute the whole essence of the thing. But not so necessarily is the genus required in a perfect definition that it cannot be perfect without the genus, for, first, there is no genus for the highest genera, such as the argument in logical invention, but their whole essence is contained in the form itself, which also includes the matter suitable to them; then it can be true that the causes themselves occur more easily than the genus which is their symbol.

32. *Ibid.*, XI, 113.

Hence if the definition is made up from the causes themselves, it will be perfect; if from genus, it merely will be more succinct.[33]

"Form is the cause through which a thing is what it is." *Therefore by it a thing may be distinguished from all other things*, that is, by an essential distinction . . . ; for from form alone comes an essential distinction.

Thus the "rational soul is the form of man, since through this man is man and is distinguished from all other natures. . . .[34]

This doctrine throws considerable light on Milton's fusion of the concepts of heroic virtue and the divine image in *Paradise Lost* and *Paradise Regain'd*. If the perfect definition of the hero is the "godlike man," the "θεῖος ἀνήρ," the term "man" constitutes the "nearest genus," and the adjective "godlike" indicates the form. The "essential distinction" of the hero consists, therefore, in "godlikeness"—in the divine image. True heroism is inconceivable apart from divine resemblance.

The implications of this definition for heroic poetry seem relatively obvious. The loss of the divine image with Adam and its renovation through Christ are theological events which determine the very existence of human heroism. They are, therefore, of inevitable importance to a heroic poet, whose office is to celebrate heroic virtue. Unlike his predecessors in the epic genre, Milton goes to the root of the problem of human heroism; he takes as his arguments the theological limitations of heroic virtue—the fall and restoration of man.

In *Paradise Lost* he defines this concept largely through comparing and contrasting the three major characters. Since the Logos is the supreme exemplar of the godlike, Milton portrays in Messiah the divine archetype of heroic virtue; in the language of the *Art of Logic*, this is a "consentany argument" as to the nature of the hero. In Satan, on the other hand, he discredits a conventional poetic conception of heroism by embodying it in a figure manifestly devoid of the "essential distinction" of the hero; by this example he not only distinguishes genuine heroism from its counterfeit, but also defines true heroic virtue more clearly by describing its opposite. In Adam, finally, he delineates the original perfection of the divine image in man, its obscuration by sin, and its partial recovery through repentance and faith.

In realizing the theological implications of the definition of heroic virtue as "godlikeness" and according them a central position in his argument and fable, Milton achieved his most significant innovation

33. *Ibid.*, XI, 262–65.
34. *Ibid.*, XI, 59, 61.

on epic tradition. In retrospect it seems almost inevitable—the only logical solution to the paradoxes and contradictions that faced an author of Christian epic. But the fact remains that his achievement was unique; only a poet who was also a logician and a theologian could have made it.

3. "Faithful Champion"

The Hero of Faith

❦ In *Samson Agonistes* Milton transformed a paragon of physical strength into the exemplar of a better fortitude, a hero who demonstrates his worth in moral decision before proving it in physical combat and triumphs in suffering as subsequently in action. This metamorphosis roughly parallels that of his classical compeer, Hercules. Milton has spiritualized and deepened Samson's character just as Renaissance mythography had refined and heightened that of his Gentile counterpart.

The "agony" of the "Heroic Nazarite" has its center in the mind, and scholars have correctly interpreted it largely as psychological drama, stressing such "themes" as repentance, regeneration, and the trial of faith and patience.[1] These concepts are as vital for Milton's drama as for his theology, and their interrelationship is no less essential

First published, in somewhat different form, in *Anglia*, LXXVII (1959), 12–28.

1. For these and related interpretations, see Walter C. Curry, "*Samson Agonistes* Yet Again," *Sewanee Review*, XXXII (1924), 336–52; James Holly Hanford, "The Temptation Motive in Milton," *SP*, XV (1918), 176–94; William Riley Parker, *Milton's Debt to Greek Tragedy in Samson Agonistes* (Baltimore, 1937); F. Michael Krouse, *Milton's Samson and the Christian Tradition* (Princeton, 1949); T. S. K. Scott-Craig, "Concerning Milton's Samson," *Renaissance News*, V (1952), 45–53; E. L. Marilla, "*Samson Agonistes*; An Interpretation," *Studia Neophilologica*, XXIX (1957), 67–76, gives a brief bibliography of studies which emphasize "the problem of determining the philosophic import of the poem." See also A. S. P. Woodhouse, "Tragic Effect in *Samson Agonistes*," *UTQ*, XXVIII (1959), 205–22; G. A. Wilkes, "The Interpretation of *Samson Agonistes*," *Huntington Library Quarterly*, XXVI (1963), 363–79.

to the fable of *Samson Agonistes* than to the *Christian Doctrine*. According to Milton's treatise, both repentance and faith are "effects of regeneration," and faith itself serves as "an instrumental and assisting cause" in the "gradual progress" of sanctification.[2] In the course of the drama Samson "becomes as it were a new creature"—a man "sanctified both in body and soul, for the service of God and the performance of good works."[3] Nevertheless, since regeneration is by definition a purely internal development, we are able to trace it only in its effects. We follow its gradual progress in the utterances which express Samson's repentance and faith. On the one hand, the pattern of his struggle follows the "progressive steps in repentance" outlined in the *De Doctrina*—"conviction of sin, contrition, confession, departure from evil, conversion to good."[4] On the other hand, his trial serves to manifest the strength of his faith and patience, the progressive recovery of his virtue.

Thus neither repentance nor the trial of faith can be regarded as an exclusive "key" to the drama. Both are essentially aspects of a larger whole, the "supernatural renovation" of the elect. The dominant motif of the tragedy is the hero's spiritual rebirth, his sanctification.[5]

More specifically, however, Samson is a "faithful Champion," a hero of faith—and this characterization is fully intelligible only against the background of Milton's theological beliefs. In orienting the drama around Samson's internal development rather than around a concatenation of external events, Milton gave poetic expression to several commonplaces of Reformation theology—the relationship of faith and works; the trial of faith and patience; and the logical opposites of faith, hope, and trust. If his primary emphasis falls on what happens in the hero's soul, this psychic drama follows a moral pattern already set forth in the *De Doctrina*.

I

Milton's emphasis on Samson's faith derives[6] less from Judges than

2. John Milton, *Works* (Columbia Edition; New York, 1931–38), XV, 376–79. All references to the *De Doctrina* in this chapter are based on the Latin text and the English translation by Charles R. Sumner, in the Columbia Edition.

3. *Ibid.*, pp. 366–67.

4. *Ibid.*, 384–85.

5. *Ibid.*, 374, "Hinc regeneratio alio nomine sanctificatio dicitur, et quidem proprio: nam regeneratio metaphorica potius est." "Sanctificatio autem nonnunquam late sumitur pro quavis electione aut separatione vel gentis universae ad cultum externum, vel hominis cuiusquam ad aliquod munus." As a Nazarite, consecrated to the particular office of delivering Israel, Samson had been sanctified from birth, in the latter, more general sense. Through his regeneration he is also "sanctified" in the former, more specialized sense.

6. Parker, 236; Krouse (pp. 130–31) observes that Samson was "an exemplar of faith" from "the time of the writing of the Epistle to the Hebrews" and that Milton's drama "deals with Samson's struggle to preserve his faith against all the temptations by which Man may be tried . . . In connection with each of these temptations, it is on Samson's faith that emphasis is placed."

from Hebrews, where he is enrolled among the "heroes" of faith. Calvin's commentary on this passage is illuminating. Since the "chief thing" in the elders "and the root of all other virtues"[7] was faith, Hebrews 11:32 ascribed to faith "all that was praiseworthy" in Samson. Nevertheless, the hero's surrender to Dalila manifested how "halting and imperfect" this virtue could be.[8] Did Milton, like Calvin, believe that Samson's disastrous revelation to Dalila was an evidence of "halting" faith? If so, it explains, to some extent, why Samson should first prove the constancy of his faith in his debate with himself, with the Chorus, and with Manoa, before re-encountering his wife. It also suggests that his rejection of Dalila's entreaties in the drama should, perhaps, be regarded as an additional confirmation and seal of his faith.

Beyond the central conception of the Nazarite as a hero of faith, *Samson Agonistes* reveals other analogies with Hebrews 11. The Chorus compares Samson with Gideon and Jephthah (lines 277–91) and recites how he had "stopped the mouths of lions, . . . waxed valiant in fight, turned to flight the armies of aliens." The catastrophe clearly ranks him among those who "through faith subdued kingdoms, wrought righteousness, obtained promises, . . . out of weakness were made strong." Finally, like other Old Testament heroes of faith, Milton's champion "had trial of cruel mockings" and "of bonds and imprisonment," but, in the end, "obtained a good report through faith."

Paradoxically, Milton's hero of faith belonged to the old dispensation, when knowledge of the objects of faith was still incomplete and obscure. Nevertheless, the seventeenth-century Protestant could regard him as all the more admirable in as much as he had "received not the promise." Had not Calvin interpreted Hebrews 11:13 as an exhortation for perseverance?[9]

Saving faith, as Milton defined it, entails believing that "whatsoever

7. John Calvin, *Commentaries on the Epistles of Paul the Apostle to the Hebrews*, trans. John Owen (Edinburgh, 1853), XXX.

8. Calvin, *Commentarius in Epistolam ad Hebraeos, Corpus Reformatorum* (Brunsvigae, 1896), LXXXIII, col. 166; Owen, 302–3. Cf. Krouse, p. 74. "Samson homo rusticanus, et qui non aliis quam agriculturae armis se exercuerat, quid poterat contra tam superbos victores, quorum potentia subactus fuerat totus populus? . . . Sed quoniam Deus omnes sequuntur ducem, et eius promissione animati iniunctum sibi munus suscipiunt, spiritus sancti testimonio ornantur. Ergo quidquid laudabile gesserunt, fidei apostolus tribuit, quamquam nullus est eorum cuius fides non claudicaverit. Samson concubinae blanditiis victus suam et totius populi salutem inconsiderate prodit . . . Ita in omnibus sanctis semper invenietur aliquid reprehensibile. Fides tamen etiamsi mutila sit ac imperfecta, Deo probari non desinit. Quare non est quod nos frangant vel exanimant vitia quibus laboramus, modo fide pergamus in vocationis nostrae stadio."

9. Calvin, *Commentarius*, col. 155. "Quum Deus gratiam, quae in nos large effusa est, patribus duntaxat gustandam praebuerit, quum eminus illis ostenderit obscuram Christi imaginem, qui nunc se conspiciendum quasi sub oculos nostros offert: tamen acquieverunt, nec unquam exciderunt a sua fide: quanto nobis hodie amplior datur perseverandi materia? Si deficimus, bis sumus inexcusabiles."

things" God "has promised in Christ are ours, and especially the grace of eternal life."[10] The fact that Samson lived and died before the advent of Christ does not, however, lessen his value as a hero of faith. According to the *De Doctrina*, "the ultimate object of faith is not Christ the Mediator, but God the Father." Many "both Jews and others, who lived before Christ," were "saved by faith in God alone: still however through the sole merits of Christ."[11]

A contributing factor in Milton's conception of his protagonist's ordeal was the Protestant doctrine of justification by faith rather than by works. In stressing Samson's faith, he was emphasizing the "essential form of good works." Since "none . . . of our works can be good, but by faith,"[12] it is actually faith which makes Samson's final exploit an heroic act—a deed acceptable to God. Before describing the act itself, Milton very logically demonstrates that his hero manifests the form or essence of heroic action. Before the "trial of mortal fight" to which Samson challenges Harapha and the "trial of strength" he exhibits to the Philistines, the poet subjects him to a trial of faith.

For a similar reason Milton delineates the gradual revival of Samson's virtue as an essential preliminary to his final act. While the "primary efficient cause of good works" is God, the *proximate* causes are virtues.[13] At the beginning of the drama the once "Heroic" and "Irresistible *Samson*" is described as "one past hope, abandon'd And by himself given over," but "whose strength, *while vertue was her mate*, Might have subdu'd the Earth." Yet at the end the Semichorus relates how the same man "His fierie vertue rouz'd From under ashes into sudden flame," and concludes:

> *So vertue giv'n for lost,*
> *Deprest, and overthrown, as seem'd . . .*
> *Revives, reflourishes, then vigorous most*
> *When most unactive deem'd . . .*

In the interim Milton had shown the progressive renewal of Samson's virtue; after his moral victories over Dalila and Harapha, the Chorus is able to conceive him once again in the role of potential hero or saint —as one who may yet deliver his people through "plain Heroic magnitude of mind" or else may prove "his own Deliverer," one "Whom Patience finally must crown." Before his final victory over his country's foes, Samson exhibits in two personal encounters with his enemies the moral virtue which is the proximate cause of good works.

10. Milton, XV, 392–93.

11. *Ibid.*, pp. 402–5. "Hinc illi sub lege illustres viri, Heb. xi, verae fidei testimonio ornati, cum in Deum duntaxat credidisse dicantur; Abel, Enoch, Noe, &c."

12. Milton, XVII, 6–9.

13. *Ibid.*, pp. 26–27.

The "works of believers are the works of the Spirit itself," and "conformity not with the written, but with the unwritten law, that is, with the law of the Spirit, . . . is to be accounted the true essential form of good works."[14] Though Samson lives under the old dispensation (and as he leaves for Dagon's festival he reiterates his determination to do nothing "that may dishonour Our Law"), he demonstrates, nevertheless, a preference for "the unwritten law" of the Spirit. In the first place, his marriages with "*Philistian* women" had been prompted by "intimate impulse" and "Divine impulsion." In the second place, it is only upon the instigation of the Spirit—after feeling "Some rouzing motions in me"—that he agrees to attend the "Idolatrous Rites." To emphasize the fact that Samson is actually conforming to the law of the Spirit in contradistinction to the written law, Milton first describes him as refusing to accompany the Public Officer on the grounds that "Our Law forbids at thir Religious Rites My presence; for that cause I cannot come." Moreover, the Chorus' final words to Samson are a prayer that the Spirit of the Lord may assist him:

> *Go and the Holy One*
> *Of* Israel *be thy guide*
> *To what may serve his glory best, and spread his name*
> *Great among the Heathen round:*
> *. . . that Spirit that first rusht on thee*
> *In the camp of* Dan
> *Be efficacious in thee now at need.*

In this context, the word *efficacious* is especially apt, inasmuch as the "primary efficient cause of good works . . . is God."

Significantly, this passage alludes directly or indirectly to several of the essential attributes of good works, as defined in the *De Doctrina*: "Good works are those which we perform by the Spirit of God working in us through true faith, to the glory of God, the assured hope of our own salvation, and the edification of our neighbor."[15] For the "edification of our neighbor" Milton substitutes the suggestion that Samson's act may spread God's name "Great among the Heathen round." The hero's "true faith" had already been established earlier in the drama.

II

As "triall is by what is contrary,"[16] Milton demonstrates Samson's faith primarily through contrast with its logical opposite, doubt. This

14. *Ibid.*, pp. 8–9.
15. *Ibid.*, p. 5.
16. Milton, IV, 311; cf. VI, 178, "In *Logic* they teach, that contraries laid together more evidently appear . . ."

is a vice "to which even the pious are sometimes liable, at least for a time," and its importance[17] in *Samson Agonistes* is emphasized by the explicit references to doubt in the first and final speeches of the drama and its prominence in the first *stasimon*. Since "the object of faith is the promise, that of hope, the thing promised,"[18] Samson's initial doubt centers upon the prophecy that he should deliver Israel. His present condition seems a direct contradiction of the terms of the promise:

> *Promise was that I*
> *Should* Israel *from* Philistian *yoke deliver;*
> *Ask for this great Deliverer now, and find him*
> *Eyeless in* Gaza *at the Mill with slaves,*
> *Himself in bonds under* Philistian *yoke* . . .

It is the diametric opposition between prophecy and fact that tempts him to "call in doubt Divine Prediction." From the very beginning of the drama God's apparent failure to fulfill his promise serves as a test of faith and a stumbling block, a suggestion that he is "to his own edicts, found contradicting." The tension created by the unfulfilled promise—the paradox that the proposed liberator is himself a slave—endures throughout the play and is not resolved until the catastrophe. In the miraculous execution of the prophecy the faithful find confirmation of their faith, indubitable evidence that God is true to his word.

Since hope and trust are closely linked with faith in Milton's theology, their opposites also serve to exercise Samson's faith or to bring it into clearer definition by contrast. To manifest hope, he must struggle not merely against doubt, but also against despair, a vice which "takes place only in the reprobate."[19]

In spite of "faintings, swounings of despair, And sense of Heav'n's desertion," Samson does not abandon his belief in God's mercy or "despair . . . of his final pardon." He displays a "most assured expectation through faith"[20] that Jehovah will vindicate the glory of his name against Dagon's competition:

> *This only hope relieves me, that the strife*
> *With me hath end; all the contest is now*
> *'Twixt God and* Dagon . . . *He, be sure,*
> *Will not connive, or linger, thus provok'd,*
> *But will arise and his great name assert* . . .

17. Milton, XVII, 58–59.

18. Milton, XV, 408–9. An essential feature of saving faith (XV, 392–93) is that "we believe, on the sole authority of the promise itself" ("propter ipsam promittentis Dei auctoritatem, credimus").

19. Milton, XVII, 58–59. Doubt is opposite to both faith and hope.

20. See Milton's definition of hope (XV, 406), "certissima . . . rerum earum expectatio futurarum quae in Christo iam nostrae per fidem sunt."

As hope is an effect of faith,[21] Samson's affirmation of hope is an additional confirmation of his faith. This hope in God stands, however, in striking contrast to the absence of personal hope:

> *Nor am I in the list of them that hope;*
> *Hopeless are all my evils, all remediless . . .*

Like Abraham, Samson is one "who *against* hope believed in hope" (Romans 4:18, 19).[22]

In the strongest expression of his griefs (lines 606–51) the core of Samson's complaint is Heaven's desertion—that God "hath cast me off as never known." His terminology makes it obvious that he is struggling against "the tentation of dereliction"—a temptation he ultimately overcomes "by a strong confidence in his God."[23] In Wolleb's discussion of Christ's internal sufferings Milton had found the temptation to despair expressed in very similar terms.[24]

This stage of Samson's ordeal involves a trial of faith and hope already familiar to Protestants from theological discussion of Christ's Passion, and Milton's contemporaries should have recognized it fairly readily as a temptation to despair. The analogy is intensified by such verbal similarities as 1. "desertion," "desertionis," "*deseruisti*" and 2. "cast me off," "abjectionis," Though *Samson Agonistes* does not really seem to be a celebration of Christ's spiritual agony (as one scholar has argued),[25] Milton has nevertheless expressed the hero's temptation to despair in terms reminiscent of Christ's.

If the earlier acts of the drama are darkened by temptations to doubt and despair, the final scenes are charged with renewed hope. Samson is confident that God will pardon his transgression and finally predicts that

> *This day will be remarkable in my life*
> *By some great act, or of my days the last.*

Manoa hopes that he may procure his son's liberty and that God will restore his sight. The Chorus conceives Samson once again in the role

21. *Ibid.*, 408, "Differt spes a fide ut effectum a causa . . ."

22. *Ibid.*, 406–7.

23. John Wollebius, *The Abridgment of Christian Divinitie*, trans. Alexander Ross (3rd ed.; London, 1660), pp. 139–40.

24. *Christianae Theologiae Compendium . . . Authore Iohanne Wollebio* (Amstelodami, 1633), 124: "Internae sunt, Tristitia, Angores & Cruciatus, ex atrocitate irae divinae & conflictu cum tentatione abjectionis ac desertionis orti, qui & sanguineum ei sudorem, & miserabilem illam vocem, *Eli, Eli, lamma sabachthani, Deus mi, cur me deseruisti?* expresserunt. Etsi autem cum abjectionis tentatione luctatus sit, nec tamen desperavit, nec tentationi succubuit, sed eam fiducia firma in Deum superavit." See Maurice Kelley, "Milton's Debt to Wolleb's *Compendium*," *PMLA*, L (1935), 156–65; T. S. K. Scott-Craig, "Milton's Use of Wolleb and Ames," *MLN*, LV (1940), 403–7.

25. Scott-Craig, *Renaissance News*, p. 46.

of potential Deliverer, triumphing over his enemies or himself:

> *Either of these is in thy lot,*
> Samson, *with might endu'd*
> *Above the Sons of men . . .*

And expectation comes close to the actual fulfillment of "Divine Prediction" when the Danites, hearing the "rueful cry" from Dagon's temple, suggest that Samson—"his eyesight by miracle restor'd"—is again "dealing dole among his foes."

In these final scenes, there is a gradual orientation of hope towards its proper object—"the thing promised." For the greater part of the drama there has been a marked disparity between Samson's "assured expectation" of God's imminent victory over Dagon and his lack of hope for himself and his prophesied role as deliverer. Although he has refused to distrust the promise itself, he does not look for its fulfillment. Nevertheless, the disparity narrows significantly during the encounters with Harapha and the Philistine Officer, and in the final utterances of Samson and the Chorus it has virtually disappeared. In the event, the same act fulfills both predictions.

III

It is in the encounter with Harapha that, for the first time in the drama, Samson appears once more in his ordained role as "Defensor Fidei"—God's "faithful Champion," who thrice challenges Dagon's "Champion bold" to combat. The giant's taunts call forth an explicit avowal of the Hebrew's "trust . . . in the living God" and "confidence" in final pardon. The very jeers of his enemy are a testimony of his faith:

> *Fair honour that thou dost thy God, in trusting*
> *He will accept thee to defend his cause . . .*

Trust and *confidence* are key words in this passage, as important in Milton's delineation of his hero of faith as was *hope* in the earlier scene (lines 460, 472). According to the *De Doctrina*, trust is an inseparable companion of saving faith and may therefore be used as a synonym for faith itself. On the other hand, the term may also be used, in a slightly different sense, to indicate "a particular effect or degree of faith, or a firm hope."[26] In this second sense, trust is one of the virtues

26. Milton, XV, 396–97. The distinction between *fiducia* as 1. the *form* or essence of saving faith and 2. its *effect* was not uncommon among Reformation theologians. Cf. James Arminius, *Works*, trans. James Nichols (London, 1828), I, 318–319; Wollebius, *Abridgment*, 253–54, 324; *Theodori Bezae Annotationes Maiores in Novum Testamentum* (*s.l.*, 1594), Part II, 365.

belonging to the worship of God—"an effect of love, and . . . a part of internal worship, whereby we wholly repose on him."[27]

Samson's affirmation of his confidence in God, in the midst of his calamities, recalls Job's similar assertion of faith under trial: "though he slay me, yet will I trust in him."[28]

In the *De Doctrina* Milton distinguishes four opposites to trust in God (*fiducia*): 1. distrust of God (*diffidentia in Deum*), 2. an overweening presumption (*praefidentia sive praesumptio*), 3. carnal reliance (*fiducia carnalis*), and 4. a trust in idols (*fiducia idololatrica*).[29] All four of these serve, in varying degrees, as foils for Samson's faith; they cast into bolder relief his confidence in God.

In the final work of Milton's imagination, Hanford observes "the temptation to distrust . . . becomes a dominant and controlling motive." In "the midst of failure and personal affliction," Samson "is definitely tempted to surrender his trust in Providence because of his inability to understand its dealing with himself."[30] Though we should avoid confusing *doubt* with *distrust* (inasmuch as Milton distinguishes them as the opposites of different, though related, virtues), we should probably regard the temptation to "call in doubt Divine Prediction" as a temptation to distrust. Though the hero checks himself before expressing actual disbelief in the promise, he comes very close to distrust, as Polanus had defined it.[31] Samson is clearly tempted to "doubt the fulfillment of the promise" because of "the lack of ordinary means and the apparent impossibility of accomplishing what God has promised."

Strictly speaking, in questioning the workings of Providence (lines 23–42, 350–72), both Samson and Manoa exhibit doubt rather than distrust. Significantly, doubt is not incompatible with trust, in Wolleb's view: "Yet we teach not such a firm confidence, as if no wayes tossed with doubtings; but such a one as doth not finally yield to doubtings."[32] Again, according to Polanus, "Doubting is neither firmely to consent to the word of God, and in that word, to the promise of Grace especially, neither altogether to resist the same, but to flow, now into one part, and anon faintly to incline to the other part."[33] In

27. Milton, XVII, 52–53.

28. *Ibid.*, pp. 56–57.

29. *Ibid.*, pp. 54–57.

30. Hanford, *SP*, 190.

31. *Syntagma Theologiae Christianae ab Amando Polano a Polansdorf* (Genevae, 1612), II, cols. 710–11: "*Diffidentia erga Deum*, est peccatum, quum quis aut omnino non fidit soli, promissioni divinae, de re aliqua vel ad salutem aeternam vel ad praesentem vitam pertinente, quamvis certae: aut de promissionis illius impletione dubitat: proficiscens à nativa infidelitate hominum propter defectum mediorum ordinarium & apparentem impossibilitatem consequendi id quod Deus promisit."

32. Wollebius, *Abridgment*, 255.

33. Amandus Polanus, *The Substance of Christian Religion*, trans. Thomas Wilcocks (London, 1608), 470.

contrast to numerous references to doubt, the drama contains only one explicit allusion to distrust—Samson's regret that he has inspired "diffidence of God, and doubt In feeble hearts."

When Samson affirms his "trust . . . in the living God" and challenges "*Dagon* to the test," Harapha maintains that this confidence is really presumption:

> *Presume not on thy God, what'er he be,*
> *Thee he regards not, owns not . . .*

Samson's challenge to a "test," to "the trial of mortal fight," might indeed seem presumptuous—a case of tempting God—were it not for his extraordinary commission from Heaven. Both Ames[34] and Polanus[35] define presumption essentially as the expectation of some benefit from God without promise. But Samson refuses to mistake *fiducia* for *praefidentia* and reiterates his confidence in God.

Primarily, however, this encounter stresses the antithesis between trust in God and "carnal reliance"—between confidence in the unarmed might of God and trust in purely human force and arms. For Samson, this is a familiar dichotomy. Formerly, "weaponless himself," he had "Made Arms ridiculous" with "what trivial weapon came to hand." Now once again, in spite of his blindness, he is confident that, relying only on his "Heav'n-gifted strength"—"the power of *Israel's* God"—he can overcome a fully-armed giant with merely "an Oak'n staff." Knowing that his might is not his own, but a divine miracle, he opposes to "gorgeous arms" his "trust . . . in the living God."[36] Harapha, on the other hand, acclaims "glorious arms" as the "ornament and safety" of "greatest Heroes." Whereas Samson trusts in Jehovah alone, his adversary is one "that trusteth in man, and maketh flesh his arm."[37]

34. *Guliel. Amesii Medulla Theologica* (Amstelodami, 1648), 237: "Temeraria ista praesumptio . . . aliquando . . . nititur Deo, sed perverse sine promissione ac fide, ut cum quis sperat veniam ac salutem, quamvis maneat impoenitens, aut retineat propositum in peccatis suis vivendi, aut aliquid aliud exspectat à Deo, quod non convenit ejus naturae vel voluntati revelatae."

35. Polanus, *Syntagma*, II, col. 711: "*Confidentia temeraria*, est peccatum, quum quis aliquid ad praesentem vel futuram vitam pertinens, se posse à Deo impetrare confidit, aut potius confidere se inaniter gloriatur, aut neglectis mediis à Deo ordinatis aut adhibitis mediis voluntati Dei adversantibus quasi volens Deum ipsum antevertere: quum novam aut peculiarem non habeat à Deo extraordinariorum mediorum promissionem."

36. The antithesis between trust in God and confidence in arms also appears in Psalm 18:2, 3, which Milton quotes as an example of *fiducia* (XVII, 52–53): "Jehovah is my rock and my fortress . . . in whom I will trust, my buckler and the horn of my salvation, and my high tower."

37. Jeremiah 17:5. The opposition between Harapha and Samson can be epitomized by the antithesis between this text and Jeremiah 17:7, "blessed is the man that trusteth in Jehovah, and whose hope Jehovah is" ("benedictus vir ille qui fiduciam habet in Iehova, et cuius confidentia est Iehova"). Milton quotes these texts (XVII, 54–57) as examples of *fiducia carnalis* and *fiducia in Deo*, respectively.

Nevertheless, it is not in Harapha alone that we must look for the antithesis of Samson's trust in God. When, "swoll'n with pride,"[38] he had walked "Fearless of danger, like a petty God," he was guilty both of presumption and carnal reliance. He has learned by experience, however, not to glory in his strength.

> *God, when he gave me strength, to show withal*
> *How slight the gift was, hung it in my Hair.*

Like Manoa, he knows how unreliable is our "ever failing trust In mortal strength."

A further instance of misplaced confidence in creatures instead of the Creator is to be found in Samson's experience with Dalila. Her "wedlock-treachery endangering life" contrasts not only with Samson's trust, but also with God's fidelity to his promise. Reliance on Jehovah is counterpointed by allusions to Samson's disastrous "trust" in his wife (lines 783, 1001) and her breach of "faith" (lines 388, 750, 986, 1115). The failure of this trust in the creature emphasizes, by contrast, the reliability of God.

Finally, the contrast between confidence in God and trust in idols is fundamental both to the drama as a whole and to Samson's role as Jehovah's champion in particular. Implicit in the interview with Dalila, it receives explicit statement in the encounter with Harapha, when Samson challenges Dagon "to the test." The focal point of this antithesis, however, is the "popular Feast" to honor the Philistine idol. In this celebration both Samson and Manoa recognize a direct affront to God ("So *Dagon* shall be magnifi'd, and God . . . compar'd with Idols"), and both expect Jehovah's early and decisive answer to this challenge. Appropriately, it is when the provocation is at its height—when, drunk with idolatry and wine, the Philistines are "Chaunting thir Idol, and preferring Before our living Dread"—that the conflict between *fiducia in Deo* and *fiducia idololatrica* achieves its fullest dramatic expression. It is at this moment that God intervenes to "vindicate the glory of his name," to destroy the idolators, and to bear witness to his faithful Champion.

IV

Samson's ordeal shows most of the characteristics of the "good temptation," as Milton had defined it in the *De Doctrina*—the trial "whereby God tempts even the righteous for the purpose of proving them." First, it serves the "purpose of exercising or manifesting [his]

38. For Milton's projected drama on *Samson Hybristes*, see Merritt Y. Hughes (ed.), *Paradise Regained, The Minor Poems, and Samson Agonistes* (New York, 1937), p. 428.

faith or patience, as in the case of Abraham and Job." Secondly, it also achieves the end "of lessening [his] self-confidence, and reproving [his] weakness," so that he himself becomes "wiser by experience, and others . . . profit by [his] example." In his "sense of Heav'n's desertion" he resembles Hezekiah, "whom 'God left'—partially, or for a time—'to try him, that he might know all that was in his heart.'"[39] Thirdly, Samson's temptation has "a happy issue,"[40] for the trial of his faith is "found unto praise and honor and glory."[41]

His sufferings not only try his faith and patience, but also lead him to repentance and renewed trust in God. "Chastisement is often the instrumental cause of repentance," according to the *De Doctrina*; since God "supplies strength for our support even under those inflictions which . . . appear to us too heavy to be borne," misfortune instructs us [2 Corinthians 1:8–10] "that we should not trust in ourselves, but in God."[42] Similarly, Polanus maintains that temptations and afflictions are "impulsive causes" of trust in God.[43]

On the whole, Samson's trial follows the causal and temporal pattern suggested by James 1:3 ("the trying of your faith worketh patience") and Romans 5:3–4 ("tribulation worketh patience; And patience, experience"). If the crisis of faith is strongest at the beginning of the drama, the test of patience is most pronounced during the interval between Manoa's departure to seek the Philistine lords and Samson's own departure with the Philistine Officer. Both Samson's lament (lines 606–51) and the immediate observations of the Chorus (lines 652–66) emphasize his need for patience. His petition for "speedy death" is patently an instance of "impatience under the divine decrees; a temptation to which the saints themselves are at times liable."[44] There is little difference in substance between this outburst and similar outcries of impatience from Elijah, Jonah, and Job:

1 Kings xix. 4. "he requested for himself that he might die."
Job iii. 2, c. "Let the day perish wherein I was born."
Jonah iv. 3. "it is better for me to die than to live."[45]

At this point the Chorus comments on the inutility of "sayings of the wise" extolling "Patience as the truest fortitude," to comfort the afflicted. Yet, immediately after the scenes with Dalila and Harapha, the same Chorus hails Samson as one whom patience may crown. After

39. Milton, XV, 88–89.
40. *Ibid.*, pp. 88–89, "Et felicem exitum promittit Deus."
41. 1 Peter 1:7. Cf. Milton, XV, 88–89.
42. *Ibid.*, pp. 388–89.
43. Polanus, *Syntagma*, II, col. 709. "*Causae impellentes* nos ad eam [fiduciam in Deo] sunt tentationes & afflictiones in quibus versamur . . ."
44. Milton, XVII, 68–69.
45. *Ibid.*, p. 69.

the sense of Heaven's desertion, he experiences "Favour renew'd" and "internal peace." His trial teaches him patience—to "acquiesce in the promises of God, through a confident reliance on his divine providence, power, and goodness, and bear inevitable evils with equanimity, as the dispensation of the supreme Father, and sent for our good."[46] Finally, the outcome of his temptation, the "great event," leaves his companions with "new acquist Of true experience."

In reply to Samuel Johnson's objection that *Samson Agonistes* lacks a middle, modern scholarship has stressed "Milton's inward interpretation of his theme."[47] This orientation is hardly surprising. Regeneration is, by definition, a "change operated" in the *inward* man,[48] and Milton's doctrine of the relationship of faith and works made it virtually imperative to place his primary emphasis on Samson's spiritual changes rather than on the movement of external events. Although a complex and tightly-knit structure of cause and effect underlies the drama, this pattern is essentially moral and theological. It is not until Samson is regenerated in understanding and will, until his repentance and faith demonstrate his sanctification in body and soul, that he is ready "for the service of God, and the performance of good works."[49] Nevertheless, Dr. Johnson's observation is not altogether unjust, for Milton has, in part at least, stressed the development of character over that of the plot and emphasized the motions of the mind and will rather than the movement of events. Though there *is* a causal sequence in the drama—a nexus of causes fully as "probable" and "necessary" as Aristotle demanded it should be—it is, on the whole, internal rather than external, psychological rather than explicitly dramatic.

If "nothing passes between the first Act and the last, that either hastens or delays the Death of *Samson*," the primary reason is to be found in Milton's theology. According to the Protestant conception of the relation of faith to works, the spiritual regeneration of the inward man, was the really significant factor in heroic activity. The true causes of good works were to be found in a pattern of internal events—a spiritual "plot"—rather than in a sequence of causes entirely outside the mind and will of the agent. External events could provide an *occasion* for moral action—good or bad—but the primary causes were to be found within the soul itself.[50]

46. *Ibid.*, pp. 66–67.

47. James H. Hanford, *A Milton Handbook* (4th ed.; New York, 1947), p. 286; Parker, p. 23; M. E. Grenander, "*Samson's* Middle: Aristotle and Dr. Johnson," *University of Toronto Quarterly*, XXIV (1955), 377–89.

48. Milton, XV, 366–67.

49. *Ibid.*, pp. 366–67.

50. In "*Samson Agonistes* and the Hellenic Drama," R. C. Jebb condemns Johnson's criticism as "far too strongly expressed": "Samson's will is the agent of the catastrophe. Everything, therefore, which helps to determine Samson's will and to define his purpose leads to the catastrophe." (See *Proceedings of the British Academy*, III [1908], 1–8).

A similar emphasis on the internal event was fostered by the Protestant attitude towards suffering. The chief significance of external misfortunes resided in their moral effects on the sufferer. Possessing little intrinsic interest in themselves, they were primarily important as instrumental causes of repentance and the trial of faith and patience.

Although the crowning event of *Samson Agonistes* is an external act, Milton invests it with probability and verisimilitude by presenting it as the logical culmination of a spiritual process rather than as the effect of purely external causes. To have led up to the final catastrophe in any other way would have blunted the whole point of the test of faith. The trial of Samson's faith and patience depends essentially on the apparent impossibility of fulfilling the promise that he should deliver Israel. If Milton had constructed his plot differently, around a chain of events pointing inevitably towards this catastrophe, he would have sacrificed the very foundation of the temptation motif.

4. The "Suffering Servant"

Messianic Ministry As Epic Exemplar

❦ In the Christ of *Paradise Regain'd* recent scholarship has recognized Milton's answer to the classic problem of the Renaissance epic poet—the choice of an exemplary hero. In both of his epics the perfect "pattern of a Christian hero"[1] he exhibits not in a secular "king or knight," but in the Son of God himself—the "Most perfect *Heroe*, try'd in heaviest plight Of labours huge and hard, too hard for human wight." In the protagonist of *Paradise Regain'd* Hughes saw "the culmination of the faith of the Reformers in an exemplar Redeemer, the Word of Saint John's Gospel, as it fused with the cravings of the critics and poets of the later Renaissance for a purely exemplary hero in epic poetry."[2] Kermode found in this figure an ideal of Christian heroism surpassing that of the pagan worthies both in virtue and

First published, in somewhat different form, in *The Harvard Theological Review*, LIV (1961), 29–43.

1. In addition to previous references, see A. S. P. Woodhouse, "Theme and Pattern in *Paradise Regained*," *University of Toronto Quarterly*, XXV (1956), 167–82; see also Arnold Stein, *Heroic Knowledge: An Interpretation of Paradise Regained and Samson Agonistes* (Minneapolis, 1957); Stein's "underlying assumption" (p. 17) is "that *Paradise Regained* is a dramatic definition of 'heroic knowledge,' not of heroic rejection; and that the contest is a preparation for *acting transcendence in the world*, by uniting intuitive knowledge with proved intellectual and moral discipline"; cf. *ibid.*, 205, "The key for Milton is knowledge, the self-knowledge of thought tested by deed, heroic knowledge maintained against the pressing claims of immediate knowledge and action."

2. Merritt Y. Hughes, "The Christ of *Paradise Regained* and the Renaissance Heroic Tradition," *SP*, XXXV (1938), 277.

in rewards: "We learn . . . why Christ is the exemplary hero by watching him in the act of confuting or transcending all the known modes of heroism. We are taught the rewards of Christian heroism by a demonstration based on the superseded rewards of the old heroes."[3] Finally, Woodhouse has focused attention on "two ideas . . . embodied in the Christ of *Paradise Regain'd*"—"the idea of obedience to God as the beginning and end of virtue, and the idea of Christian heroism as something new and distinctive, different not simply in degree, but in kind, from every other."[4]

Nevertheless, the attempt to interpret Milton's Christ against the background of Renaissance heroic tradition involves us in a certain paradox. While acknowledging that Christ himself provides the heroic norm *par excellence*, we may find ourselves, notwithstanding, in the position of regarding him as the embodiment of ethical concepts which are extrinsic to the Biblical Messiah—of explaining his character as a reflection of Milton's personal preference for a particular heroic ideal: magnanimity or charity, action or contemplation, doing or suffering, the military fortitude displayed in "Warrs" or "the better fortitude Of Patience and Heroic Martyrdom."

In actuality (Milton would have insisted) the true heroic paradigm is implicit in Christ, and any valid conception of the heroic norm must inevitably be derivative from his example. He is, strictly speaking, the *archetype* rather than the *embodiment* of Christian heroism. As the perfect "pattern of a Christian hero" is, *ipso facto*, Christ himself, Milton modeled his exemplary hero not on any ideal extrinsic to the Biblical Messiah, but on the character of the historic Christ as revealed in the Scriptures and interpreted by Protestant theologians. He did not "lay" the heroic norm in this figure, as he might have done in the case of some "king or knight, before the conquest."[5] Instead, it was precisely from the Son of God that he derived his heroic paradigm.

The norm of heroic excellence in both epics is Biblical both in origin and in authority. In the lineaments of his poetic Christ, Milton sought to imitate those of the historic Messiah—the "suffering servant" of Isaiah's prophecy, the redeemer in "the form of a servant" of Philippians. In both of these poems the supremely heroic enterprise is Messiah's ministry of redemption, and in the twofold aspects of this ministry—Messiah's humiliation and exaltation—lies the perfect exemplar of Christian heroism and its rewards. This is the true prototype of the heroic pattern in both *Paradise Lost* and *Paradise Regain'd*, and for

3. Frank Kermode, "Milton's Hero," *RES*, N.S. IV (1953), 330.

4. Woodhouse, p. 167.

5. See "*The Reason of Church Government*," in *The Prose Works of John Milton* (Bohn Library; London, 1883), II, 478.

the characterization of Christ in either poem the concepts of Renaissance ethical theory are of secondary importance.

Milton's search for the ideal exemplar of Christian heroism led him, then, from the inferior imitation to the archetype, from the Christian "king or knight" to Christ himself. In choosing the Messiah as his "pattern of a Christian hero," he pursued to its logical conclusion an axiom of Renaissance poetic theory—that the poet must imitate the idea. Poetry is more philosophic than history, Aristotle had insisted, "since its statements are of the nature rather of universals, whereas those of history are singulars."[6] In such epic heroes as Achilles, Odysseus, Aeneas, and Godfrey, Renaissance critics had recognized the "idea" of a valiant warrior, a prudent commander, a virtuous leader, or a Christian prince. Similarly, in looking for some "king or knight, before the conquest," in whom he might "lay the pattern of a Christian hero," Milton had been seeking an appropriate vehicle for the *idea* of Christian virtue—a particular historical example, in which he might delineate the universal norm. In the case of all of these secular worthies the heroic paradigm is an ideal really extrinsic to the men themselves, a universal which the poet may *embody* in a particular individual. In the instance of Milton's Christ, however, the relationship of the historical particular to the universal norm is radically different. Here the example is himself the Idea; the historical individual is himself the universal norm. In Christ, the suffering servant, Milton found the very archetype of Christian heroism.

I

Not only is Christ himself the heroic exemplar in both of Milton's epics, but his ministry of redemption is likewise the supremely heroic or "godlike" enterprise. At best, the secular worthy could bring a superficial and temporary deliverance to a mere fraction of humanity. Christ's satisfaction, on the other hand, enabled him to offer a genuine and eternal deliverance to all mankind—"to save . . . the whole Race lost," "to save A World from utter loss." Moreover, the secular hero achieved fame largely through acts of destruction. Messiah, on the other hand, not only surpassed them in destructive might (witness his victory over the rebel angels), but also was capable of a still loftier mode of valor—both to create and to restore his fallen creation; "to create," the angelic choir reminds us, "is greater than created to destroy." Finally, the earthly conqueror had inevitably been overcome by Sin and Death. Messiah, on the other hand, overcame both of these "grand foes" in his ministry of redemption. The ministry of redemption is thus

6. Aristotle, *On the Art of Poetry*, trans. Ingram Bywater (Oxford, 1951), p. 43.

the supremely heroic act of the "Most perfect *Heroe*," and it is to the dual aspects of this ministry—Christ's humiliation and exaltation[7]—that we must look for the archetypal pattern of Christian heroic virtue and its reward.

Christ's humiliation and exaltation (Milton declared in the *De Doctrina Christiana*) provide a normative pattern for all Christian believers. The conformity[8] of the faithful to his image was a major objective of his ministry of redemption: "The second object of the ministry of the Mediator is, *that we may be conformed to the image of Christ, as well in his state of humiliation as of exaltation.*"[9] Like Christ, the faithful must endure suffering, but, with Christ, they would receive an eternal "reward" or "recompense"[10] of heavenly glory:

Rom. viii, 29, "to be conformed to the image of his Son . . ."; [Rom.] viii, 17, "if so be that we suffer with him, that we may be also glorified together . . ."; 2 Tim. ii, 11, 12, "if we be dead with him, we shall also live with him . . ."; 1 Pet. iv. 13, "rejoice, inasmuch as ye are partakers of Christ's sufferings, that when his glory shall be revealed, ye may be glad also."

John xii. 32, "I, if I be lifted up from the earth, will draw all men unto me."; [John] xvi. 22, "the glory that thou gavest me, I have given them."; Ephesians

7. See Milton's *Christian Doctrine*, trans. Charles R. Sumner, in *Prose Works*, IV, 304, "Having treated of the mediatorial office, and its threefold functions, we are now to consider the manner in which it is discharged. This includes the state of humiliation to which our Redeemer submitted, as well as his state of exaltation." For the relationship of the theology of the *De Doctrina* to that of *Paradise Lost*, see Maurice Kelley, *This Great Argument* (Princeton, 1941).

8. In representing Christ himself as the heroic exemplar in both of his epics, Milton was following not only the theological doctrine of "the conformation of the faithful to the image of Christ" (*Prose Works*, IV, 309), but also the Renaissance critical principle of conformity to the moral example of the epic hero. Thus Tasso maintains, in his *Discorsi del Poema Eroico*, that heroic poems and discourses on their composition should be especially dear to those who seek to conform their minds to the example of their fathers' virtues. The intellect acts like a painter, depicting in the soul the forms of fortitude, temperance, prudence, justice, and other virtues, both acquired and infused. Torquato Tasso, *Prose*, ed. Francesco Flora (Milan and Rome, 1935), p. 319.

9. Milton, IV, 316. Cf. Amandus Polanus, *The Substance of Christian Religion*, trans. Thomas Wilcocks (London, 1608), p. 121, "The state of the humiliation of Christ, was that state of his in which hee did abase himselfe, that so by his obedience, hee might satisfie for our disobedience." According to John Wolleb's *Abridgment of Christian Divinitie*, trans. Alexander Ross (London, 1660), 135, "The state of Humiliation is, in which he took the forme of a Servant being in the forme of God, and gave obedience to his Father for us . . .: And in this State he so performed his Prophetical, Sacerdotal, and Regal office, that in a manner he stript himselfe of the forme and glory of the Divinity." In *The Reason of Church Government*, Milton declared (II, 483) that "the form of a servant was a mean, laborious, and vulgar life, aptest to teach; which form Christ thought fittest, that he might bring about his will according to his own principles, choosing the meaner things of this world, that he might put under the high."

10. Milton, IV, 317, "So far, therefore, as regards the satisfaction of Christ, and our conformity to his humiliation, the restoration of man is of merit; in which sense those texts are to be understood which convey a notion of recompense and reward."

ii. 5, 6, "God hath quickened us together with Christ . . . and hath raised us up together, and made us sit together in heavenly places in Christ Jesus."

Again, in a passage Milton cites frequently in his chapter "Of the Ministry of Redemption," St. Paul exhorts the Philippians (2:5–9) to imitate the example of Christ's humiliation:

> Let this mind be in you, which was also in Christ Jesus: Who, being in the form of God, thought it not robbery to be equal with God: But made himself of no reputation, and took upon him the form of a servant, and was made in the likeness of men: And being found in fashion as a man, he humbled himself, and became obedient unto death, even the death of the cross. Wherefore God also hath highly exalted him, and given him a name which is above every name.[11]

In Christ's humiliation and exaltation—an example normative for all believers—Milton found his ideal "pattern" of Christian heroism and its reward.

II

In Messiah's humiliation Milton found an ethical pattern diametrically opposed to that of the secular hero. Where the worldly hero sought glory, Christ had voluntarily renounced glory for shame. Where the worldly hero strove to win "high repute," Christ had made himself of "no reputation." Where the worldly hero aspired to regal dignity, Christ had assumed the form of a servant. Where the worldly heroes had usurped divine titles ("and must be titl'd Gods, Great Benefactors of mankind, Deliverers, Worship't with Temple, Priest and Sacrifice; One is the Son of *Jove*, of *Mars* the other"), Christ had resigned the "form of God" and the privileges of divinity. In this concept of heroic humility—a heroism characterized by obedience, lowliness, and suffering—Milton found the antithesis of the world's opinion of the hero.

Let us briefly examine the use Milton makes of this conception of the "suffering servant" as heroic archetype, first in *Paradise Lost* and afterwards in *Paradise Regain'd.*

Christ's humiliation (Milton declared in the *De Doctrina*) is "that state in which under his character of God-man he voluntarily submitted himself to the divine justice, as well in life as in death, for the purpose of undergoing all things requisite to accomplish our redemption." The first object of his ministry of redemption was "the satisfaction of divine justice on behalf of all men"; and in accomplishing this satisfaction he "fulfilled the law by perfect love to God and his neighbor, until the time when he laid down his life for his brethren, being made obedient unto his Father in all things."[12]

11. *Ibid.*, pp. 304–8, 316–17; cf. pp. 118, 145.
12. *Ibid.*, pp. 304, 309–10.

In *Paradise Lost* these concepts emerge with exceptional clarity in the celestial council of Book III. Here the Son of God "voluntarily submits himself to the divine justice" on man's behalf. The particular virtues he manifests on this occasion—"immortal love To mortal men" and "Filial obedience"—are the moral qualities especially demanded for his satisfaction. In accepting the Father's challenge to "satisfie for Man," he displays that "magnanimous resolution to die,"[13] which, in Tasso's opinion, characterized the ideal epic hero. In this scene he voluntarily makes "himself of no reputation" and becomes "obedient unto death."

> *Account mee man; I for his sake will leave*
> *Thy bosom, and this glorie next to thee*
> *Freely put off, and for him lastly die*
> *Well pleas'd, on me let Death wreck all his rage....*

In this passage, crucial for the celestial strategy in the Holy War, the heroic norm is clearly based on the doctrine of Christ's humiliation. After first presenting the Messiah in "the form of God" and as "equal to God," Milton shows him volunteering to "take upon him the form of a servant," for the sake of accomplishing his ministry of redemption. This deliberate renunciation of glory for shame ("no reputation") stands in striking opposition to Satan's motivation in the analogous scene in Hell ("the high repute Which he through hazard huge must earn").

Again, Milton stresses Messiah's humiliation in Book X, when the Son of God assumes "the forme of servant" immediately after passing judgment on Adam and Eve:

> ... *[He] disdain'd not to begin*
> *Thenceforth the forme of servant to assume,*
> *As when he wash'd his servants' feet, so now*
> *As Father of his Familie he clad*
> *Thir nakedness with Skins of Beasts, or slain ...:*
> *Nor hee thir outward onely with the Skins*
> *Of Beasts, but inward nakedness, much more*
> *Opprobrious, with his Robe of righteousness,*
> *Araying cover'd from his Fathers sight.*

Later, in his mediatorial function, he intercedes with the Father (X, 228; XI, 21–44) on behalf of the guilty pair. Finally, in Book XII, Michael recapitulates the essential details of Christ's humiliation and satisfaction (XII, 390–435):

> *The Law of God exact he shall fulfil*
> *Both by obedience and by love, though love*

13. Tasso, p. 368, "ma l'illustre de l'eroico è fondato ... sopra il magnanimo proponimento di morire...."

Alone fulfil the Law; thy punishment
He shall endure by coming in the Flesh
To a reproachful life and cursed death. . . .

In this passage, as in Book III, the poet emphasizes the two allied virtues, obedience and love—both requisite for Christ's mission "to satisfie for Man." It is from Michael's account of Christ's humiliation that Adam learns the better fortitude of "suffering for Truth's sake" and the merit of obedience.

If Messiah's humiliation constitutes the norm of Christian heroism in *Paradise Lost*, his exaltation provides the pattern of the Christian's reward—a *remuneratio aeterna* of celestial glory:

The exaltation of Christ is that by which *having triumphed over death, and laid aside the form of a servant, he was exalted by God the Father to a state of immortality and of the highest glory, partly by his own merits, partly by the gift of the Father, for the benefit of mankind; wherefore he rose again from the dead, ascended into heaven, and sitteth on the right hand of God. . . .* This exaltation consists of three degrees; his resurrection, his ascension into heaven, and his sitting on the right hand of God. . . .[14]

In Book III the Son himself prophesies his triumph over death and his victorious return to Heaven "with the multitude of my redeem'd" (III, 247–65). That his exaltation is the reward for his humiliation is stated, however, even more explicitly by the Father (III, 305–17):

Because thou hast, though Thron'd in highest bliss
Equal to God, and equally enjoying
God-like fruition, quitted all to save
A World from utter loss, and hast been found
By Merit more than Birthright Son of God,
Found worthiest to be so by being Good,
Far more than Great or High; because in thee
Love hath abounded more than Glory abounds,
Therefore thy Humiliation shall exalt
With thee thy Manhood also to this Throne;
Here shalt thou sit incarnate, here shalt Reigne
Both God and Man, Son both of God and Man,
Anointed universal King. . . .

Again, in Book III, Michael foretells Messiah's exaltation and entrance into glory and foresees the heavenly reward of the faithful (XII, 456–65).

14. Milton, IV, 307–8.

III

In *Paradise Regain'd,* as in the earlier epic, the heroic norm is to be found in Christ's ministry of redemption—in the humiliation which precedes his ultimate exaltation. Although the temptation is itself an aspect of this humiliation, the poet's primary emphasis falls on future events. The temptation is basically an "apprentissage"—a schooling in spiritual combat preliminary to a greater battle. In this preparatory "exercise" the protagonist must "first lay down the rudiments Of his great warfare" against Sin and Death. As he is to conquer these "grand foes" not by physical weapons, but by "Humiliation and strong Sufferance," he must learn the particular virtues requisite for his future satisfaction—obedience, humility, reliance on Providence (I, 290–93), and patience. These are the necessary moral equipment for his "reproachful life" and the supreme agony of the crucifixion—a death "ignominious in the highest degree." In this epic, as in its predecessor, the virtues Milton stresses as normative for Christian heroism are those particularly characteristic of the "suffering servant"—obedience and the "better fortitude" of patience. Both of these virtues are actually based on the concept of Messiah's humiliation, and it is significant that Milton's Christ recognizes that suffering and obedience, exercised in "humble state," are necessary prerequisites for his ultimate exaltation (III, 188–97):

> *What if he hath decreed that I shall first*
> *Be try'd in humble state, and things adverse,*
> *By tribulations, injuries, insults,*
> *Contempts, and scorns, and snares, and violence,*
> *Suffering, abstaining, quietly expecting*
> *Without distrust or doubt, that he may know*
> *What I can suffer, how obey? who best*
> *Can suffer, best can do; best reign, who first*
> *Well hath obey'd; just tryal e're I merit*
> *My exaltation without change or end.*

In the spiritual duel between Christ's wisdom and Satan's "hellish wiles," Milton skillfully exploited the antithesis between the "form of God" which Messiah had laid aside and the "form of a servant" which he had assumed, for some highly effective irony. Throughout the poem Satan has assayed to discover the identity of "this glorious Eremite"—

> *In what degree of meaning thou art call'd*
> *The Son of God, which bears no single sense;*

yet it is not until the third and final temptation that he realizes that the "Son of *Joseph* deem'd" is identical with Jehovah's "first-begot," whose "fierce thunder drove us to the deep." And this he learns by a miracle; only when Messiah is able "to stand upright" on the "highest Pinnacle" does his adversary recognize him.

Satan's inability to recognize the Son of God in the state of humiliation is quite consistent with the belief (shared by several Reformation theologians) that Christ's divinity was "hidden" in the state of his humiliation, but nevertheless manifested itself on occasion in miracles. Polanus maintained that "Christ humbled himselfe in respect of his Deity . . . by hiding it under the forme of a servant which he had assumed. . . ."[15] Wolleb asserted that when Christ "stript himself of the forme and glory of the Divinity," he "did not cast off the Divinity, but hid it in the assumed form of a servant: And . . . the Deity of Christ did manifest it selfe in the state of his Humiliation, chiefly by miracles. . . ."[16] Milton exploits this conception poetically for the sake of complicating his Fable. It enables him to achieve "the finest form of Discovery"—"one attended by Peripeties, like that which goes with the Discovery in *Oedipus*."[17]

It is the essential identity of the Son—the continuity of his divine Sonship in the state of humiliation as in that of exaltation—that the "Angelic Quires" emphasize in their final hymn:

> *True Image of the Father, whether thron'd*
> *In the bosom of bliss, and light of light*
> *Conceiving, or remote from Heaven, enshrin'd*
> *In fleshly Tabernacle, and human form,*
> *Wandr'ing the Wilderness, whatever place,*
> *Habit, or state, or motion, still expressing*
> *The Son of God, with Godlike force indu'd*
> *Against th' Attempter of thy Father's Throne. . . .*

Whether in the "form of God" or in the "form of a servant," Messiah remains the "first-begot" of the Father, and it is to "His Father's business"—the ministry of redemption—that the final lines of the angelic chorus commit him:

> *. . . on thy glorious work*
> *Now enter, and begin to save mankind.*

Humiliation and suffering—these are, paradoxically, the "matchless Deeds" whereby he must "express [his] matchless Sire."

Negatively, the pattern of Christ's humiliation determines in part the character of the "manlier objects . . . such as have more show Of

15. Polanus, 150. Cf. *Paradise Regain'd*, III, 21–23, "These God-like Vertues wherefore dost thou hide? Affecting private life, or more obscure In savage Wilderness . . . ?"

16. Wolleb, 135–36. For Milton's indebtedness to Wolleb, see Maurice Kelley, "Milton's Debt to Wolleb's *Compendium Theologiae Christianae*," *PMLA*, L (1935), 156–65; T. S. K. Scott-Craig, "Milton's Use of Wolleb and Ames," *MLN*, LV (1940), 403–7.

17. Bywater, 47. Cf. Merritt Y. Hughes (ed.), *Paradise Regained* (New York, 1937), 531n.; Ida Langdon, *Milton's Theory of Poetry and Fine Art* (New Haven, 1924).

Worth, of honour, glory, and popular praise," whereby his antagonist attempts to try his constancy. Wealth, honor, arms, arts, kingdoms, empires, glory, fame (IV, 368–69, 536)—these are not merely inferior to the *remuneratio aeterna* which Messiah merits for mankind; they are also fundamentally at variance with the nature of his mediatorial office, with the theological purpose of his humiliation. In order to carry out "His Father's business"—the ministry of redemption—Messiah must reject all ends or means incompatible with the character of the "suffering servant." The enterprises and rewards which Satan proposes are, indeed, characteristic of secular opinions of heroic activity, but, inasmuch as they are diametrically opposed to the Messianic pattern of humiliation, they are obstacles, rather than means, to his destined enterprise—the redemption of mankind.

If, on the one hand, Satan attempts to divert Messiah from his mission of redemption by tempting him to choose ends and means inconsistent with his humiliation, on the other hand he depicts the Messianic norm of humiliation as an evil to be eschewed. He pretends to find in the stars a prediction of ignominy and death, and he interprets this pattern of adversity as an obstacle to the execution of the Biblical prophecies concerning the Messiah, rather than as a means to their fulfillment (IV, 382–88, 477–80):

> *Now contrary, if I read aught in Heaven, . . .*
> *Sorrows and labours, opposition, hate,*
> *Attends thee, scorns, reproaches, injuries,*
> *Violence and stripes, and lastly cruel death.*
>
> *If thou observe not this, be sure to find,*
> *What I foretold thee, many a hard assay*
> *Of dangers, and adversities and pains,*
> *Ere thou of* Israel's *Scepter get fast hold. . . .*

As Satan elsewhere shows familiarity with the prophecies[18] about the future Messiah (III, 178; IV, 381, 502), it seems apparent that he has in mind the Scriptural predictions concerning the suffering servant and is deliberately wresting them to his own purposes. Certainly, Christ himself recognizes in these prophecies the pattern of humiliation and suffering (I, 259–67), and his mother is likewise aware that the future contains not "Honour," but "trouble" (II, 86–87).

> *This having heard, strait I again revolv'd*
> *The Law and Prophets, searching what was writ*

18. Nevertheless, despite his knowledge of these prophecies Satan does not really understand the means whereby Christ will establish his kingdom; cf. *Paradise Regain'd*, IV, 152–53, "Means there shall be to this, but what the means, Is not for thee to know, nor me to tell."

> *Concerning the Messiah, to our Scribes*
> *Known partly, and soon found of whom they spake*
> *I am; this chiefly, that my way must lie*
> *Through many a hard assay even to the death,*
> *E're I the promis'd Kingdom can attain,*
> *Or work Redemption for mankind, whose sins*
> *Full weight must be transferr'd upon my head.*

The phrase "many a hard assay" appears first on Christ's lips and afterwards on Satan's.[19] By this verbal echo Milton attempts to underscore the contrasting attitudes of the two figures towards the Biblical prophecy of the suffering servant. Whereas Christ, recognizing that his humiliation must precede his exaltation, rejects all alternatives to his destined ministry of redemption, Satan attempts to seduce the hero from the Messianic path of humiliation by proposing contrary ends or means on the one hand and by presenting the idea of the suffering servant as a degradation to be shunned, on the other. Christ, in his "wisdom," interprets the Old Testament prophecy of a suffering Messiah in its correct sense. Satan, by his "hellish wiles," deliberately distorts it.

In this context, the emphasis that Reformation discussions of Messiah's humiliation and exaltation placed on proof texts concerning the Old Testament prophecies of the suffering servant seems especially significant. Polanus[20] cited Luke 24:26, with its specific application of these predictions of Jesus: "O fools, and slow of heart to believe all that the prophets have spoken: Ought not Christ to have suffered these things, and to enter into his glory? And beginning at Moses and all the prophets, he expounded unto them in all the scriptures concerning himself." Similarly, Wolleb, explaining that in the state of humiliation Christ administered his regal office "in gathering together a Church by his word and Spirit, so, that in their [*sic*] appeared no sign of Regal Majesty," adduced the following corollary: "In vain do the Jews dream of *Messiah's* corporal and earthly Kingdome."[21] In support of this "Rule" he cited three Old Testament prophecies concerning the suffering servant—Isaiah 42:2 and 53:2–3 and Zechariah 9:9,

> He shall not cry, nor lift up, nor cause his voice to be heard in the street.

19. Instead of achieving his kingdom "in short time with ease" (*Paradise Regain'd*, IV, line 378), as Satan proposes, Christ must attain it only by "many a hard assay" and in the "fulness of time." Satan not only attempts to persuade Jesus to employ means contrary to those set forth in the Messianic prophecies, but also tries to induce him to act prematurely. Christ manifests his obedience through his willingness to await the "due time" which "The Father in his purpose hath decreed" (*Paradise Regain'd*, III, 182–86), whereas Satan argues that the present moment is "full age, fulness of time, thy season" (*Paradise Regain'd*, IV, 380).

20. Polanus, 120–21.

21. Wolleb, 156.

. . . he hath no form nor comeliness: . . . He is despised and rejected of men; a man of sorrows, and acquainted with grief: . . . he was despised, and we esteemed him not.

. . . behold, thy King cometh unto thee: he is just, and having salvation; lowly, and riding upon an ass. . . .

In these prophecies of his humiliation Christ could recognize an ideal absolutely contradictory to the ends and means Satan proposed to him.[22] From the same prophecies[23] his tempter could acquire some knowledge of the nature of the ministry of redemption and evolve a strategy designed to frustrate the Messianic way of humiliation.

IV

In Messiah's ministry of redemption Milton found the norm of Christian heroism for both of his epics, but not (paradoxically) an epic subject. Except for the incomplete lines on "The Passion," he never, apparently, devoted a poem to what would seem to be the logical material for a Christian heroic poet—the crucifixion and resurrection.[24] Though both of his epics represent these "godlike acts" as the supremely heroic enterprise, the actual arguments of both poems concern events preliminary to this "glorious work." In *Paradise Regain'd* the heroic norm is the "great warfare" on the cross, whereby Messiah is to defeat Sin and Death; but instead of taking the victory over Death and Sin as his subject, Milton chooses the theme of the temptation in the wilderness, where Christ is acquiring the "rudiments" of his subsequent warfare. In *Paradise Lost* the poet declares that Messiah is to triumph through his death and resurrection—by paying "the rigid satisfaction, death for death," and afterwards rising "Victorious" to "subdue" the "vanquisher"; the real argument of this poem, however, is not Christ's triumph, but Adam's fall. Milton never assayed a *Christiad*, the logical objective for a Christian poet.

22. Satan's offer of "the kingdoms of the world, and the *glory* of them" obviously constitutes a direct challenge to the whole concept of Christ's humiliation. Cf. *Paradise Lost*, III, 238–40 ("I for his sake will leave Thy bosom, and *this glorie next to thee* Freely put off, and for him lastly die") and 311–14 ("because in thee Love hath abounded *more than Glory abounds*, Therefore thy Humiliation shall exalt With thee thy Manhood also to this Throne"). Italics mine.

23. Satan attempts to wrest the prophecies to his own ends, either by representing the values he offers as means of fulfilling the Old Testament predictions concerning the Messiah, or else by maintaining that the prophecies themselves are not absolute but conditional—that their fulfillment is contingent upon Jesus' adopting the means and occasions he offers. Cf. *Paradise Regain'd*, III, 177–80, 351–56; IV, 106–8.

24. The Trinity Manuscript does, however, contain a brief outline of a drama on "Christus Patiens." See James Holly Hanford, *A Milton Handbook* (4th ed.; New York, 1947), 181n.

Perhaps the fact that Vida ("Cremona's Trump") had anticipated him served as a deterrent. Nevertheless there was an additional, and possibly more cogent, objection to writing an epic on the Passion and Resurrection. The detailed account in the Gospels left the poet little scope to invent, to alter and rearrange his materials in the interests of verisimilitude and the epic marvellous, or to adapt his sources to the laws and conventions of heroic poetry. In the subjects Milton *did* choose—the fall of man and the temptation of Christ—the brevity of the Biblical narrative was a distinct asset; it afforded him ample opportunity for "feigning." It is significant that both Tasso and Milton's own nephew recognized the advantages of a subject brief or obscure enough to leave scope for invention and fiction. "In [sacred] histories of the first quality," declared Tasso, "the poet scarcely dares to extend his own hand. . . . Feigning is hardly permissible in such cases, and the writer who does not feign and imitate . . . is not really a poet, but a historian." In choosing his subject (Tasso continues) the poet should select his argument from the history of a remote nation or period since it affords greater freedom in imitation. For Edward Phillips, "it is not a meer Historical relation, spic't over with a little slight fiction . . ., which makes a *Heroic Poem;* but it must be rather a brief, obscure, or remote Tradition, but of some remarkable piece of story, in which the Poet hath an ample feild to inlarge by feigning of probable circumstances, in which . . . Invention . . . principally consisteth. . . ."[25]

In both of Milton's epics the supreme exemplar of heroic virtue and its reward—the perfect pattern of that "suffering for Truths sake" which is "fortitude to highest victorie" and receives a recompense of celestial glory—is ultimately based on Christ's humiliation and exaltation. Though manifested *par excellence* in Messiah himself, this heroic norm of the "suffering servant"[26] who endures "Universal reproach" or violence in his single-handed obedience to the divine will and his isolated witness to the divine truth also recurs on the angelic and purely human levels in such "heroes of faith" as Abdiel, the faithful

25. Torquato Tasso, *Prose Diverse*, ed. Cesare Guasti, I, 110–11: "L'istoria di secolo o di nazione lontanissima pare per alcuna ragione soggetto assai conveniente al poema eroico; però che, essendo quelle cose in guisa sepolte nell'antichità, ch'a pena ne rimane debole ed oscura memoria, può il poeta mutarle e rimutarle, e narrarle come gli piace." See J. E. Spingarn (ed.), *Critical Essays of the Seventeenth Century* (Oxford, 1908), II, 267.

26. For a bibliography of studies on the "suffering servant" of Isaiah 53, see Christopher R. North, *The Suffering Servant of Isaiah: An Historical and Critical Study*, 2nd ed.; (London, 1956), 240–53. "Until the close of the eighteenth century," North observes (p. 1), "Christian writers—with almost the sole exception of Grotius, who thought of Jeremiah—were unanimous that Isa. liii was Messianic prophecy"; cf. *ibid.*, pp. 23–27.

"Servant of God," who maintains "against revolted multitudes the Cause of Truth," in the occasional "Just Man" of Old Testament history (Enoch, Noah, Abraham, etc.), and finally in the persecuted minority of Christians who bear witness to the Gospel in its purity and "in the worship persevere of Spirit and Truth."

5. *"Taught by His Example"*

Adam and the Prophesied Redeemer

❦ In the final books of *Paradise Lost* Michael fulfills a divine injunction to "reveal to *Adam* what shall come in future days," intermixing "My Cov'nant in the woman's seed renew'd." This revelation (as Parish has pointed out) represents a fusion of epic convention and theological tradition. While the device is "obviously derived from the great epic poems of antiquity," it also reflects the belief—shared by both Catholics and Protestants—that Adam died a Christian, that during his lifetime the divine clemency vouchsafed him a foreknowledge of his redeemer.[1]

Instances of this tradition, varying widely as to the time, place, manner, agent, and recipient of the revelation, have been noted in such different works as *The Gospel of Nicodemus*, *Cursor Mundi*, English mystery-cycles, and Bullinger's *Der Alt Glaub*.[2] Additional parallels occur, however, in other writings—Moslem, Hebrew, and Christian—though they sometimes disagree on the identity of the revealing angel and on the nature, object, and time of Adam's enlightenment.

In Milton's version the prophecy of the redeemer is delivered to Adam by Michael immediately before the expulsion from Paradise. Its purpose is to mitigate his grief, to instruct him in the beliefs essential

First published, in somewhat different form, in *Studies in Philology*, LVI (1959), 214–25.

1. John E. Parish, "Pre-Miltonic Representations of Adam as a Christian," *Rice Institute Pamphlet*, XL, No. 3 (1953), 1–24.

2. *Ibid., passim.*

for his justification by faith, and (by demonstrating the final triumph of supernal grace over sinfulness of man) to "assert Eternal Providence, And justifie the wayes of God to men." It follows an historical survey of Adam's posterity, and it culminates in his personal confession of faith. Although most of these features can be paralleled in other works, the particular combination Milton presents in *Paradise Lost* is by no means typical of the tradition as a whole. In other versions the immediate recipient of the revelation may be Seth or Eve. The foreknowledge of a saviour may reach Adam indirectly through their report, or directly through the medium of vision or prophecy, with or without the intervention of an angel. The identity of the divine messenger varies; Adam may hear the Gospel from God himself, from Michael or Raziel, or from an anonymous angel. The prophecy may center around the Protevangelium (Genesis 3:15) or around other texts—Genesis 3:22 and Genesis 5:1. Sometimes it occurs in the context of a vision of his posterity. His knowledge of a future redeemer may date from 1) before his fall, 2) the interval between his crime and his expulsion, or 3) after his expulsion and indeed as late as the hour of his death. In non-Christian versions, the primary object of his admiration may be David, Mohammed, or some highly gifted rabbi (Akiba, Jehuda bar Simon, Joshua ben Karcha),[3] rather than Christ.

I

In the *Palestine Targum* God prophesies Messiah's advent in Adam's hearing, at the moment of pronouncing judgment on the serpent:

> And I will put enmity between thee and the woman, and between the seed of thy son, and the seed of her sons; and it shall be when the sons of the woman keep the commandments of the law, they will be prepared to smite thee upon thy head; but when they forsake the commandments of the law, thou wilt be ready to wound them in their heel. Nevertheless for them there is a medicine, but for thee there will be no medicine; and they shall make a remedy for the heel in the days of the King Meshiha.[4]

In the *Spelunca Thesaurorum*, an apocryphal work attributed to St. Ephraem, God himself prophesies the Incarnation, in order to comfort Adam at the moment of his expulsion:

> And when they had gone forth in sadness, God spoke to our father Adam and exhorted him, saying: "Do not grieve, Adam, that you have departed under

3. J. Dreyfus, *Adam und Eva nach Auffassung des Midrasch* (Strassburg, 1894), pp. 18–19, 36.

4. J. W. Etheridge (trans.), *The Targums of Onkelos and Jonathan Ben Uzziel on the Pentateuch; With the Fragments of the Jerusalem Targum from the Chaldee* (London, 1862), I, 166. The same interpretation appears in the *Jerusalem Targum*: ". . . for these there shall be a remedy for the heel in the days of the king Meshiha."

condemnation from Paradise, for I shall return you to your inheritance.... Go and be not sad; for after the fullness of time that I have set for your exile without in the Land of Curses [i.e. in land accursed]: lo, I shall send my own Son to you. He shall descend to earth for your salvation and shall dwell in the womb of a Virgin and shall put on a body, whereby there shall be a redemption for you and a return."[5]

The tradition that Adam possessed a foreknowledge of Christ appears in other Syriac writings. According to the *Historia Apocrypha Virginis Deiparae*, at the point of death he communicated to Seth both the promise of Messiah's advent and the prophecy of his own resurrection: "And the future Messiah shall come and shall suffer under impious men and shall die, and in his death there shall be a resurrection for all men. And the third day he shall rise again and bear with him my body into Heaven."[6]

In a fragmentary *Testamentum Patris Nostri Adam*, Adam informs Seth that God had told him of Christ's advent in the interval between his sin and his expulsion. Through Messiah's death and resurrection he would achieve divinity, as he had desired: "And all these things he showed me in the midst of Paradise, after I had plucked the fruit in which Death lay concealed. And he said unto me: 'Adam, be not afraid, You desired to be made a god, and I shall make you a god—yet not now, but after a long period of years.'"[7]

In another work, however, Adam foresees Christ's crucifixion long before his fall. After creating him and endowing him with life and prophetic powers, God bids him declare what he sees: "And Adam said, 'I see the Messiah crucified....' This is the first prophecy that our father Adam made concerning Christ."[8]

Messiah's future advent is a reiterated theme in the Ethiopic *Book of Adam and Eve*. Immediately after the expulsion from Paradise, God promises to send "the Word that created thee, and against which thou hast transgressed," to save Adam when 5500 years have passed. "But God had before that made this covenant with our father, Adam, in the same terms, ere he came out of the garden, [when he was] by the tree

5. Michael Kmosko, "Preface," *Testamentum Patris Nostri Adam*, in *Patrologia Syriaca*, Part I, Vol. II, 1313.

6. *Ibid.*, p. 1315.

7. *Ibid.*, pp. 1345–49. This work also alludes to the tradition that Adam brought with him from Paradise the gifts of gold, frankincense, and myrrh which the Magi subsequently carried to Christ. Kmosko also reprints variant texts of the *Testamentum* fragment, which likewise assert that God's revelation of Christ's advent was made in Paradise after Adam's crime but before his expulsion (1341–44). In one of these versions Adam describes his informant as Messiah himself (1339–40): "Audivi, fili mi Seth, Messiam de caelo venturum esse et nasci de virgine.... Nam ipse Messias dixit mihi in paradiso, cum carpsissem de fructu, in quo mors latebat."

8. *Ibid.*, p. 1318.

whereof Eve took [the fruit] and gave it him to eat." Frightened by the altered appearance of the forbidden tree, Adam "trembled and fell down; but God in His mercy lifted him up, and then made this covenant with him." The promise is repeated at the moment of expulsion, when the protoplasts are terrified by the sight of the angel at the gate. Adam goes forth "comforted with that which God had told him. For He had told him how He would save him."[9]

In *La Leggenda d'Adamo ed Eva*, Adam repents after his expulsion from Paradise and, imploring God for the oil of mercy,[10] receives a promise of Christ: "And beholding Adam's penitence and the tears he shed for his sin in disobeying the divine command, God the Father felt pity and compassion for him. And the Lord said to Adam that when the time was complete his own Son should come into this world below and then Adam should receive the oil of mercy."[11] In a *Vita Adae et Evae*, Michael extends a similar promise to the dying Adam through Seth and Eve: "Then shall the Son of God come upon earth to raise up the body of Adam your father and the bodies of other dead men. And the Son of God himself shall be baptized in the river Jordan. And . . . then he shall anoint with oil of myrrh all who believe in him. . . . And the Son of God himself shall lead your father into Paradise."[12]

II

Adam's vision of his posterity is a recurrent tradition in numerous Moslem and Hebrew works. In some versions this revelation occurs before the fall and apparently bears no direct relation to his transgression and redemption. According to one analogue, God gave him a book comprehending his entire posterity until the time of the resurrection

9. S. C. Malan (trans.), *The Book of Adam and Eve* (London and Edinburgh, 1882), pp. 4–5. God reiterates this promise of redemption (12, 41, 44–45, 54), foretelling his own death, burial, and resurrection and promising Adam the fruit of the Tree of Life and the Water of Life. Kmosko (1316) cites a Coptic fragment of a Moses-Adam Apocalypse, in which God prophesies Christ's passion to Adam: "O Adam mein Geschöpf. . . siehe, mein Sohn ist zu dir herabgekommen und hat alle diese Leiden, bis dass er dir deine Sünden vergebe, erduldet. Maria ist es, bei der mein Sohn eingekehrt ist." This was published by Harnack and Schmidt in *Sitzungsberichte der Akad. der Wissenschaften zu Berlin* (1891), p. 1905. Kmosko observes that similar fragments were cited by Tischendorf in his preface to *Apocalypses Apocryphae* (Lipsiae, 1886).

10. Cf. Parish, pp. 8, 11, on this tradition.

11. Alessandro d'Ancona (ed.), *La leggenda d'Adamo ed Eva; Testo inedito del secolo XIV* (Bologna, 1870), pp. 9–10. In the Tree of Knowledge Seth beholds a boy whom the angel identifies as "lo figliuolo di Dio," *ibid.*, p. 16.

12. An edition without indication of place or date is preserved in the Bodleian Library at Oxford (Auct. I. Q. VI. 43). The title appears only in the colophon: "Vita Ade et Eve absoluta est feliciter." Michael gives Seth a branch with three leaves from the Tree of Knowledge to bear to Adam, who hails it as "Ecce mors et resurrectio mea."

of the dead.[13] A similar tradition appears in the commentaries on Genesis 5:1 ("This is the book of the generations of Adam") in the *Zohar*:

Said R. Isaac: "God showed Adam the visages of all future generations, of all the wise men and all the kings that were destined to rule over Israel. When he saw David, who was destined to die as soon as he was born, he said, 'I will lend him seventy years from my life,' and so it came to pass. . . . God also showed him the wise men of each generation. When he came to R. Akiba and saw his great learning, he rejoiced, but when he saw his martyrdom he was sorely grieved. Nevertheless, he exclaimed: 'How precious in mine eyes are thy companions, O God, how mighty are the chiefs of them' (Ps. cxxxix, 17)."[14]

See now what R. Simeon has told us, in explanation of the verse "This is the book of the generations of Adam," that God showed Adam every generation and its students, etc. This does not mean that he saw through the spirit of prophecy, that they were destined to come into the world, like one who in wisdom foresees the future, but it means that he literally saw with his eyes the form in which they were destined to exist in the world. He was able to do this because from the day on which the world was created all the souls which were destined to come to life among mankind were existing before God in that very form which they were destined to assume on earth . . . and so Adam saw them with his eyes.

When God showed Adam all future generations, he saw them all in the Garden of Eden in the form which they were destined to assume in this world. When he saw David . . . with no span of life at all apportioned to him, he was grieved, and gave him seventy years of his own; that is why Adam lived seventy years short of the thousand, the rest being given to David.[15]

As in *Paradise Lost*, Adam beholds the "future generations" while he is still "in the Garden of Eden"—i.e., prior to his expulsion.

According to Tha'alibi, God showed Adam all his posterity—weak and strong, sick and healthy, well-made and deformed. It was by such diversity, the Creator explained, that his creatures rendered thanks to their maker. In Ibn Abbas' opinion, all Adam's posterity were assembled in the form of intelligent ants in the valley of Nooman near Mount Arafat, to acknowledge God as their sovereign master.[16]

Mahomet Rabadan's *Mahometism Fully Explained* refers to Adam's foreknowledge of the advent of Mohammed. After years of penance,

13. Dreyfus, p. 19. Cf. E. C. Baldwin, "Some Extra-Biblical Semitic Influences upon Milton's Story of the Fall of Man," *JEGP*, XXVIII (1929), 366–401.

14. *The Zohar*, trans. H. Sperling and M. Simon (London, 1931), I, 176.

15. *Ibid.*, pp. 298, 300. Cf. Dreyfus, p. 36. According to a similar tradition, Adam gave David forty years of his own life. See *The Encyclopaedia of Islam* (Leyden and London, 1913), *s.v.* "Adam."

16. M. d'Herbelot, *Bibliothèque Orientale* (Paris, 1697), p. 54. "Mais l'Auteur de Lebab prétend que ce fut dans la plaine de Dahia aux Indes." Cf. the vision of the Lazar-house in *Paradise Lost*, Book XI.

Adam hears hymns of praise; these, God informs him, are chanted by the soul of Mohammed: "He is now invoking *that Light* which I have deposited in thee, and thy precious and elected Progeny." Adam must bequeath the Light to his posterity, "until it be finally center'd on that *Honourable* Man, (viz. *Mahomet*) relinquished by all thy Sons, and fixed in him."[17]

III

Several Renaissance writers besides Milton allude to Adam's hope and faith in a future redeemer. Andreini's *L'Adamo* concludes the drama of the fall on a note of joy. In the final act Michael promises Adam and Eve immortality and triumph over their infernal foe:

> *. . . è già la guerra*
> *In pace convertita,*
> *Fatta è la Morte, Vita;*
> *Quindi Adamo mortal fatto è immortale,*
> *Ed Eva morta mille parti avviva. . . .*
> *Pugna, resisti, e forte*
> *Co 'l nemico Serpente ogn' hor guerreggia,*
> *Che avverrà che 'l Huom deggia*
> *Vincer l'Inferno, e trionfar di Morte.*[18]

Genebrardus believed that, though Adam had lost his original knowledge, righteousness, and virtue through his sin, he retained his hope of recovering them through faith in his redeemer: ". . . citra spem eorum recuperandorum, nisi ex solo redemptoris beneficio & fide, per quam novam justificationem fuit consequutus, tam ipse, quàm reliquum humanum genus."[19]

Like Bullinger,[20] Whately maintained that Adam understood the promise of a saviour shadowed in the Protevangelium and recognized it as a "covenant of grace" with himself and his posterity. This was the chief benefit which God bestowed on the protoplasts after their fall:

> The chiefe was the promise of a Saviour, *viz.* The seede of the Woman to tread on the Serpents head, that is, to destroy the Divell, and the workes of the Divell,

17. Mahomet Rabadan, *Mahometism Fully Explained*, trans. Jos. Morgan (London, 1723), I, 54–55. According to the title-page this work was written "in *Spanish* and *Arabick* in the Year MDCIII for the Instruction of the *Moriscoes* in *Spain*" by "an *Arragonian* Moor."

18. Gio. Battista Andreini, *L'Adamo, Sacra Raepresentatione* (Milano, 1617), p. 174. Cf. pp. 172–73.

19. Gilb. Genebrardus, *Chronographiae libri quatuor* (Paris, 1600), p. 8. Adam is described as "propheta, in Seder Olam cap. 21, sive prophetico spiritu imbutus."

20. Parish, p. 18.

and to deliver them from the mischiefe which Satan sought to bring upon them. By which words he did make the Covenant of grace with them and their Posterity, providing a remedy equall to the disease, and the meanes of revealing it to all, in that he manifested it to them that they might teach it to their children, and so one to another till all knew it . . .[21]

Lightfoote similarly emphasized Adam's comprehension of the promise and his faith in the future saviour:

Christ is promised before the man and the woman are censured. . . . *Adam* apprehendeth and layeth hold upon the promise by Faith, and in evidence of this his faith he calleth his wives name *Eve* or *Life*, because she was to be the mother of Christ according to the flesh, by whom life should come; and of all beleevers that by faith should live in him, for an outward signe and seal of this his Faith, and for a further and more lively expression of the same. . . .[22]

In both of these interpretations, as in Bullinger's treatise, the author "contends that Adam heard the curse . . . and that Adam understood its mystical meaning."[23]

In *Paradise Lost*, however, Adam does not understand the true meaning of the prophecy by his own powers. He is dependent on a further revelation, and this he does not receive until his repentance has prepared him for faith.[24] It is only when Michael prophesies "the true Anointed King *Messiah*," born of a virgin through "The Power of the most High," that Adam comprehends

What oft my steddiest thoughts have searcht in vain,
Why our great expectation should be call'd
The seed of Woman:

He has, apparently, reflected long and deeply on the meaning of the curse and correctly surmised (X, 1031–35) that the serpent is "our grand Foe *Satan*." Nevertheless he has been unable to identify the woman's seed. Michael's prophecy, however, gives him the key he

21. William Whately, *Prototypes, or, The Primary Precedent Presidents out of the Booke of Genesis* (London, 1647), p. 7. This "late Pastour of *Banbury*" counsels his readers to imitate Adam and Eve in repentance and faith (8): "Againe, let us be carefull to follow them in all good deeds which they did; O let us repent and beleeve in Christ hoping for life by him according to the Covenant of grace, as they did when they had broken the Covenant of Workes." Cf. *ibid.*, 12, "But againe, wee must bee incouraged to repent of sinne and to crave pardon of it . . ., for even this sinne of our first Parents is to them pardoned. . . . *Adam* which cast all into sinne . . ., even this *Adam* is in Heaven himselfe, yea *Eve* . . . shee is in Heaven."

22. John Lightfoote, *A Few, and New Observations, upon the Booke of Genesis* (London, 1642), pp. 5–6.

23. Parish, 17.

24. Cf. *Christian Doctrine*, Book I, Chapters 19 and 20 (Milton, *Prose Works* [Bohn's Standard Library; London, 1883]), on repentance and faith as "effects of regeneration."

had sought in vain, and he immediately turns it to unlock the mystery that had baffled him. The remainder of Michael's revelation to Adam and Adam's report to Eve (XII, 375–623) is, in large part, an extended interpretation of the covenant of grace[25] obscurely adumbrated in Book X, lines 179–81.

IV

According to Reuchlin's *De arte cabalistica*[26]—a dialogue between 1) Simon, a Jew learned in the Cabala, 2) Philolaus, a Pythagorean, and 3) Marranus, a Moslem—Genesis 3:22 constituted a promise of future restoration. Overhearing this divine statement to the angels, Adam left Paradise with hope in the midst of his sorrows:

Hence the Lord said to the angels, in Adam's hearing: "And now [*nunc*] lest he put forth his hand and partake of the tree of life and eat and live forever." And the Lord God ejected him from the paradise of delight. This was the last word that the miserable Adam heard from the mouth of God when he was expelled from the garden. Nevertheless in the midst of so many griefs and laments he received thereby this firm hope in regard to his Creator—namely, that in the course of time the horrible sentence could be revoked through God's mercy. And this the very words of the oracle indicated to him. For God had said, "Now [*Nunc, sive iam*], lest he put forth his hand and partake of the tree of life." Not in vain did God add the word "now" [*nunc, vel iam*]. Thereby he designated the present time, insinuating that the sentence would not be perpetual, but that it could be abolished in a future time, when there should come a man [i.e. Christ] destined to eat of the tree of life [*siquando veniret homo ad vescandum de ligno vitae destinatus*]. . . .[27]

To console and instruct Adam further, God sent the angel Raziel[28] to teach him the future reparation of his fall and the expiation of his sin through a just man born of his seed and bearing a name containing the

25. For Milton's conception of the covenant of grace, see *ibid.*, Book I, Chapters 14 and 26: "There was a promise made to all mankind, and *an expectation of the Redeemer*, more or less distinct, *even from the time of the fall.* Gen. iii. 15." (Italics mine.) "The Covenant of Grace itself, on the part of God, is first declared Gen. iii. 15."

26. For discussions of Renaissance cabalism, see Francis Barham, *The Life and Times of John Reuchlin, or Capnion, the Father of the German Reformation* (London, 1843); Denis Saurat, "The *Zohar* and the Kabbalah," *Milton: Man and Thinker* (London, 1944), pp. 231–47; Harris Francis Fletcher, *Milton's Semitic Studies* (Chicago, 1926).

27. Johannes Reuchlin, *De arte cabalistica libri tres* (Frankfurt, 1603), p. 627. This edition appears in the same volume with *P. Galatini de arcanis catholicae veritatis.*

28. According to the *Zohar* (I, 176–77), "when Adam was in the Garden of Eden, God sent down to him a book by the hand of Raziel, the angel in charge of the holy mysteries. In this book were supernal inscriptions containing the sacred wisdom. . . ." After his transgression, "the book flew away from him," but was subsequently returned by Raphael. Cf. *Encyclopedia Judaica* (Berlin, 1928), *s.v.* "*Adam.*"

letters I.H.V.H.[29] This revelation constituted the first delivery of the Cabala,[30] the first annunciation of future salvation:

> Lest he should leave Adam destitute of all consolation, the most merciful Father continually sent an angel from whom Adam should learn more fully the future reparation of his great ruin. (For so the Cabalists declare in their commentaries on the Sepher Yetsirah.) . . . The preceptors of the fathers (they assert) were certain angels; and Adam's instructor was the angel Raziel. At the behest of the highest God he showed Adam the way of expiation and explained to him the divine word allegorically in the Cabalistic manner, which regards no word or even the slightest letter or pointing as written in vain.[31]

As in *Paradise Lost,* Adam transmits the angel's prophecy of a redeemer to his wife: "singula haec Adam uxori suae palàm renunciasset. . . ." His faith in this promise was also reflected in the name given his grandson, Enos.[32]

Like Milton, Reuchlin regards consolation as the immediate object of this revelation; it is intended to relieve Adam's despair at his expulsion and to awaken hope.[33]

29. In the final book of the dialogue Marranus converts the Tetragrammaton into the name of Jesus (770). Cf. Reuchlin's *De Verbo Mirifico* (Lugduni, 1552). See also Barham's discussion of Reuchlin's conception of the Tetragrammaton (106).

30. Cf. Reuchlin, *De arte cabalistica*, p. 625: "Tum Simon, Rectè verò, & est profectò aliud nihil, quàm post ruinam primordialem generis humani universalis restauratio, quae à nobis ישועה, & à Latinis salus nominatur. Eius ipsius extat omnium prima nostrae speciei facta revelatio, si examussim universa mundani exordij pondero, qua nulla fuit prior."

31. *Ibid.*, pp. 627–29: "Missus est igitur Angelus Raziel ad Adam collapsum & moerore plenum, ut consolaretur eum, cui sic dixit, Ne supra modum conficiaris gemitu & molestia, quod te duce genus humanum in summam corruit perditionem. Quoniam originale peccatum hoc expiabitur. Nam ex tua propagatione nascetur homo iustus & pacificus, vir heros, cuius nomen continebit in miserationibus, etiam has quatuor literas I. H. V. H. & ille per rectam fidem & placidam oblationem mittet manum suam, & sumet de ligno vitae, & eius ligni fructus erit omnium sperantium salus. Quo sermone finito, ille damnatus & aerumnosus Adam inter miserias omnes, in quas incidit, inter dolorem, inter luctum, quo in tanta calamitate fuerat affectus, confidens in Deum mutandi delicti spem concepit, & idcirco incredibili erga factorem suum amore actus divinae clementiae gratiam habuit. Haec fuit omnium prima Cabala, primordialis salutis nuncia. . . . Haec est illa revelatio sanctissima & summa, in quam omnes divinae revelationes reducuntur. . . ."

32. *Ibid.*, pp. 629–30: "Denuo Simon ait, Pater noster Adam, rursus ex Seth nepotem suscepit, memor eius Cabalae quam sibi Raziel tradiderat, quòd ex sua propagatione nasceretur homo futurus salvator. Quare vocatus est Enos .i. homo, tunc putabatur & quidem valde speratum fuit eum appellandum fore iuxta Cabalam angelicam per nomen quatuor literarum I.H.V.H. vel saltem magis Cabalisticè in miserationibus per *Sin* literam de medio quatuor literarum I.H.V.H."

33. *Ibid.*, p. 627: "Hic inquam, hic ad imminentis desperationis, quo morbo nihil perniciosius, efficax subsidium divina revelatione opus erat, ac ne tunc figmentum suum fictor Deus omnino deseruerat, sed spem quandam iniecit, fore non impossibile hoc ipsum quamvis immane crimen & contra infinitam maiestatem admissum, tamen tractu temporis finito, aboleri, tolli & extingui."

V

This version shares several significant features with *Paradise Lost.* 1) God sends an angel with the express mission of consoling Adam for his loss of Paradise by promising the future Messiah. 2) The revelation involves a detailed explanation of a divine sentence Adam had overheard but not fully understood. 3) Adam communicates these tidings to Eve. On the other hand, Milton and Reuchlin diverge on two important points—the identity of the revealing angel and the particular sentence which Adam overhears and the angel expounds. In both details Milton's account is not only more orthodox, but also much closer to traditional treatments of Adam's illumination. Whereas Raziel lacked Biblical warrant, Michael was not only well-authenticated in Scripture but had already appeared as the agent of Adam's revelation in such works as the *Vita Adae et Evae* and the *L'Adamo.* Milton's preference for Genesis 3:15 over Genesis 3:22 as the basis of the angel's prophecy of the redeemer was likewise more conventional; it was the former text which his predecessors had usually expounded in describing Adam's foreknowledge of Christ. Although Milton may have been influenced by *De arte cabalistica,* he retained few traces of Reuchlin's cabalistic esotericism.[34]

In the final books of *Paradise Lost* the poet combined details derived from various traditions concerning the protoplasts—Adam's vision of his posterity, the familiar interpretation of the woman's seed as the Messiah, the promise of salvation as a consolation for expulsion from Paradise, and the role of the revealing angel, Raziel or Michael. This fusion of conventional elements represents, on the whole, an original contribution to a fairly common theme—Adam's foreknowledge of Christ his redeemer. Through this fresh combination of traditional details Milton's version acquired probability and verisimilitude without forfeiting its essential originality.

34. In *Magia Adamica* Thomas Vaughan likewise maintains that after his fall Adam received the promise of "a future and glorious restitution. For God having ordained a second, eternal Adam did by some mysterious experience manifest the possibility of His coming to the first, who being now full of despair and overcharged with the guilt of his own sin was a very fit patient for so Divine and Merciful a Physician." God's declaration in Genesis 4:21, "Behold an Adam like one of us, knowing good and evil," refers not to the first Adam but to the "Second Adam, Christ Jesus, Who knew the evil but did not commit it and therefore was 'like one of us,' that is, like one of the Trinity, knowing good and evil and yet no way guilty of the evil. This primitive and compendious gospel was no sooner imparted to the angels but they became ministers of it . . .; and their administration to man took beginning with this oracle." Hence "Raziel the angel was presently dispatched to communicate the intelligence to Adam. . . ." See *The Works of Thomas Vaughan,* ed. Arthur E. Waite (London, 1919), 144–46.

6. The Tree of Life As Messianic Symbol

❦ In the celestial banquet at the end of *Paradise Regain'd* Professor Kermode has justly recognized both the complement of the diabolical banquet of sense in Book II and an example of the "new rewards proposed for the new hero," which supersede the "old rewards of heroism."[1] Nevertheless, as this scene also serves as a focal point for a fairly complex cluster of ideas associated with the Biblical tree of life, it merits re-examination in the light of Renaissance interpretations of the *arbor vitae* of Genesis. For the most part, Reformation theologians exhibit little variation on this point. Milton's *De Doctrina Christiana* agrees, on the whole, with the traditional conception of the tree of life, but displays a greater degree of independence on the question of its sacramental nature. More controversial is the interpretation by the Renaissance Cabalist, John Reuchlin. Despite his theologically eccentric explanation of Genesis 3:22, Reuchlin's application of this text to the Messiah may conceivably have contributed to Milton's picture of Christ's banquet on "Fruits fetcht from the tree of life."

First published, in somewhat different form, in the *Review of English Studies*, N.S. XI (1960), 384–91.

1. Frank Kermode, "Milton's Hero," *RES*, N.S. IV (1953), 317–30.

I

An early interpretation of the fruit of the tree of life as a heavenly recompense for obedience appears in the Jerusalem Targum on Genesis 2:9. The tree itself signifies the law, and its fruit is acquired through obedience: "He prepared the garden of Eden for the righteous, that they should eat, and delight themselves with the fruit of the tree, because they had kept the commandments of the law in this world. . . . For the law is the tree of life; whoever keepeth it in this life liveth and subsisteth as the tree of life. The law is good to keep in this world, as the fruit of the tree of life in the world that cometh."[2]

Reformation theologians frequently regarded the *arbor vitae* as a sacrament signifying eternal life on the condition of obedience. Calvin, explaining that "The name of sacrament . . . generally comprehends all signs that God ever committed to men in order to render them more certain and secure of the truth of his promises," classified the tree of life as an example of a sacrament "in natural things" (*in rebus naturalibus*). Thus "he gave the tree of life to Adam and Eve in earnest-money [*arrhabonem*] of immortality, so that they might securely rely on this promise as long as they ate of that fruit."[3]

Polanus cited Genesis ii. 9 and Revelation ii. 7 as proof texts for the doctrine that "the tree of life in paradise was a type of eternall life"—a sacrament promising immortality: "The tree of life was a Sacrament, by which there was signified and sealed to our first parents, eating the fruit of this tree, that immortall life should in the Sonne of God be continued unto them, if they continued in the obedience of God."[4] Wolleb believed it to be a sacrament ratifying eternal happiness under the covenant of works:

> The Covenant of works was confirmed by a double Sacrament; to wit, the Tree of Life, and the Tree of Knowledge of good and evil. . . . They had a double use. 1. That man's obedience might be tried by using of the one, and abstaining from the other. 2. That the tree of life might ratifie eternal happiness to those that should obey, but the Tree of knowledge should signifie to the disobedient the loss of the greatest happiness, and the possession of the greatest misery.[5]

Similarly, John Diodati, commenting on Genesis ii. 9, declared that God had set the tree of life in the garden of Eden ". . . for a Sacrament,

2. J. W. Etheridge (trans.), *The Targums of Onkelos and Jonathan Ben Uzziel on the Pentateuch; with the Fragments of the Jerusalem Targum from the Chaldee* (London, 1862), I, 169.

3. *Institutionis Christianae Religionis Libri Quatuor* (Genevae, 1617), f. 265.

4. Amandus Polanus, *The Substance of Christian Religion* (Genevae, 1617), pp. 168, 297.

5. John Wollebius, *The Abridgment of Christian Divinitie*, trans. A. Ross (3rd ed.; London, 1660), p. 68.

of the subsistence and spirituall life of man, in the grace and communion of the Lord, so long as he should persevere in Justice and Obedience. And to it is correspondent Jesus Christ, in the heavenly Paradise."[6] Rivetus also stressed the causal relation between obedience and the celestial fruit:

But that tree [of life] was so called because it was a Sacrament or divine sign and testimony not only that Adam would be preserved in this earthly life but also (and chiefly) that he would be translated to a celestial life if he would persist in obedience to God's mandates, but that by transgressing them he would draw death upon himself. Hence by exclusion from the tree of life God wished to signify that Adam had lost that right to life.[7]

Milton, on the other hand, rejected the interpretation of the *arbor vitae* as a sacrament, and laid primary emphasis on its significance as a symbol of immortality: "The tree of life, in my opinion, ought not to be considered so much of a sacrament, as a symbol of eternal life, or rather perhaps the nutriment by which that life is sustained. Gen, iii. 22. 'Lest he take also of the tree of life, and eat, and live for ever.' Rev. ii. 7. 'to him that overcometh, will I give to eat of the tree of life.' "[8]

In view of Milton's denial that the tree of life is a sacrament, we can scarcely regard the "Celestial Food" of *Paradise Regain'd* as sacramental in nature. Nevertheless, it does, apparently, exhibit at least one sacramental characteristic according to Milton's definition—"a visible sign ordained by God, whereby he sets his seal on believers." Nor is its meaning remote from the interpretation Polanus attached to the tree of life, "by which there was signified to our first parents, eating the fruit of this tree, that immortall life should in the Sonne of God be continued unto them," if they remained obedient. In fact, Milton's Messianic banquet is precisely such a "signifying" and "sealing" of "immortall life . . . in the Sonne of God"—a divine confirmation of "Recover'd Paradise to all mankind."

II

These interpretations of the biblical *arbor vitae* stress several points which seem basic to Milton's own treatment of these "Fruits . . . from the tree of life"—their significance as (1) a "symbol of eternal life," (2) a reward merited specifically by obedience to God's commandments, and (3) a detail particularly characteristic of Paradise. Milton could have expected his "fit audience" to be well acquainted with these concepts

6. *Pious Annotations upon the Holy Bible* (London, 1643), p. 4; cf. p. 7.

7. Andreas Rivetus, *Theologiae & Scholasticae Exercitationes CXC. in Genesin* (Lugduni Batavorum, 1633), p. 204.

8. *A Treatise on Christian Doctrine*, trans. C. R. Sumner, in *Prose Works* (Bohn's Standard Library; London, 1883), IV, 222.

and, accordingly, to be able to utilize them as a frame of reference for interpreting the symbolism of the celestial banquet. In the light of these traditional explanations of the *arbor vitae* we may more readily evaluate its significance for the development of Milton's theme and the structure of his fable.

1. In the first place, as a conventional symbol of eternal life, the "Fruits . . . from the tree of life" occupy an important position in the ethical structure of *Paradise Regain'd*. They are an integral part of the inherent pattern of contrasting ideals of heroic virtue and its rewards, in which Kermode has recognized the basic moral concern of this epic: "The whole poem . . . is concerned to establish the character of Christian heroic virtue as distinct from pagan, and to establish the heavenly nature of the rewards which supersede the earthly recompense of the old heroes." After overcoming his third and final temptation (Kermode observes) Milton's hero receives "his supernatural rewards, heavenly glory, and the banquet of celestial love."

More particularly, Kermode interprets the heavenly banquet as a reward for the temperance Christ has displayed in rejecting the sensual feast of Book II:

> . . . Milton balances this celestial banquet with a banquet of sense, which Jesus rejects so that he may attain to the higher angelic banquet. . . . At the end of the poem he has his proper reward:
>
> *A table of Celestial Food, Divine*
> *Ambrosial, Fruits fetcht from the tree of life,*
> *And from the fount of life Ambrosial drink.* (IV, 588–90)
>
> In place of the sensual banquet, the material gratifications of the conqueror, he has a celestial banquet, a banquet of love and of heavenly glory.[9]

Nevertheless, the primary significance of the celestial banquet for Milton's pattern of contrasting rewards lies in the conventional symbolism of the *arbor vitae* as a "type" of eternal life. The principal reason why Christ's heavenly feast transcends "the earthly recompense of the old heroes" is to be found not so much in its intrinsic superiority to the "sensual banquet" *qua* banquet or even in its heavenly nature, as in the fact that it signifies an *eternal* recompense. In this scene Milton has exploited the familiar Christian concept of everlasting life as a *remuneratio aeterna*.

Again, it is as a symbol of eternal life that the celestial feast highlights Christ's superiority to the "old type" of hero. Messiah alone is able to conquer the "two grand foes," Sin and Death, and he is appropriately rewarded with a symbol of eternal life. The conventional

9. Kermode, pp. 324–25, 329.

"conquering hero," on the other hand, is corrupted by sin and recompensed with death:

> *Till Conqueror Death discover them scarce men,*
> *Rowling in brutish vices, and deform'd,*
> *Violent or shameful death thir due reward.*

The celestial banquet of *Paradise Regain'd* is antithetical, moreover, not only to the stately feast Satan offers the Messiah in this epic, but also to the "Fruit of that Forbidden Tree" in *Paradise Lost.* The secular banquet and the forbidden fruit are linked not only as logical opposites of the heavenly feast, but also by Milton's explicit comparison between the elaborate "Cates" offered to Christ and "that crude Apple that diverted *Eve.*" Furthermore, at least one recent scholar has recognized in the "banqueting scene" of Book II the influence of "Protestant-Catholic controversy about the *cibus ligni vetitus.*"[10]

The antithesis between the logical contraries Death and Life underlies both of Milton's epics and is clearly symbolized by the two trees of Paradise. Tasting the fruit of the one brought death and the "loss of *Eden*"; partaking of the other constituted an affirmation of eternal life and "*Eden* rais'd in the wast Wilderness." This contrasting symbolism had, moreover, been clearly expressed in Book IV of *Paradise Lost*:

> *. . . and next to Life*
> *Our Death the Tree of Knowledge grew fast by. . . .*
>
> *. . . that onely Tree*
> *Of knowledge, planted by the Tree of Life,*
> *So neer grows Death to Life. . . .*

In the "Fruits fetcht from the tree of life" of *Paradise Regain'd* we must recognize the antithesis of the fatal fruit of the tree of knowledge in *Paradise Lost,*

> *. . . the Fruit*
> *Of that Forbidden Tree, whose mortal tast*
> *Brought Death into the world, and all our woe. . . .*

2. The pattern of contrasting rewards in both epics involves considerably more than the opposition of different heroic ideals and the sort of recompense they seek and achieve. Underlying the structure of both poems there is a more obvious, but fundamental, antithesis—the simple moral opposition between true virtue and sin, between obedience and disobedience and the contrasting rewards they merit—eternal life and death. On the one hand, everlasting life is the "fruit" and

10. See E. M. Pope, *Paradise Regained: The Tradition and the Poem* (Baltimore, 1947), pp. 70–79. Kermode (p. 324n.) disagrees with Miss Pope's interpretation.

reward of Christ's obedience; on the other hand, the "fruit" of disobedience, the "wages of sin," is death.

As the fruit of the *arbor vitae* had been traditionally regarded as a reward for conforming to God's commands, we should recognize in Christ's celestial feast a conventional recompense for obedience. The "table of Celestial Food" is remuneration for far more than the mere rejection of the sensual banquet, just as the "heavenly glory" represented by the angelic hymn is recompense for considerably more than the mere renunciation of worldly glory. They are a reward Christ earns through his *entire* ordeal—a recompense for his "firm obedience fully tri'd | Through *all* temptation" [italics mine]. The "Celestial Food" he receives represents the divine approbation of his unshaken obedience.

3. In the third place, these "Fruits fetcht from the tree of life" are an unequivocal sign of "Recover'd Paradise." They provide, therefore, an appropriate conclusion to an epic whose announced theme is Paradise *regained.*

As the tree of life was peculiarly indigenous to Paradise, Christ's participation in its fruits signifies that he has regained "the blissful Seat"—that "A fairer Paradise is founded now | For *Adam* and his chosen Sons." With this clear-cut symbol of "*Eden* rais'd in the wast Wilderness," Milton brought his epic fable to its logical conclusion. The heroic poem (Aristotle and Tasso had taught him) is an "imitation of an action"[11] and the particular action he had chosen to imitate ("Recover'd Paradise") had been explicitly stated in the first lines—and, indeed, in the very title—of his poem. This final section of the poem completes the sequence of events outlined in the first verses of the epic. After demonstrating *how* Paradise was regained ("By one man's firm obedience fully tri'd"), after leaving the Tempter "foil'd | In all his wiles, defeated and repuls't," Milton must logically conclude his action with "*Eden* rais'd." This concept he conveyed symbolically through Christ's celestial banquet on the fruits of the *arbor vitae* and explicitly through the angelic hymn of praise:

> *. . . now thou hast aveng'd*
> *Supplanted* Adam, *and by vanquishing*
> *Temptation, hast regain'd lost Paradise. . . .*

This allusion to the tree of life reinforces the antithesis between the loss of Paradise through Adam and its recovery through Christ. The *arbor vitae* was not only characteristic of "the happy Garden," but also

11. Torquato Tasso, *Prose*, ed. F. Flora (Milan and Rome, 1935), p. 331: "il poema eroico è una imitazione d'azione illustre," &c. Cf. Aristotle, *On the Art of Poetry*, trans. Ingram Bywater (Oxford, 1920), p. 35.

indirectly involved in man's expulsion. God's avowed reason for exiling Adam (Gen. iii. 22) was "lest he . . . take also of the tree of life, and eat, and live for ever." And it was "to keep the way of the tree of life" that cherubim (Gen. iii. 24) with fiery arms had been stationed at the entrance to the garden.

Nevertheless, it is not to the Garden of Eden but to the heavenly Paradise that Milton's lines refer. As the "seat of earthly bliss" has "fail'd," the *arbor vitae* is now peculiarly indigenous to Heaven. The "Fruits fetcht from the tree of life" are, therefore, "Celestial Food" in the fullest sense—signs or attributes of the "fairer Paradise . . . founded now | For *Adam* and his chosen Sons" rather than of the earthly Paradise Adam had forfeited.

III

When ministering angels set before Messiah "Fruits fetcht from the tree of life," they are not only testifying to his recovery of Paradise. They are also bearing witness to his Messiahship. Traditionally, the tree of life was not only a distinctive feature of the "happy Garden"; it was also closely associated with Christ's mission as redeemer. In Reuchlin's *De Arte Cabalistica*, God's command to expel man from Paradise "lest he . . . take also of the tree of life, and eat, and live for ever" had been interpreted as a veiled prediction that a future saviour would appear, destined to eat of the tree of life ("homo ad vescendum de ligno vitae destinatus" [f. x]): ". . . & ille per rectam fidem & placidam oblationem mittet manum suam, et sumet de ligno vitae, & eius ligni fructus erit omnium sperantium salus." At least two of several commentaries on Genesis which Milton is known to have consulted—those of Rivetus and Musculus [12]—quote this passage, even though they doubt its application to Christ.[13] Milton was, therefore, in all probability familiar with it, even though he may have agreed with the scepticism expressed by Rivetus and Musculus. Nevertheless, the likelihood that he did not take this passage seriously as Scriptural exegesis did not preclude his exploiting it for essential poetic ends. Inasmuch as "Fruits

12. See A. Williams, "Renaissance Commentaries on 'Genesis' and Some Elements of the Theology of *Paradise Lost*," *PMLA*, LVI (1941), 151–64; "Milton and the Renaissance Commentaries on Genesis," *MP*, XXXVII (1940), 263–78.

13. Rivetus, p. 201; Wolfgangus Musculus, *In Genesim Mosis Commentarii* (Basileae, 1600), p. 109. After quoting Reuchlin's interpretation, Rivetus comments, "Mirum est homines doctos & pios, talibus commentis non solum fidem adhibere, sed ea etiam commendare. . . . Quis enim unquam sibi persuaderi sinet, tale mysterium sub his verbis latere?" Musculus gives a similar verdict, "Verùm torta expositio verborum istorum probari non potest, utpote quod illud, *Ecce Adam est quasi unus ex nobis*, ad hunc modum: Et nunc in praesenti hoc tempore, ne iste meus in aeternitate unicus, qui subsistit ex meipso, manum suam mittat, & sumat etiam de ligno vitae, &c., cum haec non de Christo, sed primo Adamo sint dicta."

. . . from the tree of life" had been regarded as one of the attributes of the Messiah, the introduction of this detail lends both verisimilitude and decorum to Milton's account of Christ's celestial banquet.

Moreover, in discussing this text, Reuchlin emphasizes many of the ethical characteristics prominent in the Christ of *Paradise Regain'd*—especially the rejection of worldly glory and the preference for humility and patience:

> We . . . believe that the Messiah will come to free the miserable mortals of the human race from the bonds of original unrighteousness, to remit sins, and to save the souls of the pious servants of Gods who were excluded from eternal life through our father Adam until the Messiah should make satisfaction. In order to consummate the justice of a clement and merciful God, the Messiah shall put forth his hand and partake of the tree of life and eat thereof, so that we may live through him eternally. And this satisfaction ought not to be made in royal pride nor vaunt of honor and glory, inasmuch as the original sin that the Messiah must expiate sprang from pride and elation. On the contrary, it should be made in humility and suffering. Not in chariots and horses, but in the name of the Lord our God; not in victory nor in human triumph, but in labor, fasting, vigils, fortitude of mind, contempt of vainglory, compassionate mercy, exceptional love towards God, right love towards men; and finally in a free, heroic, and voluntary death. For Virtue alone can war against Vice, and no wise man has ever found greatness in the empires, principalities, crowns, and genealogies of this world.

Thus the primary significance of Christ's celestial banquet[14] derives largely from conventional Renaissance interpretations of the *arbor vitae*. By a skillful exploitation of exegetical traditions, Milton concludes his epic of "Recover'd Paradise" with a detail closely associated not only with eternal life and the merited reward of obedience, but also with Paradise itself and the Messianic mission of redemption.

14. For hero-feasts, see Henry Estienne's *Thesaurus Graecae Linguae* (1572), *s.v.* Ἡρῶα "dicuntur etiam epulae solennes in heroum honorem."

7. *"Like Turbulencies"*

The Tempest As Adversity Symbol

❦ Recent studies of *Paradise Regain'd* have tended to stress the continuity rather than the differences between the episodes of the Second Temptation and the storm scene which concludes it. In Stein's opinion, the "night of terrors" is "not [a] new temptation," but a "subtle recapitulation [of] much of the moral drama already experienced."[1] In Taylor's view, Satan's objective is "the same as in the previous incidents of the second temptation: to lead Christ into taking possession of power or kingdom under improper circumstances and auspices."[2] Schultz has called attention to the common theme underlying the devil's "lures and threats"—the "Kingdom, its nature and limits"; "persecution must befall a would-be king who refuses Satan's help."[3]

Granted the thematic unity of this scene and its antecedents, their differences still require further interpretation. What is the ethical significance of Satan's abrupt switch from allurements to terrors? What, precisely, does the series of night terrors contribute to the moral pattern

First published, in somewhat different form, in *Modern Philology*, LIX (1961), 81–88.

1. Arnold Stein, *Heroic Knowledge* (Minneapolis, 1957), pp. 116, 121.

2. Dick Taylor, Jr., "The Storm Scene in *Paradise Regained:* A Reinterpretation," *University of Toronto Quarterly*, XXIV (1955), 370. See also William B. Hunter, Jr., "Prophetic Dreams and Visions in *Paradise Lost*," *MLQ*, IX (1948), 277–85.

3. Howard Schultz, *Milton and Forbidden Knowledge* (New York, 1955), pp. 224–25.

of Milton's epic? In what respects does it complement the earlier appeal to "all kingdoms of the world" and their "power" and "glory" (Luke 4:5–6)?

In attempting to answer these questions, let us take as our point of departure the most obvious difference between the storm scene and the preceding temptation—the conventional antithesis between trial by prosperity and trial by adversity. Though the idea is a commonplace it is essential for a proper understanding of Satan's rhetoric, of the symbolism of the tempest episode, and of the relationship of this scene to epic tradition.

I

In drawing his arguments from the logical contraries, prosperity and adversity, Satan follows standard rhetorical procedure. According to Aristotle's *Rhetoric*, the two types of deliberative oration—exhortation and dehortation—utilize contrary topics. In exhorting, the orator "always propoundeth felicity, or some part of felicity, to be attained by the actions he exhorteth unto, and in dehortation the contrary." Appeals to riches, glory, honor, health, strength, prosperity ("Which is to have all, or the most, or the greatest of those goods which we attribute to fortune") etc., are "the grounds from whence we exhort," whereas "dehortation is from the contraries of these." Moreover, "by felicity is meant commonly, prosperity with virtue, or a continual content of the life with surety"; its parts are "such things as we call good, in body, mind, or fortune."[4] An exhortatory argument, then, makes its appeal to prosperity; and, conversely, a dehortatory argument hinges on the threat of adversity. The one argues from apparent goods, the other from apparent evils.

In his attempt to "try [Christ's] constancy," Satan employs both types of argument. When he promises "Honours, Riches, Kingdoms, Glory" to induce Jesus to accept his "offer'd aid," he is arguing from the conventional "grounds" of exhortation. On the other hand, when he alters his tactics and threatens "many a hard assay Of dangers, and adversities and pains," he is exploiting the usual "grounds" of dehortation, in order to dissuade his antagonist from the alternative path, the Messianic way of humiliation and affliction. The importance of the storm scene for this dehortatory argument lies in its intermediate position between Satan's first and second prognostications of adversity (IV, 382 ff. and 460 ff.). Sandwiched between these two predictions, the tempest episode appears to lend support to both of them. It seems to confirm the earlier forecast ostensibly based on judicial astrology and, as

4. Thomas Hobbes, *A Digest of Aristotle's Rhetoric*, in *Aristotle's Poetics and Rhetoric*, ed. T. A. Moxon (London, 1953), pp. 84–85.

"a sure foregoing sign" of future "ill," to provide the foundation for Satan's subsequent threats. But, in fact, his dehortatory argument, like his exhortations, is based on false testimony. The "Tempest at this Desert" and the "many terrors, voices, prodigies" are not divine testimony "sent from God," but "false portents" inspired by diabolical agency. As their author is not a true deity, they have no "power of proof."[5]

II

In the Biblical account of the Second Temptation, there is no threat of future adversity. The offer of the "kingdoms of the world" provides the basis of an exhortatory argument but no apparent foundation for dehortation. One is confronted, accordingly, with the problem of why Milton chose to introduce the adversity episode—the question of its relevance to the matter of the Second Temptation and to the theme of the poem as a whole.

In the first place, his presentation of the temptations of the world would have been incomplete unless it had included adversity as well as prosperity. This dual aspect of the world's assault on the Christian warrior was a commonplace in the literature of spiritual warfare. According to Erasmus' *Enchiridion Militis Christiani*, the world sometimes attacks the Christian with open force, assailing him with adversity. At other times it tempts him to capitulate by offering false promises of great rewards.[6] In *The Christian Warfare against the Devill World and Flesh,* John Downame similarly maintains that "the world on every side assaulteth us; on the right hand with prosperity, on the left hand with adversitie." As the temptations of prosperity are the more dangerous of the two, Christ deliberately chose the way of affliction, as the safest example for his followers:

> . . . our danger is farre more when the World allureth us with the baits of prosperitie, than when it threateneth and afflicteth us with trouble and adversitie: from whence an ancient Father observeth, that Christ coming into the World that hee might shew us the way to Heaven, both by his doctrine and example, made choice rather of the afflicted way, than of the faire passage of worldly prosperitie, that we might follow his steps, as being farre the safest way to bring us to our heavenly Countrie.

5. In the *Artis logicae* Milton observes that "in civil and human affairs divine testimony has the power of proof in proportion as its author is a true or false god." As an example he quotes from Cicero's *In Catilinam:* "And to omit the lightning torches which did appear by night in the occident, the vehement and parching heat of the heavens, as thraws of lightnings and fire breaking out of the clouds, earthquakes, and many other such tempests which . . . did appear, so that the gods with a loud voice seemed to sing those things which now be present" (see *The Works of John Milton* [Columbia Edition; New York, 1935], XI, 278–83).

6. *The Christian Manual: Being a Translation from the "Enchiridion Militis Christiani" of Erasmus* (London, 1752), p. 2.

... shewing himselfe an example for us to follow, he refused to be made a King, and contrariwise voluntarily offered himselfe to suffer on the Crosse, hee avoided the glory of regiment, and embraced the punishment of a shamefull death; to this end, that his members might hereby learne, to flee the Worlds favours, and little to feare his threats and terrors, to love adversitie for Truth sake, and fearing prosperitie to avoid it.[7]

The contrast between these two aspects of the world's assault on the warfaring Christian—"the tentations of prosperitie" and those of adversity, "arising from trouble and affliction"[8]—is represented graphically in an illustration on the 1634 title page of Downame's book.[9] *Mundus adulans* is depicted as a woman offering such attributes of prosperity as scepter, goblet, globe, and coins. Her motto echoes Satan's promise of the kingdoms of the world ("Omnia haec tibi dabo"). *Mundus saeviens*, on the other hand, is personified as a man carrying a sword and hangman's noose and accompanied by such instruments of persecution as gallows, stocks, fetters, fire, and faggots. His motto threatens force ("Saltem vi, si non dolo"). The explanatory verses on this picture ("The Front Opened") further emphasize the world's contrasting tactics—allurements and threats—in tempting the Christian soldier to sin:

> *The* World (*Leieutenant Generall in this fight*)
> *In* Harlots habit, *fawningly allures him*
> *To sinfull, shamefull swarving from all right.*
> *This done*, Wealth, Honour, Pleasures, *she assures him.*
>
> *Which he contemning; full of* Spleene and Hate,
> *She turnes her* Smiles to Frownes, *nought else now breathing*
> *But* (*Tyrant-like*) *Fire, Faggot, Sword, and Bate,*
> *Gibbets and Gayles, no crueltie out-leaving.*

The idea expressed in this passage is a commonplace, but therein lies its significance for *Paradise Regain'd*. Its value resides less in its possible influence on Milton than in its traditional nature and in the light it throws on the characterization of Satan. The devil's character and tactics in the Second Temptation and the adversity sequence which follows it are those conventionally ascribed to the world in its warfare against the Christian. The threats of the "World Raging" (*Mundus saeviens*) complement the blandishments of the "World Fawning"

7. London, 1634, pp. 368, 372. Aspects of Downame's relation to Milton have been discussed by Merritt Y. Hughes, *John Milton, Prose Selections* (New York, 1947), p. 223n.: B. Rajan, "*Paradise Lost*" *and the Seventeenth Century Reader* (London, 1947), p. 70; and Elizabeth Marie Pope, "*Paradise Regained*": *The Tradition and the Poem* (Baltimore, 1947).

8. Cf. the title page of Parts II and III of Downame's book.

9. A reproduction of this plate appears as the frontispiece of William Haller's *The Rise of Puritanism* (New York, 1957).

(*Mundus adulans*). When the "tentations of prosperitie"—"Wealth, Honour, Pleasure," and the like—fail to allure, Satan resorts to "the tentations of the WORLD on the left hand, arising from trouble and affliction." The chronological order of these temptations—first the appeal to prosperity, afterwards the menaces of adversity—is identical with the temporal sequence of the world's assaults, as Downame describes them. Similarly, Satan's anger when his offered aid is refused is likewise characteristic of the world's behavior when her baits are contemned. When her gifts are despised, Downame's *Mundus* waxes "full of Spleene and Hate" and "turnes her Smiles to Frownes." When Satan's offers are rejected, he bends a "stern brow," "storms refus'd," and swells with "rage" and "mad despite." In his choice of contrasting arguments, his shift from allurement to threats, and his rage at the rejection of his baits, the Prince of this World resembles the *Mundus* of Christian ethical tradition.

Second, an adversity temptation is necessary for a balanced and comprehensive demonstration of Christ's virtue. If he is to be "*fully* tried Through *all* temptation," he must withstand fortune's frowns as well as her smiles, her threats as well as her promises. Milton's hero is tested, accordingly, by both sorts of fortune ("utriusque fortunae"),[10] and in the course of this ordeal he proves his ability to bear and to forbear, to *sustain* the menaces of adversity and to *abstain* from the allurements of prosperity. The Second Temptation begins with an exhibition of temperance and concludes with a demonstration of patience.

The ethical commonplace underlying this twofold battle with fortune has been lucidly summarized by the Jesuit Eusebius Nieremberg in his *Discourse of Temperance and Patience:*

> I find that *peace* and *joy* have two *handles*, whereby we may take hold of them, *Patience*, and *Temperance*. . . . Patience in adversity is temperance in prosperity. . . . beleeve with *Epictetus*, that the Quintessence of all Philosophie is squeezed into these two, Ἀνέχου, καὶ ἀπέχου, beare and forbeare. He neither obtaines, nor retaines his joy, that doth not abstain, and sustaine. . . . By refusing you obtaine, and by suffering you preserve: by refusing the favours, and suffering the spite of fortune.
>
> . . . thou hast . . . both *Temperance* and *Patience*, the best Stratagems and Countermines against the Wiles of Fortune. Her storms and suddaine furies . . . thou mayst break and overcome by bearing; Her Arts . . . by listning to Reason.[11]

10. Cf. Francesco Petrarca, *De' Remedii dell' una e dell' altra Fortuna*, trans. Giovanni Dassaminiato (Bologna, 1867), I, 49.

11. *The Works of Henry Vaughan*, ed. L. C. Martin (2nd ed.; Oxford, 1957), pp. 221–22. Cf. "What doest thou think is bearing and forbearing? It is to be even with Fortune, discreetly to abstaine, discreetly to will, and to covet nothing" (*ibid.*, p. 222).

Both the pattern of rejection in the Second Temptation and the pattern of endurance in the adversity sequence which follows it conform to the normal pattern of this conflict against prosperous and adverse fortune.[12] Christ maintains his inner peace and constancy "by refusing the favours, and suffering the spite of fortune."

Third, the adversity episode is necessary to complete the principal epistemological pattern in the poem—the conflict between truth and falsehood, divine wisdom and hellish wiles. The offer of false goods should logically conclude with a threat of false evils. In exploiting the contrast between the real and apparent significance of good and evil fortune, Milton is again making use of a commonplace of Christian ethical tradition. According to St. Ambrose's *Christian Offices*: "Blessednesse [is] to bee obtained by the undergoing of sorrowes, and necessities"; "poverty, hunger, griefe, which are thought to be evils, [are] not only . . . no impediments, but speciall adjuments to a blessed life." Conversely, the "externall goods of the body are not only no ayde, to a blessed life but a losse." Paradoxically, "what things are thought good [are] for the most part an hindrance to a blessed, and eternall life, what are thought evill [are] certain matter, and meanes of vertue, and everlasting felicity."[13]

Nieremberg similarly maintains that both the goods and evils of fortune are counterfeit and that the wise man must distinguish between their superficial appearance and their inherent reality: "All [Fortune's] *wares* are but *gilded clouds*, a *Superficiall wash*; they are not that which they seem to be . . . Her *Good*, and her *Evill* are both counterfeits. . . . The great mercy of God hath so provided, that *Evill* when it sets upon us, is but an apparition; there comes good presently after it."[14]

Justus Lipsius likewise regards external goods and evils as false, as they have no real power over the mind:

> There bee two thinges that doe assault this castle of Constancie in us, FALSE GOODS, and FALSE EVILS: I define them both to bee, *Such thinges as are not in us, but about us: And which properlie doe not helpe nor hurte the inner man, that is, the minde.* Wherefore, I may not call those thinges good or evill simplie in subiect and in definition: But I confesse they are such in opinion, and by the iudgement

12. Cf. Justus Lipsius, *Two Bookes of Constancie*, trans. Sir John Stradling, ed. Rudolf Kirk (New Brunswick, N.J., 1939), pp. 83–84, 111. Lipsius urges his reader to "imprint CONSTANCIE in thy mind amid this casuall and inconstant variablenesse of all things"; with the motto *Nec spe, nec metu*, "thou shalt be a king indeed, only subject unto God, enfranchized from the servile yoke of Fortune and affections." With constancy, "thou shalt remaine unmooved: let showres, thunders, lighteninges, and tempestes fall round about thee, thou shalt crie boldlie with a loude voyce, *I lie at rest amid the waves.*"

13. *Christian Offices Chrystal Glasse*, trans. Richard Humphrey (London, 1637), pp. 7–10.

14. *The Works of Henry Vaughan*, ed. Martin, pp. 271–72.

of the common people. In the first ranke I place Riches, Honour, Authoritie, Health, long life. In the second, Povertie, Infamie, lacke of promotion, Sicknesse, death. And to comprehende all in one word, whatsoever els is accidentall and happeneth outwardlie.[15]

The "false goods" ("Riches, Honour, Authoritie," etc.) of the Second Temptation have already engaged the attention of scholars. Let us confine ourselves, therefore, to the "false evils" of the adversity sequence. First, the actual terrors of the night are "insubstantial," like the night itself (IV, 399); the storm and the furies are external menaces only and leave their victim "unappall'd in calm and sinless peace." The "inner man"—"the minde"—remains unhurt.

Moreover, these apparent evils contribute to an end that is unequivocally good. Though Satan's intent is evil, God permits these adversities in order to "exercise" Christ's patience and constancy. He is acquiring the "rudiments" of the "great warfare" whereby he will vanquish Sin and Death and destroy Satan's reign. As Lipsius had observed, "all these great afflictions are to good end and purpose; although this blind mind of ours perceive it not. . . . For the true ends of afflictions are often hid from us":

> The cause is God's love toward us, and not hatred. The end or consequence, not our hurt, but our benefit. For this our exercising furthereth us more waies than one: it confirmeth or strengtheneth us; it trieth or prooveth us; it maketh us mirrours of patience unto others. . . . Therefore adversitie doth confirme and strengthen us. And as trees that be much beaten with the winde, take deeper roote: so good men are the better contayned within the compasse of vertue, being sometimes assaulted with the stormes of adversity.[16]

The evils of the storm scene serve a divine end; they perfect their victim in "Humiliation and strong Sufferance."

The fallacies underlying Satan's threats of future evils are subtler, but even more important for the theme of the poem. First, the devil's epistemological method is unsound. He bases (or pretends to base) his prognostications on superstitious auguries, on judicial astrology and meteorology. Renaissance distrust of these methods of predicting the future is reflected in Gabriel Harvey's "Iudgement of Earthquakes." Harvey quotes a relevant passage from Pico della Mirandola's "sixt Chapter of his sixt Booke, against Cogging deceitfull Astrologers, and Southsayers, *De rerum Praenotione, pro veritate Relligionis, contra Superstitiosas vanitates*," which specifically ascribes natural "portents" to diabolical "imposture": "Naturae opere fieri non potest, ut Ostentis, ut Monstris magni illi, seu dextri, seu sinistri eventus portendantur, et

15. Lipsius, pp. 85–86.
16. *Ibid.*, pp. 147–49.

ab aliqua pendeant proxima causa, quae et futura etiam proferat, Impostura Daemonum, ut id fiat, videri potest."[17] Satan's first prognostication is founded on a "superstitious vanity" of "Cogging deceitfull Astrologers." His second prediction is based on "false portents" which are merely an "impostura daemonum."

There is, however, a second, more ingenious fallacy in these predictions. The hardships he prophesies are actually (in Ambrose's phrase) "no impediments, but speciall adjuments," no "hindrance" but "certaine matter, and meanes" to the achievement of Christ's destined enterprise. Though the astrological and meteorological basis of Satan's forecasts is false, the *content* of his predictions is true. The way to the Messianic kingdom *does* lie through "Sorrows, and labours, opposition, hate, . . . reproaches, injuries, Violence and Stripes, and lastly, cruel death." In attempting to divert Christ from the Messianic path of humiliation, Satan presents both prosperity and adversity in false lights. The former, he argues, is a sure means to achieving the kingdom, the latter a formidable obstacle. As he cannot allude directly to the biblical predictions concerning the suffering Messiah without exposing his own fallacies, he pretends to derive his predictions from other sources—"the Starry Rubric" and the portents of the "ominous night." he mentions the "Prophecies of thee" (IV, 381), only to veer away into astrology.

The terror scene is, then, not so much a "recapitulation" of "much of the moral drama already experienced" as an altogether different type of temptation. It is the keystone of an adversity sequence which complements the earlier temptations of prosperity. It provides the grounds of a dehortatory argument, just as the kingdoms of the world had provided the foundation for exhortation. It bears the same relation to the preceding scene as *Mundus Saeviens* to *Mundus Adulans*, as hostile fortune to favorable fortune, and as false evils to false goods. Both the ethical content and the symbolism of this episode have close parallels in Renaissance epic tradition.

III

The nocturnal ordeal which concludes the Second Temptation provides a forceful contrast to the banquet scene which began it. As Stein observes, "this is the banquet reversed: not a solicitous nature

17. *The Poetical Works of Edmund Spenser*, ed. J. C. Smith and E. de Selincourt (London, 1959), p. 619. Cf. M. Y. Hughes (ed.), *Paradise Regained* (New York, 1937), p. 524n.; John C. Lapp (ed.), *The Universe of Pontus de Tyard* (Ithaca, N.Y., 1950), pp. xlviii–xlix, 72 ff.; John C. Lapp, "Three Renaissance Attitudes toward Astrology," *PMLA*, LXIV (1949), 530–48. See *Ioannis Francisci Pici Mirandulae . . . De rerum praenotione libri novem* (Argentoraci, 1507).

offering its beautiful all to its lord . . ., but an angry nature threatening with an excess of horror for the sake of excess." This final "impostura daemonum," designed to frighten its victim from the Messianic way of humiliation and to "terrify" him to the devil's "will," is also a symbol of adversity "These flaws" foresignify "like turbulencies in the affairs of men." In all four respects—as adversity symbol, as infernal illusion, as deterrent to a heroic enterprise, and as counterpart to a scene of sensuous enticement—Milton's terror scene has affinities with those of Tasso's *Gerusalemme Liberata* and Gratiani's *Il Conquisto di Granata.*

In Tasso's epic, the pagan enchanter Ismeno attempts to prevent the Crusaders from building the necessary battering-rams and siege towers for their assault on Jerusalem by summoning a host of "wicked sprites" to frighten the Christians away from the nearby wood. Among their "illusions false by witchcraft wrought" are terrors similar to those Satan raises against Christ—evil spirits "with darts and dreadful weapons armed" and thunder, lightning, and tempests. These represent the deceitful arguments ("ingannevoli argomenti") which "do show us honest travails and honourable danger under the shape of evil."[18]

In Gratiani's heroic poem, the infidel sorcerer Alchindo employs similar tactics to prevent the Christians from capturing Granada. Summoning "le Furie, e i Demoni," he sends "gli horridi Spiriti" to strike terror into the Christian camp and thus deter it from battle ("Seminate nel Campo horrori, affani, Ciò, che à l'armi si niega, oprin gl' inganni"). Some of these assume terrible and monstrous shapes; others frighten the Christians with nocturnal terrors.

Later, when the Christian warrior Hernando is seeking the enchanted urn on which the safety of Granada depends ("La reliquia fatale à l'alta impresa"), Alchindo vainly raises a magical tempest and fearful monsters to stop him. These enchantments, according to the "Allegoria del Poema," represent the changes of fortune, and Hernando, who endures and overcomes them, exemplifies patience ("*magna pati*").[19]

Like Ismeno, Satan employs "ingannevoli argomenti" to represent "honest travails and honourable dangers under the shape of evil." Like Alchindo, he attempts to halt his destined victor by adverse fortune, which his opponent endures with "generosa sofferenza." The ethical significance underlying these demonic storm scenes is similar in all three poems. In certain respects, however, they also show affinities with older traditions. Inasmuch as they occur on *land* and are primarily designed to terrify, they recall the magical tempests and other

18. Torquato Tasso, *Jerusalem Delivered*, trans. Edward Fairfax, ed. Henry Morley (London, 1890), pp. 280–83, 361–65, 439. Cf. Tasso, *Il Goffredo* (Padova, 1742), p. xvi.

19. *Il Conquisto di Granata, poema heroico del Co. Girolamo Gratiani* (Bologna, 1660), pp. 368–70, 511.

supernatural terrors which knights-errant encountered in medieval romance.[20]

Moreover, supernaturally inspired storms raised by hostile spirits to hinder an epic enterprise were conventional features of heroic poetry. Poseidon tries to delay Odysseus' return to Ithaca by raising a storm to shipwreck him off the coast of Phaeacia (*Odyssey*, Book V). To prevent Aeneas from reaching Italy ("Italia Teucrorum avertere regem"), Juno bids Aeolus to stir up a tempest against the Trojan fleet (*Aeneid* i. 37 ff.). In *Os Lusiados* (Canto VI), Bacchus tries to hinder Da Gama's voyage to India by persuading Neptune to send a storm against the Portuguese ships. Tasso, Gratiani, and Milton retain the tempest's conventional role as an obstacle to the achievement of a destined enterprise, but change its setting from sea to land.[21]

IV

In the "scene of night terrors" and the "beautiful morning" which follows it, Stein finds an analogy with "the substantial pattern of the mystic experience." Satan provides the "dark night," but "with a difference": "The terrors are followed by a wonderful light, and pure meadows, and singing," as in "the divine marriage of the mystery cults," but the light and meadows and singing are "not those of the old revelation." "The dark night is over but the new revelation has not come."[22]

Though there is no need to challenge this interpretation, there is nevertheless a further reason for emphasizing the contrast between "the night so foul" and "morning fair." All things are now "more fresh and green, After a night of storm so ruinous." In "this fair change" from nocturnal terrors to "joy and brightest morn," Milton is expressing yet another characteristic of adversity—the commonplace that ill fortune lasts only for a limited duration and terminates in joy. Fortune's inconstancy was proverbial; as Nieremberg observed, "*Evill* . . . is but an apparition; there comes good presently after it." According to Lipsius, calamities contribute to the beauty and ornament of the world by providing change and variety:

> I can conceive no trimnesse in this huge engine, without a different change and varietie of things. I knowe that the sunne is most bewtifull: yet the dewie night and the mantle of that blacke dame put betweene, maketh him to appeare more

20. Cf. Roger Sherman Loomis (ed.), *Arthurian Literature in the Middle Ages: A Collaborative History* (Oxford, 1959), *passim.*

21. Besides these magical tempests over the land, Gratiani's epic also depicts the conventional supernatural storms at sea, designed to hinder the destined enterprise. These tempests are raised by the demon Hidragorre (pp. 292–94, 471–74) in order to obstruct the voyage of the Christian heroes Hernando and Consalvo.

22. Stein, pp. 121–22.

gratious. The summer is most pleasant, yet the winter doth make it more lovely. . . . But I perceive moreover another kinde of ornament, of more account and inward profit. Histories doo teach me, that al thinges become better and quietter, after the stormes of adversities.

Again, calamities are like "goblins or painted visards" which frighten children. Like hailstones which soon dissolve, adversities do not cast down a "constant settled mind," but "vanish and come to naught themselves."[23] This is precisely what happens in the case of Satan's storm. Sitting "unappall'd in calm and sinless peace," Christ maintains his constancy until the terrors vanish with the "unsubstantial" night. It is nature who changes her aspect, not he; and against the inconstancies and variations of fortune his own constancy stands out in bolder relief.

The differences between this episode and another storm scene—the tempest on the Sea of Galilee (Matt. 8:24 ff., Mark 4:37 ff., Luke 8:23 ff.)—are significant. Though Christ preserves the same unruffled calm on both occasions, he does not, in this case, exert his miraculous power to quell the storm. Instead of commanding the elements, he endures their fury and thus demonstrates the "Humiliation and strong Sufferance" whereby he is to win his decisive victory on the cross. In this episode the supernatural power is wielded not by Christ, but by Satan, and Milton's emphasis falls on the human virtue of patience.

In *Paradise Regain'd*, as in the *Gerusalemme Liberata* and *Il Conquisto di Granata*, the supernatural terrors vanish when the hero confronts them with fortitude. The basic pattern underlying this transition is less the "pattern of the mystic experience" than the ideal of heroic constancy through the outward vicissitudes of fortune. In the midst of external rage the "inner man" remains "unshaken." Christ's "constant settled mind" retains its internal peace in complete independence both of the "stormes of adversities" and the calm which follows them. Both the ethical content and the symbolism of this scene are conventional. The tempest had long been a familiar metaphor of adversity,[24] and the foul night and fair morning of *Paradise Regain'd* involve much the same contrast as the meditation of "Good Weather" in Christian Scriver's *Incidental Devotions*, written in 1671:

23. Lipsius, pp. 256, 280.

24. For the Fortuna tempest symbol see Howard R. Patch, *The Goddess Fortuna in Mediaeval Literature* (Cambridge, Mass., 1927), pp. 37, 101–7. In "Sturm und Drang: Conjectures on the Origin of a Phrase," *Simiolus, Kunsthistorisch Tijdschrift*, I (1966–67) and "Reflections on Seeing Holbein's Portrait of Erasmus at Longford Castle," *Essays in the History of Art Presented to Rudolf Wittkower* (Phaidon Press, 1967), Professor William S. Heckscher discusses the Renaissance opposition between *Tempestas* and *Tranquillitas* and its association with the revival of Stoicism.

The dense and gloomy clouds which discharge thunder and lightning, shake and terrify the earth, and water it with drenching rain, are not pleasant; but they make the herb of the field rejoice, and man and beast along with it. Light comes out of the darkness, and blessing accompanies the rain. Similar are the effects of trouble and adversity upon the mind. They cause pain and sorrow, but are succeeded by spiritual and divine satisfaction and joy.[25]

25. Christian Scriver, *Gotthold's Emblems*, trans. Robert Menzies (4th ed.; Edinburgh, 1877), p. 213.

Part II

❦

The Highest Good

❦

8. The "Happy Garden"

Felicity and End in Renaissance Epic and Ethics

❦ For many a Renaissance theorist, poetry was, if not the handmaid, at least the pedagogue of sterner disciplines—ethics, politics, and theology. Its final cause was instruction as well as pleasure. For Tasso, as for Sidney, its end (*fine*) was to "teach delightfully" (*giovare dilettando*). According to Minturno, "the end of tragic poetry" and "the office of the tragic poet . . . is nothing other than to speak in verse in such a way that he may teach, delight, and so move the minds of his audience that he is able to purge them of passions."[1]

In Milton's opinion, the poet had power to "inbreed and cherish in a great people the seeds of vertu and public civility" and to teach over "the whole book of sanctity and vertu through all the instances of example." Combining "profit" with "delight," he could instruct more effectively than the doctrinaire schoolman; Spenser was a "better teacher" than Scotus or Aquinas.

Though this consciousness of "what religious, what glorious and magnificent use might be made of Poetry in divine and humane

First published, in somewhat different form, in the *Journal of the History of Ideas*, XXIII (1962), 117–32.

1. Torquato Tasso, *Prose*, ed. F. Flora (Milan, 1935), pp. 328, 331; Antonio Minturno, *L'Arte Poetica* (Naples, 1725), p. 76; J. E. Spingarn, *A History of Literary Criticism in the Renaissance* (New York, 1925), *passim*. Italics mine.

things"[2] was by no means peculiar to the Renaissance, it was undoubtedly heightened by the psychological stresses of the Reformation and Counter-Reformation. A practical consequence of this doctrine was the emphasis which more "sage and serious" poets intentionally placed on the didactic element in their works, either incorporating moral, religious, and political concepts openly through explicit statement or else expressing them indirectly through allegory. Nevertheless, the tension between the two primary ends of poetry—"prodesse" and "delectare"[3]—confronted the poet with a peculiar problem. If the poetic art was theoretically oriented towards ethical, civil, and religious norms, in what way and to what extent should these values affect the argument, structure, and meaning of the poem? If poetry was to serve the ends of ethics, politics, and theology, how (if at all) should the poet represent these ends? For a partial answer to this problem, let us analyze the idea of beatitude or the "chief good" as it appears in the works of four poets of the Reformation or Counter-Reformation. Since Renaissance intellectual tradition regarded felicity as the *summum bonum* and the final cause of ethics, politics, and the "divine science" theology, this was a concept of the highest significance for a poet seriously committed to the didactic ends of his art.

I

"Every art and every inquiry," Aristotle had declared in the *Nicomachean Ethics*, "and similarly every action and pursuit, is thought to aim at some good; and for this reason the good has rightly been declared to be that at which all things aim." The "chief good," which we "desire for its own sake" and which is the "end of the things we do" is "happiness," and this is the special concern or "object" of ethics and politics.[4]

In defining beatitude as the end of ethics, Renaissance moralists were influenced not only by Aristotle and his medieval disciples, but also by Platonic and Augustinian tradition. For Plato, the Idea of the Good, "by whose use just things and the rest become helpful and useful," was the "object" and "greatest study" of the "science of dialectic" and "true philosophy."[5] For St. Augustine, the *summum bonum* was the end of ethics and indeed of "all philosophy":

> There remains the moral [part of philosophy], in Greek ἠθική, which inquires after the greatest good whereto all our actions have reference: and which is

2. John Milton, *Prose Works* (London, 1883), II, 68, 479–80; III, p. 474; cf. *Paradise Regain'd*, IV, 345. See also Ida Langdon, *Milton's Theory of Poetry and Fine Art* (New Haven, 1924).

3. Cf. Horace, *Ars Poetica*, ed. H. R. Fairclough (London, 1947), p. 478.

4. Aristotle, *Nicomachean Ethics*, trans. Sir David Ross (London, 1954), pp. 1–2, 12.

5. Plato, *Republic*, trans. A. D. Lindsay (London, 1958), pp. 198–206.

desired for itself only: and therefore we call it the end, as referring all the rest unto it, but desiring it only for itself. . . . This true and greatest good is God, says Plato: and therefore he will have a philosopher a lover of God, that, because philosophy aims at beatitude, the lover of God might be blessed by enjoying God.[6]

Renaissance ethics followed classical and Christian tradition in taking as its object or end the beatitude and "chief end" of man. In his *Institution Morale*, Alessandro Piccolomini argued that the study of man's "ultimo fine" and "somma felicità" pertained to moral philosophy: ". . . this civil faculty, which is also called Moral Philosophy, is the most principal science and is set above all other human sciences. . . . Hence it belongs to this civil and moral faculty to consider and treat the ultimate end and highest felicity of man."[7] According to Melanchthon's *Moralis Philosophiae Epitome*, ethics concerns the end of man—i.e. obedience to God:

Moral philosophy is entirely concerned with inquiry into the end [of man]. For this reason it is a "liberal" study, for it is base for a man not to know the end—that is, the use—of human nature. In any matter the knowledge of the end has the greatest force, because it shows the use of the thing.

Wherefore, just as by judgment of divine law, man's end is to obey God and illustrate his glory (for men were created so that God might be manifested through them), so both right reason and philosophy should establish that man's end is to obey God.[8]

In Hall's opinion, the "chief end" of ethics is felicity, and this consists "in approving ourselves to God": "The end whereof [i.e. of Ethics] is, to *see* and attain *that chief goodness of the children of men which they enjoy under the sun the whole number of the days of their life*."[9]

Curcellaeus' *Synopsis Ethices* defined ethics as "scientia morum, quibus hominem ad beatitudinem contendere oportet." Subdividing the field of ethics into two parts (ἀρετολογία and εὐδαιμονολογία), the author conceived beatitude as the end and goal of all human activities and regarded the moral virtues largely as means for achieving beatitude: "The subject treated in this science comprises morals [*mores*] and man's beatitude. Beatitude, inasmuch as it is the end and goal of all human actions. Morals, inasmuch as these are means whereby one achieves beatitude or avoids misfortune." Vices, on the other hand, were impediments to attaining felicity: "Since virtues and vices are

6. St. Augustine, *The City of God*, trans. John Healey, ed. R. V. G. Tasker (London, 1950), I, 232–33; cf. II, 231–33.

7. *Della Institution Morale di Alessandro Piccolomini Libri XXI* (Venice, 1594), p. 38.

8. Philip Melanchthon, *Moralis Philosophiae Epitome* (Lugduni, 1541), pp. 15–16.

9. Right Reverend Joseph Hall, *Works*, ed. Philip Wynter (Oxford, 1863), VIII, 223; cf. Ecclesiastes ii. 3.

comprehended under the general name of *mores*, ethics is concerned with the former *per se* (insofar as they are the right way leading to beatitude) and with the latter only *per accidens* (insofar as they are impediments to men travelling in the right way to beatitude)." For Curcellaeus, beatitude is the end and reward of virtue, man's highest good and final end: "Eudaemonologia . . . is the other part of Ethics treating of Beatitude, insofar as this is the end and reward of virtue. The term *Beatitude* signifies the ultimate end of life, or the highest and most perfect good. For these two things are equivalent, since the ultimate end and scope at which men aim in all their actions is fruition of the highest and most perfect good."[10]

According to Henry More's *Enchiridion Ethicum*, happiness is an essential part of the definition of ethics: "Ethicks are defined to be the Art of Living well and happily: Ethicks are divided into two Parts, *The Knowledge of Happiness, and the Acquisition of it.* The *Knowledge* contains the Doctrine of its Nature, and of such things as the Nature of Happiness does, in some sort, either comprehend, or else refer unto." In More's opinion, felicity pertains not to the intellect, as St. Thomas Aquinas had maintained, but to "the Boniform Faculty of the Soul"—"a Faculty of that divine Composition . . . as enables us to distinguish not only what is simply and absolutely the best, but to relish it, and to have pleasure in that alone."[11]

If the knowledge of man's felicity was essential for ethics, it was equally necessary for politics. Bodin and Milton shared Aristotle's belief that "the happiness of any individual man and the city is the same."[12] According to the former's *Six Books of the Commonwealth*:

The conditions of true felicity are one and the same for the commonwealth and the individual. The sovereign good to the commonwealth in general, and of each of its citizens in particular lies in the intellective and contemplative virtues, for so wise men have determined. It is generally agreed that the ultimate purpose, and therefore sovereign good, of the individual, consists in the constant contemplation of things human, natural, and divine. If we admit that this is the principal purpose whose fulfilment means a happy life for the individual, we must also conclude that it is the goal and condition of well-being in the commonwealth too.[13]

10. *Stephani Curcellaei Opera Theologica* (Amsterdam, 1675), pp. 982–83, 1016; cf. *ibid.*, p. 982, "Subjectum informationis est homo, quatenus bonis moribus est imbuendus, atque à pravis abducendus, sicque beatus reddendus."

11. *An Account of Virtue: Or, Dr. Henry More's Abridgment of Morals, Put into English*, trans. Edward Southwell (London, 1690), pp. 1–3, 6–7. Cf. *Enchiridion Ethicum, Praecipua Moralia Philosophiae Rudimenta Complectens . . . Per Henricum Morum Cantabrigiensem* (London, 1668), pp. 1, 3, 6.

12. Aristotle, *Politics*, trans. William Ellis (London, 1952), p. 203.

13. Jean Bodin, *Six Books of the Commonwealth*, trans. M. J. Tooley (Oxford, n.d.), pp. 2–3.

Similarly, in *Of Reformation in England*, Milton maintained that "what the grounds and causes are of single happiness to one man, the same ye shall find them to a whole state, as Aristotle, both in his Ethics and Politics, from the principles of reason, lays down." Accordingly, one must ascertain "that which is good and agreeable" to the state by what is "good and agreeable to the true welfare of every Christian . . . for God forbid that we should separate and distinguish the end and good of a monarch from the end and good of the monarchy, or of that, from Christianity."[14]

Other Renaissance moralists likewise emphasized the importance of this concept for the study of politics. Defining the whole of philosophy as a method of pursuing the highest good, Francesco Piccolomini allocated to politics the consideration of the *summum bonum* as the end of man.[15]

Sir Richard Barckley similarly identified politics as the science to which the study of felicity belongs:

> Seeing therefore that felicitie is the action of vertue, which is the last and most perfect of all the workes and labours of men: it must follow, that it is a civill facultie or science, that teacheth a man to governe himselfe and others. And what science or facultie soever, is as it were the master and commander of all other sciences and faculties, and for which all other are ordained: that science is conversant about that end and worke which is most worthy and perfect of all other, and is the felicitie of man or *Summum bonum*, wee seeke for. And because policie and governement of a Commonwealth, is the commander of all other arts and sciences, for whose use they are ordained, therein must consist the felicitie of man.[16]

Like ethics and politics, theology had as its end the beatitude of man. In Arminius' opinion, "The end of Theology is the blessedness of man; and that not animal or natural, but spiritual and supernatural. It consists in fruition, the object of which is a perfect, chief, and sufficient Good, which is God." The "end of Theology is *the union of God with man*, to

14. Milton, *Prose Works*, II, 391.

15. *Universa Philosophia de Moribus a Francisco Piccolomineo Senese* (Venice, 1583), pp. 477–78: ". . . Universam Philosophiam nil aliud esse, nisi methodum assequendi summum bonum: Quod summum bonum varia & distincta ratione in variis eius partibus consideratur. Dum .n. consideratur primò, ut finis hominis in nostris actionibus collocatus, ad quam universa humanae vitae institutio dirigenda est; hac ratione ad civilem Philosophiam pertinet, qui est Architectus humanae vitae: cuius officium est omnes hominum gradus & conditiones perpendere, pertinentia ad humanas actiones componere, cunctaque in summum hominis bonum pro facultate dirigere. Sic Aristoteles in prooemio Moralium Nicom. declaravit, hoc summum bonum ad civilem scientiam pertinere; & usus est hac ratione: Id, quod est optimum, & finis postremus; ad eam scientiam pertinet, quae est princeps & domina." The author also assigns the study of the *summum bonum* to physics and metaphysics.

16. Sir Richard Barckley, *The Felicitie of Man, or, His Summum Bonum* (London, 1631), pp. 290–91.

the salvation of the one and the glory of the other."[17] For Francis Junius, the primary end of theology was the glory of God; its secondary end was man's present and future good.[18] According to Wolleb's "Praecognita of Christian Divinity," God himself was "the principal and supreme end of Divinity," but its "subordinate end" was "our salvation, which consisteth in the union and fruition of God." As "the cheif [*sic*] end, and the cheif good, are one and the same thing, it is manifest that Christian Divinity only doth rightly teach us concerning the cheif good."[19] Barckley likewise regarded man's beatitude as the end of true religion:

So that religion, which is a reconciliation to God, is the way that leadeth us to our felicity and *Summum bonum*, or soveraigne good. . . . That therefore is the onely true religion, that leadeth us directly to that passage, by whose conduction we find out the right way over it: which onely leadeth us to the end of religion, that is, mans salvation. . . .

Unlike the majority of moralists, Barckley drew a sharp distinction between *felicity* and *beatitude*, referring the former to this life and the latter to the life to come:

. . . because there is a great difference not onely in continuance, but also in greatnesse betweene the happinesse of this life, and the life to come: wee will distinguish betweene the words, and call the happinesse of this life, Felicitie, and that of the heavenly life, Beatitude, or blessednesse, and *Summum Bonum*, or Soveraigne good.[20]

Ursinus' *Summe of Christian Religion* defined the end of man in terms of his beatitude. Though the "last and principall end of man's creation" was "the glory and praise of God," its secondary end was "*the felicitie and blessedness of man*, which is the fruition and everlasting participation of God, and heavenly blessings."[21] Another theologian, Amandus Polanus, insisted on an essential distinction between beatitude (i.e. enjoyment of the highest good) and the highest good itself (i.e. God).[22]

17. James Arminius, *Works*, trans. James Nichols (London, 1828), I, 299–300 ("The Author and End of Theology"); II, 320 ("On Blessedness, the End of Theology").

18. *Francisci Junii de Theologia Vera* (In Officina Sanctandreana, 1604), Chap. 16.

19. John Wollebius, *The Abridgment of Christian Divinitie*, trans. Alexander Ross (3rd ed.; London, 1660), p. 13.

20. Barckley, pp. 682–84, 370–71.

21. Zacharias Ursinus, *The Summe of Christian Religion*, trans. D. Henry Parry (London, 1663), pp. 40–41, 48.

22. *Syntagma Theologiae Christianae ab Amando Polano a Polansdorf* (Geneva, 1612), cols. 4, 21: "Philosophis Summum Bonum & Beatitudo sunt unum & idem: sed Theologia haec duo distinguit. Nam secundum eam SUMMUM BONUM creaturarum rationalium: ac proinde & hominis, est Deus ipse solus, tanquam primum principium & finis ultimus omnis boni. . . . Quicquid nos verè beatos reddit, id est, summum nostrum bonum. Summum enim bonum est causa verae beatitudinis nostrae, & nos ab omni malo, & ab omni miseria liberos facit. Beatitudo creaturarum rationalium, est fruitio Summi Boni, nimirum Dei: seu quod eodem reddit, est communio creaturarum rationalium cum Deo . . ., qui solus est verè Summum Bonum illarum, quod illas aeternùm beatas efficit. Nominatur salus Dei Psal. 50.23."

II

Thus, despite some variation in terminology, Renaissance moralists and theologians recognized beatitude as the end of ethics, politics, and divinity. A corollary of this doctrine was that, like the human and divine "sciences" it served, poetry should have beatitude as its end. This logical inference from the didactic function of poetry and its relation to the final causes of the moral, civil, and theological sciences found theoretical expression in the *Lezzioni* of Benedetto Varchi. The purpose of poetry, he declared, was "removing the vices of men and inciting them to virtue, in order that they may attain their true happiness and beatitude."[23]

For the dedicated poet, the end of "delightfull teaching" involved considerably more than "fayning notable images of vertues [and] vices."[24] In depicting these aids or obstacles to felicity, he ought to emphasize their relation to beatitude—moral, political, or theological. This was precisely what Dante had achieved in the *Divina Commedia*, delineating the civil felicity of the active life in the Earthly Paradise of the *Purgatorio* and representing the ultimate beatitude of the contemplative in the *visio Dei* which concludes the *Paradiso*. "The *branch of philosophy* which regulates the work in its whole and its parts," according to his letter to Can Grande della Scala, "is morals or ethics," and "the end of the whole and of the part is to remove those living in this life from the state of misery and lead them to the state of felicity."[25] In varying degrees a similar orientation towards the idea of felicity can be found in Renaissance epic. Tasso, Gratiani, Spenser, and Milton employ different aesthetic methods to delineate it, but the concept of beatitude is of fundamental importance in the works of all four poets.[26]

1. In the *Gerusalemme Liberata*, as in *Il Conquisto di Granata*, the idea of felicity is conveyed through the allegory rather than by the letter. On the literal level, both epics describe the conquest of a besieged city from its infidel garrison. On the allegorical level, however, this action represents the achievement of political happiness; both Jerusalem and Granada are identified with "la felicità Civile." In both poems the factors which help or hinder the Christian forces in their conquest

23. Spingarn, 35; Benedetto Varchi, *Lezzioni lette nell' Accademia Fiorentina* (Florence, 1590), p. 578.

24. G. Gregory Smith (ed.), *Elizabethan Critical Essays* (London, 1950), I, 160.

25. *The Latin Works of Dante* (London, 1940), p. 351; cf. Lodovico Dolce, *La Divina Commedia di Dante* (Venice, 1794), pp. 8, 393, 410, 463, 523, 571; *The Convivio of Dante Alighieri*, trans. Philip H. Wicksteed (London, 1940), pp. 79, 316, 337–40; Étienne Gilson, *Dante et la Philosophie* (Paris, 1939), pp. 130–200.

26. For the Renaissance, felicity is the proper end or reward of heroic virtue. Cf. the "Allegoria" in Girolamo Garopoli, *L'Aurena, poema heroico* (Bologna, 1640), "Quella Giostra poi, che segue tra gli Dei e gli Heroi, denota la comune allegrezza, che fan tutte le creature doppo che l'huomo con le virtù Heroiche al sublime grado della felicità se ne ascende."

symbolize the external and internal aids or impediments the public man encounters in his pursuit of civil felicity.

According to Tasso's "Allegory of the Poem," the Christian army, "signifieth Man, compounded of soul and body, and of a soul . . . divided into many and diverse powers. Jerusalem the strong city placed in a rough and hilly country, whereunto as to the *last end* are directed all the enterprises of the faithful army, doth here signify the *civil happiness* which may come to a Christian Man . . . which is a good very difficult to attain unto, and situated upon the top of the alpine and wearisome hill of Virtue; and unto this are turned, *as unto the last mark, all the actions of the Public Man.*" The infidel armies and the internal dissensions within the Crusaders' camp symbolize, in turn, "the impediments which a man finds as well within as without himself" in his pursuit of happiness:

> And because that, through the imperfections of human nature and by the deceits of his enemy, *Man attains not this felicity without many inward difficulties, and without finding by the way many outward impediments*, all these are noted unto us by poetical figures. As the death of Sirenus and his companions, not being joined to the camp but slain far off, may here show the losses which a civil man hath of his friends, followers, and other external goods, *instruments of virtue and aids to the attaining of true felicity*. The armies of Africa, Asia, and unlucky battles, are none other than his enemies, his losses, and the accidents of contrary fortune. But coming to the inward impediments, love, which maketh Tancredi and the other worthies to dote, and disjoins them from Godfrey, and the disdain which enticeth Rinaldo from the enterprise, do signify the conflict and rebellion which the concupiscent and ireful powers do make with the reasonable. The devils which do consult to hinder the conquest of Jerusalem are both a figure and a thing figured, and do here represent *the very same evils which do oppose themselves against our civil happiness, so that it may not be to us a ladder of Christian blessedness.*

Further obstacles to felicity are the "two devilish temptations" symbolized by the "two magicians, Ismen and Armida"—"the Errors of Opinion" and "those of the Appetite."

The "outward and inward helps, with which the civil man, overcoming all difficulty, is brought to this desired happiness" are likewise represented "by poetical figures." The diamond shield signifies "the special safeguard of the Lord God." The angels represent "heavenly help" or "inspiration." The hermit symbolizes "supernatural knowledge received by God's grace," while the wise man stands for "human wisdom." Through these aids natural justice is restored, and "civil happiness" (symbolized by Jerusalem) can be achieved. The "Ireful Virtue" (Rinaldo), once more subject to the "Understanding" (Godfrey), is now "armed with reason against concupiscence" and can "resist and drive away whatsoever impediment to felicity. . . . The Army wherein Rinaldo and the other worthies by the grace of God and advice of Man, are returned and obedient to their Chieftain, signifieth Man brought again into the state of natural justice and heavenly obedience: where the superior powers do command, as they ought, and the inferior do obey, as they should. Then the wood is easily discomfited; that is, *all external impediments being easily overcome, man attaineth the politic happiness.*"

Nevertheless, "politic happiness" is only an earthly and temporal objective. As a Christian poet, Tasso, like Dante, must point beyond it to a higher and ultimate end—to the "contemplation of eternal blessedness":

But for that this politic blessedness ought not to be the last mark of a Christian man, but he ought to look more high, that is, to everlasting felicity; for this cause Godfrey does not desire to win the earthly Jerusalem, to have therein only temporal dominion, but because herein may be celebrated the worship of God, and that the holy sepulchre may be the more freely visited by godly strangers and devout pilgrims. And the poem is closed with the prayers of Godfrey, whereby it is showed that the Understanding being travailed and wearied in civil actions, *ought in the end to rest in devotion, and in the contemplation of the eternal blessedness of the other most happy and immortal life.*[27]

2. Gratiani's epic argument is likewise allegorized as the acquisition of civil felicity ("Stimo, che la Conquista di Granata possa prendersi per l'acquisto della felicità civile"), but the "Allegoria del Poema" does not discuss this concept in detail. As in the *Gerusalemme Liberata*, various internal and external factors aid or hinder the achievement of beatitude. The Spanish monarchs Ferdinand and Isabella signify the union of prudence and piety. The Christian knights Hernando and Consalvo represent "le due parti della fortezza"—*Magna facere, & magna pati*. The pagan magician Alchindo symbolizes "la conversatione civile," and his two daughters, Aretia and Belsirena, represent virtue and vice. Granada is defended by the council of the Saracen king Baudele, by the force of his warriors Almansorre and Orgonte, and by the enchantments of Alchindo: "and in this the poet seems to teach that the pursuit of felicity is hindered by various impediments—an evil and badly chosen rule of life, a fierce and stolid ferocity, and the strange and unforeseen changes of variable and inconstant fortune."

The councilor Almireno, who advises Baudele to surrender his kingdom, represents "our native conscience, which (with the light communicated to it by the Author of Nature to pursue an honorable end and shun the more pernicious evils) impels us to works difficult,

27. Torquato Tasso, *Jerusalem Delivered*, trans. Edward Fairfax, ed. Henry Morley (London, 1890), pp. 436–43; cf. Tasso, *Il Goffredo* (Padua, 1742), x–xxiii. Italics mine.

painful, and irksome on behalf of another." Finally, the fact that Baudele is not slain, but is converted shows that "a passionate rule of life is not to be cut off, but amended, for united to piety it renders the mind capable of true felicity, even though the latter is natural [rather than supernatural]."[28]

3. Besides these allegorical representations of civil felicity, both epics introduce visions of eternal blessedness. In a dream of heaven reminiscent of the *Somnium Scipionis* the soul of the dead Crusader Hugo contrasts the insignificant "reward of goodness" on earth—"servile empire" and "dumb fame"—with "heaven's bliss" and promises Godfrey that after death he too shall reign here "Amid the saints in bliss."[29] In Gratiani's epic, Queen Isabella is similarly vouchsafed an "alta vision" of the glories of heaven. In a passage strongly influenced by the *Divina Commedia*, she beholds the spheres, the angels, the throne of God, and the Beatific Vision. Her gaze is directed "to the First Good," and she enjoys "for a moment the excess of every good and every content."[30]

Though Spenser does not mention the concept of beatitude in his letter to Raleigh (the end his principal hero pursues is "glory"), he does emphasize the idea of celestial blessedness[31] at an important point in the First Book of *The Faerie Queene*. After his release from Orgoglio's dungeon, Redcrosse is brought to the "house of Holinesse," to learn repentance and the three theological virtues. Here, like Tasso's hero and Gratiani's heroine, he is granted a vision of eternal beatitude. Through the aid of the sage "heavenly *Contemplation*," whose meditations are directed towards the *summum bonum* ("God and goodnesse"), he is taught "the way to heavenly blesse [sic]." Hailing him as "Thrise happy man," the hermit promises to show him "the way . . . That never leads the traveiler astray, But after labours long, and sad delay, Brings them to ioyous rest and endlesse blis." Redcrosse is shown the heavenly Jerusalem, "Wherein eternall peace and happinesse doth dwell," and is promised "a blessed end" and the glory of the saints. Through this vision of eternal beatitude he perceives how far the glory of the Celestial City surpasses that of Cleopolis, the seat of the Fairy Queen, and by comparison he learns how "fruitlesse" are the joys of

28. *Il Conquisto di Granata, Poema Heroico del Co. Girolamo Gratiani* (Bologna, 1660), "Allegoria del Poema."

29. Tasso, *Jerusalem Delivered*, pp. 290–93.

30. Gratiani, pp. 390–407.

31. Though glory is not identical with beatitude, the two concepts coincide in the case of the heavenly glory of the saints. According to Milton (*Prose Works*, IV, 491), the "perfect glorification of the righteous . . consists in eternal life and perfect happiness, arising chiefly from the divine vision." St. Thomas Aquinas had identified "the goal of blessedness" as "heavenly glory"; Thomas Aquinas, *Selected Writings*, ed. Father M. C. D'Arcy (London, 1950), p. 11.

the world. A similar contrast between temporal vanity and eternal blessedness recurs at the end of the Mutability fragment.

4. In all three of these epics, the concept of felicity is largely extrinsic to the epic action. It is important less for its rôle in the development of the fable than for its contribution to the total meaning of the poem. The arguments of the *Gerusalemme Liberata* and *Il Conquisto di Granata* are quite intelligible on the literal level, without the allegorical identification between the besieged cities and "la felicità Civile." If the dreams of Godfrey and Isabella further the epic enterprise, this effect is due primarily not to their glimpse of eternal beatitude but to other aspects of their visions. The chief purpose of Godfrey's dream is to reconcile him with Rinaldo, whose assistance is indispensable for the conquest of Jerusalem; "Only from exile young Rinaldo call," Hugo advises him. Isabella's vision occurs at a crucial moment when infernal spells have disheartened the Christian forces; in the "Divina Idea" she beholds the future glories of the House of Este, and in answer to her prayers her army regains its hope and discipline. In Spenser's allegory of Holiness, it is logical that instruction in the three theological virtues should culminate in contemplation of the eternal felicity to which they traditionally lead.[32] Nevertheless, despite the fact that this experience strengthens and encourages Redcrosse for his ensuing combat with the "old Dragon," it does not directly affect the development of the fable.

III

In Tasso, Gratiani, and Spenser, the idea of felicity had been largely extrinsic to the epic argument; in Milton's epics it is intrinsic. Selecting as his subjects the loss and recovery of beatitude—the "happy State" lost and regained—he gives prominence *on the literal level* to a concept his predecessors had treated allegorically. In *Paradise Lost* and *Paradise Regain'd*, the happiness of man is central not only to the meaning, but also to the argument and structure. Through this orientation of the epic towards the concept of felicity, he observes the conventional orientation of Renaissance ethics, politics, and theology towards beatitude as the end and chief good of man. Happiness is the common end of church, state, and the Christian individual, and the poet serves all three

32. Cf. Dante's *De Monarchia* (*Latin Works*, 277), "providence . . . has set two ends before man . . .; the blessedness . . . of this life, . . . figured by the terrestrial paradise, and the blessedness of eternal life, . . . understood by the celestial paradise. Now to these two as to diverse ends it behoves him to come by diverse means. For to the first we attain by the teachings of philosophy, following them by acting in accordance with the moral and intellectual virtues. To the second by spiritual teachings which transcend human reason, as we follow them by acting according to the theological virtues; faith, hope . . . and charity." Cf. Gilson, pp. 196–99; Curcellaeus, p. 983.

by demonstrating poetically the true "grounds and causes" of blessedness—obedience to God.

In *Paradise Lost* (Dryden observed) the "design is the losing of our happiness." From the first reference to the "loss of *Eden*" through disobedience, to the final scene where the exiles look back on "Paradise, so late thir happy seat" and behold the gate barred by "dreadful Faces . . . and fiery Arms," the poem is concerned with the nature, conditions, and loss of original happiness. After depicting the *external* delights of "blissful Paradise," a "happy rural seat of various view," Book IV passes to the "happier *Eden*" of holy wedlock, to the *moral* grounds of man's "happiest life, Simplicity and spotless innocence," and to the *conditions* of their "happy state"—obedience to the injunction "not to taste that only Tree of knowledge." Nevertheless, in describing man's original felicity, Milton does not neglect the demands of his fable, and ironically our (and Satan's) first glimpse of this beatitude contains the seeds of its destruction. "*Satan's* first sight of *Adam* and *Eve*" (Milton informs us) makes him "wonder at thir excellent form and happy state," but it also strengthens his "resolution to work thir fall." He perceives their felicity only to experience "grief" at their advancement "into our room of bliss." He learns its moral conditions only to make these a "foundation" for "thir ruin." The representation of original happiness is thus overshadowed by the threat of imminent woe.

The nature and conditions of beatitude are developed further in the following books. In Book V, the Father sends Raphael to advise Adam "of his happy state, Happiness in his power left free to will," and of the enemy who is "plotting now The fall of others from like state of bliss." Adam is encouraged to "enjoy . . . what happiness this happy state Can comprehend, incapable of more," but he is also warned that his felicity is contingent upon his obedience:

> . . . *That thou art happy, owe to God;*
> *That thou continu'st such, owe to thyself,*
> *That is, to thy obedience. . . .*

The angelic hymn which concludes the account of Creation in Book VII ends with an encomium of man's original happiness:

> *Thrice happy men,*
> *And sons of men . . . : thrice happy if they know*
> *Thir happiness, and persevere upright.*

Adam "knows his happiness," even though he does not "persevere"; and Book VIII is concerned in large part with this knowledge. From God himself he learns that "this happy State" is contingent on obedience, and the same divine colloquy also emphasizes the difference between the "happiness" of God and that of man (VIII, 365, 399, 405 ff.). Raphael's parting admonitions further stress the interdependence of obedience, love, and happiness. After declaring that there is "without Love no happiness," the angel bids Adam "live happy, and love, but first of all Him whom to love is to obey, and keep His great command."

Though the angels enjoy a higher state of bliss than man, its moral grounds are the same, as Raphael explains:

> *Myself and all th' Angelic Host that stand*
> *In sight of God enthron'd, our happy state*
> *Hold, as you yours, while our obedience holds;*
> *On other surely none . . .:*
> *And some are fall'n, to disobedience fall'n, . . .*
> *From what high state of bliss into what woe!*

In both cases the loss of happiness results from disobedience; in both cases, moreover, the act of disobedience itself results from discontent with the happiness appointed by God—a happiness appropriate to the nature and state of the creature—and a pursuit of felicity through forbidden means. Satan transgresses through rejecting the beatitude proposed to the angels in Messiah's reign:

> *Under his great Vice-gerent Reign abide*
> *United as one individual Soul*
> *For ever happy: him who disobeys*
> *Mee disobeys, breaks union, and that day*
> *Cast out from God and blessed vision, falls*
> *Into utter darkness. . . .*

The intent of this decree, as Abdiel explains, is not "to make us less," but "rather to exalt Our happy state under one Head more near United." In rejecting this beatitude, Satan is justly punished with the loss of blessedness. Eve also sins through a misconception of the beatitude appropriate to her nature. In her dream the tempter represents the forbidden fruit as a means to greater happiness:

> *Here, happy Creature, fair Angelic* Eve,
> *Partake thou also; happy though thou art,*
> *Happier thou may'st be, worthier canst not be:*
> *Taste this, and be henceforth among the Gods. . . .*

In Book IX, he employs a similar argument; in partaking of the fruit Eve should merit praise for "achieving what might lead To happier life, knowledge of Good and Evil."

After the fall, the idea of beatitude acquires additional emphasis both through Adam's recognition of his lost happiness and through Michael's revelation of his future restoration. Conscious of "growing miseries" without and worse sorrows within, Adam laments that, "miserable of happy" and "accurst of blessed," he must "hide me from the face of God, whom to behold was then my highth Of happiness." Michael's "tidings bring Departure from this happy place, our . . . only consolation left." But, paradoxically, Michael brings a greater consolation than the garden they must leave—the promise of "a paradise within thee, happier far." At Christ's Second Coming, "the Earth Shall all be Paradise, far happier place Than this of *Eden*, and far happier days." Adam and Eve are to pass their remaining days, "cheer'd With meditation on the happy end."

As Satan and his companions have lost their original beatitude and have received no promise of restoration to a felicity "far happier" than that they have forfeited, they must seek a substitute for the *summum bonum* denied to them.[33] Having lost their true end and final cause, they must look for an alternative. Aware of "lost happiness and lasting pain," they attempt to mitigate the pain of this awareness by rationalizing their predicament. Thus Satan argues, paradoxically, that the "loss" of "the happier state In Heav'n" is a political asset, securing "a safe unenvied Throne Yielded with full consent." Their alienation from "good" is, therefore, an "advantage . . . To union":

> *. . . where there is then no good*
> *For which to strive, no strife can grow up there*
> *From Faction. . . .*

Moloch draws a different inference from their lost felicity; having forfeited their original bliss, they can still seek the happiness of annihilation:

> *. . . what can be worse*
> *Then to dwell here, driv'n out from bliss, condemn'd*
> *In this abhorred deep to utter woe* [?]
> [*God may*] *reduce*
> *To nothing this essential, happier far*
> *Than miserable to have eternal being. . . .*

Belial argues that in time even Hell can yield a sort of happiness:

> *This horror will grow mild, this darkness light,*
> *. . . our present lot appears*
> *For happy though but ill, for ill not worst. . . .*

Mammon urges his companions to "seek Our own good from ourselves, and from our own Live to ourselves," to create "Useful of

33. For a fuller discussion of the dilemma of the fallen angels, see C. S. Lewis, *A Preface to Paradise Lost* (London, 1949), pp. 92–104.

hurtful, prosperous of adverse." Others "charm" their pain with arguments "Of happiness and final misery." There is, however, no real substitute for the supreme good they have lost, and the empire they establish is a political order established on a logical absurdity; founded on evil and perpetual misery, it cannot achieve the true political ends of a state—happiness and the common good.[34] Realizing that "all Good to me is lost," Satan dedicates himself to the only end left to him—its logical contrary, the pursuit of evil:

> *Evil be thou my Good; by thee at least*
> *Divided Empire with Heaven's King I hold. . . .*

IV

Like its predecessor, *Paradise Regain'd*[35] is based on the idea of beatitude, but its argument is diametrically opposite. The theme of "Recover'd Paradise . . . By one man's firm obedience" complements that of "the happy Garden . . . By one man's disobedience lost." By "vanquishing temptation" Christ founds a "fairer Paradise" than the "seat of earthly bliss" Adam had forfeited. The contrasting themes of the two epics reflect a theological commonplace ultimately derived from the Adam-Christ parallel[36] of Romans v. 19—that in Christ mankind recovered the happiness and chief good lost through Adam. According to Sir Richard Barckley's *Discourse of the Felicitie of Man, or His Summum Bonum*, "the onely meanes we have to attaine to blessednesse or *Summum Bonum* againe, which we lost by the fall of our first parents, is by the merits and mercie of Christ, to returne to *God* againe: and seeing that God is the greatest and chiefest good of all things, from whom all things have their being and goodnesse, in him is to be sought that *Summum Bonum* and blessednesse or Beatitude we looke for, and no otherwhere":

> . . . as man is the end of the world, so God is the end of man. . . . But . . . man . . . fell out of his favour . . . ; because he would not continue and rest in his felicitie, wherein God had first placed him; that is, in the contemplation of his

34. Cf. Aristotle, *Politics*, pp. 81–83, 201–8.

35. For the ethical pattern and background of *Paradise Regain'd*, see, besides previous references, Howard Schultz, *Milton and Forbidden Knowledge* (New York, 1955), and the introduction and notes in Merritt Y. Hughes's edition of this poem (New York, 1937).

36. M. Y. Hughes (ed.), *Paradise Regained*, p. 445n.; C. A. Patrides, "Milton and the Protestant Theory of the Atonement," *PMLA*, LXXIV (1959), 7–13. In *Milton and the Christian Tradition* (Oxford, 1966) Dr. Patrides examines "Milton's conception and presentation of the principal themes of the Christian faith" against the background of "historical and traditional Christianity" and "the specifically Protestant manifestation of the cumulative Christian tradition as reflected in the current of thought contemporary with Milton." "Milton's peculiar power," he suggests, consisted in his ability to use "traditional ideas in such a way that they were transformed into seeming novelties."

Creator: but would needs seeke his felicity some othere where. . . . The only meanes we have to be restored to our felicity and soveraigne good, is to returne to God againe (from whom by the disobedience of our first parent we are fallen) by way of true Religion, which teacheth us our duty towards God, and assureth us of his favour by the mediation and merits of his only Sonne Christ Jesus. . . .[37]

Similarly, for Viret, man's *summum bonum* and sole means of felicity is the knowledge of God in Christ.[38]

Like the *Gerusalemme Liberata, Paradise Regain'd* centers upon the causal relation between obedience and happiness—but with two significant differences. First, whereas Tasso's method is allegorical, Milton's is essentially literal and historical. Secondly, whereas Tasso is concerned largely with "politic blessedness" and introduces "everlasting felicity" almost as an afterthought, the beatitude Milton portrays is "eternal blessedness." Thus, whereas Tasso's epic ends with Godfrey's conquest of Jerusalem, Milton's poem concludes with the foundation of a "fairer Paradise" for the elect—an achievement which receives poetic expression in the hero's banquet on "Fruits fetcht from the tree of life, And from the fount of life Ambrosial drink."[39] As in *Paradise Lost*, beatitude is inseparable from obedience ("thy will . . . to fulfil is all my bliss," "Whom to obey is happiness entire").

Nevertheless, the ordeal of *Paradise Regain'd* is intellectual as well as moral. Christ is "to vanquish by wisdom hellish wiles," and, in Professor Stein's opinion, the "key" to the poem is "heroic knowledge."[40] If the hero regains beatitude for mankind through his obedience, he also demonstrates his knowledge of man's true beatitude by rejecting false or inferior goods. Unlike the multitude who "resist and oppose their own true happiness," he is not misled by spurious, secular conceptions of felicity. Instead, he possesses that "only high valuable wisdom" which Milton had defined earlier as the knowledge "of God, and of his true worship, and *what is infallibly good and happy in the state of man's life*, what is in itself evil and miserable, *though vulgarly not so esteemed*." As

37. Barckley, pp. 371, 667, 712; cf. p. 708.

38. *De Vero Verbi Dei . . . Ministerio . . . Autore Petro Vireto* (*s.l.*, 1553), 1, "De summa hominis foelicitate, & de cognitione Dei, & fide": "Hominem Deus quum ad suam effinxit imaginem, idque eum ut suae faceret divinae naturae & immortalitatis participem, & ad beatam aeternamque vitam perduceret, in qua summo illo bono perfrueretur, quo solo verè effici beatus potest; eaque vita atque summum bonum, in ipsius Dei per Christum filium cognitione posita sint, extra omnem controversiam esse debet, hanc Dei in Christo cognitionem, tum eandem esse cum fide, tum unicam, qua ad eam foelicitatem perveniatur, viam: aut certè tantum habere cognationis inter se & affinitatis, ut altera pro altera accipi posse videatur. Cuius rei nobis Christus ipse locupletissimus testis est, quum ait, Haec est vita aeterna, ut cognoscant te solum verum Deum, & quem misisti Iesum Christum. Et aliis in locis toties, Qui credit in Filium, habet vitam aeternam."

39. See Frank Kermode, "Milton's Hero," *RES*, N.S. IV (1953), 317–30.

40. Arnold Stein, *Heroic Knowledge* (Minneapolis, 1957), p. 205.

the "True Image of the Father," he displays that "likeness to God" which is the "happiest end" of the individual and the state:

. . . to govern well is to train up a nation in true wisdom and virtue, and that which springs from thence, magnanimity, (take heed of that,) and that which is our beginning, regeneration, and happiest end, likeness to God, which in one word we call godliness; and . . . this is the true flourishing of a land, other things follow as the shadow does the substance.

It is, moreover, precisely his knowledge of the supreme good—of the true end and beatitude of man—which sets him apart from fallen humanity and makes him at once the prototype and efficient cause of regenerate man. In the state of the fall, mankind not only suffers the oppression of sin, "the heaviest of all evils, as being contrary to the chief good, that is, to God," but has also lost "that right reason which enabled man to discern the chief good." Conversely, through "the new spiritual life" and "comprehension of spiritual things" which the regenerate are to receive through Christ, they are to "know all that is necessary for eternal salvation and the *true happiness of life*."[41] The wisdom that Milton's hero displays in distinguishing between eternal and temporal goods, the true and false felicity of man, mark his immunity to the domination of sin and spiritual death which have obscured the knowledge of the chief good in other men.

Christ's pursuit of the *summum bonum*—his effort to know and do "publick good" and to fulfill his "end of being on Earth, and mission high"—leads him beyond the "politic happiness" sought by Tasso's hero, to eternal felicity. If he is indeed "To earn Salvation for the Sons of men," he must inevitably reject the kingdoms of the world and aim at the highest good, reunion with God. For, as Barckley had pointed out, salvation and beatitude are inseparable: "This salvation of man is his beatitude, his beatitude is to be joyned with God. For neither the world, nor anything in it, maketh a man happy or blessed, but God onely that made man, maketh him happy."[42]

As in *Paradise Lost*, the idea of beatitude acquires further emphasis through the contrast with Satan's alienation from the true good and committal to evil and final misery. Heaven itself inflames his torment by "representing Lost bliss"; "the happy place Imparts to [him] no happiness." The "worst" (he declares) is "my Port, My harbour and my ultimate repose, The end I would attain, my final good." By contrast, the end he proposes to Christ is the *summum bonum*, or rather what appears to be the *summum bonum*. In urging his antagonist to accept the

41. Milton, *Prose Works*, II, 390–91, 473–74; IV, 265–66, 343. Italics mine.
42. Barckley, p. 684.

kingdoms of the world, he is falsely identifying the chief good with a secular object, the "politic happiness" of an earthly kingdom. The Messiah's "endless reign" (the devil argues) will be "The happier reign the sooner it begins," and it is "best" and "Happiest both to thyself and all the world, That thou who worthiest art shouldst be thir King." The fallacy in this argument is, of course, that the civil felicity Satan proposes is not the *summum bonum*; the beatitude Christ must regain is eternal blessedness, a beatitude not of this world, but of heaven. It is no worldly kingdom or "seat of earthly bliss" which is "founded now," but an eternal and "fairer Paradise" of the spirit.

Like *Paradise Lost, Paradise Regain'd* represents a conscious reorientation of the epic towards the end and final cause of ethics, politics, and theology—the *summum bonum* and true felicity of man. To a limited extent, the earlier epics of Tasso, Gratiani, and Spenser had attempted a similar reorientation through the medium of allegory. Milton, on the other hand, imitates the "happy state" through the medium of the letter; in both of his epics the idea of beatitude is the cornerstone of his argument and fable.

9. *The Christian Hercules*

Moral Dialectic and the Pattern of Rejection

❦ Milton's final epic, a recent critic has argued, is "a dramatic definition of 'heroic knowledge,' not of heroic rejection"; "to see Christ's answers, not as a positive process of self-definition, but as a retreating series of refusals, is to assume the dramatic perspective of Satan."[1] This is, however, an unnecessary antithesis. "Heroic rejection" and "heroic knowledge" are, in fact, complementary concepts rather than mutually exclusive alternatives. In *Paradise Regain'd*, rejection is grounded in knowledge, and knowledge in turn is perfected through rejection; the "process of self-definition" is accomplished by and through the "series of refusals." Christ *rejects* his Adversary's offers precisely because he *knows* their relative value in comparison with the Kingdom of Heaven. In the "dialectical drama" of the Second Temptation, rejection and knowledge are actually inseparable; and to dismiss the rejection-motif simply because it is Satan who sums it up (IV, 156, 368–71, 467, 536–7) is to ignore the fact that Christ also

First published, in somewhat different form, in the *University of Toronto Quarterly*, XXXI, No. 4 (1962), 416–30, by the University of Toronto Press.

1. Arnold Stein, *Heroic Knowledge: An Interpretation of Paradise Regained and Samson Agonistes* (Minneapolis, 1957), pp. 17, 131. See also Elizabeth Marie Pope, *Paradise Regained: The Tradition and the Poem* (Baltimore, 1947); A. S. P. Woodhouse, "Theme and Pattern in *Paradise Regained*," *UTQ*, XXV (1956), 167–82; Northrop Frye, "The Typology of *Paradise Regained*," *MP*, LIII (1956), 227–38; Burton O. Kurth, *Milton and Christian Heroism* (Berkeley and Los Angeles, 1959).

summarizes his ordeal in terms of refusal (IV, 496). If previous scholars have emphasized rejection at the expense of knowledge, Professor Stein's assumption stresses knowledge at the expense of rejection—a concept central to the Biblical accounts of the temptation and to Milton's interpretation of the Second Temptation in his discussion of magnanimity.[2]

Actually, the patterns of knowledge and rejection are complementary—dual aspects of the same philosophical and rhetorical *agon*—and to see them in their proper perspective one must examine them against their intellectual background. In this respect two traditions are of primary importance: first, the motif of heroic *judgment*, the moral crisis in which the youthful hero chooses his future way of life from two or more proposed alternatives; and, secondly, the ethical definition of the true and highest good through a method of systematic negation and the progressive elimination of false conceptions of the *summum bonum*.

I

"Reason is but choosing,"[3] and choice involves rejection as well as knowledge. In the act of moral decision, the wise man not only discriminates between better and worse; in the process of selecting the best, he also considers and eliminates lesser alternatives. His virtues appear not only in what he elects, but also in what he refuses.

Paradise Regain'd is not simply a "drama of knowledge"[4] any more than it is simply an epic of rejection. It is both and more; it is an ordeal of initial (and, in a sense, final) choice—a crisis of judgment. In this respect it resembles not only the moral ordeal of the first Adam, but also two familiar temptations of classical tradition—the judgment of Paris[5] and the choice of Hercules.

The parallel between Christ's ordeal and Hercules' derives part of its argumentative force from the fact that the latter had long been regarded as an antitype of the former. For Budé, Christ was the "heavenly Hercules" and the Christian analogue of the classical hero ("Hercules

2. See Merritt Y. Hughes, "The Christ of *Paradise Regained* and the Renaissance Heroic Tradition," *SP*, XXXV (1938), 254–77; Stein, pp. 29–33; *The Prose Works of John Milton* (Bohn Standard Library; London, 1884), V, 95.

3. *Prose Works*, II, 74; cf. 67–68.

4. Stein, p. 5.

5. Like Paris, Milton's Christ is a young man meditating in solitude on the ends and means of the *triplex vita*. For the traditional interpretation of the Judgment of Paris in terms of the active, contemplative, and voluptuous lives, see Edgar Wind, *Pagan Mysteries in the Renaissance* (London, 1958), 78–79; Sears Jayne, "The Subject of Milton's Ludlow *Mask*," *PMLA*, LXXIV (1959), 535. See Howard Schultz, *Milton and Forbidden Knowledge* (New York, 1955), pp. 73, 225–26, for the "ethical ladder" in which Satan arranges his "lures" and their organization in terms of the *vita voluptaria*, the *vita activa*, and the *vita contemplativa*.

ille noster"). For Goropius Becanus, the name *Hercul* signified "him through whom all things were created, . . . the Son of God made man." Christ, "the true Hercules," has "purged us of Cacus' venom and led us with himself to the ambrosial feast prepared for his victory." Nicolas Vuinmannus allegorized the myth in terms of the Christian soldier's warfare with the flesh. A woodcut on the title-page shows Hercules as "Christianus miles" victorious over Antaeus ("the type of the world, the flesh, and the devil") and receiving a garland from the Muse, "who rewards virtue and victorious fortitude." Latin verses by Vuolfgangus Vuinthauserus observe that the myth denotes the ways to heaven and hell—the way of divine life and that of the flesh:

> *Divinae Alcides signat vestigia vitae,*
> *Antaeus ditis monstrat advie domum.*
> *Haec tibi perpetuae fuerint certamina pugnae,*
> *Ni victo carnis tramite victor eris.*[6]

Like Prodicus' Hercules, the Christian Alcides stands at moral crossroads. At the beginning of their public careers, both heroes must choose their future course of action from alternative ways of life and contrasting ends and means. In both cases, these reflections occur in the wilderness. In both cases the moral decision is preliminary to the hero's public life, but it is also final, for he is selecting the path which he will subsequently follow to the end.

After his baptism, "the Son of God" is found "Musing and much revolving in his breast" how to achieve his mission of salvation,

> *How best the mighty work he might begin*
> *Of Saviour to mankind, and which way first*
> *Publish his God-like office now mature. . . .*

In order to "converse" the better "with solitude," he withdraws to "the bordering Desert wild" and pursues his "holy Meditations" there. In Prodicus' story, the son of Jove retires to the wilderness for similar reflections: "For he says that Hercules, when he was advancing from among children to puberty (in which the young, already becoming their own masters, show whether they will turn to living by the path through virtue or the path through vice), having come out into a solitary place, sat down, perplexed as to which of the paths he should take to."

6. See *G. Budaei . . . De Transitu Hellenismi ad Christianismum* (Paris, 1535), pp. 35, 55, 112; *Opera Ioan. Goropii Becani* (Antwerpiae, 1580), pp. 22, 119, 171. For the Renaissance interpretation of the Hercules-Antaeus myth as the victory of "reason" over "earthly appetites," see Merritt Y. Hughes (ed.), *Paradise Regained* (New York, 1937), pp. 408–9, 531–32n. Cf. *Hercules cum Antaeo Pugnae allegorica ac pia interpretatio, Christiano militi non minus utilis quam iucunda lectu, autore Nicolao Vuinmanno* (Norimbergae, 1537); Vuinmannus allegorizes the Hercules myth in terms of the Christian soldier's warfare with the flesh.

Like Hercules, Christ must distinguish between true and false felicity. He must choose between the difficult path which leads to true happiness and the easy way which leads to ultimate misery. Satan warns him of "many a hard assay/Of dangers, and adversities and pains,/Ere thou of *Israel's* Scepter get fast hold." The devil's "offer'd aid," on the other hand, "would have set thee in short time with ease/ On *David's* Throne; or Throne of all the world. . . ." In Prodicus' narrative, Vice employs similar arguments:

> "I see you, Hercules, hesitating by what road you should enter upon life. If then you make me your friend, I shall lead you by the most pleasant and most easy way. . . . Do you perceive, Hercules, how difficult and long a road this woman [Virtue] points out to you to enjoyments? But I will lead you an easy and short way to happiness."

Virtue, on the other hand, refuses to "deceive . . . with prefaces of pleasure" and instead relates "with truth realities as the gods have appointed them." As the gods "give none of the good and honourable things that exist to men without labour and care," Hercules must first "accustom the body to obey the mind, and must exercise it with labours and sweat." In contrast to the false happiness offered by Vice ("My friends call me Happiness, but those who hate me . . . call me Vice"), the labours proposed by Virtue will lead to "the most blessed happiness."[7]

If there is a basic similarity between Christ's moral situation in the Second Temptation and that of Hercules, there are also some significant differences. In the first place, Milton's literary method is essentially literal rather than mythical and allegorical. Instead of personifying Virtue and Vice as beautiful women, he presents these concepts largely through the medium of argument. The role of Virtue, with her insights into the true "realities as the gods have appointed them," is assigned to Christ; Satan, in turn, performs the deceptive role of Prodicus' Vice. Christ plays, in fact, two roles—that of Hercules and that of Virtue; like the former he must meditate and choose between alternative paths, but like the latter he illuminates and instructs.

Second, Milton's conception of vice is broader than Prodicus' view. Though Satan employs Vice's appeal to sensuous pleasure—"savoury dishes" and "costly wines"—in the banquet-scene, he also exploits some of the arguments of Prodicus' Virtue in later appeals—"to be honoured," "to enrich yourself," "to advance yourself by means of

7. E. L. Hawkins (ed.), *A Literal Translation of Xenophon's Memorabilia of Socrates, Book II* (2nd ed.; Oxford and London, 1902), pp. 13–17; cf. *Paradise Regained*, ed. M. Y. Hughes, p. 477n., for a further parallel with Prodicus' narrative. For a survey of the tradition of Hercules' Choice, see Erwin Panofsky, *Hercules am Scheidewege und andere antike Bildstoffe in der neueren Kunst*, Studien der Bibliothek Warburg, XVIII (Leipzig and Berlin, 1930); and *idem*, *Studies in Iconology: Humanistic Themes in the Art of the Renaissance* (New York, 1939).

war," "to liberate your friends and to subdue your enemies" by "the arts of war."[8] In Milton's epic these are no longer objects to be attained by the "difficult and long . . . road"; instead they are the very means which (Satan argues) would enable the hero to achieve his kingdom "in short time with ease." This shift in emphasis and value is significant of the ethical gulf between Prodicus' secular hero and Milton's Christian archetype.

Finally, the pattern of rejection in *Paradise Regain'd* is actually far more pronounced than in the judgments of Paris and Hercules. Both of the latter accept one of the two or three alternatives proposed to them. Hercules rejects Vice and elects Virtue. Paris refuses the *vita activa* and *vita contemplativa* and chooses the *vita voluptuosa* instead. Milton's hero, however, rejects *all* that his tempter proposes.

II

In the tradition of Hercules' choice, knowledge is a precondition of rejection; through an examination of ends and means the hero is able to select the better path and reject the alternative way. But rejection can also be a precondition of knowledge, an integral part of logical demonstration and moral dialectic. From Aristotle to Sir Richard Barckley, Western moralists had utilized a method of systematic negation in achieving a definition of true felicity. By the progressive elimination of false conceptions of the *summum bonum*—wealth, pleasure, fame, and so on—they attempted to demonstrate the true nature of the highest good. In *Paradise Regain'd* Milton employs a similar method. Christ demonstrates his insight into the true happiness, end, and chief good of man by analyzing and rejecting the false or inferior goods which Satan proposes to him. Two of the most important structural features of the Second Temptation—the method of systematic rejection and the "ethical ladder" of the voluptuous, active, and contemplative lives—can be traced back as far as the *Nicomachean Ethics*. After defining the chief good, happiness, as "an activity of soul in accordance with perfect virtue," Aristotle proceeds to refute the popular conceptions of felicity as "pleasure, wealth, or honor":

> A consideration of the prominent types of life shows that people of superior refinement and of active disposition identify happiness with honour; for this is, roughly speaking, the end of the political life. But it seems too superficial to be what we are looking for, since it is thought to depend on those who bestow honour rather than on him who receives it. . . .

As for riches, "wealth is evidently not the good we are seeking; for it is merely useful and for the sake of something else." Of the three "prominent types of life," the *vita voluptuosa* or "life of enjoyment," the

8. Hawkins, pp. 14–15.

"political" or active life, and the "contemplative life," Aristotle prefers the third as offering the highest happiness, "the activity of philosophic wisdom." The life of pleasure he dismisses as merely servile and bestial: "Now the mass of mankind are evidently quite slavish in their tastes, preferring a life suitable to beasts, but they get some ground for their view from the fact that many of those in high places share the tastes of Sardanapalus."[9]

Aristotle's method left its mark on both medieval and Renaissance ethical procedure. Eustratius' commentary on the *Nicomachean Ethics* devotes a chapter to refuting false opinions of felicity.[10] In the *Summa contra Gentiles*, St. Thomas Aquinas argues that man's "ultimus finis. . . ., *felicitas* sive *beatitudo*" is "cognoscere Deum," and explicitly rejects alternative conceptions of human happiness—carnal delights; honors; glory; riches; secular power; bodily goods; acts of moral virtue, such as deeds of fortitude; prudence; and art.[11]

Beroaldus' *De Felicitate* employs a similar method—examining and refuting false opinions of beatitude, such as pleasure, glory, power, riches, and virtue.[12] Suessanus likewise follows Aristotle in denying that pleasure, riches, honor, or virtue constitute the highest good.[13]

Francesco Piccolomini calls attention to the variety of opinions held by the ancient philosophers or by the common people concerning the highest good.[14] In discussing this variety of popular and philosophical

9. Aristotle, *Nicomachean Ethics*, trans. Sir David Ross (London, 1954), pp. 5–7, 24, 264.

10. *Aristotelis Stagiritae Moralia Nichomachia cum Eustratii, Aspasii, Michaelis Ephesii, Nonnullorumque Aliorum Graecorum Explanationibus, Nuper a Ioanne Bernardo Feliciano Latinitate Donata* (Parisiis, 1543), fol. 11–13. For Milton's knowledge of Eustratius' commentary, see F. A. Patterson and F. W. Fogle, *An Index to the Columbia Edition of the Works of John Milton* (New York, 1940), *s.v.*, "Eustratius." Cf. *Flaminii Nobilii Lucensis . . . De Hominis Felicitate Libri Tres* (Lucae, 1563), I, vi: "Neque in voluptate, neque in honore esse ponendam felicitatem; ac philosophorum etiam sententiam posse validis argumentis oppugnari."

11. *S. Thomae de Aquino, . . . Summa contra Gentiles* (Romae, 1934), pp. 251–62. The development of the argument proceeds (much as in *Paradise Regain'd*) through a series of negative propositions, which refute popular conceptions of happiness: "Quod felicitas humana non consistit in delectationibus carnalibus," "Quod felicitas non consistit in honoribus," "Quod felicitas hominis non consistit in gloria," etc. One may note a further analogy between Milton's method of argument and that of the moral philosophers. Both begin with appearance and common opinion, but by rejecting them succeed in establishing reality and reasoned truth. Thus in the *Summa Theologiae* St. Thomas Aquinas begins with the summary of the doctrine he intends to refute ("It *seems* that," etc.), then proceeds to refute it point by point ("I answer that," etc.).

12. *Philippi Beroaldi de Felicitate Opusculum* (n.d.).

13. *I Ragionamenti di M. Agostino da Sessa . . . sopra la Filosofia Morale d'Aristotele* (Venice, 1554), 27: "Havendo noi secondo l'opinione del Filosofo conceduto, che nè i piaceri, nè la ricchezza, nè l'honore, nè la virtù istessa, da per se sola possa far l'huomo felice, bisogna investigare hora qual sia questo SOMMO BENE, al quale ogni bene disposto animo naturalmente aspira."

14. *Universa Philosophia de Moribus a Francisco Piccolomineo Senese* (Venetiis, 1583), p. 480. "Hinc nonnulli in honore & gloria, ut viri civiles; alii in divitiis & fortunae bonis, ut viri vulgares & avari; nonnulli in sanitate, ut laborantes; vel in forma & naturae bonis, ut

ideas of the *summum bonum*, Alessandro Piccolomini emphasizes four false opinions of the highest good—pleasures of sense, honor, virtue, and riches.[15]

Polanus' *Syntagma Theologiae Christianae* applies the method of rejection to the whole complex of worldly values. Arguing that God alone is man's highest good and that no earthly thing can give him true beatitude, Polanus attempts to remove "some false opinions concerning the highest good." Quoting Ecclesiastes 1:2 and 12:12 ("Vanitas vanissima: omnia sunt vanitas"), Polanus declares that, as all worldly things are vain and bring unrest instead of tranquillity ("omnes res mundanae sunt vanae, & animum non tranquillant, sed tantummodo perturbant"), no worldly object can be the highest good. Man's *summum bonum* consists neither in human wisdom, nor in glory, nor in carnal pleasure, nor in dignity and supreme power, nor in riches, nor in virtue, nor in immortality, nor in the favour and grace of princes, nor in fortune, nor in an arbitrary human religion.[16]

In *The Felicitie of Man*, Sir Richard Barckley also approaches the problem of human happiness through a method of negation. As he explains in his "Preface to the Reader," an "erroneous opinion, and wrong estimation of things" have hindered worldly men from "attaining to the end of their desires. For every man desireth a happy estate, but because they doe not advisedly consider wherein felicitie or

---

foeminae & viri effoeminati; alii in voluptate, ut Epicurus & viri voluptarii; nonnulli in animi tranquillitate, ut viri solitarii; quidam in vita naturae legibus consentanea, ut Diogenes Cinicus; nonnulli in habitu virtutis, ut Stoici; quidam in actione ex virtute prodeunte, vel in conspiratione omnium, vel multorum ex numeratis bonis: summum bonum collocarunt."

15. *Della Institution Morale di M. Alessandro Piccolomini Libri XXI* (Venetia, 1594), pp. 40–43 (Book II, chap. 3, "Di varie openioni di qual sia l'ultimo fine dell' huomo, & in che modo sono fallaci"): "... tutti gli huomini, cosi quei del volgo, come i più saggi, ancora convengano unitamente nel nome di questo ultimo fine, chiamandolo il lor sommo bene, & la lor felicità; ... nondimeno in esprimer poi, qual sia questa vita prospera, & questa felicita, & in che consista, ... varie sono state, & sono le openioni. percioche alcuni la pongono nella sanità, alcuni nelle ricchezze, altri nella dignità, altri nella bellezza, & nella gagliardia, & infiniti nel piacer del senso; & finalmente secondo che sono à qualche effetto disposti gli huomini, in quello senz' altro discorso, o ragione si propongono il sommo bene." Cf. Flaminius, 27: "Alii igitur ... felicitatem ponunt ... in voluptate, in valetudine, in divitiis, in gloria. ... Alii vero ... sapientiam, prudentiam, virtutem."

16. *Syntagma Theologiae Christianae ab Amando Polano a Polansdorf* (Genevae, 1612), cols. 7–21. "Quapropter, ut falsas aliquot de summo bono opiniones removeamus, nulla res mundana est summum hominis bonum, quod illum beatum efficit: tum quia quaelibet illarum est vanitati subiecta, mutabilis, instabilis, fluxa, caduca: tum quia nulla illarum mentem tranquillam reddit, sed potius perturbat. Hinc necessariò conficitur, nullam rem mundanum esse summun hominis bonum, nullam illarum efficere hominem beatum. SAPIENTIA HUMANA ... non est summum hominis bonum. ... Neque GLORIA, id est, laus humana ac celebritas nominis ... est summum hominis bonum. ... Neque VOLUPTAS CARNIS est summum hominis bonum. ... Neque DIGNITAS ET POTESTAS SUMMA in republica est summum hominis bonum. ... Neque DIVITIAE sunt summum hominis bonum. ... Neque VITA HAEC TERRENA ET TEMPORALIS est summum hominis bonum. ... Denique (ne plures opiniones falsas de summo bono enumerem,

happinesse consisteth, nor direct the course of their life the next way to it, but mistake some other thing for that they seeke after, they never finde that they would have." Observing "the errours and passions of those who have set their felicity in pleasures, riches, honour & glory, and such like worldly vanities, which to all, except they be well used, are hinderance to felicity, and have brought many to extreme misery," he devotes the first four books of his treatise to a systematic refutation of these false opinions of beatitude:

In the first I have offered to prove . . . that the felicity of man consisteth not in pleasures: In the second not in riches: in the third, not in vertue, or in the action of vertue, after the Academicks and Peripateticks, nor in Philosophicall contemplation.

Three things . . . the most part of men greedily hunt after. . . . Some desire to live in pleasure, many seeke for riches, others labour for honour and glory; in these things according to their severall inclinations they put their felicitie. But how farre they are from the true felicitie, shall hereafter . . . appeare. . . .[17]

In *Solomon's Ethics or Morals,* Joseph Hall similarly explains "Wherein Felicity is not" before asserting. "Wherein Felicity is." True happiness, he declares, cannot be found in pleasure, wealth, magnificence of estate and works, honour, long life and issue, "learning and human knowledge," or "in any human thing." Again, in *Heaven upon Earth: or, Of True Peace of Mind,* Hall includes among temptations which "distemper the mind not without some kind of pleasure" the familiar triad of "the vanity and unprofitableness of riches," honor, and pleasure.[18]

The pattern of systematic rejection which Milton employs in his treatment of the Second Temptation is, then, a standard method of Western ethical tradition. His hero demonstrates his knowledge of the *summum bonum,* his insight into the nature of the "public good" and what is "best" and "happiest" for mankind, through a process of negation already well established in classical and Christian approaches to the highest good.

Far from underplaying the rejection-motif, *Paradise Regain'd* really carries it considerably further than the Biblical account. Whereas Satan's offer of "all the kingdoms of the world" and their "power" and "glory" (Luke 4.5–6) involves an appeal to the active life, Milton

---

quarum ducentas & octoginta quinque diversas Varro commemorat,) neque STATUS BONORUM OMNIUM corporis, & (ut vocant) fortunae aggregatione adeptioneque perfectus, est summum nostrum bonum. . . ."

17. Sir Richard Barckley, *The Felicitie of Man, or, His Summum Bonum* (London, 1631), p. 10, and "Preface to the Reader." Cf. pp. 672–73.

18. Right Reverend Joseph Hall, *Works,* ed. Philip Wynter (Oxford, 1863), VIII, 223–26; VI, 26–30.

expands this temptation to include values of the voluptuous and contemplative lives. Through this variation he not only strengthens the analogy with the judgment of Paris, but also provides a more comprehensive survey of ethical values. Extending the pattern of rejection to all three branches of the *triplex vita*, he emphasizes the sweeping character of the act of refusal and at the same time focuses attention, by contrast, on the values which his hero does *not* reject. Christ does not renounce the entire *triplex vita*; he refuses only those aspects which Satan has proposed to him ("aught/By me propos'd in life contemplative,/ Or active, tended on by glory, or fame"). The means and ends which the Prince of this World has offered him are secular and hence incompatible with the spiritual nature of Christ's kingdom and office. The pursuit of "glory" and "fame" in either the active or the contemplative mode of life is inconsistent with the Messianic path of humiliation.[19] The power and wisdom of the world are unnecessary for "Christ the power of God, and the wisdom of God" (1 Cor. 1.24). It is consistent with the "heavenly" character of the Second Adam ("the Lord from heaven") that he should reject the "earthy" values his Adversary proposes (1 Cor. 15.45–9). Thus the worldly and transitory objects he rejects serve to emphasize the heavenly and eternal objects he does not refuse. He declines the worldly delights Satan offers him, but he achieves a spiritual "Eden." He refuses the kingdoms of the world, but he gains the Kingdom of Heaven. He contemns the world's wisdom, but he possesses the heavenly wisdom of the Scriptures and the Spirit, and as Logos he is himself the "wisdom of God." Milton is concerned, as Professor Kermode has pointed out, "to establish the heavenly nature of the rewards which supersede the earthly recompense of the old heroes," and these "new rewards" are "suggested by the very rewards they displace."[20] This antithesis holds true for the values of all three modes of the *triplex vita*.

This pattern of affirmation complements and reinforces the basic pattern of rejection. Milton's Christ discriminates finely between true and false glory and between true and false wisdom, but this insight actually strengthens the theme of *contemptus mundi*.[21] It is precisely this recognition of the relative value of the secular and celestial which enables Milton's hero to spurn Satan's offers with confidence. The Biblical antithesis between "treasures upon earth" and "treasures in heaven" (Matt. 6.19–20) is paralleled in Milton's epic by the hero's distinction between "false glory" on Earth and "true glory and renown" in Heaven and between the "true wisdom" of the Scriptures

19. See Chapter IV, *supra*.
20. Frank Kermode, "Milton's Hero," *RES*, N.S. IV (1953), 323, 329.
21. Stein, pp. 31, 80, 90, 100, 109, 130–31; cf. Hughes, p. 257.

and its "false resemblance" in Gentile doctrine. In contrasting true and false values, heavenly and worldly ends, Milton complements the method of negation with a method recommended by Thomas Traherne:

Felicity is a Thing coveted of all. . . . Nevertheless Great Offence hath been don by the Philosophers . . ., many of them in making Felicity to consist in Negativs. They tell us it doth not consist in Riches, it doth not consist in Honors, it doth not consist in Pleasures. . . . Ought they not to Distinguish between true and fals Riches as our Savior doth; between Real and fained Honors? between Clear and Pure Pleasures, and those which are Muddy and unwholsom? The Honor that cometh from abov, the True Treasures, those Rivers of Pleasure that flow at his right hand for evermore are by all to be sought and by all to be desired.[22]

Similarly John Downame maintains that "earthly Honours, Riches and pleasures, are base and are of no worth, in comparison of the treasures, glory, and joyes of heaven."[23] Ursinus likewise contrasts the eternal good which Christians pursue with the transitory values extolled by the Gentile philosophers and "the vulgar sort":

Touching which *principall good*, without the Scripture and word of God, *So many men, so many opinions* are broached. The Epicures seate and place this supreame good in *sensuality and pleasure*: the Stoics in a decent moderation *and bridling of the affections*, or, *in the habit of vertue:* the Platonicks *in their Ideas*: the Peripateticks *in the action and exercise of vertue:* the vulgar sort *in honours, riches, power and sway amongst men*. But all these are flitting transitory toys, either lost in time of life, or left behind us at the terme of death. Now, that principall good wee hunt after is such as fadeth not, nor vanisheth, no not in death.[24]

In his pursuit of the highest good Milton's Christ employs a familiar method of Christian moralists, comparing and contrasting the true and eternal values of Heaven with the false and transitory goods of the world. Nevertheless, far from contradicting the method of rejection and the idea of *contemptus mundi*, this process of distinction usually provides Christian ethics with an additional argument for despising the goods of this world as inferior to those of Heaven.

III

Though the two traditions we have examined seem to assign a different priority to the interrelated processes of knowing and rejecting, this apparent difference does not entail a real contradiction. In one case

22. *Centuries, Poems and Thanksgivings*, ed. H. M. Margoliouth (Oxford, 1958), I, 108–9.

23. *The Christian Warfare against the Devill World and Flesh* (London, 1634), p. 698.

24. Zacharias Ursinus, *The Summe of Christian Religion*, trans. D. Henry Parry (London, 1633), p. 32.

the act of rejection is essentially *moral*; in the other it is essentially *logical*. The one involves an act of the will, the other an act of the intellect. In the tradition of Hercules' choice, knowledge is a precondition of *moral* rejection; Hercules rejects Vice and elects Virtue on the basis of his rational insight into their contrasting claims and promises. In the philosophical and theological tradition concerning the *summum bonum*, on the other hand, the method of *intellectual* rejection is a tool of logical demonstration; the progressive elimination of the false helps to prove and substantiate the true. In *Paradise Regain'd*, which builds on both traditions, the hero's act of rejection is both intellectual and moral. Just as Milton's Satan makes a twofold attack on understanding and will, seeking to blind the former by false opinion and to enslave the latter through carnal appetite,[25] so Milton's Christ achieves his victory through a dual rejection—an intellectual refutation of the secular ends and means his Adversary proposes and a voluntary act of renunciation. In this way he proves his dual immunity from the spiritual death which had reigned since the Fall; his understanding is clear "to discern the chief good," and his will is free to pursue it.[26]

The interdependence of knowledge and rejection in the Second Temptation raises a further question—the problem of how much the hero already knows. Does he actually acquire further knowledge through the act of intellectual refutation, or is this (like the complementary act of moral renunciation) based entirely on prior knowledge? Does he really learn through his dialogue with the devil, or does it yield no additional insight? Is Milton's Christ being educated by Satan, one may legitimately ask, or does he know all the answers in advance?

Though he undoubtedly knows *some* of the answers already, there is no indication that he knows *all* of them in advance, and for several reasons the former seems the more satisfactory alternative. In the first place, Milton has already (I, 203–4) taken pains to stress his hero's need to "learn" in order to "know" and "do/What might be public good," to characterize him as precociously eager to "improve [his] knowledge." One purpose of this passage, it seems, is to establish relatively early in the poem the particular characterization which is to be developed in the following books. Second, Christ himself raises the issue of the limitations to his knowledge. At first he does not know why

25. In offering the goods of the *triplex vita*, Satan reinforces his arguments with a direct appeal to the senses. In the case of the *vita voluptuosa* he presents the sensuous enticements of the regal banquet. In the case of the *vita activa* and *vita contemplativa* he heightens verbal persuasion through the visual presentation of the kingdoms of the world and the schools of Athens.

26. *Prose Works*, IV, 265.

he is being led into the wilderness: "to what intent/I learn not yet; perhaps I need not know;/For what concerns my knowledge God reveals" (I, 291–93). Nor does he know "how to begin" and "to accomplish best His end . . . and mission." Moreover, he is deliberately evasive concerning his knowledge of the Greek philosophers ("Think not but that I know these things; or think/I know them not"). Third, his very awareness of these human limitations to his knowledge accentuates his complete reliance on divine wisdom. In trusting in Providence for guidance when he himself is ignorant of the divine intent, he demonstrates his obedience and provides further confirmation of his divine Sonship. Similarly, his preference for the "true wisdom" of divine revelation over the fallacious wisdom of the world ("he who receives/Light from above, from the fountain of light,/No other doctrine needs, though granted true") proves the soundness of his epistemology; he refuses to ground his knowledge on fallible and uncertain wisdom and bases it instead on a higher and infallible source of truth.[27] As he himself recognizes, the fact that he has been sent into the world as God's "living Oracle . . ., to teach his final will" does not mean that his knowledge is already complete or that he cannot attain a clearer and more comprehensive insight into God's will in the course of his wilderness-ordeal.

Fourth, the recognized analogy between *Areopagitica* and *Paradise Regain'd* in their treatment of the "temptation motive"[28] suggests that the intellectual ordeal in the latter work may involve the process of "knowing good by evil." Even though Milton's Christ is unique in bringing "innocence into the world" rather than "impurity," his trial has much in common with that of the "true wayfaring Christian."[29] He too is tried "by what is contrary." He too engages "in the contemplation of evil, and knows . . . the utmost that vice promises her followers, and rejects it." He too demonstrates that he "can apprehend

27. For sixteenth- and seventeenth-century views of scepticism as an aid and support to religious faith, see Louis I. Bredvold, *The Intellectual Milieu of John Dryden* (Ann Arbor, 1956), pp. 16–46. Cf. Charron's argument (Bredvold, 35–36) "that all the learning of the world is but vanity and falsehood," but that "the principles of Christianity" were "delivered to us from Heaven, brought us by its Ambassador, completely assured of divine authority."

28. See J. H. Hanford, "Temptation Motive in Milton," *SP*, XV (1918), 176–94.

29. Cf. M. Y. Hughes's note in John Milton, *Prose Selections* (New York, 1947), p. 223. In support of this reading ("wayfaring") there is not only the authority of the first edition, but also the possibility that this passage in *Areopagitica* had been influenced by the tale of Hercules' choice between the two ways of Virtue and Vice. Milton refers to "the utmost that vice promises to her followers"; Prodicus' Vice promises "to my followers authority to benefit themselves from every source." The fact that Milton uses the expression "a youngling in the contemplation of evil" and personifies Virtue and Vice as female figures may also be significant. Hercules is described as "advancing from among children to puberty," and Prodicus' Virtue and Vice are represented as "two fine women."

and consider vice with all her baits and seeming pleasures, and yet abstain, and yet distinguish, and yet prefer that which is truly better." In the wilderness of *Paradise Regain'd* as in the "world" of *Areopagitica*, "the knowledge and survey of vice" is instrumental in "the constituting of human virtue, and the scanning of error to the confirmation of truth." Emphasizing Christ's humanity as well as his divinity, Milton has stressed the similarities between his temptation in the desert and the Christian's trial "in the field of this world," where "the knowledge of good is so involved and interwoven with the knowledge of evil, and in so many cunning resemblances hardly to be discerned, that those confused seeds which were imposed on Psyche as an incessant labour to cull out, and sort asunder, were not more intermixed."[30]

Fifth, in certain respects Christ's knowledge is undeniably clearer, more comprehensive, and more precise at the end of his temptation than at the beginning. He certainly knows more about the divine "intent" which has led him into the wilderness and brought him thence "By proof the undoubted Son of God." His initial uncertainties about "how to begin" and to accomplish his mission have been resolved, and he possesses, accordingly, a deeper insight into God's will.[31] Through his detailed examination and refutation of the secular values Satan had proposed, he has demonstrated logically that the chief good and beatitude of man is to be found in no worldly object; it must be sought, therefore, in and from and through heaven alone. Separating the false from the true, the apparent from the real, the temporal from the eternal, the earthly from the heavenly, he is left with the pure salt of the spirit.

Moreover, in solving the problem he shares in common with Hercules ("by what road [he] should enter upon life"), he has produced a systematic outline of Christian ethical doctrine—an orderly statement of the *philosophia Christi*. He brings to the wilderness a swarming "multitude of thoughts"; he carries from it a rationally constructed system of morality. The Second Temptation, as Milton presents it, is essentially an ethical dialogue in poetic form, and its method and structure are (as we have seen) those which classical and Christian moralists alike had employed in defining the ultimate end, highest good, and true happiness of man. In utilizing this method of systematic negation to demonstrate the other-worldly character of the "public good" and the "salvation" his hero seeks for mankind, Milton

30. *Prose Works*, II, 67–68.

31. At the commencement of his ordeal Milton's Christ has, however, already learned much that is essential for his mission. The "true wisdom" of the Law and Prophets has taught him the grounds of public happiness and misery ("What makes a Nation happy, and keeps it so,/What ruins kingdoms, and lays Cities flat"), and from the same source he knows that his ministry of redemption involves the "hard" way (I, 260 ff.).

probably had in mind the moral instruction of his audience, but—within the context of the poem, at least—it also serves as an index and yardstick of the Messiah's progressive increase in wisdom.

Finally, this demonstration of Christ's increase in knowledge is an essential element in his manifestation of the divine image—that "likeness to God" or "godliness" which is the "happiest end" of man.[32] The hero of *Paradise Regain'd* is himself "the great mystery of godliness," and in the course of his ordeal he proves his divine Sonship by exhibiting the salient features of the Father's "True Image"—righteousness, holiness, and knowledge. As understanding and will are free from the corruption of sin, he is able both to "prove what is that good will of God" and "to will and to do" God's behest.[33] Through his dual reorientation of the human understanding and will towards the "chief good" he shows his divine resemblance and thereby proves that he is the Son of God. The knowledge-rejection motif is instrumental both in the trial of his humanity and the proof of his divinity.

32. See Chapter 8, *supra.*
33. *Prose Works,* IV, 289, 195, 319, 329.

Part III

Logic and the Argument

10. *"Man's First Disobedience"*

The Causal Structure of the Fall

❦ What, in Milton's opinion, were the real causes of Adam's disobedience? In what way did the poet's conception of these causes influence the argument and structure of *Paradise Lost* or affect his avowed intent to "justifie the wayes of God"? For raising these questions Milton scholarship is deeply indebted to Professor Leon Howard's invaluable pioneer study, which takes its point of departure from the "particular analysis of the logic of causation" in Milton's *Artis Logicae.*[1]

Tracing the "apparent use of that analysis in *Paradise Lost* in connection with the 'efficient' cause," Professor Howard drew the following conclusions: "God is the remote first cause, who moves in so mysterious a way that human reason can find a force for teaching only in those more proximate causes with which he works. Adam, impelled by a 'deficience' of nature within him [the 'proegumenic' cause], was the principal of 'all our woe.' Eve provided the occasion [the 'procatarctic' cause] of his first disobedience. And Satan was the instrument by which the catastrophe was brought about."[2]

First published, in somewhat different form, in the *Journal of the History of Ideas,* XXI (1960), 180–97.

1. Leon Howard, "'The Invention' of Milton's Great 'Argument': A Study of the Logic of 'God's Ways to Men,'" *Huntington Library Quarterly,* IX (1945–46), 149–73; I am indebted for this reference to Miss K. M. Lea of Lady Margaret Hall, Oxford.

2. Howard, p. 161. In his *Artis Logicae Plenior Institutio* (*Works* [Columbia Edition; New York, 1931–38], XI, 32–33), Milton defines the efficient cause as that "by which the thing is or is brought about" ("Efficiens est causa, à qua res est, vel efficitur").

As it is largely through delineating the causes of the fall that Milton attempts to justify God's ways to men, this approach sheds undeniable light on the central event of the poem. Nevertheless, the three centuries which separate us from Milton's *Art of Logic* and his epic make it extremely difficult for the modern scholar to employ the technical terms of the *Artis Logicae* with precision. It is useful, therefore, to know how Milton's immediate predecessors and contemporaries regarded the problem, and to consult some sixteenth- and seventeenth-century conceptions of the causes of man's first apostasy.[3]

I

Milton's own theological treatise says relatively little about the causes of man's first sin. According to the *De Doctrina*, it originated in 1) "the instigation of the devil" and 2) "the liability to fall with which man was created."[4] Unlike many other Reformation theologians, he does not attempt a more detailed breakdown of the efficient cause of the fall in terms of logical analysis.

On the other hand, both Wolleb and Ames offer more complex explanations. According to the former's *Compendium*, the "Procatertical [*sic*] or external cause [of Adam's disobedience], was the instinct and perswasion of Satan that subtile Serpent." The "Proegumene or internal cause was the will of man, of it self indifferent to good or evil, but by Satan's perswasion bent to evil."[5] Ames's *Medulla Theologica* employs other logical terms. Dividing the causes of the fall

3. For Milton's logical theory and his relation to such theologians as Polanus and Keckermann, see Thomas S. K. Scott-Craig, "The Craftsmanship and Theological Significance of Milton's *Art of Logic*," *Huntington Library Quarterly*, XVII (1953), 1–16; *idem*, "Concerning Milton's Samson," *Renaissance News*, V (1952), 45–53. For the influence of Wolleb and Ames on Milton's *De Doctrina Christiana*, see Maurice Kelley," "Milton's Debt to Wolleb's *Compendium Theologiae Christianae*," *PMLA*, L (1935), 156–65; *idem*, *This Great Argument* (Princeton, 1941); Arthur Sewell, *A Study in Milton's Christian Doctrine* (London, 1939), pp. 35–45; Scott-Craig, "Milton's Use of Wolleb and Ames," *MLN*, LV (1940), 403–7. For the influence of Ramism in the Renaissance, see Walter J. Ong, S. J., *Ramus, Method, and the Decay of Dialogue* (Cambridge, Mass., 1958); *idem*, *Ramus and Talon Inventory* (Cambridge, Mass., 1958); Rosemond Tuve, *Elizabethan and Metaphysical Imagery* (Chicago, 1947); J. Milton French, "Milton, Ramus, and Edward Phillips," *MP*, XLVII (1949), 82–87; P. Albert Duhamel, "Milton's Alleged Ramism," *PMLA*, LXVII (1952), 1035–53.

4. Milton, *Works*, XV, 181.

5. John Wollebius, *The Abridgment of Christian Divinitie*, trans. Alexander Ross, (London, 1660³), p. 74; cf. *Christianae Theologiae Compendium . . . Authore Iohanne Wollebio* (Amsterdam, 1633), pp. 63–64. In his note on this passage Ross distinguishes the "direct" and "indirect" causes of man's fall (74): "The direct cause of sin was mans owne will; the indirect cause was Satan, by perswasion and suggestion. For no externall thing can necessarily move the will, but the last and onely. Satan may internally work upon the phantasie, by representing forms to it; and upon the appetite by moving it to passion by means of the spirits and the heart; but he cannot work upon the understanding and will."

into two categories ("una principalis, aliae adjuvantes"), he declared that man himself was the principal cause through the abuse of his free will:

The principall cause was man himselfe, by the abuse of his free will. *Eccles*.7.29. For he had received that righteousnesse, and grace by which he might have persisted in obedience if he would. That righteousnesse and grace was not taken from him before he had sinned, although that strengthening and confirming grace by which the act of sinning should have been actually hindered, and the contrary act of obedience brought forth was not granted unto him, and that by the certaine, wise, and just counsell of God. God therefore was in no wise the cause of his *Fall:* neither did he lay upon man a necessity of falling, but man of his own accord, did freely *Fall* from God.

Although the assisting or "adjuvant causes were the Devill, and the Woman," the former's temptation did not necessitate man's sin: "But the Devill was not the compelling cause, neither the cause of sufficient direct necessary or certaine efficacy in procuring that sin: but only the counselling and perswading cause, by tempting, whence also it is that he hath the name of the tempter." (*Mat.* 4.3.) Satan's instrument in seducing Eve was the serpent; in tempting Adam, he employed Eve herself as "instrumentum ejus."[6]

According to Arminius, the efficient cause was twofold. The immediate and proximate cause was man himself, "who of his own free will and without any necessity either internal or external, . . . transgressed the law which had been proposed to him." The "remote and mediate efficient cause" was the Devil, who envied "the Divine glory and the salvation of mankind" and therefore "solicited man to a transgression of that law." The instrumental cause was the serpent, "whose tongue Satan abused for proposing to man those arguments which he considered suitable to persuade him." These arguments could be regarded as both *intus moventes* (i.e., proegumenic) and procatarctic causes. In addition to these persuasions, man was moved from without by two qualities which God had imparted to the fruit, "that the tree was good for food, and that it was pleasant to the eyes."[7]

In Ursinus' opinion, Satan's will was the efficient cause of his own fall and the impulsive cause of Adam's lapse; Adam's will, in turn, was the principal cause of his own transgression:

The first sinne of man sprang not from God, but from the instigation of the Divell, and from the free-will of man. For the Divell provoked man to fall

6. William Ames, *The Marrow of Sacred Divinity . . . Translated Out of the Latine* (London, 1652), pp. 55–60, "he chose a *Serpent* for his instrument"; "the Woman serving the Divill, as his instrument did tempt *Adam.*" Cf. *Guliel. Amesii Medulla Theologica* (Amsterdam, 1648), pp. 52–55.

7. James Arminius, *Works*, trans. James Nichols (London, 1828), II, 152. Arminius suggests that in tempting mankind "the grand deceiver" may have "made a conjecture from his own case; as he might himself have been enticed to the commission of sin by the same arguments."

away from God; and man yeelding to the inticing allurements of the Divell, freely revolted from God, and wilfully forsooke him. . . . The Divell then was the cause of the first sinne, or of the fall of our first Parents in Paradise, provoking man to sinne; and with the Divell man's will freely declining from God, and yeelding obedience to the Divell. . . . Many are the testimonies of Scripture, which teach us that God is not the author of sinne, . . . but that the originall of evill springeth from man himselfe, by the instigation of the Divell. . . . We conclude therefore that sinne hath his beginning *not from God*, who forbiddeth evill, but *from the Divell, and the free election of man*, which was corrupted by the Divells falshood. And therefore the Divell, and mans corrupted will obeying him, are the most true cause of sinne.[8]

Matthias Martinius stresses the same dual cause of sin—man's free will and Satan's deception: "In accordance with these covenants God has acted in such a way as to allow men their liberty. Deceived by the Devil, these have fallen into sin through their own fault and are justly punished by God."[9]

Keckermann subdivided the causes of the fall of man into "externa irritans" (procatarctic) and "interna movens" (proegumenic). In respect to Eve, the *causa externa irritans* was the devil, along with the beauty of the forbidden fruit. In Adam's case, Satan's suggestions constituted the remote external cause, but the *causa propinqua* was Eve's charms ("coniugis illecebrae"). Though several internal causes were common to both Adam and Eve, one *causa interna* was peculiar to Adam alone—"immoderatus & inordinatus amor coniugis; utpote, cuius illecebris tam facile assentitur." The instrumental cause was the serpent.[10]

According to Polanus, the devil was the impulsive cause of man's lapse, but the "principium internum" was the latter's free will: "Now our first parents fell both willinglie, and by Gods *providence* also. That they fell willingly, it appeareth heerby, because they were endued with a will of their owne, which was free, and could not be compelled. . . . That they fell by Gods providence, it appeareth in the *Proverb.* 16.4. *Rom.*11.32. *Galat.*3.22." As there was no necessity constraining the free will of Adam and Eve, they fell contingently, of their own volition. Since Adam was not deceived by the serpent, the cause

8. Zacharias Ursinus, *The Summe of Christian Religion, . . . First Englished by D. Henry Parry, and Now Againe Conferred with the Best and Last Latine Edition of D. David Pareus* (London, 1633), pp. 45–47, 64–67. Cf. *Zachariae Ursini Vratislavensis . . . Volumen Tractationum Theologicarum* (Neustadt, 1587), p. 219.

9. My translation; see *Epitome S. Theologiae Methodice Dispositae . . . Auctore Matthia Martinio* (Bremen, 1614), p. 58.

10. *Systema SS. Theologiae . . . per Bartholomaeum Keckermannum* (Hanau, 1602), pp. 236–41. Keckermann (236) cites 1 Timothy 2:14 as evidence that "Adami respectu causa externa irritans, id est, principium externe movens ad transgressionem, fuit Eva."

of his transgression was Eve ("mulier seducta, causa transgressionis fuit").[11]

Pareus regards Satan as the external first cause of man's sin. While the internal cause was the latter's free will, the external proximate cause was man's eyes, hands, and mouth. Though the primary guilt for Adam's apostasy belongs to Satan, the proximate blame falls on man's free will, for he had consented voluntarily to the devil's impostures.[12]

Francis Junius distinguished two kinds of temptation—external ("unum externum & foris proritans") and internal "(alterum internum & intus, paulatim provocanti occasioni acquiescens"). In the external temptation of Eve, the devil himself was the principal efficient cause, whereas the serpent was merely the *causa instrumentalis*—the instrumental or adjuvant cause. The instruments of the internal temptation, however, were sight and hearing: "By these instruments the woman was led first to turn her eyes in concupiscence towards the object of temptation, secondly to take and eat, and thirdly to give the fruit to her husband ('ut *viro quoque ministraret*')." In this way she became the instrumental cause of Adam's trespass:

... to her husband also she was a cause of transgression. For just as Satan had counselled Eve, so she counselled Adam to commit freely and imprudently an act which God had wisely forbidden. ... For this affair Satan employed as the instrument of common perdition not the serpent, as before, but the woman, whom God had joined to Adam as a companion and consort. ... Hence Satan assailed Eve by means of the serpent, which he employed as an involuntary instrument acting contrary to its nature; but he assailed Adam through an instrument who was both friendly and voluntary. Adam was the more prone to fall, the closer his connection with Eve, whom nature and God's institution had made one flesh with himself.

11. Amandus Polanus, *The Substance of Christian Religion*, trans. Thomas Wilcocks (London, 1608), pp. 78–80; *Syntagma Theologiae Christianae ab Amando Polano a Polansdorf* (Geneva, 1612), II, col. 11. Cf. *idem*, *Syntagma Logicum Aristotelico-Ramaeum* (Basel, 1605), p. 112, "The *causa impulsa* is that which acts after being moved by some other cause, but which nevertheless acts freely and without coercion. It is moved either by itself through an internal force (à se interna vi suâ), or else by some external factor acting from without (aut ab alio principio externo adveniente foris). ... The devil was moved of his own accord by an internal motion to rebel against God (à se & per se motus est interno motu suo). Eve was the cause of the first fall of man, but she was impelled (impulsa) and seduced by the serpent. Adam was moved to transgress through Eve (motus per Evam)." (My translation.)

12. *In Genesin Mosis Commentarius ... Authore Davide Pareo* (Frankfurt, 1609), col. 519, "Here the proper causes and grades of sin should be observed. The first external cause (causa prima exterior) is Satan, with his external and internal impulses, according to John 8:44, *Diabolus mendax & homicida ab initio Pater mendacij*. The proximate external causes (proxima exterior) were man's eyes, hands, and mouth. For through external senses and members the allurements of sin penetrate to the heart and internal appetite. The internal cause was the will, which voluntarily turned from God and became subject to the Devil, thrusting out the knowledge and reverence of God's law. ... Finally, the forbidden fruit stimulating the appetite and concupiscence in various ways through flesh, eyes, and hands." (My translation.)

Unlike the devils, who had fallen entirely through a "principium internum" without the influence of any "externo principio," Adam had been moved to crime by external as well as internal causes. His will—the "principium internum in Adamo a se quidem ipso motum" —had first been moved by an external cause ("prius ab externo principio motum"), the action of the devil ("a superiore principio singulari daemonis agentis in ipso"). Nevertheless, Satan had moved the will of Adam and Eve only as a "counselling cause" ("causa consulente") rather than as the efficient cause *per se*; "nam principium & causa efficiens in ipsis per se fuit voluntas intellectiva, ultro & consilio electione sua, quamvis seducta, monitis eius consentiens." Compelled by neither necessity nor coercion, Adam had sinned of his own free will, "pura . . . voluntate libera eo inclinante libere, & intellectu a vero . . . aberante [*sic*]."[13]

In the opinion of Henry Jeanes, Adam's free will was the "sufficient cause" of his sin, and Satan was merely an "imperfect cause":

> . . . Satan was the cause of our first parents fall, or sin, only *per modum suadentis*, not *per modum efficaciter determinantis*, he was only a *counselling, and perswading* cause, and that's only an imperfect cause, only *a morall cause*, he was not of sufficient efficacy to make them sinne, for, nothing can be the sufficient cause of sinne unto man, besides his own will, as *Aquinas* rightly [says] . . .; nothing can compell, or determine him thereunto. . . .[14]

In *Christian Religion: Substantially . . . Treatised*, Thomas Cartwright classifies the causes of the fall as external and internal ("either from things without man, or from man himselfe"). The former are "Either principal, as the Divell; or instrumental, as the Serpent, in and by whom the Divell spake." On the other hand, "the causes that rise from our parents themselves" are "either outward things of the bodie, or the inward affections of the minde moved by them."

13. *Libri Geneseos Analysis . . . Francisci Junii Biturigis. Accedit . . . De Peccato Primo Adami, & Genere Causae quâ ad Peccandum Adductus Est* (*In officina Sanctandreana* [Heidelberg ?], 1604), pp. 22–24, 101–2. (My translation.)

14. Henry Jeanes, *A Second Part of the Mixture of Scholasticall Divinity, with Practical* (Oxford, 1660), p. 349. Cf. *The "Summa Theologica" of St. Thomas Aquinas*, trans. Fathers of the English Dominican Province (London, 1917), II. II. Q. 43, A. 1, "nothing can be a sufficient cause of a man's spiritual downfall, which is sin, save his own will. Wherefore another man's words or deeds can only be an imperfect cause, conducing somewhat to that downfall." Elsewhere in the *Summa Theologiae* (I. II. Q. 75, A. 3), Aquinas explains that "the internal cause of sin is both the will, as completing the sinful act, and the reason, as lacking the due rule, and the appetite, as inclining to sin. . . . Hence it follows that nothing external can be a cause of sin, except by moving the reason, as a man or devil by enticing to sin; or by moving the sensitive appetite, as certain external sensibles move it. . . . Therefore something external can be a cause moving to sin, but not so as to be a sufficient cause thereof: and the will alone is the sufficient completive cause of sin being accomplished."

What are the outward things of the bodie?

They are the abuse of the tongue and of the eares . . .: or of the eyes, and of the taste. . . . For in that it is said, *it was delectable to looke on*, the eyes are made an instrument of this sinne; and in that it was said, *it was good to eate*, the taste is made to be an instrument of it.[15]

Keckermann's *Systematis Logici Plenioris Pars Altera* contains a logical analysis signed "Gregorius Martini" and entitled "Lapsus Primorum Parentum Adami & Evae." While the immediate cause of the fall was "Gustus & esus ille pomi de arbore boni & mali decerpti," the mediate (or less principal) causes were either instrumental or impulsive:

The impulsive or proegumenic cause was the pride and ambition whereby they aspired to be like God. . . . The procatarctic causes were 1) the beauty of the fruit and 2) the Devil, who employed a persuasive argument and calumniated Jehovah's words and wickedly twisted them to his own ends.

The instrumental causes of the fall were the fruit, the serpent, and Eve:

The instrumental causes were 1) the fruit of the tree of knowledge of good and evil, whose violation the Devil foreknew would entail man's fall and perdition; 2) the serpent, into which the Devil transformed himself and which he used as his assistant for deceiving man; and 3) Eve, whom (as the weaker sex) he cleverly won to his opinion and afterwards employed as a convenient instrument and hook for inducing the man also. . . .[16]

Curcellaeus regards the Devil as the "occasio . . . & causa impulsiva" of man's lapse, the "causa moralis peccati";

The Devil was the moral cause of sin, inasmuch as he seduced Eve by his tricks and Adam through her. But in no way did he compell them to violate God's command; if he had done so, they would have been immune from guilt. Though they had been armed with sufficient strength to resist him, they freely allowed themselves to be persuaded.

As neither God's decree nor his foreknowledge had made his transgression necessary, Jehovah could not be accused of being the author of sin:

Much less is it to be believed that God imposed on man any necessity of sinning. For this would be inconsistent with the hate with which he prosecutes sin, as well as with the severe interdict he imposed on Adam and with the punishment with which he vindicated the transgression. . . . So far as God's foreknowledge is concerned, it is certain that it can impose no necessity on anything. . . . Nor

15. Thomas Cartwright, *Christian Religion: Substantially, Methodicallie, Plainlie, and Profitablie Treatised* (London, 1611), pp. 34–39. The cause of Satan's attempt to seduce Adam and Eve (34) was "his hatred to mankinde, and his envie of his happie estate. . . ." Cartwright regards Eve as an instrumental cause of Adam's fall, observing (41) "how dangerous an instrument is an evill and deceived wife. . . ."

16. Bartholomaeus Keckermannus, *Systematis Logici Plenioris Pars Altera* (Hanau, 1609), pp. 653–59. (My translation.)

did it result from any decree of God, so that Adam could have sinned by necessity. Not from an effective decree, because in such a case God would be the author of sin, and such an opinion of the deity would be blasphemous. Nor did it result from a permissive decree. For the fact that God decreed not to impede man's fall by his own omnipotence did not impose any necessity of sinning. . . . Nor, finally, was any *concursus Dei* in eating the fruit of the tree of knowledge of good and evil the cause, so that man should necessarily eat from the tree: for no such concurrence can be attributed to God, as it would make him the author of sin.

Adam sinned "through an excessive desire of pleasing his wife ("nimio placendi uxori suae studio"), so that he preferred to die rather than remain alive after her death."[17]

In his "Analysis Logica" of Genesis 3, Piscator distinguishes three types of "causae procreantes" of man's first disobedience—1) the agents, 2) their action, and 3) the quality of mind their action effected in man:

In describing man's crime Moses indicates first the "procreant causes," secondly the crime itself, and thirdly its effects in man. There are three types of procreant causes—the agents ("substantiae agentes"), their action, and the quality of mind produced in man by this action. Two agents are indicated—the devil and the serpent. . . . From these details it is evident that the devil was the principal cause of the seduction and that the serpent was the instrumental cause.

The "secundum causae genus" was the devil's action through the serpent, "videlicet sermocinatio ad decipiendum mulierem, & adducendum ad transgressionem mandati Dei." Finally, the "causae genus tertium" was the "qualitas animi in muliere per illam sermocinationem effecta: unde postea immediatè transgressio profecta fuit":

Moses speaks of this matter in Genesis 3:6 as follows: *Et vidit mulier, quod bona esset arbor illa cibum, & quod concupiscentia esset* (i.e. res valde concupiscenda) *oculis & desiderabilis arbor ad efficiendum prudentem.* In these words Moses explains the woman's judgment or opinion of the forbidden fruit, and likewise indicates the affections it aroused. Her opinion (he explains) was twofold. First, she judged the fruit to be pleasant to the taste. . . . Secondly, she believed that it could confer prudence—the divine sapience promised by the serpent. . . . Moses indicates that the procreant cause of the former opinion was the judgment of the eyes . . ., but he leaves the procreant cause of the second opinion to be inferred from the preceding passage. For any attentive person can perceive that the woman had been led to this opinion by the serpent's promise. . . .[18]

17. *Stephani Curcellaei Opera Theologica* (Amsterdam, 1675), pp. 127–30. (My translation.)

18. *Commentarius in Genesin . . . Authore* [*Ioanne*] *Piscatore* (Herborn, 1601), pp. 63–67. (My translation.)

Another causal analysis of the fall in terms of Ramist logic appears in a meditation on sin in Richard Rogers' *Practice of Christianitie*. In analyzing the "cause efficient" of sin, Rogers warns the "rebellious soule" not to lay "the blame upon the Lord neither make him the author of thy sinne." Although it is indeed true that the "divell, . . . using the subtill Serpent for his instrument, did offer the first occasion of sinning; whereby he became an externall cause of sinne, and is called a murtherer from the beginning, and the author and father of all deceit, Ioh. 8.44: yet man had power to have resisted him if he would, which he not doing, became the true and proper efficient cause of corrupting himselfe and all his posterity; who likewise . . . became also the proper and immediate causes of their owne sinnes."[19] This analysis was subsequently reprinted in the translator's preface to *A Compendium of the Art of Logic and Rhetorick in the English Tongue* (London, 1651).

From these discussions it is evident that the problem of the causes of Adam's fall was a commonplace of sixteenth- and seventeenth-century theology.[20] Several of the theologians we have considered had published works on Ramist logical theory in addition to their religious writings.[21] To treat the fall of man in terms of its causes and effects was a familiar approach in Reformation theology, and available to both Milton and his readers was an extensive theological tradition which had analyzed the causal pattern of "Man's First Disobedience" in terms of Aristotelian, Ciceronian, or Ramist logic. Even without the *Artis Logicae* (which did not appear until five years after the first publication of *Paradise Lost*), Milton's audience should have recognized in the causal structure of his epic action a familiar logical pattern.

II

Except for certain obvious, but minor differences in terminology, there is little real divergence between these Reformation conceptions of

19. Richard Rogers, *The Practice of Christianitie* (London, 1619), pp. 312–14.

20. Cf. Melanchthon's *Loci Theologici* (*Corpus Reformatorum*, XXI, cols. 643–52, 668–78): "The causes of sin are the Devil's will and man's will, which freely and voluntarily turned from God (who neither willed nor approved this rebellion) and which, wandering beyond the law, adhered to objects against God's command, as Eve's will (turning from God's voice and straying beyond the law) adhered to the apple." "The efficient causes of the first fall of man are the Devil and the will of Adam and Eve, which assented to the Devil and freely turned away from God's command. Moreover, causes which merit something are 'efficient' (Dicuntur autem et efficientes caussae, quae merentur aliquid). Thus Adam and Eve are 'caussae efficientes,' who merited guilt for themselves and their descendants. . . ." (My translation.) For a Roman Catholic analysis of the causes of Adam's sin, see *Ioannis Delphini . . . De Salutari Omnium Rerum* (Camerini, 1553), p. 112, "The cause of that sin which Adam actually committed was his own free will." (My translation.)

21. Scott-Craig (*HLQ*, XVII, p. 3) cites Polanus' *Syntagma logicum Aristotelico-Rameum* (Basel, 1611). See also William Ames, *Demonstratio Logicae Verae* (Leyden, 1632), and (among Piscator's numerous writings on logic) *Animadversiones Joan. Piscatoris Arg. in Dialecticam P. Rami* (London, 1583).

the efficient cause of Adam's fall and the results modern scholarship should obtain by analyzing *Paradise Lost* in terms of the principles of the *Artis Logicae*. In most essentials Professor Howard's interpretation does not differ radically from these traditional views. Where it does differ, however, there is warrant (either in Milton's epic or in his logic or in both) for preferring the theological convention.

The causal structure of man's disobedience in *Paradise Lost* can be summarized as follows:

1. Milton's own statements make it clear that he regarded man's free will as the principal efficient cause of the fall. In Book III of the poem the argument whereby God "clears his own Justice and Wisdom from all imputation" is that he had "created Man free and able enough to have withstood his Tempter";

> *So will fall*
> *Hee and his faithless Progenie: whose fault?*
> *Whose but his own? ingrate, he had of mee*
> *All he could have; I made him just and right,*
> *Sufficient to have stood, though free to fall.*
> *Such I created all th' Ethereal Powers*
> *And Spirits, both them who stood & them who fell.*
> *Freely they stood who stood, and fell who fell.*

Created free, they cannot "justly accuse Thir maker, or thir making, or thir Fate":

> *. . . they themselves decreed*
> *Thir own revolt, not I:*

Adam and Eve have "themselves ordain'd their fall," and trespass,

> *. . . Authors to themselves in all*
> *Both what they judge and what they choose; for so*
> *I form'd them free, and free they must remain*
> *Till they enthrall themselves:*

Again, in Book X, God reiterates the fact that man fell of his own free will:

> *. . . no Decree of mine*
> *Concurring to necessitate his Fall,*
> *Or touch with lightest moment of impulse*
> *His free Will, to her own inclining left*
> *In even scale.*

In representing man's free will as the principal cause of his lapse, Milton was following a well-established theological convention. Both

Ames and Ursinus had specifically designated it as such ("causa principalis," "principaliter efficiens . . . causa"); but it had also been described as 1) the sufficient cause (Jeanes), 2) the "internal cause" (Wolleb, Pareus, Polanus), 3) the "direct cause" (Ross), and 4) the immediate and proximate cause (Arminius).

2. According to the *Artis Logicae*, the *causa minus principalis* (or *causa adjuvans & ministra*) is either 1) impulsive (impelling and moving the principal) or 2) instrumental. The former contains two subdivisions: a) proegumenic (moving the principal from within) and b) procatarctic (moving the principal from without).[22]

Although Professor Howard regards Satan as the instrumental cause of man's first disobedience, it seems certain that the serpent is really the instrumental cause. In the first place, this is the opinion of most of the theologians we have cited. Secondly, in Book X of *Paradise Lost*, Milton explicitly states that Satan made the serpent an "instrument Of mischief, and polluted from the end Of his Creation." Thirdly, according to the *Artis Logicae*, instruments do not act of themselves; they merely assist some other cause, or are used by it.[23] Since Satan obviously acts of himself, he is not an instrumental cause.

3. The procatarctic, or external, cause of Eve's transgression is Satan, but Eve herself is the procatarctic cause of Adam's sin. Both of these interpretations are traditional. Wolleb regards the devil's persuasion as "the procatertical or external cause" of the fall. According to Keckermann he was the *causa externa irritans* in the seduction of Eve and the remote external cause in Adam's temptation. In Arminius' opinion, he was the "remote and mediate efficient cause"; for Ross, he was the "indirect cause." Polanus and Ursinus regard him as the impulsive cause of the fall. Piscator identifies him as the principal cause of Eve's seduction, and Junius declares him to be the principal cause of the external temptation. For Keckermann, the proximate external cause of Adam's sin was "coniugis illecebrae." Thus, in the strictest sense, "Femal charm" is the procatarctic cause of Adam's sin. In Eve's case, it is (strictly speaking) the devil's "perswasive words," together with

22. See Milton, *Works*, XI, 30–51; cf. Howard's discussion and diagram of Milton's conception of the efficient cause, pp. 155–56. According to the *Artis Logicae* (34–35), trans. Allan H. Gilbert, "the efficient cause works alone, or with others. And of these last often one is principal, another less principal or a helping and servant cause [adjuvans & ministra]." "A principal cause of the lower order [causa minus principalis], as some put it, is either impulsive, in some way impelling and moving the principal, or it is instrumental." "The two sorts of impulsive cause are called by accepted Greek names either *proegumenic* or *procatarctic*. The first moves the principal from within [intus], the second from without [extrinsecus]; if it is genuine it is called the *occasion*, if feigned the *pretext*."

23. Milton, *Works*, XI, 36–37, "Instruments also are reckoned among the helping causes [in causis adjuvantibus]. . . . Instruments, however, do not act of themselves, but are used or help [aguntur aut adjuvant]."

the beauty of the forbidden fruit ("which to behold Might tempt alone") and "the smell So savorie of that Fruit."

4. The proegumenic, or internal, cause of Adam's sin is less the inherent "deficience" in his nature than uxoriousness—"immoderatus & inordinatus amor coniugis." Milton himself makes this point absolutely clear in Book IX; Adam (he declares) is "fondly overcome with Femal charm" and "resolves through vehemence of love to perish" with his wife.[24]

The proegumenic cause of Eve's default, on the other hand, is her false conception of the "Vertues" of the forbidden fruit, her desire for wisdom and Godhead, and her "eager appetite" and "desire, Inclinable now grown to touch or taste."

III

As the above analysis is based on the mode whereby the efficient cause "works with others" ("causa efficiens . . . efficit . . . cum aliis"), we must consider two additional aspects of the efficient cause: 1) "quod procreet, aut tueatur" and 2) "causa efficiens per se efficit, aut per accidens."[25]

To the former category belong "omnium rerum inventores, auctores, conditores, conservatores," Thus Satan is the author, or procreant cause, of sin and death and their works (*Paradise Lost*, II, 864; VI, 262; X, 236), and Adam and Eve are the procreant causes of their own transgression—"Authors to themselves in all" (III, 122). They sin, moreover, not *per accidens*, but *per se*. "*A cause works by accident which works by some external power*, that is by a power not its own, when the beginning of the effect is without the efficient and is an external principle opposed to the internal, for thus the efficient cause acts not through itself, but through another. *This is true of those things which are done by coercion or fortune*, for these two are external principles opposed to the internal ones, namely, nature and will or thought."[26] Milton repeatedly emphasizes the fact that neither coercion nor fortune (i.e., fate or providence)[27] compell "our Grand Parents" to sin. To prevent them from pleading ignorance or *imprudentia*[28] as an excuse,

24. See *Artis Logicae* (40–41), "the impulsive cause, whether proegumenic or procatarctic . . .; these are not so much causes associated with or aiding [sociae aut ministrae] the principal cause, as modes of the efficient cause, through which either impelled by some affect, or because some occasion has been furnished, under the guidance of thought a man does this or that. . . ."

25. *Ibid.*, pp. 32–39.

26. *Ibid.*, pp. 42–43.

27. *Ibid.*, pp. 48–51.

28. *Ibid.*, pp. 46–47, "under other conditions *prayer for pardon* [*deprecatio*] is for the most part *rested on lack of foresight*, and surely there is sometimes room for excuse here."

"to render Man inexcusable," Raphael is sent "to admonish him of his obedience, of his free estate, of his enemy near at hand";

> . . . *this let him know*
> *Least wilfully transgressing he pretend*
> *Surprisal, unadmonisht, unforewarnd.*

"*A cause works of itself which works by its own power*, that is, which produces an effect from an internal principle."[29] Of these, some work by nature (and therefore by necessity), others by *consilio* (and therefore freely).[30] As Adam disobeys God's command not through the necessity of nature, but through rational choice, he falls of his own free will. By virtue of his rational nature, he possesses freedom *ex hypothesi*—the power to obey or to disobey:[31]

> Absolutely, God alone freely does all things, that is whatever he wishes, and is able to act or not to act. The Bible frequently asserts this. Those causes merely which work according to reason and thought, as angels and men, act freely *ex hypothesi*—on the hypothesis of the divine will, which in the beginning gave them the power of acting freely. For liberty is the power of doing or not doing this or that, except, to be sure, God wished otherwise, or force from some other quarter assailed them.

Hence the God of *Paradise Lost* repeatedly stresses man's native liberty, "the high Decree . . . which ordain'd Thir freedom":

> *Happiness in his own power left free to will,*
> *Left to his own free Will, his Will though free,*
> *Yet mutable. . . .*

To "justifie the wayes of God to men," Milton demonstrates 1) that God himself was not the author of "Man's First Disobedience," 2) that Adam himself was primarily responsible for his transgression and its evil effects for himself and his posterity, and 3) that the punishment for his sin was just. Thus the causal structure of the fall in *Paradise Lost* serves essentially to exonerate God and to place the principal blame for man's sin and misery on man himself.

This was a conventional theme in Reformation discussions of the causal pattern of the fall. Thus Melanchthon insists that God is not the author or cause of sin:

> . . . God is not the cause of sin, nor does he will the existence of sin, nor does he impell the wills of his creatures to commit sin, nor does he approve sin. . . .

29. *Ibid.*, pp. 38–39.
30. *Ibid.*, pp. 40–41, "What men do by nature they do of necessity; what they do after planning [consilio] they do freely."
31. *Ibid.*, pp. 42–43.

God is not the cause of sin, nor was sin established or ordained by God; on the contrary, sin is the horrible destruction of God's own work and of the divine order.[32]

Wolleb denies God's responsibility for Adam's sin:

Neither God, nor Gods Decree, nor the denial of special Grace, nor the permission of sin, nor the stirring up of natural motion, nor finally the government of that sinne, were the causes of *Adam* and *Eves* transgression. Not God; because he most severely prohibited the eating of that fruit. Not his Decree, because that infers a necessity only of immutability, not of coaction, neither doth it force any man to sin. Not the denyal of special Grace . . ., for God was not bound to give that grace to man, which he gave him. . . . Not the permission of sin; for he was not bound to hinder it. . . . Not the stirring up of naturall motion; because motion of it self is not sin. Not the government of his fall; because to turn evil into good, is rather to be the author of good, than of evil.[33]

Ames maintains that God was in no way the cause of the fall "Deus igitur nullo modo fuit causa lapsus"), nor "did he lay upon man a necessity of falling."[34]

Similarly, in the *De Doctrina*, Milton declares that "on account of the infinite holiness of the Deity, it is not allowable to consider him as in the smallest instance the author of sin." God "does not effect his purpose by compelling any one to commit crime, or by abetting him in it, but by withdrawing the ordinary grace of his enlightening spirit, and ceasing to strengthen him against sin. . . . Again, as God's instigating the sinner does not render him the author of sin, so neither does his hardening the heart or blinding the understanding involve that consequence. . . .[35] According to the *Artis Logicae*, "fate or the decree of God forces no one to do evil; and on the hypothesis of divine prescience all things are certain though not necessary."[36]

In *The Doctrine and Discipline of Divorce* Milton uses Adam's "native innocence and perfection" as an argument to prove that God is not "the author of sin";

Yet considering the perfection wherin man was created, and might have stood, no decree necessitating his free will, but subsequent though not in time yet in order to causes which were in his owne power, they might, methinks be perswaded to absolve . . . God. . . .

32. Melanchthon, XXI, col. 644. (My translation.)

33. Wollebius, trans. Ross, p. 73. Cf. *ibid.*, p. 72, "God cannot be called the author of sin without blasphemy." Delphinus similarly observes (112) that "sin cannot in any way be imputed to God, nor can it be committed with God as its author. Instead, it should be entirely imputed to the human will, because this alone wickedly rebels against its duty." (My translation.)

34. Ames, *Marrow*, p. 57.

35. Milton, *Works*, XV, 81.

36. *Ibid.*, XI, 48–51.

Even classical philosophy had employed this argument to justify God's ways to men; despite their ignorance of man's original righteousness, Plato, Chrysippus, and their followers "could yet find reasons not invalid, to justifie the counsels of God and Fate from the insulsity of mortall tongues: That mans own freewill self-corrupted, is the adequat and sufficient cause of his disobedience *besides Fate*; as *Homer* also wanted not to expresse both in his *Iliad* and *Odyssei*."[37]

When Milton's God asserts that neither "impulse or shadow of Fate" nor "absolute Decree Or high foreknowledge" has caused Adam to sin, he is voicing a theological commonplace.

The real reason why Milton "allowed God to dissociate himself entirely from the other 'more proximate' efficient causes" is not so much the fact that the latter "contained 'the whole force" of proving, teaching, or causing one to 'know or understand why things are so,'"[38] as the theological commonplace that God is in no sense an author or cause of sin. Although Reformation theologians would have regarded divine providence as the first cause of all things, they would have denied that God was an efficient cause of Adam's transgression.

In declaring that "I made him just and right, Sufficient to have stood, though free to fall," Milton's God was again giving expression to an argument often employed by Reformation theologians to prove that the divine will was not the cause of human sin. The fact that man had been created good exempted his Creator from blame. In proof of this thesis Henry Jeanes quotes Ecclesiastes 7:29, "Lo, this only have I found, that God hath made man upright, but they have sought out many inventions":

> In the verse foregoing, Solomon complaines of the generall depravation of mankind . . .; now lest any, should hereupon throw the blame of this upon God, for giving man so depraved a nature, he cleareth God, by laying downe *two conclusions*.
>
> The *First*, concerning the state of man by creation, *God made man upright*.
>
> The *second*, concerning the state of man by his apostacy, and defection from God; *but they have sought out many inventions*.
>
> . . . in relation unto that depravation of mankind . . .: *this only have I found;* to wit, as touching the cause of it, first, *negatively;* that God is not the cause of it; *for he made man upright:* secondly, *affirmatively;* that man himselfe is the cause of it; *But they have sought out many inventions*.

Thus "the principall thing, that is to be remarked, touching the sinfullnesse of men is; that God was not the cause of it, by his creation of

37. *Ibid.*, III, Pt. 2, 441.
38. Howard, p. 158; Milton, *Works*, XI, 36–39.

man's nature; but that our first parents were authors thereof, by their fall from that rectitude, in which God created them. . . ."[39]

Ursinus contrasts "*mans originall excellency* before his fall, and *his originall misery* since the same," so that "*the cause and fountaine of our misery being discovered, it might not be imputed unto God*." Inquiring "What manner of Creature Man was made by God," he attempts to show "how man was created by God without sinne, and that therefore God is not the author of our sinne, corruption, and misery."[40]

God is the cause of no sinne: as is proved, 1. By testimonies of Scripture, *God saw those things which he had made, and they were very good*. . . . 2. Because God is exactly and perfectly good and holy, so that no effect of his is evill. 3. Because he forbiddeth all sin in his law. 4. He punisheth all sinne most severely, which hee could not rightly doe, if he wrought or caused it. 5. He himselfe destroyeth not his owne Image in man: therefore he causeth not sinne, which is the destruction of his Image. The proper and only efficient cause of sinne is the *will* of Divels and men, whereby they freely fell from God, and robbed and spoyled themselves of the Image of God.[41]

Now, although God left man destitute in his temptation, yet hee is not the cause of his fall, or sinne, or destruction of man. For in that dereliction or forsaking of man, God neither intended, nor effected any of these; but hee proved and tried man, to shew how impotent and unable the creature is to doe, or retaine ought that is good, God not preserving and directing him by his spirit: and together with his triall of man, hee in his just judgement suffered the sinne of man to concurre, but hee was no cause or efficient of it.[42]

After explicitly refuting several objections which regard God as the cause of sin,[43] Ursinus asserts that the cause of Adam's fall and of all other sins was not the deity, but the will of devils and men ("sed diabolorum & hominum voluntatem, quae sponte à Deo & obedientia se avertens, peccato se contaminavit").[44] Among these rejected arguments is the thesis that God was the remote cause of sin:

This is also objected: *Hee that is the cause or the efficient of a Cause, is also the author of the Effects of that cause, if not the next, yet a farre off. But God is the cause of that Will, which is the cause of sinne: therefore is hee the cause of the Effect of the Will that is, of sinne.*

39. Jeanes, pp. 346–49.

40. Ursinus, trans. Parry, pp. 39–40.

41. *Ibid.*, p. 64.

42. *Ibid.*, p. 46. Cf. p. 47: "Wee must know that man was created of God without sinne, lest God bee imagined the author or cause of sinne."

43. *Ibid.*, pp. 67–71; cf. Ursinus, *Volumen Tractationum Theologicarum*, pp. 221–24, 242.

44. Ursinus, *Volumen*, p. 224; cf. *ibid.*, pp. 218–19. In arguing that God is not the cause or author or "effector" of sin, Ursinus cites as proof-texts Genesis 1: 31 ("*Vidit Deus quae fecerat & erant valdé bona*") and Ecclesiasticus 15:11–13 ("Ne dicas defeci impulsu Domini: nam quae ille odit, ut non debes facere. Ne dicas ipse me induxit in errorem: neque enim improbo viro ei est opus. Omne nefas odit Dominus, nec probatur ijs qui eum timent, & impiè agere nemini praecepit, nec cuiquam dedit licentiam peccandi").

Ursinus answers this objection by the distinction between causes *per se* and *per accidens:*

But when the cause which is a farre off a cause, either doth not move the next cause of the effect, or doth not intend or minde the effect, neither is appointed thereunto: it cannot be said to be a cause of that effect but by an accident. . . . Wherefore it followeth not at all, that God is the cause of those things which are committed by his creatures, depraved and corrupted of themselves.

A similar objection is that, since "second causes are able to doe nothing without the first cause, which is good, . . . neither is sin brought forth, neither do they deprave themselves, but that also the first cause worketh it with them." Ursinus replies "to the Antecedent" as follows: "The second causes doe nothing *without the first cause*, that is, without the first cause preserve and move them to doe, so farre forth as it is good which they doe: but they doe without the first cause concurring with them to the bringing forth of evill, as it is a fault, or of sinne."[45]

These logical analyses of the fall tend to confirm Howard's emphasis on the importance of the efficient cause in Milton's treatment of this theme. To consider the problem of "Man's First Disobedience" primarily in terms of its causes and effects was a common approach among Reformation theologians.[46]

On the other hand, there seems little ground for regarding cause as the "great Argument" of *Paradise Lost*. Although, in Howard's opinion, cause is not only "the 'great' argument in Milton's logical system," but also ("rather than any conventionally heroic narrative or any theological doctrine") the "highest concern and hence the 'Great Argument' of the author of *Paradise Lost*,"[47] the "great Argument" of the poem is really not so much the *causes* of the fall, as the fall itself. Significantly, the allusions to "argument" and "higher Argument" in the opening lines of Book IX have precisely the same referent as the "great Argument" of Book I—"Man's First Disobedience":

> *. . . foul distrust, and breach*
> *Disloyal on the part of Man, revolt,*
> *And disobedience: On the part of Heav'n*

45. Ursinus, trans. Parry, pp. 69–70.

46. Keckermannus, *Systema SS. Theologiae*, p. 236, "Two things are to be considered in the fall of man—namely, its causes and effects." Translation mine. Ursinus (*Volumen*, 199) lists four things to be learned from Scripture "ad agnitionem peccati & miseriae nostrae"—1) "Quid sit peccatum," 2) "Quae sint praecipuae peccatorum species, sive differentiae," 3) "Quae sint causae peccati," and 4) "Qui sint effectus peccati." According to Ames's *Medulla* (51–52), two things should be considered in the perpetration of Adam's sin—"causa, & consequentia ejus." Cf. Piscator, p. 63; and Cartwright, p. 34, "*What do you consider in the fall?* The causes of the fall, and the fall it selfe."

47. Howard, p. 152.

Now alienated, distance and distaste,
Anger and just rebuke, and judgement giv'n,
That brought into this World a world of woe,
Sinne and her shadow Death, and Miserie
Deaths Harbinger:

In these lines, as in the initial lines of Book I, Milton is not referring to the causes of man's first sin, but rather to the sin itself and its subsequent effects. In both passages he employs the word "argument" not as a logical term, but in a perfectly familiar literary sense, as "Subject-matter of discussion or discourse in speech or writing; theme, subject."[48]

IV

Thus far we have examined the efficient causes of the Fall in terms of the poem as a whole. Let us re-examine them now in a different but more personal context, through the eyes of three of the principal characters: Adam, Eve, and Satan. All three speeches exhibit the torments of an "evil conscience." All three are confessions, and serve therefore as "testimony" (inartificial proof) to pin the guilt on the speaker and exonerate the justice of God. Despite one profound ethical difference (Satan is unregenerate and cannot repent, whereas Adam and Eve are partially regenerate and *do* repent), the content of the speeches is remarkably similar. All three stress the misery of sin and place the primary responsibility on the speaker himself.

In the soliloquy on Mount Niphates, Satan finds in his own free will the "principal efficient cause" (in Ramist terminology) of his fall:

Hadst thou the same free Will and Power to stand?
Thou hadst: whom hast thou then or what to accuse,
But Heav'n's free Love dealt equally to all?

The "Proegumenic" causes of his sin were, in turn, "Pride and worse Ambition." (The divine decree proclaiming the Messiah as "King anointed" was merely the procatarctic cause—the occasion—of his revolt.)

In the judgment scene both Adam and Eve had extenuated their crime by putting the blame on external (or procatarctic) causes. He had accused his wife, and she the serpent. In their later speeches, however, immediately prior to their reconciliation, each acknowledges his own guilt. In this respect both exhibit a clearer insight into the causes of their transgression; and, as this awareness is due largely to their partial regeneration, it may be appropriately contrasted with their

48. *N.E.D., s.v. Argument.*

attitudes immediately after their fall, when both "in mutual accusation" had spent "fruitless hours, but neither self-condemning." Each had "upbraided" the other "as the cause of [his] transgressing," but neither had confessed that the principal cause resided in his own will. Their "vain contest" had centered entirely upon external, procatarctic causes. Each blames the other for the *occasion* of Eve's sin. Adam censures her "desire of wand'ring" and her rash attempt to "seek needless cause to approve" her faith. Eve, in turn, accuses him of responsibility in permitting her to go:

> *Hadst thou been firm and fixt in thy dissent,*
> *Neither had I transgress'd, nor thou with mee.*

Had Adam stood firm, there would have been (in other words) no occasion for her sin, nor would she have occasioned his own.

The reconciliation scene in Book X reveals a marked change in attitude. Adam's soliloquy, like Satan's, exhibits not only an intense awareness of his own misery, but an equally intense recognition of his own responsibility for it. "I deserv'd it," he confesses, and acknowledges that God's "doom is fair." He is also to blame (as he realizes) for the miseries of his posterity, the "propagated curse" on mankind:

> *. . . all from mee*
> *Shall with a fierce reflux on mee redound,*
> *On mee as on thir natural centre light*
> *Heavy, though in thir place.*

Absolving God of blame, he accuses himself as the procreant cause of the inherited guilt of "all mankind," condemned "for one man's fault":

> *. . . all my evasions vain*
> *And reasonings, though through Mazes, lead me still*
> *But to my own conviction: first and last*
> *On me, mee only, as the source and spring*
> *Of all corruption, all the blame lights due . . . .*

Eve likewise blames herself as the "cause of misery" to their posterity and to Adam. She alone is "sole cause to thee of all this woe" and the "only just object" of God's ire. Her transgression is greater than Adam's, and she is therefore the "more miserable" of the two:

> *. . . both have sinn'd, but thou*
> *Against God only, I against God and thee. . . .*

If the progressive regeneration of Adam and Eve appears first in their repentance, the latter appears most significantly in their analysis of efficient causality. Instead of emphasizing the procatarctic cause (as both had done earlier to extenuate their own guilt), each accuses himself as the principal efficient cause.

In *Samson Agonistes* one encounters a similar emphasis on efficient causes. Like Adam, the hero exonerates divine justice by acknowledging his own responsibility for his sin and the miseries it has entailed. His insight, moreover, is progressive. At first he blames his own strength as the procreant cause of his present wretchedness:

> *Suffices that to mee strength is my bane,*
> *And proves the source of all my miseries. . . .*

Later he accuses the disproportion in his natural (or supernatural) gifts—extraordinary strength coupled with merely ordinary wisdom—as the impulsive cause that "drove me transverse." Nevertheless, even from the beginning, he recognizes his own responsibility. Though tempted to question divine Providence, he refuses to "call in doubt Divine Prediction" and blames "mine own default": "Whom have I to complain of but myself?" Though Dalila provided the occasion (the procatarctic cause) of his fall, he realizes that the chief responsibility is his own; he himself is the principal efficient cause of his plight:

> *. . . of what now I suffer*
> *She was not the prime cause, but I myself. . . .*

Nor is God's Providence to blame; the cause of his misery is not "heavenly disposition" but his own "folly":

> *Nothing of all these evils hath befall'n me*
> *But justly; I myself have brought them on,*
> *Sole Author I, sole cause. . . .*

As in *Paradise Lost*, Milton clears divine justice by putting the responsibility for man's sin and its consequent misery squarely on man himself. To "justify the ways of God to men" he relies, in both poems, on the analysis of efficient causality.

Yet this is only half the picture. To "assert Eternal Providence" the poet must place equal, if not greater, stress on final causes. God permits Samson's temptation and fall in order to achieve Israel's deliverance. He allows Adam's in order to bring greater good out of evil and set the stage for the entrance of a divine *persona*, the advent of "one greater Man." In Adam's case, as in Samson's, "highest dispensation . . . haply had ends beyond [his] reach to know"; poetically as well as theologically, it is through these final causes that the "ways of God" are ultimately justified.

In both of these poems, and also in *Paradise Regain'd*, efficient and final causes are tightly interwoven; and the pattern in that well-knit fabric is fully discernible only "at the close," as a providential design. Insofar as the structure of the poem embodies this design, the poem itself becomes the mirror, if not the vehicle, of providence. As the imitation of an action it depicts the execution of a supernal decree. In the disposition and economy of its fable it imitates "divine disposal" and the "economy" of divine government. The chain of "probable" or "necessary" events that compose the plot becomes the bond of divine law, acquires (in appearance at least) the inevitability of providence. This was one of the advantages of writing a "divine poem," and Milton made the most of it. His Urania served him well.

To "assert Eternal Providence" most forcefully Milton must withhold the final revelation until the end. To "justify the ways of God" most dramatically he must emphasize their inscrutability, their mystery. To "discern things in thir Causes" and to "trace the ways of highest Agents" are not man's prerogatives; and Milton assigns this boast to Satan—significantly, in the temptation-scene. For the greater part of the poem not only must God's ends (the final causes) remain obscure; the occasion and means (procatarctic and instrumental causes) whereby he intends to accomplish his intent must also be left in darkness. In *Paradise Lost* the prophecy concerning the Woman's Seed (the principal efficient cause of man's salvation) remains an enigma until Michael reveals its true meaning. In *Samson Agonistes* the hero's companions do not realize until after the event that the Dagonalia (the occasion of Samson's deepest humiliation and grief) will also prove the occasion for his greatest triumph nor that the very pillars of the idol's temple will serve as the instrument of his vengeance. In *Paradise Regain'd* Satan bases his arguments not only on final causes (or ends) but also on procatarctic and instrumental causes (occasion and means). In rejecting these allurements, the hero demonstrates his faith and obedience by leaving both means and occasion to providence. Though these remain obscure throughout the poem, the reader is well aware of them. The occasion of Christ's major victory will be in "due time," his passion at Jerusalem, and its instrument the cross.

11. *Satan and the Argument from Equality*

❦ Milton's indebtedness to Isaiah for his account of Satan's rebellion is common knowledge.[1] Following patristic tradition and literary convention, he applies the prophet's denunciation of the king of Babylon to the archangel's revolt and fall. Satan's trust "to have equal'd the most High" (*Paradise Lost,* I, 40) echoes Lucifer's boast (Isaiah xiv. 14), "I will ascend above the heights of the clouds; I will be like the most High." Yet there is a significant difference. Equality and likeness are not synonymous; and, in noting Milton's debt to Isaiah, scholars have usually overlooked the distinction between attempting to "be like" Jehovah and to "equal" Him. In Milton's *Art of Logic,* however, this difference is of fundamental importance for logical and rhetorical argument. "Equals" (*paria*) and "likes" (*similia*) represent two distinct types of comparison. It is essential, therefore, to re-examine the Biblical sources of Satan's insistence on equality with

First published, in somewhat different form, in *Archiv f.d. Studium d. neueren Sprachen u. Literaturen,* CCII (1966), 347–60.

1. Cf. Merritt Y. Hughes (ed.), *Paradise Lost* (New York, 1935), pp. xxxii, 9, 173–74; F. A. Patterson and F. R. Fogle, *An Index to the Columbia Edition of the Works of John Milton* (New York, 1940), *s.v.* Isaiah; James H. Sims, *The Bible in Milton's Epics* (Gainesville, Florida, 1962), p. 259. Though patristic commentators apply Isaiah's prophecy literally to the king of Babylon, they regard it as an allegorical reference to the devil. Cf. Haymo of Halberstadt, *Patrologia Latina* (Paris, 1879), CXVI, and Herveus, *Patrologia Latina* (Paris, 1854), CLXXXI.

God and his rhetorical exploitation of the "argument of the equal" (the *argumentum paris*) in justifying his rebellion and exhorting his companions to revolt.

I

The most common translation of Isaiah xiv. 14 represents Lucifer's crime as a quest for divine likeness rather than equality. According to the Septuagint, he desires to be "like the most high": ἔσομαι ὅμοιος τῷ ὑψίστῳ or (as the Polyglot Bible translates it), "*ero similis altissimo.*"[2] In the Vulgate, in Pagninus' version, and in Sebastian Münster's translation from the Hebrew, the boast is "similis ero Altissimo."[3] In Castellion's version, "Excelsa scandam nubila supremo similis,"[4] and in Piscator's translation "assimilabo me excelso."[5] In the "Great" Bible and the "Bishops" Bible Lucifer declares that he "will be like the highest of all."[6] In the "Geneva" Bible and the Authorized Version he brags that he "will be like the most high."[7]

The alternative reading ("equal") is much more rare. The Zurich Latin Bible reads "altissimo aequalis ero," but the marginal gloss notes that the Hebrew means "Assimilabo me."[8] The Tremellius-Junius version translates the Hebrew as "*me* aequabo excelso."[9] As this is the translation on which Milton relied for the proof-texts of his *De Doctrina Christiana*,[10] it is probably the immediate source of the line in *Paradise Lost* (I, 40):

He trusted to have equal'd the most High . . .

Unlike the Zurich version, both Milton and Tremellius employ "equal" as a verb rather than as an adjective.

II

On the surface this difference in translation appears slight. Logically and rhetorically, however, it is highly significant, for it involves two

2. *Vetus Testamentum* (Alcalá de Henares, 1514–1517).

3. *Biblia Sacra Vulgatae Editionis* (Antverpiae, 1603); *Biblia Hebraica. Eorundem Latina Interpretatio Xantis Pagnini Lucensis*, ed. Benedictus Arias Montanus (Antverpiae, 1584); *Hebraica Biblia Latina Planeque nova Sebast. Munsteri tralatione* (Basileae, 1534).

4. *Biblia Interprete Sebastiano Castalione* (Basileae [1551]).

5. *Johannis Piscatoris Commentariorum in Omnes libros veteris testamenti tomus tertius* (Herbornae Nassoviorum, 1644).

6. *The bible in Englishe* (London, 1562); *The holie Bible* (London [1568]).

7. *The Bible* (London, 1576); *The Bible* (London, 1611).

8. *Biblia Sacrosancta Testamenti Veteris & Novi* (Tiguri, 1544).

9. *Biblia Sacra*, trans. and annotated Immanuel Tremellius and Franciscus Junius (Londini, 1593).

10. See Maurice Kelley, *This Great Argument* (Princeton, 1941), p. 70; Harris Francis Fletcher, *The Intellectual Development of John Milton* (Urbana, 1956), *passim; idem, Milton's Rabbinical Readings* (Urbana, 1930), *passim.*

distinct types of argument. "Equals" and "likes" entail two different types of comparison—in quantity and in quality. Whereas "equals are those things that have the same quantity,"[11] "like things are those that have the same quality." Although there is (as Milton observed) "great affinity of equals with likes," they nevertheless "differ especially in that equals do not admit of superiority or inferiority, but likes admit it, for even the things most alike can be greater or less, but equals cannot."[12]

This distinction is of considerable importance for Milton's representation of Satan's crime. In asserting his equality with God, the archangel is, in effect, denying Jehovah's superiority and his own inferiority. Yet such would not have been the case had he merely affirmed his *likeness* to God. Logically, he could have asserted his similitude with God without denying that Jehovah was the greater and he himself the lesser of the two. Moreover, there is graver moral danger in seeking equality than likeness with the "most High." Not only is the desire for likeness to God compatible with the highest virtue; it is essential for true holiness, wisdom, truth, and liberty, inasmuch as the original dignity of man and angel alike lies in the divine image in which both have been created. Not until the desire for divine resemblance involves usurpation of God's prerogatives, aspiration toward divine power, honors, and majesty, does it become vicious. On the other hand, to seek equality with God (unless God himself confers it as a free gift, as in the case of Father and Son) is sacrilege and blasphemy. Milton gives clearer definition to Satan's criminal intent by following the less frequent reading ("equal") rather than its more conventional alternative.

To be sure, he draws on both interpretations of Isaiah. Satan attempts to imitate God (to "be like the most High") as well as to "equal" Him. Yet Milton's primary emphasis, throughout the poem, falls on Satan's desire for equality rather than on likeness. Equality is a principal end or final cause of his rebellion, and his intent to equal God is a "proegumenic cause"[13] of his disobedience. In persuading his companions to revolt, he attempts to justify his rebellion through the argument of equality.

Having introduced the motif of equality in the opening lines of *Paradise Lost*, Milton develops it in greater detail in his history of the angelic war. In the course of the narrative the term assumes several different meanings. Satan desires to equal God in regal power, in

11. John Milton, *Artis Logicae Plenior Institutio* (*Works* [Columbia Edition; New York, 1931–38], XI, 155). Milton is referring not only to "mathematical quantity"—i.e., magnitude and number, but also to "logical quantity."

12. *Ibid.*, p. 193.

13. Cf. *ibid.*, p. 35.

strength, in freedom, in reason, in glory. The most common meaning, however, is parity in might.

In predicting Satan's strategy, the Father summarizes the rebel's purpose as equality in royal dignity and military power rather than mere likeness. The archangel (V, 922 ff.)

> *... intends to erect his Throne*
> *Equal to ours throughout the spacious North*

and to "trie in battel, what our Power is, or our right." Subsequently, Milton informs us that Satan's ambition to "be like" God in regal state is really an attempt to equal Him. When the archangel calls his royal seat the "Mountain of the Congregation" in "imitation" of the mount where Messiah had been divinely proclaimed, he is actually "affecting all equality with God" (V, 760 ff.).

When Satan exploits the *argumentum paris* in urging his followers to revolt, he is on dangerous ground. The arguments he raises against the Son's monarchy can, with even greater plausibility, be turned against his own desires for regal dignity. In aspiring to "set himself in Glory above his Peers" (I, 39), he is violating equality by affecting superiority to his equals. To avoid arguments that would too obviously refute his own claims, he uses the term "equality" in an equivocal sense. Though the angels are "not equal all" in titles and degree, they are nevertheless "equally free" and hence not subject to Messiah's jurisdiction (V, 788 ff.). It is unjust that the Son, their equal, should reign over them:

> *Who can in reason then or right assume*
> *Monarchie over such as live by right*
> *His equals, if in power and splendor less,*
> *In freedom equal?*

Abdiel refutes this "argument of the equal"[14] by an *argumentum imparis*, the "argument from the greater." Satan is inferior to the Son, for the effect is necessarily inferior to the cause[15] and the creature to the Creator (V, 828 ff.):

> *But to grant it thee unjust,*
> *That equal over equals Monarch Reigne:*
> *Thy Selfe though great and glorious dost thou count,*
> *Or all Angelic Nature joined in one,*

14. Cf. *ibid.*, p. 157.

15. Cf. Aristotle, *Treatise on Rhetoric*, trans. Theodore Buckley (London, 1851), p. 47, "Again, if one be a principle and the other not; and for the same reason if one be a cause, the other not; since without a cause or principle, existence or production is impossible." See also Thomas Hobbes, *A Brief of the Art of Rhetorick* (*ibid.*, p. 283), "the Beginning is a *greater Good*, or *Evil*, than that which is not the Beginning; ... And the Cause, than not the Cause."

Equal to him begotten Son, by whom
As by his Word the mighty Father made
All things, ev'n thee . . .

Abdiel's argument derives from the commonplaces of cause and effect,[16] and to refute it Satan denies that the angels had been created and that God had been their efficient cause. Instead, they are "self-begot, self-rais'd By [their] own quick-ning power" (V, 857–58).

Both Waldock and Empson find this reasoning plausible. In the former's opinion, Satan "makes two not ineffective rejoinders" to Abdiel's account of the creation of the angels: "first, that the point is new; and second, that Abdiel's account of the creation of himself and other angels must necessarily be based on hearsay."[17] Empson argues that Satan's assertions are more or less sincere; not until "Uriel has convinced him that God created the world" does he "become convinced . . . that God created Satan too."[18] Yet there are recognizable fallacies in Satan's argument. Aside from the fact that both premise and conclusion are false (inasmuch as the angels *were* created by the Son), the archangel confuses cause and effect and ignores the etiological argument for God. It is not altogether true that Abdiel's account of the creation of the angels must necessarily be based on "hearsay." It can just as well be based on reason, as the analogy with Adam indicates. Satan's denial of his creation and Creator stands in striking contrast to Adam's affirmation of both. Correctly reasoning from effect to efficient cause, Adam realizes that his own existence argues the existence of a Creator (VIII, 270 ff.):

But who I was, or where, or from what cause,
Knew not; . . .
. . . how came I thus, how here?

16. For Milton, "the first of all arguments is *cause*" (*Works*, XI, 29). "The effect . . . argues causes and is in turn argued by them, but not on the same ground; for the effect proves that the cause is or has been . . .; but the cause demonstrates why the effect should be . . . The causes are prior and clearer; the effect as posterior, argues less weightily." (*Ibid.*, p. 71). Nevertheless, "sometimes the effects, not through themselves indeed, but as better known to us, more plainly argue the causes than they are argued by the causes." (*Ibid.*, p. 73.) In employing the argument "from the greater," Abdiel reasons from cause to effect: God created Satan, hence Satan must (*a fortiori*) be less than God. In replying, Satan reasons from the effect, denying Abdiel's conception of his efficient cause and substituting another. For Abdiel, God is the "principal" efficient cause of the angels. For Satan, the angels ("self-begot" and "self-rais'd") are themselves their own "principal" efficient cause, and nature and fate ("fatal course") are merely assisting causes. (See *ibid.*, p. 35.) If Satan's argument does indeed seem plausible to his hearers (as Waldock argues), the chief reason is that in this case the effect is "better known" to them than the cause and hence seems to argue "more plainly" and clearly.

17. A. J. A. Waldock, *Paradise Lost and its Critics* (Cambridge, 1947), p. 71.

18. William Empson, *Milton's God* (London, 1961), p. 62.

Not of my self; by some great Maker then,
In goodness and in power praeeminent; . . .

For Milton and many of his contemporaries such *a priori* reasoning would have seemed irreproachable. The poet was blissfully unaware of the weaknesses his descendants would find in the etiological argument; for him, as for most seventeenth-century thinkers, it still constituted valid proof not only of God's existence but also of his supreme goodness and power. As the *De Doctrina Christiana* put it, there could be "no doubt that every thing in the world, by the beauty of its order, and the evidence of a determinate and beneficial purpose which pervades it, testifies that some supreme efficient Power must have pre-existed, by which the whole was ordained for a specific end."[19]

Though Satan does not deny God's existence, he does deny that He is the "supreme efficient Power" and the Creator of Heaven and the angels. Though greatly superior to Adam in natural intelligence and in experience, the rebel archangel nevertheless fails to utilize the argument that the latter had been capable of making at the very dawn of consciousness. The contrast between them reflects discredit on Satan's argument and sincerity. If Adam (who has not yet beheld his Creator and whose reason is primarily "Discursive" rather than "Intuitive") can reason from his own existence and the beauty of the world to the fact of his creation by a supreme power, "some great Maker," surely Satan (who has looked on God and possesses the additional advantage of angelic intelligence) is capable of making the same inference both from his own existence and from the "beauty" and "order" of Heaven.[20] The fact that Adam—the inferior of the two in natural intellect—can draw this inference casts doubt on the interpretations advanced by Empson and Waldock. Unless one assumes that Satan's intelligence has become so corrupt that it cannot make the etiological argument, it is highly improbable that Satan really regards himself as "self-begot." Under the circumstances it seems far more likely that (like Abdiel and Adam) he realizes that he has been created by a "supreme efficient Power." Indeed, in the soliloquy on Mount Niphates he frankly acknowledges that God had created him (IV, 42 ff.):

. . . he deserv'd no such return
From me, whom he created what I was
In that bright eminence, and with his good
Upbraided none; . . .

19. Milton, *Works*, XIV, 27.

20. This "argument from the lesser" seems inescapable if one compares Satan and Adam in their reflections on creation and their use of the etiological argument.

There is little in this speech to support Empson's thesis that Satan has acquired an insight into his own creation only through Uriel's discourse. The probability is that, like Adam and Abdiel, he was perfectly aware that he had been created by a supreme "Maker." His claim to have been "self-begot" is essentially a rhetorical argument designed to strengthen his pretense to equality with God and to justify his revolt.

Nor is Waldock's summary of Satan's argument altogether accurate. The archangel does not argue that Abdiel's account of the angelic creation "must necessarily be based on hearsay." The gist of his argument, couched in the form of rhetorical questions, is an appeal to *experience*[21] (V, 856):

> *Doctrine which we would know whence learnt: who saw*
> *When this creation was? remember'st thou*
> *Thy making, while the Maker gave thee being?*

Once again, the contrast with Adam is illuminating. He too has had no experience or memory of this "making"; instead, he achieves his knowledge of his creation and his Creator through *a priori* reasoning. The essential defect in Satan's argument (which Waldock fails to recognize) is that it appeals to experience rather than reason as the authority for denying a Creator and creation.

Whether or not Abdiel's "point" is as "strange" and "new" as Satan (and Waldock after him) declares is not altogether clear. In Waldock's opinion, "the point *must* be new, or [Satan] could not in full assembly say it was." Abdiel is "exceptionally well informed, . . . just as . . . the rebel angels appear to have been kept in the dark about a number of other facts that good angels know."[22] Yet, in fact, there is no need to assume that the rebels "have been kept in the dark" about the fact of their creation nor that Abdiel has been "exceptionally well informed" on the point. Such *might* be the case if Abdiel's report of their creation really *were* "based on hearsay"—but it is much more likely that, like Adam, he has reached his conclusions by reasoning[23] from the fact of his existence to the role of "some great Maker" and efficient cause. Satan wrongly denies this inference, but since it *is* primarily an inference he can reject it "in full assembly" without arousing opposition from his followers.[24]

In denying his creation, Satan employs arguments that Milton had

21. Experience, strictly speaking, is an inartificial rather than an artificial argument. Cf. Milton's *Art of Logic* on experience as testimony (*Works*, XI, 291).

22. Waldock, p. 71.

23. Abdiel's reasoning would, of course, have been primarily "intuitive" whereas Adam's was largely "discursive."

24. As this is one of the cases where the effect is "better known" than the cause, Satan's argument might well seem more convincing to his audience than Abdiel's.

specifically rejected as false in the *De Doctrina*. Maintaining that the angels were "self-begot" and had been "self-rais'd"

> *... when fatal course*
> *Had circl'd his full Orbe, the birth mature*
> *Of this our native Heav'n,*

Satan is actually arguing from the topics of fate and nature. For Milton, such reasoning was self-contradictory, since it implied the existence of the very Creator it attempted to deny:

> There are some who pretend that nature or fate is the supreme (efficient) Power: but the very name of nature implies that it must owe its birth to some prior agent, or, to speak properly, signifies in itself nothing; but means either the essence of a thing, or that general law which is the origin of every thing, and under which every thing acts; on the other hand, fate can be nothing but a divine decree emanating from some almighty power.
>
> Further, those who attribute the creation of every thing to nature, must necessarily associate chance with nature as a joint divinity; so that they gain nothing by this theory, except that in the place of that one God, whom they cannot tolerate, they are obliged, however reluctantly, to substitute two sovereign rulers of affairs, who must almost always be in opposition to each other.[25]

In admitting the rule of fate ("fatal course") and nature ("*birth* mature Of... *native* Heav'n")[26] Satan commits the errors that Milton had specifically denounced in the *De Doctrina*. Finally, there is a further contradiction in the archangel's argument. If his "procreant causes"[27] are nature and fate, he can hardly be "self-begot" and "self-rais'd" by his "own power."

For most seventeenth-century thought at least, Satan's attack on the doctrine of creation would seem fallacious. Yet it serves its purpose. By denying that God was his Creator, he attempts to refute Abdiel's argument that God is therefore greater than he. By asserting that he had been "self-begot" by his own "power," he argues that his "puissance is [his] own" and that he can, accordingly, equal God in force (V, 861 ff.):

> *... our own right hand*
> *Shall teach us highest deeds, by proof to try*
> *Who is our equal: ...*

The rhetorical function of his views on creation is to strengthen his argument for his equality with God.

25. Milton, *Works*, XIV, 27.

26. Cf. Milton, *Works*, XI, 211–19, on conjugates. *Nature* and *native*, being "derived from the same root," are true conjugates, whereas *nature* and *birth* are "conjugates, in in the sense merely and not in sound."

27. Cf. *ibid.*, pp. 29, 489.

Satan's "confidence to equal God in power" (VI, 343) is shaken when his first wound and first experience of pain reveal that he is "not matchless," as he had believed. Nevertheless, he refuses to surrender the claim to equality; better weapons can make his forces equal or superior to their foe (VI, 438 ff.):

> *. . . perhaps more valid Armes,*
> *Weapons more violent, when next we meet,*
> *May serve to better us, and worse our foes,*
> *Or equal what between us made the odds,*
> *In Nature none: . . .*

The question of equality retains its central importance, but its terms have varied. In this instance the issue is not so much Satan's equality with God as the relative strength of the two opposing armies. The rebels have thus far fared the worse and seek to equalize the "too unequal work . . . Against unequal armes" (VI, 453–454) by employing new weapons—cannon and gunpowder.

Satan has subjected to the test of battle his claims to equality with the most High, and the outcome of the conflict demonstrates their falsity. In two days of fighting without success he never encounters the full might of his divine adversary. The combats between the two angelic armies—"Equal in their Creation" (VI, 690)—demonstrate their relative power, but neither prove nor disprove Satan's vaunt to equal God. The final proof that shatters this claim is the Son's single-handed victory over the rebel army (VI, 818 ff.):

> *That they may have thir wish to trie with mee*
> *In Battel which the stronger proves, they all,*
> *Or I alone against them, since by strength*
> *They measure all . . .*

Messiah's victory refutes Satan's claim by an *argumentum imparis*, since the outcome demonstrates the latter's inferiority. But it also serves as an "inartificial argument" to rebut the devil's fallacies. Both as an act of God and as "trial and proof" it dispels Satan's pretensions by divine testimony.[28]

After his fall Satan acknowledges his inequality with Jehovah in strength, but continues to assert his equality in other respects. Recognizing that God has "provd" the "stronger . . . with his Thunder"

28. See *ibid.*, pp. 279–93; cf. Sister Miriam Joseph, *Shakespeare's Use of the Arts of Language* (New York, 1947), pp. 309–11.

(I, 92 ff.), he confesses that God is "mightiest," and his "Compeer" Beelzebub agrees on the same grounds:

> ... *whom I now*
> *Of force believe Almighty, since no less*[29]
> *Than such could have orepow'rd such force as ours ...*

Both have been convinced of their inequality with God in power through an *argumentum imparis.*

Nevertheless, Satan still exaggerates his strength. In hailing his troops as "Powers Matchless, but with th' Almighty" (I, 622–23), he confesses their inferiority to Jehovah in power, but ignores their parity with the faithful angels. (As God has temporarily "suspended" the "doom" of the rebel angels, the two forces had been almost evenly matched.) Moreover, even in acknowledging his own inferiority to God in strength, Satan insists on his equality in reason (I, 248–49):

> *Whom reason hath equald, force hath made surpream*
> *Above his equals.*

Even though "Thunder hath made [Jehovah] greater," Satan is still "all but less[30] then hee" (I, 257–58), and the illusion of equality still lingers in the divine worship his followers accord him (II, 478–79):

> ... *and as a God*
> *Extoll him equal to the highest in Heav'n: ...*

Despite his demonstrated inferiority to God, the terms of his Luciferian boast still echo after his fall. They will subsequently recur in *Paradise Regain'd* (I, 145–46), where Satan summons his potentates for counsel and assistance,

> ... *lest I who erst*
> *Thought none my equal, now be over-match't*

III

Like many another motif in *Paradise Lost,* the theme of equality with God is developed by variation and counterpoint. Satan's example emerges all the more clearly and forcefully through comparison or contrast with other characters in the poem—Moloch, Messiah, and

29. Cf. Milton, *Works,* XI, 159, on "negations of unequals," such as "*not more, not less.*"

30. This too is a "negation of unequals," but not a direct assertion of equality. Cf. *ibid.,* p. 161, "the negation of the greater or the less separately is never the sign of equals ..."

Adam and Eve. Moloch has shared Satan's vain confidence to equal the Almighty (II, 46–48):

> *His trust was with th' Eternal to be deem'd*
> *Equal in strength, and rather than be less*
> *Car'd not to be at all; . . .*

Nevertheless, despite his recognition that God is superior in might, he argues—irrationally—that the fallen angels can counter Jehovah's thunderbolts with hellfire (II, 64 ff.):

> *. . . when to meet the noise*
> *Of his Almighty Engin he shall hear*
> *Infernal Thunder, and for Lightning see*
> *Black fire and horror shot with* equal rage
> *Among his Angels; . . .*

In contrast to Satan and Moloch, the Son of God renounces his parity with the Father in order to assume a lower nature. "Thron'd in highest bliss Equal to God, and equally enjoying God-like fruition" (III, 305 ff.), he quits all "to save a World from utter loss." His humility is the contrary of Satan's pride, and the exaltation he ultimately receives as recompense is the contrary of Satan's final humiliation. In emphasizing this contrast, Milton expresses the same opposition that Herveus had stressed in his commentary on Isaiah xiv. 14.—the antithesis between Christ's renunciation of divine equality and Satan's ambition to be like God.[31] Like Herveus, Milton utilizes Christ and Satan as contrary examples in arguments drawn from *paria* and *similia*, "equals" and "likes."

The arguments of equality and likeness also assume central importance in the temptation of man. When Satan first learns of the injunction concerning the forbidden fruit and conceives his design to "excite [the] minds [of Adam and Eve] With more desire to know," he intends to employ the argument that "knowledge might exalt [them] Equal with Gods" (IV, 522 ff.). This is, on the whole, the same *argumentum paris* that he had utilized to justify his own revolt and persuade his companions. The parallel with his own crime is obvious, and Biblical

31. *P.L.*, Vol. 181, cols. 165–66: "Nam ille (Christus) ait: 'Discite a me, quia mitis sum, et humilis corde (*Matth.* xi)', et iste (Satanas) 'est rex super omnes filios superbiae (*Job* xli 25)'. Ille, 'cum in forma Dei esset, non rapinam arbitratus est esse se aequalem Deo (*Philip*, ii, 6)', iste per rapinam usurpare similitudinem Dei, quam naturaliter non habuit cupiens: 'Similis, inquit, ero Altissimo.' Sicut ille est caput omnium justorum, et omnes justi membra ejus, sic et iste caput est omnium iniquorum, et omnes iniqui membra hujus. Sicut ille super omnia est Altissimus, sic et iste infra omnia dejectissimus, et omnibus modis omnino contrarii sunt Satanas et Altissimus."

commentators had called attention to it. As Calvin observed, in discussing Isaiah xiv. 14, "the ungodly . . . fight against [God] when they exalt themselves more than they ought; hereby attributing that to themselves which is proper unto him: which is as much in effect, as if they meant to pluck him out of his seate. And what did satan else when he deceived the first man? You (saith he) shall be as gods. Gen, 3.5."[32] Biblical exegesis had emphasized the parallel between Lucifer's boast in Isaiah and Satan's argument in Genesis, and Milton in his turn also develops the analogy.

Strictly speaking, the Biblical text describing Eve's temptation (Gen. iii. 5) employs the "sign" or *nota* of "likes" rather than of "equals."[33] The serpent promises Eve not that she and her husband will be "equal" to gods, but that "ye shall be *as* gods." In the Tremellius-Junius Bible this appears as "vos fore sicut Deos," and in Piscator's version as "eritis sicut dij." In the *Art of Logic* Milton lists the adverb *sicuti* among "the proper signs of similars"[34] or "likes."

Nevertheless, even though the Biblical text employs the sign or *nota* of likeness, Piscator's commentary interprets the passage as a promise of equality. By eating the forbidden fruit Adam and Eve will become "equal to God in happiness." "Deo evaderetis aequales in felicitate." The text "Et eritis sicut dii" really means "eritis aequales tribus illis personis sanctae Trinitatis," and verse 22 suggests that Eve must have employed the same argument in persuading Adam to partake of the fruit: "ita fierent dii, seu aequales diis: hoc est, personis illis divinis sanctae Trinitatis."[35] Thus, for Piscator as for Milton, Satan's temptation of man, like Lucifer's original crime in Heaven, involved the aspiration to "equal the most High."

In his account of Eve's temptation, Milton retains the *nota* of likeness instead of substituting that of equality. Echoing the Biblical promise ("Ye shall be as Gods"), Satan offers divinity, but does not explicitly declare that man will become equal to Jehovah. However great Eve's desire for "God-head," the *argumentum paris* appears primarily in her attitude towards her husband. She hopes that the "odds of Knowledge" will "render [her] more equal, and perhaps . . . somtime superior" to Adam (IX, 820 ff.). In tempting Eve, Satan actually employs the *argumentum imparis* rather than the *argumentum paris*. He urges her to seek divinity on the ground that no creature in the visible universe equals her in beauty (IX, 608–9):

32. John Calvin, *A Commentary upon the Prophecie of Isaiah*, trans. C. C[otton] (London, 1609), p. 157.

33. See Milton, *Works*, XI, 157, 195.

34. *Ibid.*, p. 195.

35. Piscator, pp. 22–25.

. . . no Fair to thine
Equivalent or second . . .

In Eve's case, as in Satan's, there is a significant distinction between likeness and equality. She is Adam's "likeness" (VIII, 450), but not his equal (IV, 295–96), and her inferiority provides one of the topics for Adam's indictment after the fall. Employing the "argument from the unequal," God argues that Adam should not have disobeyed a divine injunction and his own judgment in order to obey Eve; in heeding his inferior, he has neglected his superior (X, 146 ff.)[36]:

. . . was shee made thy guide,
Superior, or but equal, that to her
Thou did'st resigne thy Manhood . . . ?

IV

The *argumentum paris* owes its prominence in *Paradise Lost* partly to Milton's recognition of the rhetorical possibilities inherent in the Tremellius-Junius version of Isaiah xiv. 14.[37] As this emphasizes equality rather than likeness, Milton's account of Satan's revolt tends to stress the "argument of the equal" and its contrary rather than arguments derived from similitude or dissimilitude.[38] His description of man's first disobedience, on the other hand, tends to combine the two types of comparison. Although Eve aspires to "Godhead," she does not (unlike Lucifer) explicitly state her intent to "equal" Jehovah. Though she clearly hopes to equal or surpass her husband, she does not express a desire to "equal the most High."

Like Calvin and numerous theologians before him, Milton emphasizes the parallels between Lucifer's boast to "be like the most High" and Satan's promise to Eve to "be as gods," between Lucifer's fall and the fall of man. Though he heightens the analogy through a

36. Both God and Raphael utilize the *argumentum imparis* in bringing home to Adam his inequality with God, on the one hand, and with Eve, on the other. Cf. VIII, 406 ff.

37. Besides explicit allusions to Lucifer's claim to equality with the "most High," there are further echoes of Isaiah xiv. 14 in *Paradise Lost.* Satan himself admits (IX, 163 ff.) that he had "contended with Gods to sit the highest" and "to the hight of Deitie aspir'd . . ." The Father asserts that Lucifer had "trusted to have seis'd" His throne, "This inaccessible high strength, the seat of Deitie supream" (VII, 140 ff.). Abdiel accuses Satan (VI, 131 ff.) of hoping "to have reacht The highth of thy aspiring unoppos'd, The Throne of God unguarded . . ."

38. The argument from similitude or dissimilitude nevertheless plays an important role in Milton's treatment of Satan and other characters in the epic.

variety of devices, one of his favorite methods is to apply the arguments of equality and likeness to both cases, to adapt Lucifer's vaunt to man and devil alike. Having vainly aspired to equal God in strength and majesty, Satan sets out to tempt mankind to equal God in knowledge. The *argumentum paris* underlies both transgressions.[39]

39. See the following studies for other aspects of Milton's logic and rhetoric: Donald Leman Clark, *John Milton at St. Paul's School* (New York, 1948); *idem*, *Rhetoric and Poetry in the Renaissance* (New York, 1922), John S. Diekhoff, *Milton's "Paradise Lost": A Commentary on the Argument* (New York, 1946); Wilbur E. Gilman, *Milton's Rhetoric: Studies in his Defense of Liberty*, *University of Missouri Studies*, XIV (1939), 1–193; Leon Howard, "The Invention of Milton's Great Argument: A Study of the Logic of God's Ways to Men," *Huntington Library Quarterly*, IX (1946), 149–73; Wilbur Samuel Howell, *Logic and Rhetoric in England, 1300–1700* (Princeton, N.J., 1956).

Part IV

❦

The Heroic Idol

❦

12. *"Men of Renown"*

Heroic Virtue and the Biblical Giants

❦ Milton's heroic idol—the specious heroism of Satan and his peers—is many-faceted. It reflects an infinite variety of lights, Biblical and secular, literary and historical. Sometimes it distorts them—magnifying or diminishing the patterns it reflects, reducing the grandiose to burlesque and the heroic to parody. Though Milton's Hell is scarcely Looking-Glass Land, it is nevertheless an image in an enchanted glass.

As the classical elements in this portrait are the most obvious, they have, not unnaturally, attracted the majority of commentators. Epic conventions—the themes of warfare, conquest, and revenge; the catalogue of heroes; councils, heroic songs, and games; the conception and execution of an enterprise; the resort to force or fraud—place the fallen angels squarely in the epic tradition. Preserving "epic decorum," these details link Milton's rebels with heroic prototypes in Homer and Hesiod, Statius and Virgil. Direct allusions to classical epic heighten the parallel. Satan is "as huge" in bulk as the Titans and giants who "warr'd on *Jove*." His legions, who march like "Heroes old" to Dorian

First published, in somewhat different form, in (a) *Philological Quarterly*, XL (1961), 580–86; (b) *Modern Language Notes*, LXXV (1960), 551–53; (c) *Journal of English and Germanic Philology*, LX (1961), 786–95; (d) *Milton Studies in Honor of Harris Francis Fletcher* (Urbana, 1961), pp. 178–87.

music, exceed in "force" both the "Giant brood of *Phlegra*" and the "Heroic Race . . . That fought at *Thebes* and *Ilium*." In their "*Typhoean* rage" they "Rend up both Rocks and Hills," as Hercules had uprooted "*Thessalian* Pines." Satan's journey through Chaos is more hazardous than the Argonauts' voyage or Ulysses' passage through the Straits of Messina.

The poet reinforces these explicit analogues with classical heroes through implicit parallels with Greek or Latin epic. Satan resembles Ulysses in his wiles, his disguises, his skill at tuning his speech to a particular audience or adapting his tactics to the demands of the situation. Like the Ithacan king and the Trojan wanderer, he assumes the role of the "faithful Leader" and endeavors (or pretends to endeavor) to save his companions. The tears he sheds at their plight, the rousing addresses he utters to encourage them, the efforts he makes to suppress his misgivings and conceal his despair recall Aeneas' behavior after the shipwreck off the Libyan coast. In fierceness, implacability, and lust for revenge he resembles Achilles and Turnus.[1] In his pride and contempt of deity he shows affinities with Capaneus and Mezentius.

Beëlzebub, in turn, fills the role of epic confidant, like Patroclus and faithful Achates. The architect of Pandaemonium falls from Heaven like his mythical antitype, the classical Mulciber. In mellifluous oratory, Belial resembles Nestor. Like the Homeric heroes, the rebellious angels are skilled "in Counsel, or in Fight." Like the giants in Hesiod's *Theogony*, they hurl mountains in battle. Such devices as the well-established bee-simile, suggesting the multitude of fallen spirits, provide further links with the epics of Homer and Virgil.

Nevertheless, the heroic *eidolon* is not exclusively classical in character. The heroic tradition had never been limited strictly to epic and myth, and Milton expands his allusions to Thebes and Ilium to comprehend the romantic tradition and the heroes associated with Arthur and Charlemagne. By a historical reference to the Germanic migrations, he likens the infernal legions to the "barbarous Sons" of the "populous North," who had laid waste the provinces of the Roman empire. Like these conquerors of a later heroic age, the fallen angels represent the forces of discord and confusion. They too are destined to overthrow peace and established order by destructive might and "infinite

1. For discussion of revenge as a heroic motif, see Torquato Tasso, *Discorsi del poema eroico* (*Prose*, ed. Francesco Flora [Milan and Rome, 1935]), III, 432–35: "L'obbligo de la vendetta ne l'uno e l'altro [Achille ed Enea] era eguale: obbligo non picciolo, se la vendetta è giusta ed onorevole fra i principi e i cavalieri, come estima il Bernardo ed il Possevino." The "terrible words" that Aeneas addresses to Turnus as he slays him are justified by "quella religione de' gentili" into which Virgil had been born. "Questa fu dunque la vendetta, lecita al cavaliero gentile (il quale non può esser riputato crudele da' gentili, o in comparazione de gli altri). . . ."

Manslaughter." Proleptically, they are spiritual Vandals, who will devastate the newly-created world.

In *Samson Agonistes* the heroic idol includes the "gorgeous arms" and "embattled Armies" of the Philistine host. In *Paradise Regain'd* it embraces the conquests of Alexander, Scipio, and Caesar. Similarly, in *The History of Britain* Milton reproaches his countrymen for lacking the wisdom that ought to complement valor and insure the fruits of victory. His heroic *eidolon*—his "grand illusion"—encompasses the whole tradition of worldly might—ancient and modern, legendary and historical.

Though the ideal itself is secular—one of the "vain imaginations" of a corrupted world—its ultimate source, for Milton, was Biblical. Foreshadowed in the scattered texts describing Lucifer's revolt and fall, it entered human history with the heroic age, the exploits of the giant "men of renown."

Adam's vision of the giants born from the union of the "sons of God" and the "daughters of men" provides a point of departure for Michael to condemn both a conventional, but vicious conception of "Valour and Heroic Vertu" and a false opinion of fame. Though this episode is based on Genesis 6:4 ("There were giants in the earth in those days; . . . mighty men which were of old, men of renown"), the extent of Milton's indebtedness to this text—both for the characterization of the giants and the terminology of his critique of heroic virtue—has been underestimated. Thus, after quoting lines 685–93 as evidence of the poet's "fuller feelings about the old ideal of military prowess," Sir Maurice Bowra concludes that there is little "justification in *Genesis* for this view of the Giants, and Milton's outburst shows that he felt a need to say what he really thought of the old heroic ideal."[2]

In actuality, the poet's remarks on the giants owe much to conventional interpretations of Genesis 6:4. His statement that "in those dayes Might onely shall be admir'd, And Valour and Heroic Vertu call'd" had been foreshadowed in Castellion's Latin translation of the Scriptures. Whereas the Vulgate described the giants as *potentes* and the Authorized Version called them *mighty men*, Castellion preferred the title of *Heroes*: "Erant ea tempestate in terris Gigantes. Accedebant eò ex illis potentum connubijs nati Heroes, homines ab omni memoria celebres."[3] Here the concepts of might and heroic virtue are practically interchangeable. Calvin's *Commentaries on Genesis* likewise referred to the giants as heroes, but emphasized the vicious character of their exploits: "Interea tamen sub *magnifico* heroum *titulo* crudeliter dominati sunt, et ex fratrum iniuriis ac oppressione sibi acquiesierunt potentiam

2. C. M. Bowra, *From Virgil to Milton* (London, 1945), pp. 197–98.
3. *Biblia Sacra ex Sebastiani Castalionis Postrema Recognitione* (Basileae, 1573), col. 9.

ac nomen."[4] Milton did not have to look far for his Might-Heroism equation nor for the "magnific titles" in which his "Giant Angels" delight.

In characterizing the giants in terms of "violence . . . and Oppression, and Sword-Law," Milton was following several conventional interpretations of this text. In addition to the usual translation as *giants*, the word *Nephilim* had also been rendered as οἱ ἐπιπίπτοντες (*assailants*) and οἱ βιαῖοι (*the violent*).[5] The Midrash described them as "the greatest of all masters of the arts of war."[6] A gloss in the Geneva Bible referred to them as *tyrants*.[7] Magius explained the term "giants" as a reference to their warlike disposition: ". . . & per Gigantes ibi, non procerae monstruosaeque magnitudinis homines, sed potius bellicosos praepotentesque significare nobis voluisse . . . reverendus auctor, videtur."[8] Calvin interpreted their name etymologically in terms of violence and devastation.[9] The giants were robbers and tyrants who devastated the world as storms lay waste the countryside. Milton likewise represents the giants as *latrones*, who ravage the countryside and carry off spoils and "Bootie."

The Junius–Tremellius Bible, in turn, explained the word "giants" as a metaphorical epithet, emphasizing their impiety and apostasy: "Gigantes . . . id est, impii defectores, & audacissimi ac sceleratissimi apostatae Deum protervè oppugnantes Gigantum more."[10] The *Gibborim* ("mighty men") also possessed characteristic features of Milton's giants. The Midrash stressed their massive bone structure,

4. *Corpus Reformatorum*, LI, ed. G. Baum, E. Cunitz, and E. Reuss (Brunsvigae, 1882), col. 116. See Arnold Williams, "Renaissance Commentaries on *Genesis* and Some Elements of the Theology of *Paradise Lost*," *PMLA*, LVI (1941), 151–64; *idem*, "Milton and the Renaissance Commentaries on *Genesis*," *MP*, XXXVII (1940), 263–78. Italics mine.

5. Herbert E. Ryle, *The Book of Genesis* (Cambridge, 1914), p. 95n.; Fridericus Field (ed.), *Origenis Hexaplorum Quae Supersunt*, I (Oxonii, 1875), 22; cf. *P.L.*, XXIII, col. 949; XXIV, col. 658; XCIII, col. 293; CLXVII, cols. 339–40.

6. *Midrash Rabbah*, trans. H. Freedman and Maurice Simon (London, 1939), I, 217; this conception of the Zamzumin (one of "seven names" for the Biblical giants) appears in the commentary on Genesis 6:4.

7. *The Bible* (London, 1594). Cf. G. W. Whiting, "Before the Flood: *Paradise Lost* and the Geneva Bible," *N & Q*, 19 Feb. 1949.

8. *Hieronymus Magius de Gigantibus* (Rotterodami, 1697), p. 462.

9. *Op. cit.*, col. 115: "*Gigantes fuerunt super terram.* Inter plurimas corruptionum species quibus referta erat terra, unam peculiariter hoc loco Moses commemorat: quod violenter et tyrannice grassati sunt gigantes. Caeterum non arbitror de cunctis illius saeculi hominibus haberi sermonem, sed de certis quibusdam, qui aliis valentiores quum essent, robore et potentia sua freti, sine lege et modo se extulerunt. . . . Verior mihi videtur eorum sententia, qui similitudinem esse dicunt sumptam a labe vel impetuosa procella: nempe quod sicut tempestas et labes violenter cadens agros vastat et perdit: ita suis irruptionibus latrones isti perniciem et vastationem mundo intulerint."

10. *Biblia Sacra . . . Scholiis Illustrati ab Immanuele Tremellio & Francisco Junio* (Genevae, 1630), p. 9. For Milton's reliance on this translation in his *De Doctrina Christiana*, see Maurice Kelley, *This Great Argument* (Princeton, 1941), pp. 42, 70.

observing that "The marrow of each one's thigh bone was eighteen cubits long."[11] Milton describes them similarly, as "Giants of mightie Bone, and bould emprise."

Calvin excoriated their tyranny, pride in their own strength, and contempt of God[12] and man. Like Milton he recognized in these "men of renown" an unworthy conception of fame. Like Milton, he regarded as vicious the exploits for which they had won glory on earth, and condemned as vain the titles they had achieved through ambition and oppression.[13]

For Milton, as for Calvin, these pretensions to fame through conquest are merely "inanes titulorum fumos." The men of renown possess no valid claim to their "high titles." Though "styl'd great Conquerours, Patrons of Mankind, Gods, and Sons of Gods," they are "Destroyers rightlier call'd and Plagues of men." Appropriately, the giants are first to enter "The Lymbo of Vanity" of those "who in vain things Built their fond hopes of Glorie or lasting fame":

> *First from the ancient World those Giants came*
> *With many a vain exploit, though then renownd. . . .*

Like the "men of renown," Milton's "Grand Thief" is an "honorificus latro" who "glories in his crimes" and "vaunts his vain titles."

Milton had Biblical authority for regarding the giants as the world's first heroes. These "mighty men" are the prototypes of a heroism that he consistently delineates as vicious—a pattern embodied in the "Giant Angels"[14] of *Paradise Lost*, the brutish conquerors of *Paradise Regain'd*, and the giant Harapha in *Samson Agonistes*. In all three instances, might is the norm of heroic virtue, and military prowess the basis of the hero's fame. In all three instances, this spurious heroism is grounded in evil—in impiety and violence. In all three instances, it results from the corruption of man's nature once "Sin With vanity had filled the works of men." In all three instances, it contrasts with the patience of the just man who endures violence or reproach in his witness to the Truth.

In *Paradise Lost* its influence appears chiefly in Milton's critique of heroic virtue and fame. Here the word "might" patently recalls the

11. *Midrash Rabbah*, I, 217. Ambrosius Calepinus, *Dictionarium undecim linguarum* (Basileae, 1598), *s.v. Heros*, regards *gibbor* as the Hebrew equivalent of *hero*.

12. *Op. cit.*, col. 116.

13. *Ibid.*, col. 116: "Addit Moses, *fuisse viros nominis*, quo significat, gloriatos esse in suis sceleribus, et fuisse honorificos latrones, ut loquuntur. Nec vero dubium est quin aliquid habuerint vulgo excellentius, quod illis conciliaret gratiam in mundo et gloriam. . . . Sed quum semper vitiosa sit ambitio, tum vero ubi accedit tyrannica ferocia, ut potentior minoribus insultet, malum est non tolerabile: multo autem indignius, dum sibi ex sceleribus dignitatem comparant improbi, et quo quisque audacior est ad nocendum, eo insolentius inanes titulorum fumos iactat."

14. See R. H. West, "Milton's 'Giant Angels,'" *MLN*, LXVII (1952), 23.

Biblical phrase "mighty men," and his allusions to "men of high renown" and "renown on Earth" echo the scriptural reference to "men of renown." Indirectly, the basic ideas in this text are reflected in the characterization of the rebel angels. Milton stresses their "imbodied force," their "prowess," their resemblance to "Hero's old Arming to Battel," and (as in his own description of the giants in Book XI) their skill in fight and council. Like the giants, they seek fame by deeds that merit infamy, and Raphael characterizes them in words reminiscent of the Nephilim ("In might . . . wondrous and Acts of Warr, Nor of Renown less eager"). The same Might-Heroism equation underlies Satan's characterization as one who "hard'ning in his strength Glories." In *Paradise Regain'd* the same concepts reappear in Christ's condemnation of the fame achieved by conquest as a "false glory, attributed To things not glorious, men not worthy of fame."

In *Samson Agonistes* the giants again emerge as a norm (though an inferior one) of heroic virtue. Samson's early exploits are acts heroic "beyond The Sons of *Anak*." As Milton probably realized, there is a verbal link between the giants of Genesis 6:4 and the "giants, the sons of Anak," in Numbers 13:33. In the Hebrew text both are called Nephilim—the only instance of this word in the Scriptures.[15] As the Nephilim of Genesis had been traditionally renowned for their military prowess, it was logical for Milton to attribute warlike exploits likewise to "the Nephilim, the sons of Anak."[16]

Again, a possible echo of the Biblical conception of the giants as "men of renown" occurs in Harapha's description of his own lineage as a "stock renown'd/As *Og* or *Anak* and the *Emims* old."

This boast about his noble ancestry is not unfounded, even though it does embody a false criterion of nobility. According to Calvin, the giant "men of renown" were the world's first noblemen—a nobility that exalted itself through contempt and dishonor of others.[17] Unlike the low-born Braggadocchio—the braggart buffoon to whom critics have compared him—Harapha may justly claim descent from a "stock renown'd." The abuse he heaps on Samson is quite consistent with the character of the giants as Calvin had described it—a nobility elevated "ex aliorum despectu et contumelia." Since Harapha belongs to an heroic race, it is hardly surprising that he appeals to heroic tradition in extolling the "glorious arms Which greatest Heroes have in battle worn."

15. John Skinner, *A Critical and Exegetical Commentary on Genesis* (2nd ed.; Edinburgh, 1930), p. 146.

16. Ryle, 95n.

17. *Op. cit.*, col. 116: "Atque haec prima fuit mundi nobilitas: ne quis longa et fumosa imaginum serie nimium sibi placeat: ea, inquam, nobilitas, quae nonnisi ex aliorum despectu et contumelia in sublime se attollit." Milton would not, however, have regarded this "prima mundi nobilitas" as direct ancestors of Harapha, inasmuch as the descendants of the original giants would have perished in the flood.

Finally, the words of the Chorus at the end of this episode strongly suggest that Milton may have modeled Harapha's character on that of the antediluvian giants:

> . . . *the mighty of the Earth, th' oppressor,*
> *The brute and boist'rous force of violent men*
> *Hardy and industrious to support*
> *Tyrannic power, but raging to pursue*
> *The righteous and all such as honour Truth. . . .*

It is as one of "the mighty of the Earth"—a figure of "brute and boist'rous force" like the ancient Nephilim—that Milton conceived the giant of Gath.[18]

III

Milton's reference to Satan and his forces as "the Giant Angels" has usually been interpreted in terms of classical mythology or Renaissance demonology. The passage seemed to involve either a "comparison . . . between the rebellious Angels and the Giants of classical mythology who sought to expel Zeus and the gods from Olympus,"[19] or an exegetical tradition that interpreted two Old Testament words for giants (*anakim* and *rephaim*) "as designating devils also."[20] Besides these influences, however, other factors may also have contributed to Milton's phrase. In the first place, Johannes Drusius had already employed a similar expression in his commentary on the *Historia Sacra* of Sulpicius Severus: "Sunt etiam qui hos *gigantes angelos* fuisse putant, in queis Jonathan Uzielides . . ., Cave sequaris."[21] Secondly, a conventional etymology of the word Nephilim (Genesis 6:4) from a root meaning *falling* or *assailing* made the comparison of the defeated angels to giants particularly appropriate. Thus Jerome, commenting on this text ("Gigantes autem erant super terram in diebus illis"), explained *Annaphilim* in terms of falling and violence.[22] The *Midrash Rabbah* also

18. In *A Milton Handbook* (4th ed.; New York, 1947), pp. 285–88, James H. Hanford regards Harapha as a symbol of "physical force" and "brute menace."

19. A. W. Verity (ed.), *Paradise Lost* (Cambridge, 1936), II, 548.

20. West, "Milton's 'Giant Angels,'" p. 23, cites examples in Cornelius Agrippa and Pierre Le Loyer.

21. *J. Drusii ad Historiam Sacram Sulpicii Severi Commentarius Liber sive Notae* (Franekerae, 1607), 27. Italics mine. Cf. Sulpicius Severus, *Historia Sacra* (*P.L.*, XX, col. 97): "ex quorum coitu Gigantes editi esse dicuntur, cum diversae inter se naturae permixtio monstra gigneret." Drusius himself rejected the suggestion that the giants of Genesis 6:4 were angels, and in both of his epics Milton gave contradictory interpretations of the "sons of God" mentioned in this text. The Palestine Targum (commonly known as the Targum of Jonathan Ben Uzziel) identified the "sons of the great" as fallen angels, but did not actually equate the giants of Genesis 6:4 with angels.

22. *Liber Hebraicarum Quaestionum in Genesim* (*P.L.*, XXIII), col. 997. Cf. Bede (*P.L.*, XCIII, col. 293) and Rupertus Tuitiensis (*P.L.*, CLXVII, cols. 339–40). "In Hebraeo ita habet: *Cadentes erant in terra in diebus illis*, id est ANNAPHILIM (הנפלים). . . . Pro cadentibus, sive gigantibus, *violentos*, interpretatus est Symmachus. Et angelis autem et sanctorum liberis convenit nomen cadentium."

derived the Hebrew word for giants from a root signifying *falling*: "Nefilim denotes that they hurled (*hippilu*) the world down, themselves fell (*naflu*) from the world, and filled the world with abortions (*nefilim*) through their immorality."[23] Drusius, on the other hand, rejected Jerome's suggestion that Nephilim meant *cadentes* and derived it instead from *irruendo* (assailing).[24] Calvin traced the word Nephilim to a Hebrew verb meaning *to fall*, but observed that grammarians disagreed as to its meaning:

> Some think they were so called because they stood out [*excidessent*, literally "fell out"] from the common stature. Others explain that the vulgar crowd of men lost courage [*caderet*, literally "fell"] at their sight, because of their vast bulk of body; or that all people prostrated themselves in terror of their size. In my opinion, however, the truer explanation is that the simile was taken from ruin or impetuous storm. For just as tempest and ruin falling violently devastate and destroy the fields, so those robbers by their irruptions brought destruction and devastation to the world.[25]

These explanations of Nephilim[26] in terms of violence and attack, hurling and falling, made the epithet "Giant" particularly suitable for the rebel angels, whom Milton had described as attacking with "devilish Enginry" (VI, 553), hurling hills "with jaculation dire" (VI, 665), and falling from Heaven (VI, 871). Moreover, the term had become closely associated with Satan's fallen legions. Ryle observes that "among Patristic commentators, the word [Nephilim] was connected with 'the fallen angels,'"[27] and Friedlander has noted a similar interpretation in rabbinical tradition: "These 'fallen angels' were called Nephilim (the fallen ones). 'Giants' is the usual rendering of this term."[28] In this dual interpretation of Nephilim to mean both *giants* and *fallen angels* Milton could have found a suggestion for his phrase "the Giant Angels."

23. *Midrash Rabbah*, I, 218.

24. Drusius, 27. Drusius overlooked the fact that Jerome had translated this word as *irruentes* in his commentary on Isaiah 66:7 (*P.L.*, XXIV, col. 658): "Geneseos quoque narrat liber (*Cap.* vi), quod postquam coeperunt homines multi fieri, . . . et filiae eis natae sunt, acceperunt eas, non Angeli, sed filii Dei, de quibus orti sunt gigantes: sive ut in Hebraeo scriptum est ἐπιπίπτοντες, id est, *irruentes*." Cf. Field, *Origenis Hexaplorum*, I, 22: "Gigantes vocantur hic a Mose Nephilim, ut alij existimant, ab cadendo; ut ego, ab irruendo. Naphal enim & irruere significat, ut apud Davidem, *irruit validis suis in turbam attritorum*. Etymo huic firmando est interpretamentum Aquila Pontici, ἐπιπίπτοντες, irruentes, quod male Hier. exponit, cadentes."

25. Calvin, *Commentarius in Genesim*, LI, col. 115. See footnote 9.

26. For discussion of this word, see A. Dillmann, *Genesis Critically and Exegetically Expounded*, trans. Wm. B. Stevenson (Edinburgh, 1897), I, 240–43; S. R. Driver, *The Book of Genesis* (4th ed.; London, 1905), p. 84; Skinner, *Commentary on Genesis*, pp. 139–47.

27. Ryle, *The Book of Genesis*, p. 96n.

28. Gerald Friedlander (trans.), *Pirkê de Rabbi Eliezer* (London, 1916), p. 160n.

The fact that Eusebius regarded this text as the origin of the classical legends of the Titans and giants[29] would have made the comparison all the more appropriate—an instance of Biblical, as well as literary, decorum.

In Hobbes's *Leviathan*, finally, Milton could have encountered still another tradition concerning the Biblical giants. Hobbes not only equated them with the ancient heroes, but also specifically associated them with Hell: "The place after judgment of those who were never in the kingdom of God, or having been in, are cast out" is designated in Scripture as "the congregation of giants."[30]

IV

Like the fallen angels, the "Giant *Harapha* of *Gath*" bears a significant resemblance to the antediluvian giants. But for the unfortunate detail—the fact that they had all perished in combat or by drowning—he could have boasted a lineage not merely "dating from the Flood" but indeed *pre*dating it. Ethically he has much in common with the giants of Genesis, as Biblical exegesis had interpreted them.

Other aspects of his character are less venerable, and for these one need not search beyond the Flood for a prototype. A more nearly contemporary ancestor stands conveniently close at hand, and this (paradoxically) is his own son. In this case, at least, Wordsworth's dictum is plausible: "The child *is* father of the man."

Like most pedigrees, his literary parentage has proved a controversial subject for genealogists. In Parker's opinion, "Harapha had some Euripidean blood in his veins,"[31] "the introduction of an insolent giant, the frank depiction of a noisy quarrel; the tendency to mix laconic insult with formal debate—these are all things which we expect from Euripides."[32] Gilbert, on the other hand, suggested a derivation from romances of chivalry. "Harapha," he maintained,

29. J. Chaine, *Le livre de la genèse* (Paris, 1949), p. 105; *P.G.*, XXI, cols. 323–26; cf. Philo Judaeus, "On the Giants," in *Philo*, trans. F. H. Colson and G. H. Whitaker (Loeb, London, 1929), II, 475; Hermann Gunkel (ed.), *Genesis, Handkommentar zum alten Testament* (Göttingen, 1902), pp. 51–52.

30. Thomas Hobbes, *Leviathan*, ed. Michael Oakeshott (New York, 1962), pp. 330–31: "Again, because those mighty men of the earth, that lived in the time of Noah, before the flood (which the Greeks call *heroes*, and the Scripture *giants*, and both say were begotten by copulation of the children of God with the children of men), were for their wicked life destroyed by the general deluge; the place of the damned, is therefore also marked out, by the company of those deceased giants; as *Proverbs* xxi. 16, *The man that wandereth out of the way of understanding, shall remain in the congregation of the giants*; and *Job* xxvi. 5, *Behold the giants groan under water, and they that dwell with them. . . .* And Isaiah xiv. 9, *Hell is troubled how to meet thee . . . and will displace the giants for thee. . . .*"

31. William R. Parker, "Milton's Harapha," *TLS*, 2 January 1937, p. 12.

32. William R. Parker, *Milton's Debt to Greek Tragedy in Samson Agonistes* (Baltimore, 1937), p. 123.

"is a boastful knight, own brother to Spenser's Braggadocchio."[33] Boughner believed that "the giant of Gath is . . . a figure conceived in the comic spirit and woven out of the same comic stuff that Milton so sweepingly disparages in the preface." The cowardly braggart of Renaissance Italian comedy contributed the salient characteristics of this figure—

> Harapha's emphasis on his "honour," which he has won by "mortal duel"; his knightly disdain for Samson's feats of strength and unchivalric equipment, and a preference for the "glorious arms" worn in battle by heroes and for a combat "in camp or listed field"; his pretended lament that "fortune" in the past has prevented the two from meeting and now makes it impossible for a "noble warriour" to stoop to such an unworthy "match"; and his taking refuge, when directly challenged by Sampson, in the pretext that "no man of arms" would fight with a condemned man.

This behavior, Boughner argued, reflected the influence of Renaissance dramatists, who had "ordinarily made the soldier the victim of a situation in which he must either accept a challenge and by fighting run the risk of wounds or blows, or decline the challenge on some pretext by which the code of arms permitted him to retain his honor. . . ."[34]

Actually, there is no need to look so far afield. For one prototype of the braggart giant, with his brazen trust in arms, Milton could have turned simply to the account of Goliath in I Samuel 17. Many of Harapha's attributes could have been derived from the Biblical portrait of his son.

In describing this figure as a "Giant . . . of *Gath*" and the "Father of five Sons All of Gigantic size, *Goliah* chief," Milton was exploiting the Hebrew word for giant (*raphah*)[35] and the Biblical references to "the sonnes of Haraphah," who had been "borne unto Haraphah at Gath, and fel by the hand of David, and by the hands of his servants" (2 Samuel 21:16–22; I Chronicles 20:4–8). Of these four "children of Haraphah," one (Lahmi) had been identified as "the brother of Goliath the Gittite, whose spearestaffe was like a weavers beame." In investing the father with characteristics of his more famous son, Milton

33. Allan Gilbert, "*Samson Agonistes* 1096," *MLN*, XXIX (1914), 161n.

34. Daniel C. Boughner, "Milton's Harapha and Renaissance Comedy," *ELH*, XI (1944), 297–306. For criticism of Boughner's view, see F. Michael Krouse, *Milton's Samson and the Christian Tradition* (Princeton, 1949), p. 129.

35. Parker, "Milton's Harapha"; E. N. Adler, "Milton's Harapha," *TLS*, 16 January 1937, p. 44; Jacob Leveen, "Milton's Harapha," *TLS*, 23 January 1937, p. 60; H. Loewe, "Milton's Harapha," *TLS*, 23 January 1937, p. 60; Merritt Y. Hughes (ed.), *Samson Agonistes* (New York, 1937), pp. 588n., 596n.; James Hastings (ed.), *A Dictionary of the Bible* (Edinburgh, 1902), *s.v. Rapha.*

was following one of the cardinal principles of the poetic art—decorum, "the grand masterpiece to observe."[36]

Goliath and Harapha share several affinities besides their father-son relationship: Both are giants of Gath. Both are champions of the Philistines. Both hurl insults at the Israelites. Both boast of exploits they never fulfill. Both invoke Philistine gods.[37] Both scoff at the "trivial" weapons of their adversaries, and mock the latters' disregard for the conventional armaments of warfare. Both are finally humiliated[38] by the Hebrew opponents they have scorned.

Conversely, despite differences in age, experience, and renown, David and Samson play comparable roles—in championing Jehovah's cause against the principal Philistine champions, in disregarding armor and arms, in discounting their own physical handicaps and trusting in Jehovah's aid.

Samson's catalogue of the giant's "gorgeous arms" includes many items listed among Goliath's paraphernalia—helmet, coat of mail, greaves, spear, and shield.[39] Though Milton amplifies this list, to underline still further the giant's reliance on arms ("Brigandine," "Vant-brass," "Gauntlet"), he adds two further details strongly reminiscent of Goliath. Like his son, Harapha wears helmet and body-armor of brass. Like Goliath's, his spear-shaft resembles "A Weaver's beam."[40]

On the other hand, Samson (like David) bears only the most trivial weapons. Though the "Oak'n staff" with which he threatens his opponent has no parallel in Judges, there is a suggestive analogue in the staff David carries in 1 Samuel 17:40—a weapon Goliath despises ("Am I a dog, that thou comest to me with staves?"). Harapha's "knightly disdain for Samson's . . . unchivalric equipment, and a preference for the 'glorious arms' worn in battle by heroes"[41] are paralleled by Goliath's contempt for David's rustic arms and the Biblical emphasis on the giant's own massive weapons and armor.

36. John Milton, *Of Education* (Bohn Standard Library, London, 1883), III, 474. In "Milton's 'Grand Master Peece,'" *American Notes & Queries*, II (1963), 54–55, Thomas Kranidas suggests that "in Milton's use of the word, *master peece* comes closer to meaning master trick or plot than master rule." Cf. *idem*, *The Fierce Equation: A Study of Milton's Decorum* (The Hague, 1965). See also Marvin T. Herrick, *The Fusion of Horatian and Aristotelian Criticism, 1531–1555* (Urbana, 1946).

37. I Sam. 17:43 ("And the Philistine cursed David by his gods"); Milton's Harapha invokes Baal-zebub (I. 1231) and swears by Astaroth (I. 1242).

38. It is interesting to note that the Vulgate uses the word *humiliavit* in describing the victory of David and his warriors over four Philistine giants (I Chron. 20:4): "percussit Sobochai Husaithites, Saphai de genere Raphaim, et humiliavit eos."

39. I Sam. 17:5–7. The Biblical account of the victory of David and his men over the four giant "sonnes of Haraphah" (see Geneva version) likewise stresses the giants' arms and armor (II Sam. 21:16, 19; I Chron. 20:5).

40. See Hughes, p. 1120n.

41. Boughner, p. 298.

Analogous too are the giants' emphasis on "mortal duel," their "preference for . . . a combat 'in camp or listed field,'" and their disdain for their Hebrew antagonists as "an unworthy 'match.'"[42] In the Biblical account, Goliath ("a champion out of the camp of the Philistines") had challenged the Israelites to "choose you a man for you" for single combat to the death, in full view of the two armies in "battle . . . array." This "mortal duel" became a favorite theme for Renaissance Biblical epic, and Milton could have encountered the theme of the *Monomachia* of David and Goliath in several heroic poems.[43] Unlike the Renaissance playwrights cited by Boughner, these poets treated the single combat as a heroic theme, rather than as a subject "for farce."[44]

Like Harapha, who despises Samson as "no worthy match for valour to assail," Goliath feels contempt for his adversary:

> And when the Philistine looked about, and saw David, he disdained him: for he was but a youth, and ruddy, and of a fair countenance.

In Du Bartas' *La Seconde Sepmaine*, Goliath warns David that this is no shepherds' contest; like Harapha, he initially refuses to fight with so unworthy an antagonist:

> *Mais non, je ne veux point, ô pucelle affetee,*
> *Souiller dedans ton sang ma dextre redoutee,*
> *Cerche* [sic] *quelque autre main, trouve un autre Atropos,*
> *Et ne fonde, insolent, sur ma honte ton los.*[45]

Harapha declares that a combat with Samson would "stain his honour"; Du Bartas' Goliath regards a duel with David as shameful to himself and disdains to soil his hand in such a fight.

In both encounters the giants' boasts prove substanceless. Goliath threatens to "give thy flesh unto the fowls of the air, and to the beasts of the field." Harapha vaunts that

> *I should have forc'd thee soon wish other arms,*
> *Or left thy carcase where the Ass lay thrown. . . .*

Both engagements culminate in the giants' humiliation. Goliath is ignominously slain by a boy armed only with the shepherd's weapons he had despised. Harapha departs "somewhat crestfall'n"—compelled

42. Boughner, p. 298.

43. For DuBellay's *Monomachie de David et de Goliath* and other epic treatments of this subject, see R. A. Sayce, *The French Biblical Epic in the Seventeenth Century* (Oxford, 1955), *passim*. See also Rudolph Walther, *Monomachia Davidis et Goliae* (Tiguri, n.d.).

44. Boughner, p. 298.

45. *The Works of Guillaume de Salluste Sieur Du Bartas*, ed. U. T. Holmes, Jr., J. C. Lyons, R. W. Linker (Chapel Hill, 1940), III, 341–42. For Du Bartas' influence on *Paradise Lost*, see George C. Taylor, *Milton's Use of Du Bartas* (Cambridge, Mass., 1934).

to "Hear these dishonours, and not render death"—a "vain boaster" and "baffl'd coward."

Despite obvious differences between the two situations[46] (Samson's victory over the giant is essentially moral, for his adversary refuses to fight), most of the salient features of the encounter between Samson and Harapha appear in the Biblical account of the duel between David and Goliath. The giant's character derives, on the whole, less from Renaissance comedy than from I Samuel 17.

In the encounter with Harapha, Krouse has recognized the third and last of "three trials of faith." The giant serves as "the instrument of temptation by violence and fear," but Samson is "ready to engage in mortal combat with Harapha because his 'trust . . . in the living God' is still strong."[47] The Biblical account of David's *monomachia* with Goliath places a similar emphasis on the Hebrew champion's reliance on God for victory. Like Samson, David is zealous for Jehovah's honor. Like Samson, he depends on divine aid rather than on arms and armor. In both encounters the essential elements are the same—on the one hand, the giant's boasts and reliance on arms; on the other, the Hebrew's disdain of fleshly weapons and an unshaken confidence in God.

Although Milton gives this antithesis its clearest dramatic expression in the Harapha episode, it recurs throughout the drama. The opening speech of the Chorus describes the hero as one "whom unarm'd No strength of man, or fiercest wild beast could withstand" and relates how, before his downfall, he

> *Ran on embattelld Armies clad in Iron,*
> *And weaponless himself*
> *Made Arms ridiculous, useless the forgery*
> *Of brazen shield and spear, the hammer'd Cuirass,*
> Chalybean *temper'd steel, and frock of mail*
> *Adamantean Proof.*

Scorning "thir proud arms and warlike tools," he had compelled seasoned warriors to turn "Thir plated backs under his heel" or soil "thir crested helmets in the dust." Fighting with "what trivial weapon came to hand, The Jaw of a dead Ass," he had slain a thousand Philistines at Ramath-lechi. Samson himself reiterates this contrast:

> *. . . on thir whole Host I flew*
> *Unarm'd, and with a trivial weapon fell'd*
> *Thir choicest youth. . . .*

46. The most obvious differences are that Samson and Harapha never come to blows, that Goliath never reveals himself a coward, and that (though Harapha first brings up the subject of the duel) it is Samson, rather than the Philistine giant, who issues the formal challenge.

47. Krouse, pp. 129–30.

Thus the essential features of Samson's challenge to Harapha had been clearly stated at the very beginning of the drama, and, significantly, the Chorus reaffirms them immediately after the Harapha episode:

> *He all thir Ammunition*
> *And feats of War defeats*
> *With plain Heroic magnitude of mind*
> *And celestial vigour arm'd,*
> *Thir Armories and Magazins contemns,*
> *Renders them useless, while. . . .*
> *Swift as the lightning glance he executes*
> *His errand on the wicked, who surpris'd*
> *Lose thir defence distracted and amaz'd.*

In 1 Samuel 17 the contrast between the virtually unarmed Israelite and the heavily armed Philistine giant had been emphasized by the detailed catalogue of Goliath's massive armaments (verses 5–7), David's explicit rejection of Saul's armor for the trivial weapons of the shepherd (38–40), and his reply to the giant's taunts (45–47): "Thou comest to me with a sword, and with a spear, and with a shield: but I come to thee in the name of the LORD of hosts, the God of the armies of Israel, whom thou hast defied. And all this assembly shall know that the LORD saveth not with sword and spear: for the battle is the LORD's, and he will give you into our hands." Could we ask for a clearer statement of the basic antithesis underlying Samson's challenge to Harapha—the ethical opposition of *fiducia in Deo* (trust in God) and *fiducia carnalis* (carnal reliance)?[48] Like David, Samson chooses to fight in God's name, for God's honor, against the blaspheming infidel. Like David, he confesses that "the battle is the LORD's":

> *. . . all the contest is now*
> *'Twixt God and* Dagon. . . .
> *. . . these Magic spells,*
> *Which I to be the power of* Israel's *God*
> *Avow, and challenge* Dagon *to the test. . . .*

Like David, he rejects the conventional paraphernalia of warfare and relies instead on divine aid. The parallel between the two Hebrew champions is still further enhanced by their physical handicaps—Samson's fetters and blindness, and David's youth: "And Saul said to David, Thou art not able to go against this Philistine to fight with him: for thou art but a youth, and he a man of war from his youth."

48. See Milton's *Christian Doctrine*, Book II, Chapter 3 (*Prose Works* [Bohn's Standard Library; London, 1884]).

The moral values Milton emphasizes in the Harapha episode had, moreover, been traditionally recognized by commentators on I Samuel 17. Procopius of Gaza observed that God did not permit David to bear Saul's weapons, lest the victory be attributed in part to arms.[49] Theodoretus stressed David's trust in divine aid and the contrast between the unarmed shepherd youth and the seasoned man of war.[50] Theodorus Prodromus likewise emphasized the gulf between the two champions in arms, size, and military experience.[51]

Calvin's *Homilae in Primum Librum Samuelis*[52] also emphasized concepts of basic importance in the Harapha episode—the giant's vaunts and blasphemies, the apparent inequality of the conflict, and (above all) the Hebrew's confidence in God. The most striking feature of the duel is its seeming inequity. An unarmed and inexperienced shepherd youth confronts a seasoned and fully equipped warrior.[53] Nevertheless, appearances are deceptive. Trusting not in his own strength, but in God, David remains unshaken by the giant's threats and superior weapons and treats the latter's vaunts and blasphemies as an occasion for magnifying God.[54] In the *Homilies*, as in *Samson Agonistes*, the Philistine's boasts prove vain ("vana gloriatio"). Both Calvin and Milton compare

49. *Patrologia Graeca*, LXXXVII (Paris, 1865), col. 1102: "Saul arma sua dedit, at David gestare non potuit. Etenim Deus hoc non concedit, sed necdum vult reportare victoriam, ne armis victoriae virtute partae pars attribuatur."

50. *Patrologia Graeca*, LXXX (Paris, 1864), cols. 566–67: "Erat adolescens quindecim aut sedecim annorum. . . . Nihil, inquit, differt a bestia qui vivit in impietate, et qui est nudatus divino auxilio. Ego autem confido in illius [Dei] auxilio. . . . Cum hac fide profectus spe non fuit frustratus: sed cum esset nudus, vicit armatum, et qui pascebat oves, eum qui erat exercitatus in bellis et tropaeis; et qui erat parvus et juvenis, eum qui de tanta se jactabat magnitudine."

51. *Patrologia Graeca*, CXXXIII (Paris, 1864), col. 1152: "David upilio, per aetatem pusillus corpore, Goliae procero giganti mortem infert, inermis armato. . . . Ante Philistaeorum cuneos prosiliens barbarus, provocabat ad singulare certamen virum bello instructissimum, qui visu quidem horribilis erat, sed ab exili David prostratus est. . . ."

52. *Corpus Reformatorum*, LVIII, cols. 184–253.

53. *Corpus Reformatorum*, col. 190. Cf. col. 215: "Sed quam impari certamine! Nae veluti si musca elephantum, vel formica taurum vel aliquam similem feram lacesseret. . . . Nam ipsius gigantis staturam et armaturam attendite, *erat altitudinis sex cubitorum et palmi: Et cassis aerea super caput eius: et lorica squamata induebatur. Et ocreas aereas habebat in cruribus: et clypeus aereus tegebat humeros eius.* Quibus vero contra munitus armis erat David? Nae, nudus et inermis adversum tam bene armatum gigantem progreditur. . . ."

54. *Corpus Reformatorum*, cols. 213–14, 227–29: "Quam blasphemus iste gigas, Davidi maledicens in idolis quae a Philistaeis colebantur? quasi adversus Deum possit aliquid idola gentium. Atque istis minis Davidem ille gigas terrere voluit: sed ille contra maiorem inde occasionem Dei magnificiendi capit: et blasphemi hominis in Dei maiestatem contumeliis excitatur. Nihil enim de suis viribus sibi pollicitus est, adversus gigantem Goliathum singulari certamine congredi paratus: . . . sed in Deum spem omnem collocavit, et coelitus auxilium exspectavit, de se ipso nihil sperans. . . . Talis est fiducia illa Davidis in Dei potentia. Nunquam ergo David, mente titubavit nunquam immutatus est: quam mentem habuit rusticus et opilio, et quam in Deo fiduciam. . . . Hoc sane David auxilium divinum sensit, exprobans giganti gladium et lanceam, qua Davidem se confossurum gloriabatur, sed vana gloriatione."

him to a tower: "his pile high-built and proud," "lay thy structure low."[55] Again, in Calvin's account, as in Milton's, the giant arrogantly mocks his Hebrew antagonist as below his own "quality."[56]

The marginal glosses on 1 Samuel 17 in the Geneva Bible[57] emphasize many of the same points. The note on verse 33 stresses the trial of faith:

Here Satan proveth Davids faith by the infidelitie of Saul.

The observations on verses 34, 46, and 48 call attention to David's trust in God, assurance of his cause and calling, and zeal for God's honor:

David by the experience that he hath had in time past of Gods helpe, nothing doubteth to overcome this danger, seeing he was zealous for Gods honor.

David being assured both of his cause and of his calling, prophesieth of the destruction of the Philistims.

Being moved with a fervent zeale to be revenged upon the blasphemer of God's Name.

The commentary on verses 37 and 40 declares that David's victory was due not to his own might, but to the "power of God":

For by these examples he [Saul] saw that the power of God was with him [David].

To the intent that by these weake meanes, God might onely be knowen to be the author of this victorie.

The headnote at the beginning of the chapter reiterates the essential point of verse 47, "*The Lord saveth not by sword nor speare.*"

David and Samson had long been associated (Hebrews 11:32–34) as "heroes of faith" who "out of weakness were made strong." Keckermann's *System of Sacred Theology* stressed a further point of resemblance —a point of no little significance in Milton's tragedy. The exploits of both champions were "mixed" miracles—miracles in which God controls the "second causes," both directing them and increasing their

55. Hughes, pp. 588n., 596n.

56. *Corpus Reformatorum*, col. 226; "Itaque Goliathus arroganter et fastuose adversus illum progressus despexit, quod non esset eiusdem cum ipso qualitatis . . . Davidem ludibrio habuit quod cum baculo pastorali seu pedo progrederetur, tanquam adversus canem. . . ."

57. *The Bible . . . Imprinted at London by Robert Barker* (1607). For close parallels between *Samson Agonistes* and the Geneva version's glosses on Judges, see George W. Whiting, "*Samson Agonistes* and the Geneva Bible," *Rice Institute Pamphlet*, XXXVIII, no. 1 (1951), 18–35.

forces beyond nature.[58] Samson himself, as Milton describes him, is "the miracle of men." The strength in his locks is (as old Manoa observes) "miraculous." The catastrophe of the drama is itself a divine miracle—not the "miracle" of restored eyesight that Manoa hopes for, but a more powerful and more "admirable" example of the Judaeo-Christian marvelous.

The primary source of Milton's giant is thus Biblical rather than secular. Though classical tragedy and Renaissance comedy may have been contributing influences, his character and significance derive largely from 1 Samuel 17, and his name from 2 Samuel 21. Milton introduced him into the story of Samson on the analogy of Goliath in the story of David, in order to convey the same moral opposition which had been manifested in David's duel—the antithesis between the Hebrew's trust in God and disdain of fleshly weapons and the Philistine's pride and carnal reliance. Both Goliath and Harapha trust in "glorious arms" for "safety," but this is a false security, a *vana salus*.[59] "The LORD saveth not with sword and spear," and both giants, for all their strength, are ignominiously defeated by their unarmed opponents. The true prototype of the spiritual duel between Samson and Harapha is the *monomachia* between David and Goliath. In the encounter between a physically handicapped "hero of faith" and a Philistine giant in full armor, Milton found an ideal vehicle for the ethical opposition between *fiducia in Deo* and *fiducia carnalis*.

58. *Systema SS. Theologiae . . . per Bartholomaeum Keckermannum* (Hanoviae, 1602), p. 467: "Mixta sunt, cum Deus assumit causas secundas, earumque vires supra naturam intendit & auget." Cf. Keckermann, pp. 466–67: "Talia mixta miracula multa occurrunt in sacris: quale est miraculosum illud robur Simsonis, qui naturae & temperamenti fuit robustissimi, sed ita, ut Deus vires illas naturales in eo auxerit, ut ea efficeret Simson, quae impossibile fuit efficere solis naturae viribus, ut videre est, Iud. 14.15 & 16. Sic 1. Sam. 17 David adolescens vastissimi corporis, & roboris Goliatum lapillo è funda eiecto, prosternit, adhibens naturae vires brachium & fundam; sed quae minime suffecissent ad hoc opus emoliendum, nisi naturam auxisset vis quaedam superior. Nimirum quotiescunque potest per naturae vires fieri, solet Deus adhibere naturam ad miraculosos effectus, tum ne ociosa sit natura, quando potest agere; tum ut testetur causas, secundas non pugnare, sed subordinari suae potentiae; tum denique, ut ostendit se esse autorem naturae, eamque amare, & eius vires posse prout licet vel intendere, vel remittere."

59. Cf. Rabanus' comment on the Israelites' battles with four Philistine giants in 2 Sam. 21 (*Patrologia Latina*, CIX, col. 114): "Quid autem quatuor bella ista David et servorum ejus contra Palaestinos significant, nisi bellum Christi, quod omni tempore istius vitae in membris suis contra perfidos quosque istius saeculi, et contra spiritales nequitias incessanter agit? . . . Unde Psalmista ex persona Ecclesiae confidenter dicit: 'Vana salus hominis. In Deo faciemus virtutem, et ipse ad nihilum deducet tribulantes nos (*Psal.* LIX).'" In the Authorized Version this text is Psalm 60:11; in the Vulgate, Psalm 59:13.

13. The Classical Hero

Satan and Ulysses

❦ In *The Reason of Church-Government*, Milton voices his ambition to "adorn" his native language and thus accomplish for his own country what other writers—"the greatest and choycest wits of *Athens*, *Rome* or modern *Italy*, and those Hebrews of old"—had done for theirs. Yet he had (he believed) a distinct advantage—"with this over and above of being a Christian."[1] The qualifying phrase—like the self-confidence—is characteristic of Milton, but it is also typical of an attitude shared by many Renaissance writers. It signalizes the divided allegiance that the Christian poet accorded his classical models, his ambivalent relationship to antiquity.

For the classics were also the Ethnics. The highly-lauded ancients were also the benighted Gentiles. Though they had successfully climbed Parnassus, where few Christian poets had ever established a secure footing, they had never scaled the heights of Sion or Mount Carmel. How could they teach true felicity, who had never known the Highest Good? How could they depict the way to celestial beatitude, who might (at most) attain the milder shades of Limbo or the upper terraces of Hell?

First published, in somewhat different form, in *Modern Language Review*, LII (1957), 81–85, and here reprinted by permission of the Modern Humanities Research Association and of the editors.

1. John Milton, *Works* (Columbia Edition; New York, 1931–38), III, 236.

Classical civilization could provide the rules and principles of the arts, but not their true end, not their final cause. It could offer standards and models for style and structure, but hardly the highest norms of moral conduct. For every Renaissance moralist who emphasized the instructive force of the examples left by the ancients in literature or history, there were others who placed equal stress on the inadequacies of classical ethics in the light of the Christian revelation.

The temples of the Muses stood on sand—the vain wisdom of the world—not on the solid rock of revealed truth, the cornerstone of Christian doctrine. Ignorant alike of the true God and the true good, of the real nature and end of man, Greco-Roman ethics was insufficient, and classical poetry was, for this reason, inevitably imperfect. It could not perform the proper offices of the poetic art as a vehicle of moral instruction and persuasion. It imitated badly and taught amiss. It missed the ultimate end of every art—beatitude.

Like other arts and sciences of the ancients, classical poetics required reformation on Christian principles, reorientation towards Christian ends. The same challenge confronted Protestant and Catholic writers alike, and, with varying degrees of sincerity and success, poets of the Reformation and Counter-Reformation set about meeting it. The romantic allegories of Spenser and Tasso were one answer. Camoens' *Lusiads*—two parts patriotic ardor, one part pagan mythology, and one part missionary zeal—was another. The Biblical epics of Vida and Sannazaro, Du Bartas and Du Bellay, Cowley and Milton represent a third solution.

With "this [advantage] of being a Christian," Milton could expect a loftier inspiration and hope to "soar Above th' *Aonian* Mount." In a subject based on Biblical truth, he found a "higher Argument," a theme "more Heroic" than those of Virgil and Homer. From Christian ethics he learned a "better fortitude" than the military prowess celebrated by most of his predecessors—the ideal "Of Patience and Heroic Martyrdom." In the example of Christ he recognized the perfect heroic archetype—the spiritual "King or Knight," in whom to "lay the pattern of a Christian hero."

I

Milton's technique as a poet reflects his competence as a logician. He utilizes logical contraries—heroic virtue and brutishness, merit and demerit, felicity and misery, reward and punishment—to sharpen definition through contrast. He plays diverse or contradictory meanings against one another—reality and appearance, essence and accident, truth and falsehood. He exploits the commonplaces of cause and effect. He argues from the deliberative topics of felicity and the highest good, the demonstrative topics of praise and blame, and the forensic commonplaces of justice and injustice. When convenient, he disposes of a contrary opinion by a *reductio ad absurdum*. In his hands, the conventional epic machinery acquires argumentative force, the authority of a rhetorical *exemplum*. His celestial and infernal "machines" become moral archetypes, embodying the Ideas of heroic virtue and its antithetical vice, the true and specious images of heroism. The latter he reduces to absurdity by stressing its inherent contradiction, by applying a conventional concept of "godlikeness" to the devil himself.

To be morally valid and poetically effective, the heroic idol must be demonstrably false, but in the context of seventeenth-century poetics it must also conform to Aristotelian principles of character. It must be probable, "good," "appropriate," "like the reality," and "consistent." On the last of these points Milton has frequently been condemned—accused of wantonly "degrading" the heroic Satan of the early books and arbitrarily transforming a classical hero into a grotesque fiend. Yet the inconsistency has been grossly exaggerated. Milton sustains the fiction without serious discrepancies until the moment of truth exposes its fallacy.

The basis of this portrait is both literary and theological, and the preconditions of ethical consistency are likewise dual. Since Satan is an epic character, the poet must represent him in a manner consistent with epic decorum. By classical standards, Milton succeeds far better than most of his Christian precursors—Tasso, Vida, Gratiani; Crashaw, Fletcher, and Cowley. As critics have seldom failed to recognize, the Satan of Books I and II is much closer to the *personae* of classical epic than are the grotesque fiends of his immediate predecessors. Unlike the usual devils of Renaissance epic, Milton's fiend does not appear out of place in a *heroic* poem.

Yet Milton also had to consider Biblical tradition. To be "like the reality,"[2] Satan's character must conform to the pattern already set by Scripture and its commentators. He must display the distinctive traits of Isaiah's vainglorious Lucifer, who had sought equality with God, and the belligerent Satan of Revelation, who had warred with Michael's angels and been expelled from Heaven. On the other hand, he must exhibit qualities more appropriate to the wily seducer of Eve and the future tempter of Job and Christ. The disparity between these two facets of Satan's character might well present a formidable difficulty to any poet; Milton's argument compelled him to present *both* of them—and this within the framework of a single plot. Moreover, the transition from one aspect to the other must be "probable."[3] The poet must

2. Aristotle, *On the Art of Poetry*, trans. Ingram Bywater (Oxford, 1951), p. 56.

3. *Ibid.*, p. 56. In portraying character, the poet must endeavor "after the necessary or the probable."

somehow reconcile these disparate traits as different aspects of the same character and thus preserve its consistency. Or, if he should attempt to show change or development in *ethos*, he must make the alteration seem plausible.

In the Aristotelian sense, Satan's character undergoes little change throughout the poem. His *ethos*, his "moral purpose,"[4] remains essentially the same throughout the fable. From the moment of his recovery until the end of the narrative—indeed, from his first conception of rebellion until the end of time—he is consistently the Adversary of the Almighty, the Antagonist of Heaven, the spiritual opponent of the divine will. The seduction of Eve follows logically—*probably*—from the plans partially disclosed in his first speeches to his fallen host and elaborated more fully in the infernal council. Neither strategy nor tactics undergoes any fundamental change. He accomplishes his objective—conquest of the world and its inhabitants (cf. I, 650 ff.)—by "fraud or guile" (I, 645 ff.), tactics that he had favored from the beginning.

Throughout the epic, in fact, Milton attempts to combine the characteristic features of the fraudulent tempter of Genesis and the aspiring rebel of Isaiah and Revelation. Even before his expulsion from Heaven, the Satan of *Paradise Lost* employs stratagems that foreshadow his tactics against Eve. He withdraws his troops under the "pretext" of preparing a reception for Messiah. Concealing his artillery from his foes and feigning a desire for truce, he takes his foes by surprise. In Heaven, as later on Mount Niphates, Satan is "Artificer of fraud." By introducing this conception, alien to the rebellion as described in Revelation and Isaiah, Milton gives greater continuity to the Satanic *ethos*.

The real changes in Satan's character result from the internal, spiritual effects of sin and death. But these are gradual, and Milton usually suggests them by physical rather than strictly ethical detail. (The "moral purpose" revealed in Satan's speeches shows little variation; his reasoning is almost as sophistical before his defeat as after. His degeneration appears chiefly through such details as corporeal grossness, diminished luster, vulnerability to pain, and—finally—the physical transformation that makes him as deformed as his Sin.)

There are also, of course, emotional changes; his vain ambition to equal God yields to despair. Yet, on the whole, the archangel exhibits the same traits that had led to his ruin—vainglorious boasting, ambition to reign and to "imitate" the divine majesty, hatred of the Almighty, and envy towards God's favorites. His fall contributes an additional motive—revenge—while from the ravages of spiritual death and the denial of grace there results an obdurate refusal to repent. Both of the latter traits appear in his opening speeches, and throughout the

4. *Ibid.*, pp. 38, 55.

poem they motivate his enterprise against man. They are as characteristic of the "heroic" angel of the opening books as of the wily trickster who beguiles Eve.

In general, Milton tends to reduce the contrasts between the Satan of Genesis and the Satan of Revelation and Isaiah to a shift in tactics and immediate objective. Satan continues to prosecute his war against God, but after force has failed he must resort to fraud. Since he cannot overcome the Creator Himself, he must attack Him indirectly through the creature:

> . . . *our better part remains*
> *To work in close design, by fraud or guile*
> *What force effected not: that he no less*
> *At length from us may find, who overcomes*
> *By force, hath overcome but half his foe.*

Nevertheless, the shift in emphasis from force to fraud—from the tactics of Revelation to those of Genesis—is gradual. The opening scenes of the poem show a dual orientation—towards two different aspects of Satan's character and activity as revealed in Scripture. They look forward to the temptation in Eden, backward to the battle in Heaven.

The first reference to Satan in the poem fuses the contrasting images of the Biblical narrative—the serpent of Genesis and the Lucifer of Isaiah. They were already linked in the Apocalypse, which had identified Michael's foe, the warlike "dragon," with "that old serpent, called the Devil, and Satan, which deceives the whole world." Milton, in turn, introduces Satan both as the "infernal Serpent" who deceived the "Mother of Mankinde" and as the vainglorious archangel who "Rais'd impious War in Heav'n and Battel proud . . . ." These allusions, so carefully juxtaposed, link the portrait in Book I with the tempter of Eve and the leader of the angelic revolt. They emphasize its Biblical origin and the poet's concern to frame his character "like the reality" of Scripture.

The heroic features of this portrait result in large part from Milton's desire to preserve consistency and verisimilitude by emphasizing the ethical continuity between the fallen archangel and the ambitious rebel. Similar heroic traits characterize the revolting angels of Valvasone and Valmarana, and these also—significantly—occur in the context of the celestial war. They are, however, conspicuously absent in most epics dedicated to more recent themes. Like the Satan of *Paradise Regain'd*, the devils of Tasso and Gratiani are further removed, in both time and character, from the archangelic warriors; by long practice they have become inured to fraud and guile.

II

In the opening scenes of *Paradise Lost* Milton achieved this continuity through several devices. The most obvious technique was to introduce reminiscences of the angelic war. Satan calls it the "Glorious Enterprize," and Beëlzebub hails his leader as the "Chief of Many Throned Powers, That led th' imbattelld Seraphim to Warr. . . ." Secondly, the poet described properties of the angelic nature that still survived in the fallen spirits, placing heavy emphasis on their strength and military power. Satan—no less than an "Arch Angel ruind"—boasts of "the strength of Gods And this Empyreal substance." Beëlzebub declares that "the mind and spirit remains Invincible, and vigour soon returns. . . ." The infernal hosts are "Powers Matchless, but with th' Almighty," "puissant Legions" who can scarcely "faile to re-ascend . . . and repossess their native seat." Thirdly, Milton invested his devil with the characteristic traits of Isaiah's Lucifer. Satan is still an incorrigible boaster, "Vaunting aloud" even in despair; he retains his pride and ambition, his love of glory and dominion, and his desire to imitate God's majesty. All of these factors link the pseudo-heroic portrait of Books I and II with the Satanic image of Isaiah and Revelation.

The martial character of Milton's Hell serves a variety of functions. It establishes "epic decorum."[5] It creates the heroic "idol." It preserves continuity with preceding events—especially with the angelic rebellion. It foreshadows the future City of the World. It illustrates the doctrine of permissive evil and the futility of carnal reliance; Satan and his companion escape the "*Stygian* flood" not by "thir own recover'd strength," but "by the sufferance of supernal Power." For all their "imbodied force," their strength "beyond Compare of mortal prowess," and their formidable order of battle, the Stygian powers are not permitted to deploy their military might against man. Satan must accomplish his mission not through force but through fraud.

Yet until the end of Book IV both tactics remain closely associated; Satan continues to rely on force as well as guile. The hazardous journey through space tries his strength and endurance and, above all, his courage. When his first attempt to seduce Eve by fraud is frustrated by the angelic guard, he does not hesitate to challenge Gabriel to a trial of strength. Despite his defeat, he is still a formidable antagonist, capable of "dreadful deeds" that could devastate earth and sky. Though his threats prove abortive, their menace is nevertheless real; only the Almighty can prevent the combat. Not until Satan has perceived "his mounted scale aloft" and learned "the sequel each of parting and of flight" does he desist.

5. See Torquato Tasso's *Discorsi del poema eroico* in *Prose*, ed. Francesco Flora (Milan and Rome, 1935).

Essentially, there is no ethical inconsistency in Satan's shift in tactics, no real breach of heroic decorum in his attempt to conquer through fraud rather than force. In a strictly *moral* context guile might seem the more ignoble of the two (both Dante and St. Thomas Aquinas treat fraud as a graver crime than violence). Yet in a *military* context, guile could conceivably seem the more praiseworthy, since it could achieve victory with less hazard and less bloodshed. To deceive the enemy as to one's real capabilities and intent had long been recognized as a valid principle of warfare. In *Henry IV, Part Two* Prince John had won honor and acclaim for tricking the rebel leaders into disbanding their forces. Odysseus had conquered Troy by a ruse. Prince Maurice of Nassau had penetrated an enemy fortress by stratagem—and received as reward a heroic poem devoted largely to this exploit. For Machiavelli *virtù* appeared in fraud as well as force; a prince might conquer heroically by guile as well as by violence. Satan can justly boast of the stratagem whereby he conquers the world with so trivial an instrument as an apple.

Sacred history gave Milton authority for a Satan of heroic dimensions, a warrior who thirsts for glory, who fights against superior odds, and who can be defeated only by the Almighty. These are traditional traits of the epic hero, and in ascribing them to the prince of the devils Milton took advantage of the hints that Isaiah and Revelation offered for a quasi-heroic rebel. Like the Biblical Lucifer, the heroes of classical and Renaissance epic aimed at glory and honor—the traditional objects of heroic virtue and magnanimity. Like Lucifer and Milton's Satan, they were both "insatiable of Glory" and jealous of their honor (τιμῆ). As the Biblical suggestions for the Satanic *ethos* were remarkably similar to the classical picture of the heroic *ethos*, Milton could legitimately fuse the two, reinforcing scriptural and literary tradition and embellishing his portrait of the fallen Lucifer with details reminiscent of poetic heroes.

III

Scholarship has never tired of emphasizing the classical elements in Milton's Hell. As Herford observes,

> Not only Satan, but his companions, are human warriors and counsellors of the grandest type. These fiends . . . hold sports like the comrades of Aeneas, discuss philosophy like the Stoic academe; and the debate in Pandemonium is worthy of the loftiest achievements of the Roman Senate . . ., while Pandemonium itself is a pillared fabric like the Forum or the Parthenon.
>
> Milton's classic humanism here found magnificent, and triumphant expression.[6]

6. C. H. Herford, *Dante and Milton* (Manchester, 1924), p. 34.

Milton's devils are Homer's warriors writ large, and for this very reason they have proved a stumbling-block to many critics. Not only do they invite comparison with the heroes of classical epic, but they raise the further question of ethical consistency. Stressing Satan's affinities with the traditional epic hero, scholars have frequently concentrated their attention on Books I and II, at the expense of the later books. This disproportionate emphasis, in turn, fosters the unfortunate impression that Milton drops the classical charade once he has guided Satan safely through Chaos to Mount Niphates.

In actuality, the poet shows more regard for continuity than his critics have recognized. He sustains the heroic *eidolon* until the most effective time to shatter it—at the conclusion of the enterprise and the moment of triumph. Until the transformation-scene of Book X, Satan continues to wear the mask of a classical hero. In his manifold ruses and disguises he is the ectype[7] of Homer's *polytropos Odysseus*, "the man of many wiles."

Satan's role in *Paradise Lost* is consistently conceived in terms of the "siege tradition." As in the *Iliad* and poems modeled upon it (such as Tasso's *Gerusalemme Liberata* and Alamanni's *L'Avarchide*) the action centers on the attempt to conquer a hostile citadel. In Milton's epic the siege is moral rather than physical, and the prize is the world rather than a single town. The fallen Archangel plots his enterprise, forms strategic alliances, infiltrates enemy territory, defeats its inhabitants, and returns triumphantly from the scene of conquest to report his victory in his own capital. This pattern of events parallels that of the traditional epic enterprise so closely that it could mislead even so astute a critic as Dryden, convincing him that Milton had made the devil his hero.[8]

The heroic pattern is not broken by Satan's resort to fraud rather than force to accomplish his end. In the classical epic guile and valor are not always contradictory qualities.[9] Odysseus possesses both attributes, and his sagacity outweighs Ajax's might in their rivalry for Achilles' arms.[10]

7. For a study of Milton's use of types and ectypes from classical or Biblical tradition, see Merritt Y. Hughes, "Satan and the 'Myth' of the Tyrant," in *Ten Perspectives on Milton* (New Haven and London, 1965), pp. 165 ff.

8. "And Milton, if the Devil had not been his hero, instead of Adam; if the giant had not foiled the knight, and driven him out of his stronghold, to wander through the world with his lady errant. . . ." "Dedication of the *Aeneis*," *Essays of John Dryden*, ed. W. P. Ker (Oxford, 1900), II, 165.

9. B. Rajan, *Paradise Lost and the Seventeenth Century Reader* (London, 1947), p. 97, notes that Milton links two conceptions of Satan—"the leader of all but unconquerable armies" and "someone whose characteristic qualities are cunning and subtlety rather than heroic valour."

10. In Book V of Quintus Smyrnaeus' *Fall of Troy*, trans. Arthur S. Way (London and New York, 1913), Ajax and Odysseus compete for Achilles' arms and boast the respective merits of might and wit. Cf. Ovid, *Metamorphoses*, trans. George Sandys (Oxford, 1632), XIII, 1–398.

The Trojan Brutus leads his Greek foes into ambush through a well-planned lie.[11] Xenophon's Cyrus learns the importance of deceit in warfare.[12] "Dolus an virtus, quis in hoste requirat?" demands Coroebus in the *Aeneid*.[13]

If Satan exhibits guile as well as valor, this does not necessarily mean that his character is inconsistent or even that it has degenerated. On the contrary, one could conceivably regard him as all the better warrior for this very conjunction of craft and might. Like Paradise, Troy also fell by a trick, and Satan's ruses have a precedent—and perhaps a conscious prototype—in Odysseus' stratagems.[14]

In the very orations that most critics accept as undeniably "heroic," Satan has already pointed out the superior advantages of fraud over force in the war with Heaven; Beëlzebub, in turn, has proposed force and fraud as alternative methods in the campaign against man. The infernal enterprise has been conceived largely in terms of fraud; it seeks revenge on Heaven not directly by "open war," but indirectly, by "covert guile," attacking the Creator obliquely through his creation.[15] As Satan himself had originated this strategy of fraud, it is probable and consistent that he should resort to fraud himself in executing it.

Nor is the heroic pattern broken by the Archangel's voluntary assumption of animal forms. Although conscious of their baseness, he assumes them expressly for the sake of the enterprise that he has already proclaimed in heroic language and that he clearly regards as meriting public honor. He employs them, moreover, with the same intelligent discrimination that prompts him, on other occasions, to borrow the shapes of angels.[16] Since there are as yet only two representatives of the human race, the most logical disguise for him to employ in concealing his identity must be either angelic or bestial. His choice of disguise is determined largely by circumstances, by the requirements of the situation in which he finds himself. When he selects the serpent as the most suitable vessel for the crucial engagement of his enterprise, he does so

11. Milton, *Works*, X, 9–10.

12. Xenophon, *Cyropaedia*, trans. Maurice Ashley (London, 1803), pp. 6–81. The successful commander must be "full of wiles, a dissembler, crafty, deceitful, a thief, and a robber, and must take advantage of the enemy in all manner of ways" (p. 76).

13. Virgil, *Aeneid*, trans. H. Rushton Fairclough, Book II, line 390 (London and New York, 1916), I, 320.

14. In Quintus Smyrnaeus' epic it is Odysseus who conceives the idea of the Trojan horse and the other major details of the ruse whereby Troy is taken (XII, 25–45). Similarly in *Paradise Lost* the scheme "to confound the race Of Mankind in one root" is Satan's own (II, 358–86).

15. *Paradise Lost*, I, 645–49; II, 40–42, 337 ff.

16. *Ibid.*, III, 634 ff.; X, 327, 441–43.

only after "inspection deep" and "long debate."[17] This careful accommodation of the disguise to the demands of the particular situation is at least superficially consistent with the quality of heroic prudence, and in the tactics of the "father of lies" we may perceive an analogy with the exploits of Odysseus, the classical exemplar of this virtue.[18]

Like Satan, Odysseus was a master of the ignoble disguise. In the *Odyssey* Athena transformed him into a beggar so that he might enter his palace undetected. On another occasion he penetrated Troy under a similar disguise. "Marring his own body with cruel blows, and flinging a wretched garment about his shoulders, in the fashion of a slave he entered the broad-wayed city of the foe, and he hid himself under the likeness of another, a beggar he who was in no wise such an one at the ships of the Achaeans. In this likeness he entered the city of the Trojans, and all of them were but as babes."[19]

Euripides' Hector refers to the same disguise:

> *. . . and that glib craftiest knave*
> *Odysseus . . .;*
> *Who came by night unto Athena's fane,*
> *Her image stole, and bare to Argos' ships.*
> *In vile attire but now, in beggar's guise,*

17. *Ibid.*, IX, 83 ff. In Andreini's *L'Adamo* the tempter explains in detail why he has chosen the serpent's form rather than that of another animal or that of man or angel:

> *Non volli in campo comparir guerriero*
> *Contro gran Semidea d'Angelo in foggia,*
> *Poi, ch'ella hà per costume*
> *Gli Angeli di mirar teneri, e vaghi,*
> *Non qual mi son, horrido, e fero, essendo*
> *Nato à battaglie, ed acquistarmi i Cieli.*
> *Non volli in forma humana,*
> *Disfidarla in guerra à gran certame*
> *Poi, che sà, ch'un sol huom nel Mondo alberga.*
> *Non di Tigre, over d'Orsa,*
> *O di Leon superbo,*
> *O ver d'altro animal sembianza io presi,*
> *Poi, ch'ella sà che ragionar non puote,*
> *Chi di ragione è privo. . . .*

L'Adamo Sacra Rapresentatione di Gio. Battista Andreini Fiorentino (Milan, 1617), p. 43. In the *Seconde Sepmaine* Du Bartas also explains "Why he appeared not in his own liknes: nor transformed him into an Angell of light" and why Satan preferred the serpent to other animals. Josuah Sylvester, *Du Bartas His Divine Weekes and Workes* (London, 1621), pp. 188–89.

18. In his *Discorsi dell' Arte Poetica* Tasso designates Odysseus as the type of prudence; see Torquato Tasso, *Le prose diverse*, ed. Cesare Guasti (Firenze, 1875), Vol. I. J. E. Spingarn, *A History of Literary Criticism in the Renaissance* (2nd ed.; New York, 1954), p. 122. Minturno in *De Poeta* categorizes this hero as *prudens et callidus*. C. S. Baldwin, *Renaissance Literary Theory and Practice* (New York, 1939), p. 166.

19. *Odyssey*, IV, 240 ff. (Loeb Classical Library; London, 1919).

> *He passed our gate-towers: loudly did he curse*
> *The Argives—he, their spy to Ilium sent!*
> *He slew the guards, the warders of the gates,*
> *And stole forth. Aye in ambush is he found*
> *By the Thymbraean altars nigh the town*
> *Lurking. . . .*[20]

The same dramatist alludes again to this disguise in *Hecuba*,[21] where the queen addresses Odysseus as follows:

> *Rememberest thou thy coming unto Troy*
> *A spy, in rags vile vestured; from thine eyes*
> *Trickled adown thy cheeks the gouts of gore?*

Milton himself once considered writing a heroic poem on a similar episode. In the Trinity Manuscript he noted that "A Heroicall Poem may be founded somwhere in Alfreds reigne, especially at his issuing out of Edelingsey on the Danes, whose actions are wel like those of Ulysses."[22] Professor Tillyard has cited a relevant passage in Milton's *History of Britain*: ". . . Malmsbury writes that in this time of his [Alfred's] recess, to go a spy into the Danish camp, he took upon him with one servant the habit of a fiddler; by this means, gaining access to the king's table and sometimes to his bed-chamber, got knowledge of their secrets, their careless encamping, and thereby this opportunity of assailing them on a sudden. . . ."[23]

Like Alfred and Odysseus, Satan resorts to the ignoble disguise primarily in order to penetrate enemy territory undetected on a mission of vital importance for the ultimate success of his enterprise. If such an exploit is praiseworthy in Odysseus and Alfred, it is scarcely unheroic in Satan's case. Those critics who find it so must likewise

20. *Rhesus*, ll. 498 ff. (Loeb Classical Library; London, 1912). Quintus Smyrnaeus also alludes to the theft of the Palladium by Diomedes and Odysseus (X, 343–60). Sir J. G. Frazer argues that Odysseus made two different expeditions into Troy: on one of these he entered as a spy in mean attire and was recognized by Helen; on the other, accompanied by Diomedes, he stole the Palladium. See Frazer's note in Apollodorus' *Library* (Loeb Classical Library; London and New York, 1921), II, 227–28n.; Boccaccio, *Genealogiae Deorum* (Paris, 1511), p. 85; *Commentarii in Virgilium Serviani*, ed. H. Albertus Lion (Gottingae, 1926), I, 48, 120, 133.

21. Lines 239–41 (Loeb Classical Library; London, 1912).

22. Milton, *Works*, XVIII, 243. Francis Peck, *New Memoirs of the Life and Poetical Works of John Milton* (London, 1740) declares that Milton planned "two large heroic poems: the one entitled *Arthur*, in imitation of the *Iliad*; the other, *Alfred*, in imitation of the *Odyssey*." Milton, *Works*, XVIII, 536.

23. E. M. W. Tillyard, *The Miltonic Setting, Past and Present* (London, 1949), p. 196. Milton, *Works*, X, 214. In the list of subjects for tragedies in the Trinity Manuscript Milton includes the following: "Alfred in disguise of a minstrel discovers the danes negligence sets on with a mightie slaughter about the same tyme the devonshire men rout Hubba & slay him." Milton, *Works*, XVIII, 243.

support Ajax against Odysseus and subscribe to Rhesus' condemnation of the latter:

> *No man of knightly soul would deign by stealth*
> *To slay his foe; he meets him face to face.*[24]

The gulf between the supposedly "heroic" or valorous Satan of Bks. I and II and the allegedly "degraded" or fraudulent Satan of the later books has been seriously exaggerated. Until divine justice degrades him at the moment of apparent triumph, the Archangel's character and enterprise conform to a pattern of heroism already familiar in epic and historical tradition. Since this pattern is not *justly* heroic, since it is void of true virtue in God's sight, the poet ultimately discredits it. But the force of its final rejection depends largely on the consistency with which, up to this point, Milton has described it.

IV

The transformation-scene in Book X is a *peripeteia*, a dramatic "reversal" that converts "triumph to shame." For full effectiveness, it requires that Milton sustain the heroic idol until the final moment, and only then reveal Satan's apparent heroism as brutishness, the contrary of heroic virtue.

The scene reflects the symbolism of the poetic metamorphosis, which had conventionally expressed the irrational quality of evil through allegorical fictions. The vicious man is transformed into the beast that typifies his characteristic vice. The image of the brute symbolizes the moral Idea. Conversely, the qualities of the virtuous man or the hero find poetic expression in his transformation into a god or his elevation to the stars. Sandys had given expression to this antithesis in his translation of Ovid's *Metamorphoses*,[25]

24. Euripides, *Rhesus*, ll. 510–11. In Quintus Smyrnaeus' *Fall of Troy* (XII, 67–72) Neoptolemus opposes Odysseus' scheme of the wooden horse on the grounds that guile is unheroic:

> *Calchas, brave men meet face to face their foes!*
> *Who skulk behind their walls, and fight from towers,*
> *Are nidderings, hearts palsied with base fear.*
> *Hence with all thought of wile and stratagem!*
> *The great war-travail of the spear beseems*
> *True heroes. Best in battle are the brave.*

To this objection Odysseus replies that neither Achilles' might nor all the travail of the Greeks has hitherto availed against Troy (XII, 74–83). Neoptolemus is finally compelled by a divine warning to agree to this stratagem.

25. The frontispiece expresses this moral dichotomy iconographically, in terms of the opposition between Circe's victims and an aerial chariot bearing the inscription *Ad aethera virtus*. Ovid, *Metamorphoses*, "The Minde of the Frontispiece and Argument of this Worke." Geoffrey Whitney, *A Choice of Emblemes*, ed. Henry Green (London, 1866), p. 15, explains Actaeon's metamorphosis in terms of the "fancies fonde" and "affections

But, our Will,
Desire, *and* Powres Irascible, *the skill*
Of PALLAS orders; who the Mind *attires*
With all Heroick Virtues; *by her noble Guide*
Eternized, and well-nigh Deifi'd.
But who forsake that faire Intelligence,
To follow Passion, and voluptuous Sense;
That shun the Path and Toyles of HERCULES;
Such, charm'd by CIRCE's luxurie, and ease,
Themselves deforme: 'twixt whom, so great an ods;
That these are held for Beasts, and those for Gods.

Bartolomeo Delbene's *Civitas veri sive morum* depicts heroic virtue and brutishness allegorically in similar terms. The engraving illustrating "virtute heroica, eiusque extremo feritate" follows Delbene in placing the seat of heroic virtue in the Elysian Fields, partly enclosed by a hedge of laurels, palms, and myrtles as emblems of glory. The garden contains ten *cellae* with statues of such heroes as Hercules, Theseus, Dardanus, Hector, Anchises, Rhadamanthus, Minos, Charlemagne, and St. Louis. Orpheus himself sings the "meritas HEROUM laudes." On the other hand, *Feritas* is banished to a dark cave, along with statues of such brutish men and women as Phalaris, Lamia, and Pasiphaë.[26]

Both Delbene and his commentator, Theodore Marcile, were strongly influenced by Aristotle's *Ethics*. According to the title-page, the book sets forth "Aristotelis de Moribus doctrinam, carmine et picturis complexa," and in the poem itself Aristotle conducts the poet, "his patroness Marguerite of Savoy . . . and two of her ladies-in-waiting round the 'City of Truth.'"[27] As the poem is "an allegory" of the *Nicomachean Ethics*, Marcile echoes Aristotelian conceptions of heroism and demonstrative rhetoric. Heroes are "like gods among men"; their contraries like beasts. This antithesis provides the grounds of the highest praise and basest vituperation.[28]

---

base" that cause men to appear "Like brutishe beastes." See my "Falstaff as Actaeon: A Dramatic Emblem," *Shakespeare Quarterly*, XIV (1963), 231–44. Similarly, the transformation of Ulysses' men by Circe (Green, p. 82) "showes those foolish sorte, whome wicked love dothe thrall, Like brutishe beastes to passe theire time, and have no sence at all."

26. Bartolomeo Delbene, *Civitas veri sive morum* (Paris, 1609), p. 187.

27. See Frances A. Yates, *The French Academies of the Sixteenth Century* (London, 1947), pp. 111–16.

28. Delbene, pp. 186–88: "Haec enim illa virtus est, qua qui instructi & ornati sunt, videntur tanquam Dij versari inter homines. Itaque a virtutis excellentia *divini* olim Spartae *viri* nominati. . . . Atque iidem dicti *Heroes*, unde nomen virtutis Heroicae: iidem *Semones* & *Semidei* quasi altera tantum parte homines. . . . Eiusce autem modi Heroicae virtuti opposita est Feritas. Interiectus namque inter excellentem Dei aeternamque naturam & expertes rationis pecudes, homo est. Itaque licet ei vel ad similitudinem aliquam Dei appropinquare, vel ad immanitatem beluae. . . . Inter hos Deos, & feros illos sive

For Milton, as for Delbene and his commentator, heroic virtue and brutishness are topics of eulogy and vituperation. The divine image and its deformation serve as *demonstrative* arguments for encomium and diatribe. "Divine resemblance" and the "likeness of a beast," "Godlike Virtues" and "brutish vices" constitute the extremes of praise or blame. Only the absolute extremes—God and the devil—exceed them. Heroic virtue and sanctity approach divine virtue; brutishness approximates diabolical vice.

The techniques of "demonstrative" rhetoric—praise and blame—underlie Milton's contrasting images of true and false heroism. The Messiah manifests his Sonship—his perfect resemblance to the Father—through godlike actions and virtues, thereby revealing himself as the "perfect image" of God and (*a fortiori*) the perfect hero. Satan also imitates God, displaying a superficial "resemblance to the Highest." But this is a specious likeness, and his own "perfect image" is really his daughter Sin. Her bestial change foreshadows his own and possesses the same ethical significance. Both transformations represent the distortion of the rational soul through vice. Both belong to a common literary tradition—the symbolic metamorphoses of the Renaissance.

In both cases, however, Milton deliberately exaggerates the metamorphoses by introducing the extreme topics of praise and blame—divinity and beast. Sin sprang from Satan's head "a Goddess arm'd." Now she is half-transformed into a brute, "a Serpent arm'd With mortal sting." Satan aspired to be "like God," and his followers have worshiped him "like a God." Now he is transformed into a dragon and receives their hisses instead of applause. The worldly conquerors of *Paradise Regain'd* embody the same antithesis. Though they "swell with pride, and must be titl'd Gods. . . . Worship't with Temple, Priest and Sacrifice," death exposes them as "scarce men, Rolling in brutish vices, and deform'd."[29]

This predominantly ethical conception of the metamorphosis enjoyed widespread popularity during the Renaissance—in literature, in art, in masques and interludes. It dominates commentaries on Ovid and Dante. It recurs frequently in emblem books. It appears in allegorical interpretations of Homer's Circe and in such Renaissance versions as

---

bellutos, interiecti homines: inter divinam sive heroicam *virtutem*, & feritatem media virtus hominis. . . . *Heroica* illa virtus, eximiae laudi est, ut viceversa feritas, summa vituperationi. Neque enim laus ulla praeclarior est, quam illa quae similitudinem & speciem aliquam divinitatis homini attribuit. . . . Neque maior esse potest vituperatio, quam belluarum, in specie figuraque, feritatis."

29. In the vision of the Lazar-house (XI, 504–22) man's neglect of the divine image in himself is appropriately punished by physical deformity.

the gardens of Alcina, Armida, and Acrasia.[30] Milton exploits a well-established convention, but (as usual) he radically alters it in adapting it to the epic framework. In his hands it becomes an Aristotelian reversal. It illustrates divine providence and supernal justice. It puts into execution the sentence already pronounced on the serpent in Eden. It reveals the moral reality underlying the heroic *eidolon*. Satan's metamorphosis into a beast provides a final ironic commentary on his earlier attempts to "be like the Most High." Instead of putting on "the image of God," he assumes that of a beast. Through a time-tried poetic convention—the symbolic metamorphosis—Milton dramatizes the moral antithesis between heroic virtue and its contrary vice, the logical opposition between *virtus heroica* and *feritas*.

In his epic, as in his *Artis Logicae*, he is still the dialectician.

30. For studies of the Renaissance enchantress, see Merritt Y. Hughes, "Spenser's Acrasia and the Circe of the Renaissance," *Journal of the History of Ideas*, IV (1943), 381–99.

14. *The Classical Hero*

Satan and Gentile Virtue

❦ For many critics the classical elements in Milton's Hell affirm his humanism, but challenge his Christian values. They lead to additional inconsistencies in characterization. The degraded devil of the later books is inconsistent with the heroic rebel of Books I and II. Satan's character is self-contradictory, and the contradiction springs in part from the conflict between Milton's Puritanism and his Hellenism, his "Hebrew hate of sin" and his "Greek passion for beauty." Thus, in Herford's opinion, the poet's humanism clashed with his Christianity. After "creating his glorious Satan," Milton "felt compunction lest the author of Evil should be taken for the hero of his great poem; and besides stripping him of his noble human form, and transforming him into a serpent, pursues him all through the later books of the poem with fierce abuse and reproof."[1]

The alleged inconsistency is, however, largely a figment of the critic's own imagination. It results primarily from a failure to recognize the ambivalence of Renaissance attitudes towards classical antiquity. The Ethnics had established the norms of the classical languages, and the rules of the traditional arts and sciences. In literature and art they had achieved standards of excellence that the Renaissance craftsman (whether poet or architect or sculptor) might profitably imitate.

1. C. H. Herford, *Dante and Milton* (Manchester, 1924), pp. 34–35.

In public life they had performed notable exploits in war and peace, and these might still inspire or instruct the contemporary soldier or statesman. Like Petrarch and Machiavelli,[2] many a Renaissance humanist found in classical poetry and history examples that possessed a quasi-rhetorical force as instruments of persuasion—examples that might exhort to virtue or "dehort" from vice.

On the other hand, the classics were morally inadequate—vitiated by ignorance of the true faith and its witness to the Highest Good.

I

Like other Christian humanists, Milton stood in a paradoxical relationship to the ancients. Though they could offer him models for literary imitation, their pagan status diminished their value as moral teachers, and a Christian poet might imitate their ethical content only with caution. Greek poetry was "Thin sown with aught of profit or delight," and Greek philosophy could only deceive:

> *Alas what can they teach, and not mislead;*
> *Ignorant of themselves, of God much more . . . ?*

In *Paradise Regain'd* Milton's attitude towards the moral value of classical civilization is painfully clear—so clear that it ought to resolve some of the ambiguities surrounding the classical elements in *Paradise Lost.* One would hardly expect the two poems to show marked contradictions on this point; nor, indeed, do they. The ethical postulates that lead the poet to censure classical philosophy and poetry also underlie his treatment of the fallen angels. By casting his devils in the mold of classical heroes, he achieves poetic imitation of the ancients, yet simultaneously emphasizes the gulf between Christian and pagan conceptions of heroic virtue. If his Hell is classical, it is also heathen. The devils not only pose as heathen gods; they also bear an impressive resemblance to pagan heroes. They too are infidels, unable to seek or find grace, and impotent to merit salvation by their own exertions. They too have not lost "all their virtue"—yet this serves in large part, to their eventual confusion. Indeed, the devils' apparent virtues are frequently "splendid vices"; what genuine virtues they *do* possess are Gentile, rather than Christian.

Morally, the state of the fallen angels roughly parallels that of the Ethnics. Both are alienate from God. Both tend to overlook the limitations of their fallen nature and to trust accordingly in their own

2. See R. R. Bolgar, *The Classical Heritage* (New York, 1964), pp. 253–56; 281, "The scholars who followed Petrarch . . sought for heroes, so that in their writings we find Livy valued above Tacitus . . . Where the twelfth century had seen the Greeks and Romans as paragons of learning, the fifteenth saw them as paragons of human excellence. . . ." For Erasmus' more critical attitude towards Livy, see p. 340. Cf. Federico Chabod, *Machiavelli and the Renaissance* (New York, 1965), pp. 99, 103, 169.

merits, their own virtues, their own deeds. Relying on their own strength and wisdom instead of God's, they acknowledge no need for divine grace. Their very virtues are directed towards evil ends.

Criticism of the ancients on moral and religious grounds was common among Renaissance theologians. The merits of the infidel or reprobate and the limits of Gentile virtue had been hotly debated by Catholic and Protestant alike. Against the background of this controversy, it would not have been difficult for Milton's contemporaries to appreciate the moral ambivalence of the classical elements that adorn his Hell. By making his demons talk and act like classical warriors and philosophers, the poet suggested to his audience, at the very start, a concept it had encountered already in theological controversies concerning the ancient heathen—the idea that human strength and intellect at their best belong to a nature depraved by sin and a world corrupted by death.

II

The latent parallel between the devils and the Gentiles emphasizes a cardinal doctrine of Reformed theology—the inadequacy of human works, however great and seemingly worthy, to merit an eternal reward. If the greatest works of men are surpassed by those of reprobate devils, how can fallen man expect, by his own efforts alone, to win a reward of lasting value? If Satan's heroic enterprise leads but to deeper damnation, what can frail mankind hope to achieve by its own exploits? Milton utilizes the *gesta diaboli* much as Protestant theologians had utilized the deeds of the Gentiles—as an argument for justification by faith rather than by works. By emphasizing the merits of the fallen angels, he stresses, by contrast, their exclusion from grace.

Like the Ethnics, the rebel angels ignore their fallen nature and rely on their own exploits instead of divine grace, trusting their own merits instead of those of a Mediator. Like the Ethnics, they seek their own praise rather than that of God, and their very virtues redound to their disadvantage.

In the course of Milton's epic his fallen archangel conceives and executes an enterprise of conquest and destruction closely resembling that of the conventional epic hero. Nevertheless, for a seventeenth-century Protestant, this apparently heroic exploit should have fitted into a familiar ethical category, a pattern already delineated and condemned by theologians in their discussions of pagan virtue.

Besides preoccupying Luther and Calvin, this subject had also engaged Paolo Sarpi and Richard Humfrey. These authors had advanced the following charges against the ancient Gentiles:

1. In their deeds of valor and virtuous acts, they sought their own glory instead of God's.

2. However heroic such works might appear, they were performed for a bad end and were therefore sinful.

3. The ancient Gentiles were only superficially virtuous, for they lacked inward sanctity.

4. They sought their reward on earth rather than in Heaven, pursuing worldly renown rather than celestial glory.

5. Their religion tended to fill man with pride by persuading him that he was naturally virtuous.

6. Their teachings incited him to revenge rather than to patience.

7. Since none of man's works, whether internal or external, can justify him before God, the pagan heroes might exhibit civil or political goodness and win praise in the political forum or before popular opinion, but they could not merit righteousness before God.

Most of these points could apply equally well to the "heroic" Satan of *Paradise Lost*. He expects to merit honor and praise by his perilous journey through space; in his original revolt he had sought glory as his prime end. His enterprise against man is conceived in direct opposition to the divine will; no matter how heroically he may describe it, it is, therefore, essentially sinful in end and intent. His first speech in Book IV underlines the superficiality of the apparent virtues he had displayed in reorganizing the infernal host and council. It demonstrates his loss of inner peace and internal sanctity. Despairing of regaining the beatitude of Heaven, he seeks instead the rewards and praises that Hell can give him. He believes that his natural virtues—his strength and reason—are still unimpaired by his fall and that he himself is still *naturally* virtuous. Like the Gentiles, he is motivated by desire for revenge, and the patience that he and his associates exhibit is pagan rather than Christian. Whatever deeds he performs cannot regain divine favor. Though he exhibits some of the political virtues of a skillful leader—and thereby wins praise from other devils—his actions merit shame and condemnation from God.

III

In Luther's *De Servo Arbitrio*, criticism of the merits of the Gentiles is closely associated with the doctrine of the bondage of the will. In his answer to Erasmus' *Diatribe on the Freedom of the Will*, Luther argues that the most exalted works of the Ethnics were carnal and therefore evil. In the New Testament the ground of reward is not man's merit, but God's promise. "In the matter of merit and reward, we deal with either *worthiness* or *consequence*. If you have *worthiness* in view, there is no merit and no reward. . . . If, on the other hand, you have *consequences* in view, there is nothing good or evil, that has not its reward."

Emphasizing the Biblical distinction between the carnal and the spiritual, Luther insists that all men are merely "flesh"—"both body and soul, with all their strength and works, all their vices and virtues, all their wisdom and folly, all their righteousness and unrighteousness." All are flesh and "void of the glory of God and the Spirit of God [Rom. 3:23]."

Erasmus had earlier maintained that "not every energy in man is flesh" and cited the ancient philosophers as proof. "There is an energy called the soul, and one called the spirit, by which we aspire to what is upright, as did the philosophers; who taught that we should welcome a thousand deaths sooner than commit a vile action...." To refute this argument Luther attacks Erasmus' concept of the "meritorious good" and denies the ability of the philosophers (even of "a Socrates twice or seven times over") to live up to this teaching: "Could they aspire to upright action [the meritoriously good] when they did not even know what an upright action was?"

As for the ancient worthies of Greece and Rome, they had sought their own glory rather than God's:

> If I should ask you for the most outstanding example of such uprightness, you would say, perhaps, that it was nobly done when men died for their country, for their wives and children, or for their parents; or when they refrained from lying or treachery; or when they endured exquisite torments rather than lie or betray others, as did Q[uintus] Scaevola, M[arcus] Regulus, and others. But what can you show us in all these men but the external appearance of their works? Have you seen their hearts? Why it is at once apparent from the look of their works that they did it all for their own glory, so that they were not ashamed to acknowledge and to boast that it was their own glory that they sought. The Romans, on their own confession, performed their valiant acts out of a thirst for glory. So did the Greeks. So did the Jews. So does the whole human race.

Though this apparent heroism seems meritoriously good in the sight of man, nothing is less so in God's eyes: "It is, indeed, the supreme impiety and the height of sacrilege, inasmuch as they did not do it for the glory of God...." Instead, they robbed him of his glory, and "*were never less upright and more vile than when they shone in their highest virtues.*" The faculty that Erasmus extols as the "spirit that rules" or that "principal part of man, which aspires to what is upright," is no more than "a plunderer of God's glory, and a usurper of His majesty!"

Paradoxically, Luther reduces the heroism of the ancients to vain-glorious sacrilege. The heroes themselves are the worst offenders. The insult to divine glory and majesty "*applies most of all when men are at their noblest, and are most distinguished for their own highest virtues!*"

Accordingly, there is a sharp contrast between the merits of the ancients as they appear to the world and to God; and the most excellent men in the world's opinion are vilest in God's sight: "... the brightest virtues among the heathen, the best works among the philosophers, the most excellent deeds among men, which appear in the sight of the world to be upright and good, and are so called, are really flesh in the sight of God, and minister to the kingdom of Satan; ... they are ungodly, sacrilegious, and evil in every respect."[3] For Luther, then, there is no merit at all in the works of the noblest men among Greeks and Romans. Those men of heroic excellence were, on the contrary, the vilest of mortals in God's view.

IV

Calvin's attitude towards the potential heroism of the "natural man" is less extreme than Luther's. He acknowledges the virtues of many of the ancient Gentiles, but argues that these are really due to God's special grace:

> In every age there have been persons who, guided by nature, have striven towards virtue throughout life.... [These] have by the very zeal of their honesty given proof that there was some purity in their nature, [and their examples] seem to warn us against adjudging man's nature wholly corrupted, because some men have by its promptings not only excelled in remarkable deeds, but conducted themselves most honorably throughout life. But here it ought to occur to us that amid this corruption of nature there is some place for God's grace; not such grace as to cleanse it, but to restrain it inwardly.

Among the unregenerate, God "bridles perversity of nature, that it may not break forth into action; but he does not purge it within." Some of these are restrained by shame, others by the law. "Still others, because they consider an honest manner of life profitable, in some measure aspire to it. Others rise above the common lot, in order by their excellence to keep the rest obedient to them." (Several of these motives—the dread of shame, the desire to rule over his companions, the concern to demonstrate his superior worth—will appear in Milton's Satan.)

The heroism of the natural man results from God's providence—his desire to provide effective leaders for fallen man. But the virtues of such

3. Martin Luther, *On the Bondage of the Will*, trans. J. I. Packer and O. R. Johnston (Westwood, N.J., 1957), pp. 181–82, 251–53, 276–83. Italics mine. In attacking Erasmus' views, Luther argues *a majori* (from the greater to the less). The noblest of the Gentiles rejected the truth. The "most excellent part of the most excellent men not only did not follow this method of righteousness, not only was ignorant of it, but when it was revealed and proclaimed to them, thrust it away with the greatest hate...." Paul specifically instances "the noblest among the Greeks when he says that the wiser ones among them 'became fools, and their heart was darkened,' and that 'they became vain in their own reasonings.'"

men are praiseworthy only in human eyes; in God's sight they are vitiated by ambition and their indifference to the glory of God:

Indeed, I admit that the endowments resplendent in Camillus were gifts of God and seem rightly commendable if judged in themselves. But how will these serve as proofs of natural goodness in him? . . . What power for good will you attribute to human nature in this respect, if in the loftiest appearance of integrity, it is always found to be impelled toward corruption? . . . [T]hese are not common gifts of nature, but special graces of God, which he bestows variously and in a certain measure upon men otherwise wicked. . . . For God, in providing for the human race, often endows with a heroic nature those destined to command. From this workshop have come forth the qualities of great leaders celebrated in histories. . . . But because, however excellent anyone has been, his own ambition always pushes him on—a blemish with which all virtues are so sullied that before God they lose all favor—anything in profane men that appears praiseworthy must be considered worthless. Besides, where there is no zeal to glorify God, the chief part of uprightness is absent. . . . As for the virtues that deceive us with their vain show, they shall have their praise in the political assembly and in common renown among men; but before the heavenly judgment seat they shall be of no value to acquire righteousness.

Like the heroism of the Gentiles, Satan's apparent virtues are tarnished by ambition and his refusal to glorify God. They resemble "the qualities of great leaders" and win praise in the political assemblies of Hell, but they lack the essence of righteousness and are therefore only the shadows of true virtue.

The achievements of the fallen angels in the arts or sciences—in architecture, eloquence, and philosophy—are likewise characteristic of the Gentiles. In Calvin's opinion, "the discovery or systematic transmission of the arts, or the inner and more excellent knowledge of them," is "bestowed indiscriminately upon pious and impious"; it is among the "natural gifts" corrupted by the Fall:

Whenever we come upon these matters in secular writers, let that admirable light of truth shining in them teach us that the mind of man, though fallen and perverted from its wholeness, is nevertheless clothed and ornamented with God's excellent gifts. . . . Shall we deny that the truth shone upon the ancient jurists who established civic order and discipline with such great equity? Shall we say that the philosophers were blind in their fine observation and artful description of nature? . . . No, we cannot read the writings of the ancients on these subjects without great admiration. We marvel at them because we are compelled to recognize how pre-eminent they are. But shall we count anything praiseworthy or noble without recognizing at the same time that it comes from God?

These "natural men" were "sharp and penetrating in their investigation of inferior things," and their example indicates "how many gifts the Lord left to human nature even after it was despoiled of its true good." Nevertheless, these gifts are defiled and perverted from their true end: "For with the greatest truth Augustine teaches that as the free gifts were withdrawn from man after the Fall, so the natural ones remaining were corrupted. Not that the gifts could become defiled by themselves, seeing that they came from God. But to defiled man these gifts were no longer pure, and from them he could derive no praise at all."[4]

V

At the Council of Trent, where Luther's doctrines of exclusive justification by faith were condemned as heretical, the problem of the heroic deeds of the ancients played an important part in the discussion. According to Paolo Sarpi, the Council rejected the opinion "that all human works without faith are sins," on the grounds that there are certain acts which are morally good, even though they may not win favor from God. Among these are the "virtuous deeds" of "infidels and Christian sinners" and especially "the heroic exploits so extolled by antiquity."[5]

On the other hand, Fra Ambrogio Catarino (subsequently Bishop of Minori) maintained that without special aid from God man was unable to perform any good work—not even works that were merely "morally good." Without grace all his acts must be sins. However heroic the deeds of infidels or unconverted sinners might appear in the

4. John Calvin, *Institutes of the Christian Religion*, ed. John T. McNeill, trans. Ford Lewis Battles (Philadelphia, 1960), I, 270, 273–75, 291–94. For Calvin, as for Luther, the question of the virtues of the Gentiles was closely linked with the problem of the merits of the natural man, and this, in turn, involved the issue of justification by faith or by works. Like Luther, Calvin distinguished between merit and reward; fallen man might receive recompense through divine grace, but he did not merit it by his own works, and the doctrine of human merits tended to rob God of his glory: "The first part of a good work. is will; the other, a strong effort to accomplish it; the author of both is God. Therefore we are robbing the Lord if we claim for ourselves anything either in will or in accomplishment." (p. 302) Man cannot take credit for any good work apart from divine grace. (p. 306) Calvin dismisses the doctrine of human merit as injurious to "sincere faith." None of man's works can "bear God's gaze because they are full of uncleanness." Though the Father accepts them and promises a reward, nevertheless "whatever is praiseworthy in works is God's grace; there is not a drop that we ought by rights to ascribe to ourselves. If we truly and earnestly recognize this, not only will all confidence in merit vanish, but the very notion. . . . To man we assign only this: that he pollutes and contaminates by his impurity those very things which were good. For nothing proceeds from a man, however perfect he be, that is not defiled by some spot. Let the Lord, then, call to judgment the best in human works: he will indeed recognize in them his own righteousness but man's dishonor and shame!" (pp. 789–91).

5. Ernesto Buonaiuti (ed.), *Le più belle pagine di Fra Paolo Sarpi* (Milano, 1925), p. 81: ". . . e queste sono le opere oneste degl' infedeli e cristiani peccatori, le quali è repugnanza grandissima chiamar insieme oneste e peccati, massime che in questo numero sono incluse le opere eroiche tanto lodato dall' antichità."

eyes of men, they were essentially perverse.[6] Since any "good work" must be good in all circumstances, its failure in a single particular made it corrupt. As all works performed for an evil end were necessarily tainted, the apparent heroism of the infidels was actually sinful.[7]

VI

In the preface to his translation of St. Ambrose's *Christian Offices*, Richard Humfrey compared the Gentile and the Christian heroism in detail.[8]

Like Calvin and Catarino, he argued that the virtues of the ancients were superficial rather than essential and that they were vitiated by their end:

> The practice of vertue in the Gentile, whose person the Lord accepteth not, because hee remaining in infidelity, and unconverted, aimeth not at the honour of God, nor whatsoever performance of his truth, . . . is such as is undoubtedly estranged from the life of God, without expectation of a better life, destitute of all promise of a Saviour to bring him to it. The want of faith only cuts them off for any true reputation thereby, for any acceptation at the hands of God. For without it, it is impossible to please him.

The Gentiles sought their own glory; Christian heroes seek the glory of God:

> The Heathens in their apprehension goe thus farre, that men are borne partly for their countrey, partly for their parents and friends, and some have added this also, that partly for the service of God: and therefore for the benefit of these, chiefly for their countrey and friends, they have adventured their lives thereby to attaine immortal fame: but christian philosophie binds to this, that all be done for the honour of God, making his praise the only marke at the which we must . . . aime at in all our affaires, and what is to bee done for man or nation is to bee performed subordinately, and so that it may not diminish his glory, and so that it must bee solely for his names sake.

The classical philosophers, in Humfrey's opinion, had been able to produce good citizens but not true saints. Though they "have endevored to make good men, yet have they effected no more, then to make them civilly good, morally vertuous: but where notwithstanding is inward sanctitie [?]"

6. *Ibid.*, p. 81: "Per il che tutte le opere degl' infedeli che da Dio non sono eccitati a venir alla fede, e tutte quelle de' fedeli peccatori inanzi che Dio gli ecciti alla conversione, se ben paressero agli uomini oneste, anzi eroiche, sono veri peccati, e chi le loda le considera in genere e nell' esterna apparenza; ma chi essaminerà le circostanze di ciascuna, vi troverà la perversità."

7. *Ibid.*, p. 82: ". . . ma gl' infedeli riferiscono tutto quello che fanno nel fine della loro setta che è cattivo; per il che, se ben paiono eroiche a chi non vede l'intenzione, sono nondimeno peccati. . . ."

8. St. Ambrose, *Christian Offices Crystall Glasse*, trans. Richard Humfrey (London, 1637).

In commenting on Romans 14:23 ("whatsoever is not of faith is sin"), St. Thomas Aquinas had argued that infidels do not sin in every work when the natural goodness of reason has not been altogether extinguished in them. Humfrey qualifies this doctrine. It applies only to "the substance of worke, sinne in it selfe, and civill actions; but concerning spirituall to bee so, we utterly deny, and that upon sure warrant of the holy Ghost, testifying, *that all wisdome of the flesh is enmitie against God.*"

In many respects pagan and Christian religion are diametrically opposite. The one persuades to revenge, the other to patience. The former "fills men with pride" by convincing them that they are "naturally vertuous"; the latter "abats pride of heart, and shewes that naturally wee are sinfull." The virtues of the Gentiles were superficial, for their great men did not seek internal sanctity:

They, which are guided by the rules of *Ethnick* Philosophie, cared not to be inwardly vertuous, as may appeare by the examples of those of greatest reputation among the *Romans*, as of *Caesar*, *Pompey*, *Cicero*, and even of *Cato* of *Utica* himselfe: for his heart no lesse then theirs was sore swolne with an aspiring desire devoide of humilitie, and conscionable comportment. But such as followed the precepts of Christian philosophie, sought not outwardly onely, but so to adorne their hearts, and consciences with vertues, as in truth they might best please God. . . . Among the Heathens, *Scipio African*, *Alexander*, *Cyrus*, *Archytas*, *Xenocrates*, are highly extolled for their temperance: yet this being in the outside, and by the gift of restraint only, not in the inside, it is not that which is in a Christian heart, and was in the heart of *Joseph* sanctified by the Spirit of God.

Hence there is an essential difference between the heroism of the pagan and that of the Hebrew or Christian. What is "heroicall, is not in like manner in *Ioseph*, and *Alexander*; *David* and *Scipio*. For the one sort were moved by the Spirit of sanctification; the other not so; the one sought the honour of God, as the final cause; the other shot at pompe, and policie, greatnesse of government together with their owne praise, as the upshot of all their hopes."

Similarly, the fortitude of Esther, Judith, and Jephthah's daughter was greater than that of Damon and Pythias, since it aimed at a higher end: ". . . theirs [was] true fortitude in a good cause, to the best end, with undaunted courage, this in none of these respects commendable, their cause was the preservation of the Church of God, [their] end, the honour of his Name. . . ." As for the "*Heroicks*, and noble spirits of the Heathen in peace and warre: it is the cause that must magnifie their courage, *causa fecit Martyrem, & causa facit militem palmarium;* the *Maccabees* sought the glory of God, these their own ends, and they had their immortall reward, and renowne, not in heaven, but on earth."

VII

Milton could use "the heroes of antiquity" and their "life of exertion and glory" as a standard for praising the heroes of the English Commonwealth.[9] Like Calvin, he believed that the ruins of the divine image were still perceptible in the noblest of the Ethnics despite the psychological effects of the Fall. Yet, unlike the stricter Calvinists, he recognized in fallen man some degree of moral freedom:

It cannot be denied . . . that some remnants of the divine image still exist in us, not wholly extinguished by this spiritual death. This is evident, not only from the wisdom and holiness of many of the heathen, manifested both in words and deeds, but also from what is said Gen. ix. 2 "The dread of you shall be upon every beast of the earth." . . . These vestiges of original excellence are visible, first, in the understanding. . . . Nor, again, is the liberty of the will entirely destroyed. First, with regard to things indifferent, whether natural or civil. . . . Secondly, the will is clearly not altogether inefficient in respect of good works, or at any rate of good endeavors; at least after the grace of God has called us: but its power is so small and insignificant, as merely to deprive us of all excuse for inaction, without affording any subject for boasting.[10]

Like Luther and Calvin before him, Milton is emphatic in his denunciation of the doctrine of human merits, even though he acknowledges a greater degree of liberty in fallen man. Regarding faith as the "essential form" of good works and insisting that the "works of believers are the works of the Spirit itself," he denies any real credit for them to man: "Hence may be easily discerned the vanity of human merits; seeing that, in the first place, our good actions are not our own, but of God working in us; secondly, that, were they our own, they would still be equally due; and, thirdly, that, in any point of view, there can be no proportion between our duty and the proposed reward."[11]

Observing that "as regards the satisfaction of Christ, and our conformity to his humiliation, the restoration of man is of merit," he insists that the merit belongs properly to God rather than to man:

Nor need we fear, lest in maintaining this belief we should lend any support to the doctrine of human merits. For our conformity to the image of Christ is as far from adding anything to the full and perfect satisfaction made by him, as our works are from adding to faith; it is faith that justifies, but a faith not destitute of works: and in like manner, if we deserve anything, if there be any worthiness in us on any ground whatever, it is God that hath made us worthy in Christ.[12]

9. In his *Second Defense* (*Works* [Columbia Edition; New York, 1931–38], VIII, 213–55), Milton compares Cromwell to Cyrus, Scipio, and Epaminondas.

10. See *De Doctrina*, Book I, Chapter 12 (Milton, *Works* [Columbia Edition; New York, 1933]), XV, 209, 211.

11. *De Doctrina*, Book I, Chapter 1.

12. *De Doctrina*, Book I, Chapter 16.

Again, in arguing that man is justified "by faith without the works of the law, but not without the works of faith," Milton goes out of his way to attack the doctrine of merits, citing Ephesians 2:8–10, "For by grace are ye saved through faith; and that not of yourselves: it is the gift of God: Not of works, lest any man should boast": "This interpretation . . . affords no countenance to the doctrine of human merits, inasmuch as both faith itself and its works are the works of the Spirit, not our own."[13]

Milton's classical Hell and heroic devils must be set against the background of Reformation concepts of Ethnic virtue and the vanity of human merits. In this context, many of the apparent inconsistencies that have perplexed his critics tend to disappear. His contemporaries were accustomed to thinking of the ancients as superficially heroic, yet intrinsically evil—unjustified in the sight of God. In Satan's salient features—ambition and revenge, political and military skill, pride in his own merits and works, boasting in his own strength and wisdom, pursuit of his own glory—they should have had little difficulty in recognizing the very traits that Luther and Humfrey had condemned in the ancient Gentiles. Though conventionally heroic by the standards of a fallen humanity, these characteristics were vicious by Christian standards. There would, accordingly, be no real contradiction between the merits of the "heroic" Satan of the early books and the reward he receives in Book X.

Protestant views of justification should also have placed Satan's heroic exploits in perspective. The doctrine of justification by faith rather than works and its corollary—the vanity of human merits—throw a new light on the conventional epic hero and his enterprise. The hero who relies on his own merits, boasts of his own exploits, and trusts in his own strength or wisdom to save him is inevitably doomed; in the end his enterprise must terminate in humiliation and death, as it cannot merit eternal glory or perpetual life. Whatever his merit in the eyes of men, in the sight of God the conventional "worthy" has no true worth.

Milton gives central emphasis to these concepts in *Paradise Lost*. They affect the choice of argument and the contrasting merits and rewards of the three principal persons of the poem and their exploits—the *gesta Christi*, the *gesta Adae*, and the *gesta diaboli*. In particular, Satan's fate serves as an argument *a fortiori* to dissuade fallen man from relying on his own merits and to persuade him conversely to place his faith in God. The same emphasis recurs in Milton's description of the Limbo of Vanities, full "Of all things transitory and vain,

13. *De Doctrina*, Book I, Chapter 22. For a perceptive examination of the problem of worth in Milton's epic, see Merritt Y. Hughes, "Merit in *Paradise Lost*," *Huntington Library Quarterly*, XXI (1967–68), 3–18.

when Sin *with vanity had fill'd the works of men.*"[14] The denizens of the moon—"Translated Saints, or middle Spirits . . . Betwixt th' Angelical and Human kind"—reflect both the Christian conception of the hero as saint and the Neo-Platonic conception of the hero as an order midway between man and daemon. Milton draws a deliberate contrast between the valid rewards of these true heroes and the vain recompense of the false "worthies" who inhabit the Paradise of Fools:

> *Both all things vain, and all who in vain things*
> *Built their fond hopes of Glory or lasting fame,*
> *Or happiness in this or th' other life;*
> *All who have their reward on Earth, the fruits*
> *Of painful Superstition and blind Zeal,*
> *Naught seeking but the praise of men, here find*
> *Fit retribution, empty as thir deeds. . . .*

The "degradation" of Satan in Book X and the humiliation that awaits the proud or ambitious man in the Limbo of Vanities both center on a false conceit of merit and a frustrated expectation of reward. Both emphasize the contrasting merits of fallen man or angel in the eyes of the world and in the sight of God.

The divine honors that the fallen angels bestow on their leader and that they themselves subsequently receive from a superstitious humanity provide yet another parallel with the classical heroes. In *Paradise Regain'd* Milton condemns the self-styled "Benefactors" who demanded adoration as deities. In this passage, as in his account of Empedocles in the Limbo of Vanities, he exploits the classical and patristic tradition that the ancient gods were really mortal kings and heroes who had been idolized by their contemporaries and immortalized by their posterity.[15] The epic catalogue of *Paradise Lost*, on the other hand, reflects the patristic doctrine that the Gentile deities were really devils. Both of these traditions concerning the origin of the pagan gods thus contribute to his heroic *eidolon*.

VIII

The problem of Gentile virtue reappears in a specifically literary context in Tasso's dialogue *Il Cataneo*.[16] For the three speakers—Cataneo, Vitelli, and Tasso himself—the point at issue is the propriety

14. Italics mine.

15. See Jean Seznec, *The Survival of the Pagan Gods*, trans. Barbara F. Sessions (New York, 1961), pp. 3 ff.

16. Torquato Tasso, *Prose*, ed. Francesco Flora (Milano, 1925); see especially pp. 186 ff.: "Io stimo che questi fossero uomini amici de la patria, liberatori de la Grecia, guastata da le fiere e da i mostri, ed oppressa da' tiranni, i quali soggiogarono i paesi estrani, e trionfarono de le barbare nazioni con pompa maravigliosa. . . . Noi fummo uomini

of comparing Christian rulers to pagan gods and heroes in encomiastic poetry. Thus Tasso maintains that Caro's eulogy of the King of France not only dishonors the pagan deities but also retains too much of the "odor of gentilism" to befit a defender of the faith. Vitelli, in turn, defends the honor of the ancients—valiant heroes and benefactors whom their contemporaries had honored as gods. He imagines them pleading their case as follows: Though Rome has forsaken the "lying gods" for the "true God," nevertheless "our ancient statues are still preserved, and we are honored in the verses of poets and the orations of illustrious men. Our fame seems to revive in the rimes of this new language, where we are pleased to be compared to new Caesars, New Octavii, and new Alexanders." In life we displayed fortitude and constancy and performed magnanimous deeds, and it is fitting that our glory should still resound. Even though it does not content us, as it is not the true glory, it consoles us, as our human virtues have no other reward than honorable fame.

To Vitelli's apology for the ancients, Tasso replies that the basic issue is not whether they merit glory, but whether they should be honored as divine. The deification poets confer on them is like "quella podestá maravigliosa de gli idolatri d'Egitto, con la quale gli uomini facean gli Dei. . . ." Cataneo supports this objection. In Varro's opinion, it was politically "useful" for men to feign themselves "sons of the god," because this belief in divine descent more easily inspired them to accomplish great deeds and aroused greater ardor in others. Alexander had fostered this belief in his army when he visited the temple of Jupiter Ammon, and Scipio had adored the same god on the Capitol. Nevertheless, though this artifice might be praiseworthy in the Gentiles, "who did not know true praise, as they did not know the true good," it is "false and damnable" for Christians. As "no virtue should ever be disassociated from the others," pagan worthies are not comparable to Christian heroes even in moral virtues—much less in theological virtues. "No demigod, no hero, no Gentile king ought to be equalled with any Christian prince."

The Renaissance attitude towards the ancients remained ambivalent. Princely families and their flatterers proudly traced their ancestry to the heroes of the Trojan war or to figures still more legendary—Jason and Hercules. Christian theologians occasionally admitted them to honored positions in Heaven. Indeed, Zwingli himself assigned to

valorosi, creduti Dei per lo nostro valore, e per lo giovamento fatto a' miseri mortali, che da varie calamitá erano circondati: e mentre fiorirono le cittá de la Grecia, ed ebbero quasi l'imperio del mare, e passaro con gli eserciti ne l'Asia, ponendo il freno a potentissimi re ed a popoli numerosi, fiori parimente la nostra gloria, e ci furono drizzati i tempii, e consecrati gli altari in tutti i regni de l'oriente e del mezzogiorno, e ne l'occidente ancora. . . ."

"Hercules, Theseus, Socrates, the Catos, the Scipios" a station in Paradise close to Enoch and St. Paul and not too remote from God Himself.[17]

For Milton the inherent contradictions in Renaissance ideas of heroic virtue and the merit of the pagan worthies proved a poetic asset. They gave him a traditional basis both for his heroic idol and for the standards by which he exposed its fallacy. They lent verisimilitude and probability both to his portrait of the Satanic hero and to the iconoclastic scene in which he shattered it. These discrepancies and variations in contemporary evaluations of the ancients left ample room for the poet to exercise his own originality, his plastic powers as a "creator" or "maker."

17. See Seznec, *Pagan Gods*, pp. 23–26.

Part V

❦

The Devil As Rhetorician

❦

15. "Conquest Fraudulent"

Satan and the Strategy of Illusion

❦ Criticism of the opening books of *Paradise Lost* has diverged widely in its approach to the fallen angels. To what extent should their declarations be taken at face value? To some commentators, the superficially heroic attitudes of Satan and his compeers were actually little more than postures; their logic was mere rhetoric, their arguments essentially "bluff." This tissue of lies, woven to conceal the unsightly realities of the diabolical predicament—sin against God, and in consequence, eternal damnation—should not (these critics argued) be taken literally. It served, on the whole, rather to disguise than to reveal the true nature of Hell and the true character of Hell's angels. The primary concept Milton tried to convey was not the heroism of the fallen spirits, but their mendacity—the element (conscious or unconscious) of illusion and falsehood. "Hell is always inaccurate," asserted Charles Williams[1] and C. S. Lewis;[2] "Satan lies about every subject he mentions in *Paradise Lost*."

. . . it was the poet's intention [Lewis maintained] to be fair to evil, . . . to show it *first* at its height, with all its rants and melodrama and "Godlike imitated

First published, in somewhat different form, in the *Journal of English and Germanic Philology*, LIX (1960) 640–54.

1. Charles Williams, "Introduction," *The English Poems of John Milton* (London, 1951), p. xiii.
2. C. S. Lewis, *A Preface to Paradise Lost* (London, 1949), p. 95. Cf. B. Rajan, *Paradise Lost and the Seventeenth Century Reader* (London, 1947), pp. 95–96.

state" about it, and *then* to trace what actually becomes of such self-intoxication when it encounters reality.

> But I do not know whether we can distinguish his [Satan's] conscious lies from the blindness which he has almost willingly imposed on himself . . . for far earlier in his career he has become more a Lie than a Liar, a personified self-contradiction.[3]

Waldock, on the other hand, regarded these initial speeches as the true index, the correct measure, of Satan and his companions. However frequently Milton attempted to modify or neutralize them, they remained the real norm of these characters on the "level of demonstration or exhibition." It was, therefore, Milton—not Satan or Belial—whose assertions contradicted reality.

> If one observes what is happening one sees that there is hardly a great speech of Satan's that Milton is not at pains to correct, to damp down and neutralize. He will put some glorious thing in Satan's mouth, then, anxious about the effect of it, will pull us gently by the sleeve, saying . . .: "Do not be carried away by this fellow: he *sounds* splendid, but take my word for it. . . ." We have in fact . . . two levels: the level of demonstration or exhibition, and the level of allegation or commentary; and . . . there is disagreement. What is conveyed on the one level is for a large part of the time not in accord with what is conveyed on the other. Milton's allegations *clash* with his demonstrations.[4]

The two viewpoints were thus directly opposite in their approaches to the issue of appearance and reality in Milton's epic. In Lewis' opinion, Books I and II deliberately presented "the most specious aspects of Satan." In Waldock's mind, they delineated the "real" Satan of *Paradise Lost*. Where Lewis and Williams distinguished the superficial illusions of Hell from the moral reality of evil and the spiritual reality of damnation, Waldock contrasted "the Satan Milton had in mind" with the Satan he actually portrayed, the "ghost-epic shaped in our minds from what we know very well Milton was trying to do" with the "epic that is there on pages." For the former critics, the heroic Archfiend was an illusion; for the latter, he represented (however unintentionally) a poetic truth.

Lewis' interpretation rested ultimately on the traditional conception of the devil as the father of lies: "[Milton] was relying on two predispositions in the minds of his readers, which in that age, would have guarded them from our later misunderstanding. Men still believed that there really was such a person as Satan, and that he was a liar. The poet did not foresee that his work would one day meet the disarming simplicity of critics who take for gospel things said by the father of falsehood in public speeches to his troops."[5]

3. Lewis, pp. 95, 97.
4. A. J. A. Waldock, *Paradise Lost and Its Critics* (Cambridge, 1947), pp. 77–78.
5. Waldock, pp. 144–145; Lewis, p. 98.

Waldock's opinion, on the other hand, was based on his belief in the superior validity of "the level of demonstration or exhibition" in contradistinction to "the level of allegation or commentary":

And between a comment and a demonstration . . . there can never be a real question, surely, which has the higher validity. . . . What the comment really means is that Milton has begun to realize, if vaguely, that his material has been getting out of hand.

The process begins . . . quite early in the poem. After Satan's very first speech comes the comment:

> *So spake th' Apostate Angel, though in pain,*
> *Vaunting aloud, but rackt with deep despaire.* (I, 125)

Has there been much despair in what we have just been listening to? The speech would almost seem to be incompatible with that. To accept Milton's comment here . . . as if it had a validity equal to that of the speech itself is surely very naive critical procedure.[6]

In at least one respect Waldock's own "critical procedure" was itself patently "naive." His most serious oversight was the failure to conceive the possibility of an instance where the poet's "level of demonstration" might comprehend a conscious delineation of falsehood. Hence he missed the essential point of Milton's "demonstration."

What, indeed, was Milton attempting to "demonstrate" in the speeches he assigned to the fallen angels? If (among other things) he was essaying to convey their disregard of right reason and alienation from truth, then one can hardly accept Waldock's contention that "Milton's allegations *clash* with his demonstration." By mistaking the poet's conscious delineation of falsehood for a bona fide exhibition of "real character," Waldock overlooked the true significance of the contrast between Satan's words and Milton's glosses on them. Instead of an inadvertent "clash" between the levels of demonstration and commentary, *Paradise Lost* embodied a deliberate antithesis between appearance and reality, falsehood and truth. Among the concepts that Milton was intentionally "demonstrating" in these portraits of Satan and his fellow-fiends were the ideas of mendacity, sophistry, and illusion.

6. Waldock, pp. 49, 78. Waldock's observation that there was not "much despair in what we have just been listening to" by no means invalidates Milton's comment on this speech. Satan could hardly boast and give vent to despair in the same breath. To portray him as "vaunting aloud," the poet must defer the direct expression of Satan's despair until a more suitable occasion, when there would no longer be any necessity for, or advantage in, boasting. Hence Milton, quite logically, postponed Satan's outbreak of despair until his arrival on Mount Niphates.

Similarly, Waldock's objection that Belial's words were not merely "cloath'd in reasons garb," but *were* reasonable (p. 79) is only a half-truth. Though the greater part of this speech was a valid refutation of Moloch's argument, the conclusions Belial drew (ll. 209–25) were patently false.

Lewis' interpretation, on the other hand, accorded not only with conventional demonology, but also with the principal tenets of Renaissance critical doctrine.

I

If Milton was to pay more than lip service to neo-Aristotelian poetic theory, "... that sublime art which in Aristotle's poetics, in Horace, and the Italian commentaries of Castelvetro, Tasso, Mazzoni, and others, teaches what the laws are of a true epic poem, what a dramatic, what a lyric, what decorum is, which is the grand masterpiece to observe,"[7] he could scarcely ignore its precepts in sketching the outlines of the fallen Archangel. In several respects Renaissance critical doctrine made it advisable to stress, comparatively early in *Paradise Lost*, the concept of Satan's mendacity.

Such a characterization was doubly appropriate—both on the basis of divine testimony[8] and from the nature of Milton's theme. No less an authority than Christ himself had called the devil a liar and the father of lies: "He was a murderer from the beginning, and abode not in the truth, because there is no truth in him. When he speaketh a lie, he speaketh of his own: for he is a liar and the father of it."[9] Moreover, the very argument of *Paradise Lost* necessarily entailed an emphasis on this aspect of Satan's character. In the Biblical narrative of the temptation the serpent's argument had centered upon a lie: "And the serpent said unto the woman, Ye shall not surely die: For God doth know that in the day ye eat thereof, then your eyes shall be opened, and ye shall be as gods, knowing good and evil."[10]

According to Aristotle's *Poetics*, the poet should make his characters *similis* (ὅμοιος) or "like the reality" and *aequalis* (ὁμαλός) or "consistent." He should also aim at "the necessary or the probable; so that whenever such-and-such a personage says or does such-and-such a thing, it shall be the probable or necessary outcome of his character. ..."[11]

7. John Milton, *Prose Works* (London, 1883), III, 473–74.

8. For Milton's conception of the value of divine testimony in argument, see *Artis Logicae*, Book I, Chapter 32, "De Testimonio divino" (Milton, *Works* [New York, 1935], XI, 278–83). Obviously, the judgments of God and the faithful angels—confirming, as they do, the Biblical testimony—are a more reliable index of Satan's true character than the statements of the devil and his angels.

9. John 8:44.

10. Genesis 3:4–5. See the glosses on Genesis 3 in the Tremellius-Junius Bible (Hanoviae, 1624) in regard to the serpent's "fallacia" in tempting Eve.

11. Aristotle, *On the Art of Poetry*, trans. Ingram Bywater (Oxford, 1951), pp. 55–56; Daniel Heinsius, *Aristotelis De Poetica* (Lugd. Batav., 1643), pp. 282–83; Heinsius, *De Tragoediae Constitutione* (Lugd. Batav., 1643), pp. 143–44; Lodovico Castelvetro, *Poetica d'Aristotele Vulgarizzata et Sposta* (Basilea, 1576), pp. 319–27; Torquato Tasso, *Prose* (Milan, 1935), pp. 441, 424.

To portray Satan "like the reality," Milton should logically present him as Scripture had described him—as *ψεύστης . . . καὶ ὁ πατὴρ αὐτοῦ*. To depict him as "consistent," to make his temptation of Eve seem "the probable and necessary outcome of his character," the poet should previously establish his character as a liar. Lewis' belief—that the Satan of the early books constitutes a deliberate portrait of falsehood—seems, accordingly, decidedly more probable than Waldock's view.

Far from clashing with his demonstration, Milton's passing comments—the "level of allegation or commentary"—were intended as a safeguard, to forestall the reader's overlooking the specious nature of Satan's utterances and mistaking the false appearance for reality. This device, moreover, had been specifically recommended by Tasso: ". . . and Plutarch, in his book on the manner of interpreting the poets, . . . teaches that the poet is permitted to censure and interpose his own judgment and thus first accuse wickedness. By this means he demonstrates what is useful [*utile*]. Otherwise he could harm us by the example of the things he has imitated. Reading the poets could be very dangerous indeed if, in doubtful passages, they did not show us the path of virtue and serve us as a guide."[12]

II

Lewis' interpretation of the Satan of Books I and II in terms of specious appearance and falsehood accorded, moreover, with Milton's presentation of this character elsewhere in *Paradise Lost*.[13] Since the major features of Satan's behavior in the crucial temptation scene had been fixed by Scripture and admitted little variation, they should, on the whole, have provided the real norm for his words and actions in the episodes which preceded and followed. Any details which Milton might invent to describe the Archfiend's activities before or after the temptation must—according to Renaissance poetic theory—be consistent with his role as tempter in Book IX. To make Satan *similis*, the poet should delineate him essentially as the Bible had portrayed him—as a liar and forger of illusions. To make him *aequalis*, the author should present him consistently in this role.

On the whole, Milton met the latter requirement as well as the former. From Book III onward, he portrayed Satan consistently as the

12. Tasso, p. 423.

13. *Paradise Regain'd* likewise presents Satan consistently as a forger of fallacies and lies (see Book I, ll. 375, 428, 430; III, 3; IV, 3, 491) and describes his encounter with Christ as a contest between falsehood and truth (III, 443). The learning of the Gentiles (IV, 319) contains no "true wisdom," but only "her false resemblance." Cf. also *In Quintum Novembris*, ll. 17, 79, 131.

"false dissembler," resorting to a continuous series of disguises, ruses, and deceptions. To learn the route to Paradise, Satan questioned Uriel in the form of a "stripling Cherube." On Mount Niphates he concealed his passions ("ire, envie and despair") with "outward calme,"

> *Artificer of fraud; and was the first*
> *That practisd falshood under saintly shew,*
> *Deep malice to conceale, couch't with revenge. . . .*

After entering Paradise he assumed a succession of animal disguises to avoid detection—"the shape of a Cormorant," a lion, a tiger, a toad. Detected by Ithuriel's spear—"for no falshood can endure Touch of Celestial temper"—he attempted to evade Gabriel's interrogation by lying:

> *To say and strait unsay, pretending first*
> *Wise to flie pain, professing next the Spie,*
> *Argues no Leader, but a lyar trac't. . . .*

A week later, re-entering Paradise "as a mist by Night," he chose the serpent as his

> *Fit Vessel, fittest Imp of fraud, in whom*
> *To enter, and his dark suggestions hide*
> *From sharpest sight. . . .*

Depicting the fallen Archangel consistently as a liar and deceiver, who gradually evolved his strategy and tactics of illusion with fuller knowledge of his intended victims and the potentialities of his angelic enemies, Milton laid the foundations for Satan's role in Book IX; he made the final temptation of Eve appear "the probable or necessary outcome of his character. . . ."

In Raphael's account of the war in Heaven, Satan exhibited the same bias towards illusion and falsehood. Assembling his forces under the pretense of a command "to consult About the great reception of thir King," he beguiled them

> *. . . with calumnious Art*
> *Of counterfeted truth. . . .*

Again, he resorted to ruse in concealing from the enemy his newly invented cannon until a favorable moment for firing. The Satan of Book I, whose "high words . . . bore Semblance of worth not substance," was cut from essentially the same cloth as the Satan of the later books.

One can distinguish, however, several strands in this fabric of illusions. Satan exploited various methods of deception and for diverse ends. A common mode of deception was the resort to downright lies and disguises. Another consisted in false or exaggerated claims, pretensions, and boasts. In some instances his arguments were characterized by false premises and specious reasoning; in other cases his logical errors may have been partly unintentional. The persons against whom he practiced—or attempted to practice—his deceptions included his enemies (divine, angelic, or human), his own colleagues, and perhaps himself. Though the extent of his self-deception has probably been exaggerated, he nevertheless appeared at times to believe his own lies. Such delusion was quite consistent with Milton's conception of the "evil temptations" which befell unrepentant sinners,[14] who should

> *. . . hard be hard'nd, blind be blinded more,*
> *That they may stumble on, and deeper fall. . . .*

Though some of Satan's falsehoods thus appear to have been genuine errors resulting from his alienation from truth, the majority seem to have been deliberate lies.

Among the vain pretensions which made him, in Lewis' opinion, "more a Lie than a Liar, a personified self-contradiction," were his affectation of divine honors and his spurious claim to regal status. The first of these was patently false, although the fallen angels would subsequently win notoriety among men as heathen gods. The second was likewise illusory, since the devils retained even their liberty to work evil only by divine permission. God continued to reign supreme in Hell as in Heaven, and the assertion of independence was little more than a boast. However valiantly or craftily Pandaemonium might strive, through force or fraud, to frustrate his intent, its citizens must remain inevitably the instruments and vassals of his will.

Satan's remaining pretensions were invalidated by the vicious nature of his enterprise. The affectation of heroic virtue involved such logical contradictions as a "godlike devil," a superlatively virtuous vice, and a "godlike" sin. The claim to heroic leadership entailed the inherent absurdities of an ethical and political order based on the pursuit of evil. The principles on which the infernal society was based—its "unwritten constitution," so to speak—involved fallacies which should have been obvious to any reader of Aristotle's *Politics*. Unlike a true state, it was by nature incapable of aiming at happiness or the good. Its policy was oriented towards war rather than peace.[15] Its very pursuit of liberty could result only in deeper enslavement. The cornerstone of its moral and political order was a contradiction—"Evil be thou

14. For Milton's conception of "evil temptations" and the "production of evil," see *De Doctrina Christiana*, Book I, Chapter 7 (Milton, *Prose Works* [Bohn's Standard Library; London, 1883], IV, 200–9).

15. Cf. Aristotle, *Politics*, trans. William Ellis (London, 1952), pp. 78, 81, 83, 88, 124, 205, 228–30.

my Good." Though it possessed the likeness of a well-ordered state, governed by a prudent and heroic leader, this was merely an appearance; its real foundations were (as Lewis has observed) "Nonsense."[16] The reality underlying the affectation of a sound and stable polity was not order, but spiritual confusion. Like Augustine's *civitas terrena* or Babylon, its essence was *confusio*.[17]

These pretensions to heroic virtue and heroic leadership lie at the root of the so-called "problem of Satan" and the accusations of inconsistency which have been leveled against Milton. In raising these charges, however, critics have often overlooked two highly significant factors: 1) the falsity of these pretenses and 2) their intrinsic consistency (however superficial) throughout *Paradise Lost* and their external resemblance to conventional heroic types.

First, through the substitution of evil for good, the moral and political structure of Hell has become an inverted order. Patterns of thought and behavior which could conceivably have proved heroic, if oriented towards a legitimate object, have been vitiated by their consecration to evil. Satan's prudence and fortitude have become vicious through his opposition to the divine will; they remain heroic only within a perverted ethical system where evil has become good and vice versa. His apparent heroism is, consequently, essentially a facade—shadow without substance; it lacks the essence of the truly heroic.

Second, Satan's superficial conformity to the heroic pattern is far more consistent than critics have usually conceded. Though his heroism is only a false appearance, the appearance itself is consistent. The alleged inconsistency between the "heroic" Archangel of Books I and II and the "degraded" fiend of the later books has been partly due to the reader's failure to recognize Satan's strong affinities with the Odysseus-type of hero in the crucial sections of the fable (from the end of Book II through Book X). Actually Milton invested this figure with conventional attributes of at least three different types of heroes: the Achilles-type (represented also by Ajax, Turnus, and Rinaldo), proud of his military valor, jealous of his honor, and prompted by "high disdain, from sence of injur'd merit"; the *dux* (exemplified by such generals as Agamemnon, Aeneas, and Godfrey), whose primary duty is command and whose office necessarily involves not only the direction of the war against the enemy but also the preservation of order, discipline, and unity of purpose among his subordinates; and the Odysseus-type, characterized by wiles, ruses, disguises, and deceptions—a hero who accomplishes his enterprise primarily through

16. Lewis, pp. 95–96.

17. See Augustine, *The City of God* (London, 1950), I, 312, 341. For the Augustinian "Two Cities" in *Paradise Lost*, see C. A. Patrides, *Milton and the Christian Tradition* (Oxford, 1966), pp. 230, 260.

stratagem and fraud. Satan's affinities with the two former types are most pronounced in the early books and, to some extent, in the angelic war; the third type predominates, however, in the account of the execution of his enterprise against man. The belief that Milton "degraded" Satan after the first two books arose largely from overlooking the conventional nature of this third heroic pattern.

The resort to a strategy and tactics of fraud did not, *ipso facto*, invalidate Satan's pretensions to heroic leadership. On the contrary, such military ruses as his disguises for the purpose of espionage and subversion, his attempts to lie his way out of tight situations, his concealment of his new weapons in the angelic battle, his choice of subterfuge after open force had proved impractical were quite consistent with the character of the prudent and wily hero, whose literary prototype was Odysseus.[18] In a normal military engagement this mode of behavior could be regarded as justifiable and even laudable. In a spiritual conflict against God, however, they became not only vicious, but ultimately vain. Against an omniscient enemy a strategy of deception could be little more than a shallow pretense.

In concealing his true emotions from his companions, in hiding his despair and attempting to raise their spirits with "high words" which he himself knew to be largely false, Satan's resort to illusion was again superficially consonant with heroic leadership. The *Aeneid* provided a literary precedent in so exemplary a hero as Aeneas himself.[19] Nevertheless, Satan's lies to induce his followers to revolt and subsequently to continue the war against the divine will belonged to a different category. In both of these instances his guidance proved vicious and disastrous—resulting first in damnation, then in deeper damnation. Instead of leading, he misled; he was less *Führer* than *Verführer*. In this respect the pretense of faithful leadership was clearly an illusion.

The irony underlying Milton's method in presenting the speeches of the fallen angels resulted partly from the fact that the characters he was describing were either the forgers or victims of lies—deceivers or deceived. Verisimilitude required him to present the illusions of Hell in their true nature, to portray falsehood in its proper essence as a pretension to truth, sophistry as a pretension to reason, appearance as a pretension to reality, shadow as a pretension to substance. He undoubtedly expected his readers to detect the logical absurdities underlying this delineation of falsehood. Nevertheless, in order to forestall possible misinterpretation, he introduced his own comments on the spurious quality of the values, claims, and logic of Hell. Moreover, he

18. C. M. Bowra (*From Virgil to Milton* [London, 1945], p. 223) observed that Satan's "deception of Uriel is in the best manner of Odysseus. . . ."

19. Cf. *Aeneid*, I, 189–209.

also exposed its illusions through the actions and speeches of more reliable characters—Uriel, Gabriel, Michael, Abdiel, God the Father and Son, and even (in certain instances) Satan himself. Thus the unmasking and exposure of falsehood proceeded almost *pari passu* with its development. The soliloquy on Mount Niphates revealed the emptiness of Satan's vaunts in Hell and at the same time betrayed to Uriel the spurious nature of his angelic disguise. Ithuriel's spear unmasked him in a subsequent disguise, and Gabriel's interrogation forced him to contradict himself. Adam and Eve recognized the false and irrational character of her dream. Abdiel and Michael refuted the apostate's claims and arguments in the angelic revolt.[20] Finally, Messiah's sentence of judgment on the serpent and the subsequent metamorphosis of the fallen angels constituted the divine verdict as to the true merits and character of Satan's enterprise—a decisive intrusion of divine truth into the realm of infernal illusion.

Throughout *Paradise Lost* the conflict between divine and infernal agents, the antithesis between Heaven and Hell, possessed not only moral, but also epistemological significance. It served to convey not only the ethical struggle between good and evil, order and disorder, law and sin, but also the opposition between truth and falsehood, reality and appearance, reason and sophistry, Idea and idol. The literary force of this antithesis resided not only in the portrait of truth, but also in the effective delineation of error. By providing from the beginning of the poem a convincing image of falsehood, Books I and II established the concept of Satan which was to prevail through the later books—that of the sophist and the pretender, the forger of illusions and father of lies.

III

A realistic presentation of falsehood should meet two conditions—verisimilitude and clarity. On the one hand, it should pretend to be true. On the other hand, to avoid ambiguity, the fallacy should be made obvious to the reader. Milton's portrait of Satan filled both of these requirements. It delineated him consistently in terms of specious arguments and false appearances, sophisms and *εἴδωλα*. At the same time it contained numerous indications that these pretences were false and should not be taken at face value.

Milton presented the fallen Archangel essentially in terms of illusion, as a false appearance or *εἴδωλον*. The phrase "Idol of Majestie

20. Abdiel condemns Satan's reasoning as "unsound and false." Allan H. Gilbert ("The Theological Basis of Satan's Rebellion and the Function of Abdiel in *Paradise Lost*," *MP*, XL [1942–43], 35) comments that "Abdiel has been the good logician, as Satan has been the bad one, resting his argument on false premises, while the angel has had the sure foundation of Scripture."

Divine" was actually a far more significant index of his status than critics have generally recognized. The word "Idol," as Milton employed it here, was a technical term. In affecting divine honors and heroic leadership, Satan represented the sort of εἴδωλον which Phavorinus and Suidas had defined as a fictitious likeness, which Francis Bacon had described as a false appearance, and which Plato had classified as a φάντασμα (or appearance), as distinguished from an εἰκών (or likeness).[21]

In elaborating his theory of the four idols of the human mind, Bacon employed the term *idol* as synonymous with "false appearance."[22] "I do find therefore in this enchanted glass four Idols or false appearances of several and distinct sorts. . . ."[23]

21. Jacopo Mazzoni, *Della Difesa della Commedia di Dante . . . Parte Prima* (Cesena, 1587), "Introduttione, e Sommario della difesa di Dante": "L'Idolo [declared Phavorinus] è una similitudine umbrosa, e una cosa finta, che non è veramente, una forma, che non ha subsistenza, come le persone, ch' appaiono nell' acque, e ne' specchi, e deriva dal verbo εἴδω, che vuol dire apparo, o rassomiglio." According to Suidas, "Gli Idoli sono l'effigie di cose non subsistenti, come sono Tritoni, Sphinge, Centauri. Ma le similitudini sono l'imagini di cose subsistenti, come di fiere, e d'huomini."

This was, of course, a highly specialized use of the term. Plato included as *eidola* both *eikon* (likeness) and *phantasma* (appearance). Mazzoni (¶ 16) regarded Suidas' definition as "troppo ristretto" and cited Hesychius' definition of *eidolon* as "*similitudine, imagine, et segno.*" Cf. Tasso, p. 352, on this point. Tasso likewise cited the definitions of *idol* by Phavorinus and Suidas (p. 352), but accorded them greater authority than did Mazzoni: "Definí Favorino gl' idoli (come riferisce l'istesso Mazzoni) una similitudine ombrosa, ed una cosa finta che veramente non è; una forma che non ha sussistenza, come le forme che appaiono ne l'acque e ne gli specchi: e deriva dal verbo εἴδω che vuol dire *appaio* e *rassomiglio.* Ma gl'idoli, come li definisce Suida, sono effigie di cose non sussistenti, quali sono i tritoni, e le Sfingi, e i Centauri; e le similitudini sono imagini di cose sussistenti, come di fiere e d'uomini."

On this point there is, however, a significant divergence between Mazzoni's views and those of Tasso. Partly because of his pronounced Platonic bias, Mazzoni tends to blur the distinction between image and idol and to classify poetry (whether icastic or phantastic) as a subdivision of sophistic. (See Allan H. Gilbert, *Literary Criticism: Plato to Dryden* [New York, 1940], pp. 376–70.) Tasso, on the other hand, challenges Mazzoni's classification, emphasizing the differences between poet and sophist. "Però io non posso concedere né che la poesia si metta sotto l'arte de' sofisti, né che la perfettissima specie di poesia sia la fantastica." Mazzoni's argument that "la poesia è facitrice de gl'idoli, la sofistica è facitrice de gl'idoli, adunque la poesia è sofistica" is faulty in Tasso's view. Not only are the two affirmative propositions in Mazzoni's syllogism "vicious," but its terms are ambiguous inasmuch as "il nome de gl'idoli riceve alcuna distinzione, e secondo che egli è variamente definito, cosí appertiene al poeta o al sofista il formar gl'idoli. . . . Quando diciamo adunque, il sofista è facitor de gl'idoli, intendiamo de gl'idoli che sono imagini di cose non sussistenti; perché il subbietto del sofista è quel che non è; ed in questa significazione disse S. Paolo: *Idolum nihil est.* Ma quando affermiamo che il poeta sia facitor de gl'idoli, non intendiamo solamente de gl'idoli de le cose non sussistenti; perché il poeta imita ancora le sussistenti, e principalmente le rassomiglia. Laonde quantunque il poeta sia facitor de gl'idoli, ciò non si dee intendere ne l'istesso significato nel quale si dice che il sofista è fabro de gl'idoli; ma dobbiam dir piuttosto che sia facitore de l'imagini a guisa d'un parlante pittore, ed in ciò simile al divino teologo che forma le imagini, e comanda che si facciano. . . ." See Tasso, pp. 349–53.

22. Francis Bacon, *Works*, ed. Spedding, Ellis, and Heath (London, 1857), I, 643 (*De Augmentis Scientiarum*): "Ad Elenchos vero *Imaginum*, sive *Idolorum*, quod attinet;

Bacon contrasted these *idols* of the human mind with the *ideas* of the divine mind, in terms of the antithesis between appearance and reality, falsehood and truth.[24]

In the *Theatetus* and other dialogues, Plato had contrasted the εἴδωλον with truth. In *The Sophist* he had distinguished between two species of the image-making art (εἰδωλοποιικὴν τέχνην)—icastic and phantastic. The latter "produces appearance (φάντασμα), but not likeness (εἰκόνα)," and its practitioners "abandon the truth and give their figures (εἰδώλοις) not the actual proportions [of the original] but those which seem to be beautiful. . . ."[25]

It was in this sense—as *phantasmata*, or false appearances—that Satan's pretensions to deity, to kingship, to statesmanship, and to heroic excellence were, in the final analysis, merely *eidola*. "Idol of Majestie Divine," his pretension to equality with God was counterfeit, like his imitation of the Mountain of the Congregation, his "Godlike imitated State," and Mammon's attempt to imitate God's light through the gems and gold of Hell. Though his "resemblance to the Highest" remained for a while "where faith and realtie Remain not," this too was superficial, an empty appearance. Superficial too was his outward conformity to the heroic ideal of the "faithful Leader." Though apparently aiming at deliverance, his enterprise could, in actuality, lead only to deeper spiritual enslavement. The very exercise of his virtues—such as prudence, fortitude—in this cause could result, paradoxically, only in profounder entrenchment in vice.

Hell itself was thronged with such *phantasmata* or *eidola*. The fallen angels, subsequently known by "various Names, And various Idols

---

sunt quidem Idola profundissimae mentis humanae fallaciae. Neque enim fallunt in particularibus, ut caeterae, judicio caliginem offundendo et tendiculas struendo; sed plane ex praedispositione mentis prava et perperam constituta, quae tanquam omnes intellectus anticipationes detorquet et inficit. Nam Mens Humana . . . tantum abest ut speculo plano, aequali, et claro similis sit (quod rerum radios sincere excipiat et reflectat), ut potius sit instar speculi alicujus incantati, pleni superstitionibus et spectris." Cf. Thomas Fowler (ed.), *Bacon's Novum Organum* (2nd ed.; Oxford, 1889), pp. 212–13. "*Idola* et notiones falsae, quae intellectum humanum jam occuparunt, atque in eo alte haerent non solum mentes hominum ita obsident, ut veritati aditus difficilis patent. . . ."

23. Bacon, III, 241–42 (*Valerius Terminus of the Interpretation of Nature*). Chapter 16 is entitled "Of the internal and profound errors and superstitions in the nature of the mind, of the four sorts of idols or fictions which offer themselves to the understanding in the inquisition of knowledge . . ." (p. 241). Cf. *idem*, *The Advancement of Learning*, ed. W. A. Wright (5th ed.; Oxford, 1926), p. 162.

24. Fowler, pp. 328–29; cf. pp. 204–5: "Etenim verum exemplar mundi in intellectu humano fundamus. . . . Modulos vero ineptos mundorum et tanquam simiolas, quas in philosophiis phantasiae hominum extruxerunt, omnino dissipandas edicimus. Sciant itaque homines (id quod superius diximus) quantum intersit inter humanae mentis *idola* et divinae mentis ideas. Illa enim nihil aliud sunt quam abstractiones ad placitum: hae autem sunt vera signacula Creatoris super creaturas, prout in materia per lineas veras et exquisitas imprimuntur et terminantur."

25. *Plato*, trans. Harold North Fowler (Loeb Classical Library; London, 1952), II, 39, 335. Cf. *Phaedo*, and *The Republic*, *passim*.

through the Heathen World,"[26] would eventually seduce "the greatest part Of Mankind" to false religions, adoring devils for deities.[27] The double-formed monster, Sin, was an *eidolon*, like the Tritons, Sphinxes, and Centaurs enumerated by Suidas. Death—"that Fantasm," which scarcely "substance might be call'd that shadow seem'd"—conformed to Phavorinus' conception of the *eidolon* as "una similitudine umbrosa . . ., una forma, che non ha subsistenza." The very punishments of Hell involved illusion; Satan and his colleagues were plagued with hunger for the delusive fruit which "not the touch, but taste Deceav'd."

Eve's dream was likewise an *eidolon* or *phantasma*. Plato had included the "appearances in dreams" among *eidola*,[28] and in his first temptation of Eve Satan attempted

> *. . . by his Devilish art to reach*
> *The Organs of her Fancie, and with them forge*
> *Illusions as he list, Phantasms and Dreams. . . .*

These Adam subsequently dismissed as "Imaginations, Aerie shapes" formed by "Fansie." Significantly, Eve had already displayed her vulnerability to *eidola*; her reflection in the lake was an *eidolon* by Phavorinus' definition: ". . . a form without substance, like the persons who appear in water and in mirrors. . . ."

IV

Idols could be verbal as well as visual, and in his exploitation of "false speech and false opinion" Satan displayed a striking affinity with Plato's "dissembling imitators"—the public orator and the sophist. His words which bore "Semblance of worth not substance" and his "calumnious Art Of counterfeted truth" marked him as a master of

26. Tasso, p. 352, had linked the Platonic criticism of the sophist's idols with St. Paul's denunciation of pagan idolatry (1 Corinthians 8:4): "Quando diciamo adunque, il sofista è facitor de gl'idoli, intendiamo de gl'idoli che sono imagini di cose non sussistenti; perché il subbietto del sofista è quel che non è; ed in questa significazione disse S. Paolo: *Idolum nihil est.*" Cf. Calvin, *Commentary on Epistles of Paul the Apostle to the Corinthians*, trans. John Pringle (Edinburgh, 1848), I, 275–76; David Pareus, *In . . . ad Corinthios Priorem S. Pauli Apostoli Epistolam Commentariis* (Frankfurt, 1609), pp. 486–89; James Arminius, *Works*, trans. James Nichols (London, 1828), II, 289–312 ("On Idolatry"). Calvin also quotes Habakkuk's condemnation of the idol (2:18) as "a teacher of lies," inasmuch as idols "deal falsely in pretending to give a figure or image of God, and deceive men under a false title."

27. The contrast between true religion and idolatry—between the worship of the Creator and the false adoration bestowed on the creature—was a recurring theme in Milton's epic. Both Satan and Eve aspired to divine attributes. Moreover, Eve paid "low Reverence" to the Tree of Knowledge, and Satan's colleagues not only adored their leader as a god but also solicited divine honors for themselves from fallen humanity.

28. *Plato*, II, 451.

the sophist's "art of deception."[29] Moreover, in his final exhortation to Eve his manner of delivery resembled that of classical orators. Belial, whose "words cloath'd in reasons garb" were able to "make the worse appear The better reason," was expert in the same art, and by Platonic standards both fiends were properly orators rather than statesmen.[30]

Thus Milton portrayed Heaven and Hell consistently in terms of epistemological opposites—reality and appearance, revelation and illusion, right reason and fallacy. Through this antithesis the distinction between truth and falsehood emerged in clearer focus. The true likeness served to expose the false; the image to discredit the idol.

Like Bacon, he realized the value of a knowledge of fallacies. Although a true standard of judgment might provide a criterion for both true and false reasoning ("Rectum . . . et sui index est et obliqui"), the study of elenches (a category comprising both sophisms and *eidola*) might serve as a useful guide for the detection of fallacies:

> But this art [of judgment] hath two several methods of doctrine, the one by way of direction, the other by way of caution; the former frameth and setteth down a true form of consequence, by the variations and deflections from which errors and inconsequences may be exactly judged . . . . The second method of doctrine was introduced for expedite use and assurance sake; discovering the more subtile forms of sophisms and illaqueations with their redargutions, which is that which is termed *elenches*. For . . . the more subtile sort of them doth not only put a man besides his answer, but doth many times abuse his judgment.[31]

Milton proceeded not only by the "way of caution" but also by the "way of direction." On the one hand, the divine testimony of Father and Son and the right reason of the faithful angels constituted the true norm of truth and error ("et sui index et obliqui"). In the "proud imaginations" of Satan and his peers, on the other hand, the poet created a deliberate picture of illusion, an admonitory portrait of the arch-tempter's fallacies and the *eidola* of the intellect depraved by sin. Like *Paradise Regain'd, Paradise Lost* delineates an epistemological conflict between truth and falsehood—a holy war with two supernatural champions, the Son and the Adversary of God. If the one is "True Image of the Father," the other is no more than the "Idol of Majestie Divine."

29. *Plato*, II, 445, 457.
30. *Plato*, II, 459.
31. Bacon, *Works*, I, 641 (*De Augmentis*); Bacon, *Advancement of Learning*, p. 159.

16. "Semblance of Worth"

Pandaemonium and Deliberative Oratory

❦ For many critics Milton's infernal debate is notable rather for the speakers' intellectual dilemma than for the rhetorical force of their arguments. Even though they speak with the tongues of fallen angels, scholarship has practiced the adder's wisdom and turned a deaf ear to their eloquence, stressing the defects of their eschatology rather than the competence of their oratory. Interpreting their speeches as relatively successful or unsuccessful efforts to comprehend and control the realities of their new situation, criticism has exaggerated both their logical strength and their absurdity.

For C. S. Lewis, who regards "the whole debate" as "an attempt to find some other door [out of the Satanic predicament] than the only door that exists"—i.e. "the way of humiliation, repentance, and . . . restitution"—"all the speeches are alike futile"; they illustrate the nonsense and inaccuracy of Hell.[1] Peter censures Satan's opening address for its "incoherent" logic and condemns Moloch's speech as "reverberat[ing] in a limbo of unreality"; it "peters out feebly as he adjusts himself belatedly to the real facts of their position."[2] On the

First published, in somewhat different form, in *Neophilologus*, XLVIII (1964), 159–76.

1. C. S. Lewis, *A Preface to Paradise Lost* (London, 1943), pp. 95, 101–4.
2. John Peter, *A Critique of Paradise Lost* (New York, 1960), p. 43.

other hand, the validity of Belial's reasoning has been wildly exaggerated. Waldock hails his speech as "impregnated with strong common sense," and in Peter's opinion it "is bluntly realistic and sets out their predicament to a hair." Milton's own comments are dismissed as a "perfectly brazen" attempt "to discredit Belial"; they exemplify the poet's "tendency . . . to pass derogatory comments on the devils which are inadequately related to what he has presented."[3] Such open disagreement[4] makes it imperative to re-examine this scene with its singular mixture of reason and absurdity. How far—and in what sense—do the fallen angels speak "well and wisely" or "meanly and foolishly"?[5]

In overemphasizing the assembly's preoccupation with the infernal "predicament," critics have distorted the purposes of these orations and their relation to the character of the speakers. The infernal councilors are *not* attempting to investigate reality, but to argue the merits or demerits of a proposed course of action. They have not been summoned to explore their predicament, but to decide whether it is expedient to continue the war against Heaven—and, if so, how best to conduct it. Political orators rather than philosophers, they are concerned less with knowledge than with persuasion and dissuasion. They are rhetoricians rather than dialecticians, and their arguments fall accordingly within the province of deliberative oratory.

The character of the proposals suggested is largely determined by that of the speakers themselves. The alternatives they favor are primarily indicative of the bondage of the will, secondarily of the obscuration of the understanding. If the devils reason wrongly, it is

3. *Ibid.*, pp. 43–44; A. J. A. Waldock, *Paradise Lost and Its Critics* (Cambridge, 1947), pp. 79–80.

4. Even those scholars who have recognized Milton's mastery of rhetorical principles have failed to apply these principles in detail to the council scene. Despite its emphasis on Milton's "rhetorical aids to proofs" and the similarity between the poet and the "deliberative orator," John S. Diekhoff's study of *Milton's "Paradise Lost"* (New York, 1946) does not assay a rhetorical analysis of the infernal conclave. Though T. S. Eliot's essay on "Milton" (see *Milton Criticism*, ed. James Thorpe [London, 1951]) correctly notes the "exactness. . . . with which Moloch, Belial, and Mammon, in the second book, speak according to the particular sin which each represents," it does not investigate the rhetorical structure of their arguments. Arnold Stein's *Answerable Style* (Minneapolis, 1953) calls attention to the "public rhetoric" of Satan's speech (p. 49), but does not explore its relation to deliberative oratory. Kenneth Muir's *John Milton* (London, 1955) recognizes that the "great speeches in Book 2 . . . depend for their effect on a superb use of certain rhetorical devices [and] on the way they are logically constructed, if on false premises" (p. 147), but does not elaborate this point. J. B. Broadbent's analysis of the infernal council in *Some Graver Subject* (London, 1960), pp. 110–20 does not consider the deliberative oratory underlying this scene, though other passages in this book display an interest in Milton's rhetoric. William Emp on's discussion of the Stygian debate in *Milton's God* (London, 1961), pp. 48–57, chiefly emphasizes the rebel leaders' "general state of opinion" and their "beliefs" about God rather than their rhetorical ingenuity.

5. Waldock, p. 80.

largely because they will and desire wrongly. Faced with a clear-cut practical issue, each makes his distinctive choice not so much on the basis of his own reasoning (whether valid or false) as on the grounds of his dominant vice. The arguments he advances are rhetorical proofs designed to win or seduce his companions to accept the policy most congenial to his own temperament. As such they are instruments of deception, but not always (as some scholars have argued) of self-deception.

To regard "all the speeches [as] alike futile" is to miss the subtlety of Satan's parliamentary tactics. He is deliberately disingenuous. His initial proposal to regain Heaven by force or fraud is merely a ruse to prepare the way for the real issue, the enterprise against man. By introducing a topic which can only prove pointless and fruitless, he lays the foundation for his own favorite scheme, to be elaborated by Beëlzebub. The futility of the earlier speeches plays into his hands, as he had anticipated it would.

I

The subject of the "Consultation"—"whether another Battel be to be hazarded for the recovery of Heaven" and "by what best way, Whether of open Warr or covert guile"—is a standard object of deliberative rhetoric: ". . . for nearly all the questions on which men deliberate, and on which the deliberative orator harangues, those at least of the highest concernment, are in number *five*; and these are questions of *finance*, or *war and peace* and again respecting *imports and exports*, and also respecting *legislature*."[6]

In debating this issue, some of the devils "advise it, others dissuade." These are the two characteristic approaches of deliberative oratory, for "the business of deliberation is partly exhortation, partly dissuasion; for invariably those who in their individual capacities simply advise, and those who publicly harangue, effect one of these objects."[7] The remaining "species of rhetoric," on the other hand—judicial and demonstrative—are concerned respectively with accusation and defense and with praise and blame. Neither plays a significant part in the council scene of Book II; for, like true deliberative orators, the speakers of Pandaemonium are concerned primarily with future issues rather than with the past or present, and with the question of expediency or inexpediency rather than with the problems of justice or injustice and honor

6. *Aristotle's Treatise on Rhetoric*, trans. Theodore Buckley (London, 1851), p. 29. Cf. the translation by W. Rhys Roberts, in *The Basic Works of Aristotle*, ed. Richard McKeon (New York, 1941), pp. 1318–1451.

7. Buckley, p. 24.

or disgrace. According to Aristotle:[8] "The object of the deliberative orator is the expedient and inexpedient; for he who recommends, advises you to adopt the better measures; but he who dissuades, diverts you from the worse; the other considerations either of justice and injustice, of honor or disgrace, he adjoins by the way, in addition to these two."

For a proper understanding of the infernal oratory in Book II, it is essential to recognize the limited rhetorical scope of the speakers. In the first place, as deliberative rather than judicial orators, they are not primarily concerned with a *post mortem* on their own past conduct. Though they do attempt to justify their own actions and to brand Heaven with injustice, this is really a secondary consideration, a minor point which reinforces the principal argument for continued warfare. Ethically and theologically it emphasizes their obduracy in crime; repentance would have entailed the very opposite approach—self-accusation for past sin and acknowledgment of the justice of God. Though Belial affirms that "the Law" ordaining their suffering is not "unjust," he adapts the commonplace of justice to the demands of deliberative rhetoric; he utilizes it as an argument to dissuade from warfare, just as his opponents had exploited the contrary argument as a means of persuasion to further battle.

On the whole, the infernal statesmen ignore the question of justice and injustice—the crucial issue for the fallen sinner—and when they do consider it, they pervert it. The role of positive moral judgment is left to the agency of Heaven, as in the catastrophic transformation-scene of Book X. When Satan next raises the issue of justice, in the soliloquy on Mount Niphates, his position is reversed; he accuses himself and defends the justice of God. This represents a true assessment of the past, but it comes at an untimely hour. He is still unrepentant, he is fully committed to his role as "Antagonist of Heav'n," and he has given himself wholly to his enterprise against man. The deliberative argument has outweighed the judicial, and the vital issue of justice and injustice has been eclipsed by the question of expediency. Instead of condemning their former disobedience and treason, the fallen angels plot a fresh sin for the future. When Satan does reconsider his initial crime, it is too late.

Secondly, the issue of honor and disgrace is similarly subordinated to that of expediency. Though the devils cling tenaciously to their former

8. *Ibid.*, pp. 24–25: ". . . the time proper to each of these [species of rhetoric] respectively is, to the deliberative orator, the *future*; for in exhorting or dissuading, he advises respecting things future. The time proper to a judicial pleader is the past; for it is ever on the subject of actions *already done*, that the one party accuses, and the other defends. To the demonstrative orator the *present* time is the most appropriate, for it is in reference to qualities actually possessed that all either praise or blame."

titles and deplore their shameful defeat, though they appeal occasionally to the principle of *honestas*, they are not primarily concerned with praise or blame. These arguments serve instead to reinforce the question of the expediency or inexpediency of further war against Heaven. The topics that chiefly engage the speakers are those of deliberative rather than demonstrative oratory.

Underlying the whole debate, however, there is a concealed fallacy. The conditions of Hell are incompatible with the usual objects of deliberative rhetoric. Where "there is . . . no good For which to strive," where there is no possibility of recovering true happiness, debate necessarily becomes an empty charade: ". . . for on the subject of [happiness], and what conduces to it, and of its opposites, exhortation or dissuasion is always conversant; and this, because we needs do the things which procure it or any of its constituents, or which render it greater from having been less, and refrain from doing the things which destroy or impede it, or produce its opposites."[9]

Similarly, an argument based on the "acquisition of a greater instead of a less[er] good"[10] becomes meaningless in a state of alienation from God, the *summum bonum*. In the context of stubborn hostility to God it becomes a ridiculous contradiction.

The critics who find the devils' arguments absurd are, therefore, partly correct, for the conventional objects of deliberative rhetoric—the concepts of happiness and the greater good—are ends not only inaccessible to the fallen angels, but indeed diametrically opposed to the subject of debate. The speakers must inevitably appeal to lesser goods to rationalize their alienation from the Supreme Good or to urge irreconcilable opposition to Him. With this in mind, one is better able to define the nature and limits of the council's absurdity, so drastically exaggerated by many scholars. The consultation is not utter nonsense. The individual speeches are, on the whole, characterized by considerable rhetorical subtlety. Most of them reveal no slight degree of ingenuity, and as deliberative orations all of them exhibit some fidelity to the principles of classical rhetoric.

II

Satan's initial remarks perform the functions an exordium would fulfill in a longer oration. They announce the subject of debate and attempt to foster a favorable predisposition in his audience. According to Aristotle, "the exordia of deliberative rhetoric are derived from those of judicial [rhetoric]: but this species has them naturally least of all the three; for indeed the audience are aware of the subject; and the case

9. *Ibid.*, p. 33.
10. *Ibid.*, p. 40.

needs no exordium" except when "the audience conceive of the importance of the matter otherwise than [the speaker] could wish" or when there is a necessity "for either exciting or doing away a prejudice, or for amplification or diminution."[11]

Only the final lines of Satan's speech, however, are devoted to the first of these functions—the "most necessary business of the exordium," —which consists in providing "an intimation of the subject" and in throwing "some light on the end for the sake of which the speech is made."[12] The major portion of his oration is directed towards a different, but related, end—to win his audience to give favorable consideration to his proposal of renewed warfare against Heaven. This is no easy task, especially so soon after their crushing defeat; and, as the subsequent course of the debate reveals, the majority of the councilors are reluctant to resume combat:

> *for such another Field*
> *They dreaded worse then Hell: so much the fear*
> *Of Thunder and the Sword of* Michael
> *Wrought still within them. . . .*

In such a situation it is hardly surprising that Satan deliberately avoids the realities of the infernal "predicament" and resorts instead to the sophistry that his legions are all the stronger for their defeat. Under the circumstances this is a sound rhetorical tactic. As Aristotle observes, the exordium is particularly useful to speakers "who have, or appear to have, the worse case; for it is better to pause any where than on the case itself."[13] As Satan could hardly have chosen a more difficult and unpalatable case than a resumption of warfare against an all-powerful enemy immediately after an ignominious defeat, he appropriately dedicates the greater part of his address to preparing his audience for this unwelcome suggestion. The flattering salutation "Deities of Heav'n" provides him with a point of departure for arguing that the defeated angels have not really lost their heavenly birthright. On the contrary, they have (he insists) a greater chance of winning than before, for their defeat has given them greater political solidarity:

> *With this advantage then*
> *To union, and firm Faith, and firm accord,*
> *More then can be in Heav'n, we now return,*
> *To claim our just inheritance of old,*
> *Surer to prosper then prosperity*
> *Could have assur'd us. . . .*

11. *Ibid.*, p. 255.
12. *Ibid.*, p. 252.
13. *Ibid.*, p. 254.

Peter's condemnation of Satan's rhetoric as "opaque and self-deluding"[14] is scarcely just; as the Archfiend does not really intend to hazard another battle "for the recovery of Heaven," there is little excuse for regarding him as seduced by his own oratory. Nor is his argument concerning a "safe unenvied Throne" such "cold comfort to his followers" as Peter maintains. Satan is cleverly exploiting the inescapable fact of "present pain" as an argument in favor of renewed war. In any future battle (he suggests) his followers would stand in less peril than he, for his is "the greatest share of endless pain." As his greater portion of misery places him beyond the reach of envy, it provides a distinct political and military "advantage," for, united as they are under a stronger leadership, the devils should stand a better chance of winning than before. This ingenious argument from the commonplace of adversity is not *per se* illogical. The faulty logic lies in the enterprise itself, rather than in the arguments whereby Satan urges his followers to pursue it.

Though the ostensible object of the consultations is the recovery of Heaven, the actual subject of debate, as Satan announces it, is the question of the most effective means to this end:

> *by what best way,*
> *Whether of open Warr or covert guile,*
> *We now debate. . . .*

These are conventional alternatives in deliberative oratory. In the *Rhetorica ad Herennium* they are subdivisions of security (*tuta*), which is in turn a subdivision of expediency (*utilitas*): "Haec tribuitur in vim et dolum. . . . At si nostram rationem tutam esse dicemus, divisione utemur in vim et consilium."[15]

In the debate which follows, only Moloch considers the issue strictly in terms of the two alternatives proposed in Satan's opening speech. The other speakers shift the ground to other issues. The overt subject of the debate is not the relative merits of war and peace, but whether the war for the recovery of Heaven should be waged by force or by guile. Belial and Mammon divert the course of the discussion from the best and most expedient means of warfare to the advantages of peace over war. Beëlzebub, in turn, substitutes a "third proposal"; as peace is out of the question and war to recover Heaven would be vain, the only alternative is some "easier enterprise."

The initial terms of the debate are essentially a calculated ruse, designed to steer the argument initially into a series of *culs de sac* and to

14. Peter, p. 43.
15. [*Cicero,*] *Ad C. Herennium De Ratione Dicendi*, trans. Harry Caplan (Cambridge, Mass., 1954), pp. 160, 170.

demonstrate by a process of elimination that the enterprise against man —already designed and partly proposed by Satan—is, under the circumstances, the most practical and feasible alternative. In accepting Beëlzebub's resolution, the assembly is really giving the final seal of approval to the strategy Satan had outlined earlier in his first public address (I, 621 ff.). Its concluding words ("Warr then, Warr Open or understood must be resolv'd") had announced the topic of the future debate. His argument that the "Infernal Pit" could not, in the nature of things, "hold Caelestial Spirits in Bondage" had anticipated his subsequent appeal to his cohorts as "Deities of Heav'n," in formally opening the debate. His avowed preference for fraud over force and his first suggestion of the design against mankind had foreshadowed the strategy subsequently promulgated by Beëlzebub and eventually executed by Satan himself.

Other details in the earlier address also lay the foundation for subsequent debate. The relative strength of Heaven and Hell is obviously an essential factor in considering the alternative of war and peace, but Satan introduces this topic in his initial speech to his troops rather than in the opening address of the consultation:

> *Henceforth his might we know, and know our own*
> *So as not either to provoke, or dread*
> *New warr, provok't. . . .*

This is exactly the type of knowledge that Aristotle regarded as essential for any deliberative orator debating questions of peace and war:

> Respecting questions of *war and peace*, the orator must needs be acquainted with the force of the state, how great it actually is already, and how great it admits of becoming. . . . Moreover he should know both what wars the state has been engaged in, and how it has conducted them. This must he needs know, not in relation to his own state only, but as regards frontier states also; particularly in the case of those with whom there is a likelihood of being at war, in order that towards the more powerful, pacific measures may be held, and that in regard to the weaker, it may be with his own state to make war or not.[16]

In the evolution of the infernal strategy, a major—and, on the whole, the decisive—factor is the councilors' knowledge of their own force, its performance in their recent battles, and its relative inferiority to their omnipotent enemy. This is, of course, the reason for directing their attack against frail man instead of Almighty God, against the less easily defended outlying province, the earth, instead of the impregnable citadel of Heaven. In choosing this easier enterprise the devils are

16. Buckley, p. 30; cf. p. 175.

obviously preferring war with "the weaker" frontier state rather than with "the more powerful" enemy. Towards the latter, in the opinion of Belial, Mammon, and a substantial majority, "pacific measures [should] be held." The use they make of their knowledge of their own relative strength is, on the whole, consistent with Aristotelian rhetorical theory.

Indeed, this recognition of the discrepancy between their own military potential and that of their enemy plays a greater role in determining their strategy than criticism has generally acknowledged. The awareness of divine omnipotence and omniscience[17] is, in fact, one of the major components of Satan's military and foreign policy and his parliamentary tactics. The success of the "third proposal" is ultimately due to the realization that the devils could not hope to overcome the Almighty by force or the All-knowing by fraud. This realization, in turn, stems indirectly from the terms in which Satan had couched his first proposal—terms actually designed to expose the futility of "open Warr" and "covert guile" alike against an omnipotent and omniscient foe.

III

On the issue of open war Moloch and Belial are divided—the one seeking to persuade, the other to dissuade—but in pleading their contrary causes they nevertheless exploit some of the same rhetorical arguments. Both appeal to the principles of "the acquisition of a greater instead of a less [*sic*] good; [and] of a less evil instead of a greater"—objects that Aristotle ranks among the indisputable goods to which the deliberative orator may make his appeal.[18] Thus, in exhorting his companions to open war against Heaven, Moloch employs the argument of the "lesser evil" to mitigate their fear of the consequences:

> *Th' event is fear'd; should we again provoke*
> *Our stronger, some worse way his wrath may find*
> *To our destruction: if there be in Hell*
> *Fear to be worse destroy'd. . . .*

Nothing can be worse (he argues) than their present lot. To be "worse destroy'd" would mean annihilation—a state "happier farr" than their present misery. If, on the other hand, they cannot be annihilated, they would be "at worst On this side nothing."

In countering this argument Belial appeals to the same rhetorical principle. To his adversary's contention that open war could not

17. Peter (pp. 43–45) radically exaggerates the devils' unawareness or neglect of divine omniscience.

18. Buckley, p. 40.

possibly cause them to "suffer worse," he replies with a detailed catalogue of greater evils, based both on past torments and on future fears:

> *is this then worst,*
> *Thus sitting, thus consulting, thus in Arms ?*
> *What when we fled amain. . . .: or when we lay*
> *Chain'd on the burning Lake ? that sure was worse.*

To be plunged in flames, transfixed to rocks, or enchained under the "boyling Ocean"—"this would be worse." Their present miseries are, therefore, a lesser evil than the greater torments further warfare would incur:

> *. . . better these then worse*
> *By my advice; . . . our present lot appeers*
> *For happy though but ill, for ill not worst,*
> *If we procure not to our selves more woe.*

Similarly, despite fundamental disagreement on the issue of peace or war, several of the speakers resort to the argument of ease. According to Aristotle, "men determinately choose. . . . such [things] as may *easily* be done. Easy things are such as are done either without pain, or in a short time; for difficulty is determined in reference either to the pain, or length of time."[19] Thus Moloch suggests, as an additional argument for open warfare against Heaven, that the enterprise would be easy:

> *But perhaps*
> *The way seems difficult and steep to scale*
> *With upright wing against a higher foe.*
> *Let such bethink them. . . .*
> *That in our proper motion we ascend*
> *Up to our native seat: descent and fall*
> *To us is adverse. . . . Th' ascent is easie then. . . .*

Later, when the difficulties of this proposal have been exposed, Beëlzebub exploits the same type of argument in pleading the merits of an "easier enterprize." Stressing the "weakness" of the "punie inhabitants" of earth and their vulnerability to "force or subtlety," he dwells on the strategic disadvantages of their "expos'd" position on the frontiers of Heaven and perilously near the confines of Hell:

> *Though Heav'n be shut,*
> *And Heav'ns high Arbitrator sit secure*
> *In his own strength, this place may lye expos'd*
> *The utmost border of his Kingdom, left*
> *To their defence who hold it. . . .*

19. *Ibid.*, p. 43.

Neither of these speakers regards ease as an end in itself, but rather as a characteristic of the *means* to an end; both are simply arguing that apparently difficult enterprises would, in actuality, be relatively easy to execute. Belial, on the other hand, employs the argument of ease in a very different manner. Unlike the previous speakers, he exploits this concept as an argument against undertaking any enterprise at all. Ease is for him not only a means to an end, but also an end in itself. Nevertheless, in counseling "ignoble ease, and peaceful sloath," he takes care to disguise these vices in the garb of virtue. In particular, he represents inactivity as the better fortitude of patient endurance:

> *To suffer, as to doe,*
> *Our strength is equal. . . .*

In one respect Mammon's exploitation of the argument of ease resembles Belial's, for both propose it as an end attainable only by endurance. Ethically, however, they are as different as industry and lassitude. For Belial endurance means the passive acceptance of pain, whereas for Mammon (the archetypal industrialist) it is coupled with active labor:

> *Our greatness will appear*
> *Then most conspicuous, when great things of small,*
> *Useful of hurtful, prosperous of adverse*
> *We can create, and in what place so e're*
> *Thrive under evil, and work ease out of pain*
> *Through labour and endurance.*

In pleading their different cases, the various speakers appeal to many of the "indisputable goods"[20] recognized by rhetoricians. Moloch urges the claims of honor and happiness. Overt attack may achieve revenge—frequently regarded as a sub-topic of honor—even if it does not achieve the good of victory. Destruction would be "happier farr" than the devils' present condition under sentence of eternal misery. In countering these arguments, Belial appeals to the goods of life, thought, justice, and fortitude. To Moloch's contention that death would be happier than present misery, he replies that their "present lot appeers For happy though but ill." Where Moloch had hailed "utter dissolution" as a good, Belial extols "this intellectual being, Those thoughts that wander through Eternity." Moreover, the law that ordained their torments is not "unjust," and their sufferings provide an occasion for exercising the virtue of patient endurance. Mammon, appealing to such ends as ease, magnificence, and wealth, characteristically rejects the *summum bonum*—the fruition of the divine presence—

20. Cf. *ibid.*, pp. 40–41, on indisputable goods.

as "wearisom" and proposes instead that the fallen angels "seek Our own good from our selves." Beëlzebub's plea for "revenge" is, like Moloch's, an indirect appeal to the principle of honor.

The prominent position that the theme of honor occupies in the infernal oratory is hardly surprising. Both Cicero and Quintilian rank honor (or *honestas*) with expediency (or *utilitas*) as one of the primary aims of deliberative rhetoric.[21] In Aristotle's *Rhetoric* and the pseudo-Ciceronian *Rhetorica ad Herennium*, which restrict deliberative oratory to questions of expediency, honor remains an important topic either as one of the "indisputable goods"[22] or as one of the two "aspects" or parts of expediency.[23] In the diabolical conclave it is such a recurrent argument that to ignore it is to risk distorting the whole scene. This is particularly true in the case of Moloch and Belial.

Instead of a belated adjustment to the facts, as Peter has maintained, the final lines of Moloch's speech really involve two commonplaces of honor—revenge and the preference of death to disgrace. The first had found expression in Aristotle's *Rhetoric*: ". . . the taking vengeance on a foe rather than being reconciled [is honourable]; both because to compensate is just, and what is just is honourable; and further, because it belongs to the courageous man never to be worsted."[24]

The second of these commonplaces has been stressed by the *Rhetorica ad Herennium*, which represents it as a topic of courage (*fortitudo*): "Again, from an honourable act no peril or toil, however great, should divert us; death ought to be preferred to disgrace. . . . One who prefers the consideration of honour to security will use the following topics: . . . either pain, if that is feared, or death, if that is dreaded, is more tolerable than disgrace and infamy. . . ."[25] Similarly, according to Quintilian's *Institutio Oratoria*: "Often again we shall urge that honour must come before expediency; as for instance, when we advise the men of Opitergium not to surrender to the enemy, even though refusal to do so means certain death."[26]

The rhetoric of Hell is not, of course, a true index of its moral character, and the devils' appeals to *honestas* are not a real sign of their motivation. Though they draw their arguments from apparent virtues, they are actually moved by their own dominant vices. Thus Moloch exploits the commonplaces of honor and courage, but his chief motive (as Belial perceives and as Milton repeatedly emphasizes) is despair. His preference for death over "this dark opprobrious Den of shame"

21. Cicero, *De Inventione*, trans. H. M. Hubbell (London, 1949), pp. 325, 327; Quintilian, *Institutio Oratoria*, trans. H. E. Butler (London, 1921), I, 479–83.

22. Buckley, p. 41.

23. Caplan, p. 161.

24. Buckley, p. 61.

25. Caplan, pp. 167–73.

26. Butler, p. 495.

is rooted not in courage and magnanimity, but in the characteristic vice of the suicide. Milton's gloss on the speaker's actual motives (lines 45–50) places his proposal in its correct ethical context and exposes his rhetorical camouflage.

In the speeches of Belial and Mammon the antithesis between rhetorical pretense and ethical reality is even more pronounced. Though both orators appeal to the commonplaces of *honestas*, the one is actually motivated by sloth, fear, and the desire for ease, while the other is moved by avarice. In these cases, as in the instance of Moloch, the poet's "asides" strip the ethical pretensions from these arguments and reveal the basic, underlying vices. His glosses are not, as Waldock and Peter have argued, a "brazen attempt" to discredit the speaker, nor do they contradict the speech. They merely correct it, by disclosing the true *ethos*, the latent evil under the spurious guise of honor.

Unfortunately, both critics have taken Belial's remarks at face value and have consequently ignored the verbal dexterity that enables him to harness a virtue in the cause of its opposite vice. He counsels "ignoble ease" in the name of honor, and he appeals paradoxically to fortitude in arguing a course of inaction dictated by fear. Able to "make the worse appear The better reason," he exhorts to vice in the name of the contrary virtue.

In thus pleading a dishonorable cause in the name of honor, Belial is—like most of the infernal orators—following a rhetorical principle recognized by Quintilian:

> . . . if anyone is going to urge a dishonourable course on an honourable man, he should remember not to urge it as being dishonourable. . . . Even when we address bad men, we should gloss over what is unsightly. For there is no man so evil as to wish to seem so. Thus Sallust makes Catiline speak as one who is driven to crime not by wickedness but by indignation, and Varius makes Atreus say:
>
> *My wrongs are past all speech,*
> *And such shall be the deeds they force me to. . . .*
>
> For the sole aim of the man who is deliberating about committing a criminal act is to make his act appear as little wicked as possible.[27]

Thus Moloch disguises despair as courage, Belial represents cowardice as fortitude, and Mammon depicts avarice as labor and endurance.

Parallel to this rhetorical exaltation of vice is the corresponding depreciation of virtue. While Belial correctly diagnoses Moloch's apparent "courage" as "despair", he passes beyond truth into exaggeration when he brands it as downright cowardice:

> *I laugh, when those who at the Spear are bold*
> *And vent'rous, if that fail them, shrink and fear*

27. *Ibid.*, pp. 501–3.

What yet they know must follow, to endure
Exile, or ignominy, or bonds, or pain,
The sentence of thir Conquerour. . . .

In thus belittling the suggestion of open war as "fear" of pain and, conversely, in extolling a policy of inactivity as true fortitude, he is employing rhetorical tactics recommended in the *Rhetorica ad Herennium*:

> Virtues of this kind are to be enlarged upon if we are recommending them, but depreciated if we are urging that they be disregarded, so that the points which I have made above [concerning the topics of Wisdom, Justice, Courage, and Temperance] will be belittled. To be sure, no one will propose the abandonment of virtue, but let the speaker say that the affair is not of such a sort that we can put any extraordinary virtue to the test; or that the virtue consists rather of qualities contrary to those here evinced. Again, if it is at all possible, we shall show that what our opponent calls justice is cowardice, and sloth. . . .; what he has named courage we shall term the reckless temerity of a gladiator.[28]

The same rhetorical devices recur in Mammon's speech. Motivated by avarice, but appealing to the topics of *honestas*, he resorts, like Belial, to amplification and diminution to make the worse appear the better reason. Ennobling the production of wealth by representing it as the reward of "endurance" and a sign of "greatness," he inverts the order of good and evil by associating Hell with strenuous liberty and Heaven with servile ease, "a state of splendid vassalage." His rhetorical tactics are based on depreciating the Highest Good he and his fellows have lost and misrepresenting the evil of punishment as a good.

Besides appealing to "indisputable goods," the infernal council also exploits a type of argument classified among "questionable" or "disputable" goods. According to Aristotle: ". . . in the case of questionable goods, your reasonings will be deduced from these formulae—that of which the contrary is evil, is itself a good; as is that of which the contrary is expedient to an enemy: . . . And, in a word, whatever be the things which the enemy desires and in which they rejoice, the contrary of those things appear beneficial. . . ."[29]

Satan had already utilized this type of argument in seeking the contrary of his enemy's will:

To do ought good never will be our task,
But ever to do ill our sole delight,
As being the contrary to his high will
Whom we resist. If then his Providence
Out of our evil seek to bring forth good,
Our labour must be to pervert that end,

28. Caplan, pp. 167–169.
29. Buckley, p. 41.

And out of good still to find means of evil:
Which oft times may succeed, so as perhaps
Shall grieve him, if I fail not, and disturb
His inmost counsels from their destind aim.

Wiser than his predecessor, Beëlzebub shows a better understanding of the legitimate grounds of argument. The issue of war and peace is out of the question, as the infernal powers can neither wage a successful war nor conclude a successful peace:

What sit we then projecting Peace and Warr?
Warr hath determin'd us, and foild with loss
Irreparable; tearms of peace yet none
Voutsaf't or sought....

As neither alternative is subject to their own choice or power of execution, the question is meaningless, and he diverts the debate, accordingly, to a topic on which they *can* choose and act—the easier enterprise against man. In so doing, he preserves the distinction between expediency (which is a valid topic for deliberative rhetoric) and necessity (which is not):

Some have held that the three main considerations in an advisory speech are honour, expediency and necessity. I can find no place for the last. For however great the violence which may threaten us, it may be necessary for us to suffer something, but we are not compelled to do anything; whereas the subject of deliberation is primarily whether we shall do anything.... It appears to me ... that where necessity exists, there is no room for deliberation, any more than where it is clear that a thing is not feasible. For deliberation is always concerned with questions where some doubt exists.[30]

The drift of the infernal debate, as we have traced it, is from the inexpedient to the expedient, from the impracticable to the practicable. As the speakers compare their own strength with that of the enemy, they perceive how very narrow indeed is the field of activity still viable for them. Moloch proposes "open Warr," but its impracticality is self-evident. It cannot assure positive victory, and it is motivated by despair. Belial's speech demonstrates that "Warr ... open or conceal'd, alike" is impractical,

...for what can force or guile
With him, or who deceive his mind, whose eye
Views all things at one view?...
Not more Almighty to resist our might
Than wise to frustrate all our plots and wiles.

30. Butler, p. 491.

Mammon argues that a war to recover Heaven is impractical and inexpedient:

> *Either to disinthrone the King of Heav'n*
> *We warr, if warr be best, or to regain*
> *Our own right lost. . . .*
> *The former vain to hope argues as vain*
> *The latter. . . .*

For Beëlzebub, the scope of possible activity is even more restricted. Maintaining that war and peace with Heaven are alike impossible, he urges an easier enterprise, which lies within their capabilities. In its progressive discrimination between the practical and the impractical, the Stygian council exemplifies the principles of deliberative oratory.[31]

IV

The infernal oratory is, then, essentially deliberative in character, and its arguments appear, for the most part, to have been chosen less for their relevance to the diabolical "predicament" than for their value as instruments of persuasion or dissuasion. The fact that these arguments are often false does not mean that the speaker is self-deceived, but rather that he is attempting—by whatever arguments best suit his purpose—to beguile his audience into accepting his own point of view. And his own viewpoint is largely determined by his distinctive and characteristic vice. In keeping with the principle of decorum—"the grand masterpiece to observe"—Milton portrays his devils exercising their characteristic roles as tempters. The fact that they direct their efforts towards the seduction of their own companions is merely additional evidence of their depravity. Instead of centering the debate on the issue of the public good, each speaker reorients it according to the bias of his own private evil—avarice, cowardice, ambition, despair. The particular courses of action, or inaction, that they champion are not so much the result of intellectual error (though the angelic intelligence has, of course, been partially darkened by sin) as the effect of moral depravity, the bondage of the will. The counsels offered by Mammon, Moloch, and Belial are at once the sign and result of self-enslavement. The policy devised by Satan, proposed by Beëlzebub, and approved by the entire assembly is likewise a symptom and effect of moral bondage. Aiming at revenge, it is dictated by anger and hate; it marks its proponents as passion's slaves.

Within the predetermined limits of their moral depravity, all of the devils—even Moloch—are still able to speak with enviable skill, even

31. Cf. Buckley, p. 263, "But in deliberative speeches, the orator may either contend that the circumstances will not take place, or that what he directs will indeed take place, but that it is not just, or not beneficial, or not in such a degree." Cf. *ibid.*, p. 43, on the "possible" or practicable.

though they fall short of true wisdom, even though they employ their rhetorical ingenuity in causes that are ultimately little more than folly. But one must not regard them as seduced by their own oratory. The arguments they exploit in the cause of their distinctive vices are essentially rhetorical in character and should not be mistaken for real motivation or sincere belief.

In a sense the infernal conclave is a dress rehearsal for roles the various participants will subsequently play on the stage of the world. The poet characterizes them according to their dominant vices—pride, wrath, sloth, avarice—and shows them skilfully deploying the available means of persuasion to win others to their characteristic sins. They attempt to seduce their fellows with the same types of argument they will subsequently exploit to deceive men. They are already tempters, and their rhetoric is essentially an art of pretense.

Its real character as an abuse of rhetoric is all the more pronounced when viewed against the background of classical and Christian rhetorical tradition. From Plato to Fénelon Western moralists were concerned with the moral ambivalence of eloquence, its adaptability to both good and evil ends. The *Phaedrus* contrasts its use and abuse through two set speeches by Socrates and emphasizes the dichotomy between the true master, who harnesses his art in the service of justice and truth, and the bad rhetorician who makes "the same thing appear to the same persons to be at one time just and at another time unjust," good and the "reverse of good."[32] The *Gorgias* is even severer in its condemnation of rhetorical abuses. Though Gorgias contrasts the good and bad usages of his art and insists that "one ought to use rhetoric with justice," Socrates brands it as a form of "flattery" and condemns it for aiming at pleasure instead of at a true good. It is the "*eidolon*" of politics, and as a means of persuasion it does not seek to teach, but merely to induce belief.[33] For Aristotle, rhetoric is a branch of dialectics and politics, and as such ought to serve the cause of truth and justice. There is, however, no separate name to distinguish the honest orator from the dishonest, and the same term "rhetorician" comprehends the speaker's knowledge of his art as well as his moral purpose. Though it is "wrong to persuade to what is bad," a "person, unfairly availing himself of such powers of speaking, may be, in a very high degree, injurious. . . ."[34]

Like Belial, who could make the "worse appear The better reason," Isocrates stresses the orator's power "to represent the great as lowly or invest the little with grandeur, to recount the things of old in a new manner or set forth events of recent date in an old fashion."[35] But in

32. Plato, *Works*, trans. B. Jowett (New York, *n.d.*), III, 424.

33. Cf. Plato, *Oeuvres Complètes*, ed. Alfred Croiset and Louis Bodin, *Sixième édition revue et corrigée* (Paris, 1955), III, 120–32.

34. Buckley, pp. 8–13.

35. *Isocrates*, trans. George Norlin (London and New York, 1928), I, pp. 123–25.

Longinus' opinion, this "praise of the power of words" is "almost a warning to his hearers not to trust him." Isocrates' "ambition to speak of things as bigger than they are" results in mere puerility.[36] Fénelon similarly condemns Isocrates for his "very low and vulgar notion of eloquence" and for placing "almost the whole of it, in a nice disposal of his words."[37] According to the *Dialogues sur l'eloquence*, "eloquence, . . . may be considered in three respects: as the art of enforcing truth on people's minds, and of making them better; as an art indifferent in itself; which wicked men may use as well as good; and which may be applyed to recommend injustice and error, as well as probity and truth: and, as an art which selfish men may use to ingratiate themselves with others; to raise their reputation, and make their fortune." It is to the second of these categories that the rhetoric of Pandaemonium obviously belongs. The infernal orators make an "ill use" of their "eloquence to enforce error and vice."[38]

Milton's rhetorical skill is as evident in the "bad art" (as Plato would have called it) of the council scene as in the "good art" of his Isocratic oration, the *Areopagitica*, and his political treatises. He illuminates the realities of the infernal "predicament" by means of the very fallacies with which the demonic orators attempt to disguise it. The apparent truths accentuate the real truth. The speakers' delusive arguments expose their own moral nakedness. Their irrevocable alienation from justice, truth, and the Supreme Good appears in the quality of their rhetoric. They can persuade—but only by seeming goods, by specious arguments, and to evil ends. They can utilize their art only to deceive. In the council they attempt to seduce one another. In their recreations they turn "Eloquence" into a dilettante amusement, a "pleasing sorcerie" to deaden their pain. Or else, like Satan, they may direct their "perswasive Rhetoric" against man (*P.R.*, IV, 4). The crowning example of the art of pretense is the temptation of Eve, and it is not fortuitous that Milton draws an explicit comparison between

> *The Tempter, . . . with shew of Zeale and Love*
> *To Man, and indignation at his wrong,*

and his classical counterpart,

> *. . . som Orator renound*
> *In* Athens *or free* Rome, *where Eloquence*
> *Flourished, since mute, to som great cause addrest. . . .*

36. Allan H. Gilbert, *Literary Criticism, Plato to Dryden* (New York, 1940), pp. 189–90.

37. *Dialogues Concerning Eloquence. . . . by M. de Fénelon*, trans. by William Stevenson (Glasgow, 1750), p. 9. I am indebted to Professor W. S. Howell for this reference to Fénelon.

38. *Ibid.*, pp. 13–14. For the idealized conception of the orator, see also Cicero, *De Oratore*, trans. E. W Sutton (Cambridge, Mass. and London, 1942), I, 27; *idem*, *Orator*, trans. H. M. Hubbell (Cambridge, Mass. and London, 1939), p. 315.

The oratory of Pandaemonium is cut from the same cloth as that of the temptation scene. The same type of eloquence displays itself in the inception of the infernal enterprise and in its execution. The structure of Milton's epic hinges on a perverted rhetoric.

V

In emphasizing the rhetorical element in this scene, one does not intend to minimize the importance of Character. The same speeches may involve *Ethos* as well as *Dianoia*. In interpreting such discourses, however, one should bear in mind that the two concepts are by no means identical. Though they may intermingle, Character and Thought are not at all the same thing, and in the case of sophistic oratory they may contradict one another. The dissembler, the tempter, the hypocrite assume an *Ethos* that is not properly their own. Their "rhetorical character" (assumed as a means of ethical proof) contradicts their "true" character as the poet has conceived it. When the speaker conceals his true motives and feigns a false intent designed to insinuate and ingratiate himself with his audience, this feigned character belongs (properly speaking) not to Character but to rhetoric, not to *Ethos* but to *Dianoia*. An unwary critic may confuse the two; this has happened more than once in the case of Satan and Belial. Seduced by their oratory, both Waldock and Peter have mistaken rhetorical for poetic *Ethos* and misinterpreted Thought as an index of Character.

Both Satan and Belial are masters of sophistical oratory, and in introducing them in the narrative Milton warns his audience of this fact. When he describes Satan's words as bearing only the "semblance of worth, not substance," he is characterizing the Satanic rhetoric as sophistical. Aristotle had defined sophistry as "the semblance of wisdom without the reality" and emphasized the fact that its proof was only "apparent" rather than "genuine." Belial's ability to "make the worse appear the better reason" likewise associates him with the Aristotelian conception of the sophist. Protagoras (Aristotle had informed his readers) had shocked the ancients by vaunting his power "of making the worse the better side," and Cicero credited "many other" rhetoricians with the same boast: "Protagoras Abderites, Prodicus Ceius, Hippias Eleus, aliique multi docere se profitebantur arrogantibus sane verbis, '*quemadmodum causa inferior*, ita enim loquebantur, *dicendo fieri superior posset*.'" Any reader familiar with Aristotle's *Rhetoric* and *Sophistic Elenches*[39] should have been able to recognize the significance of Milton's phrases; they served to characterize the demonic speaker and his discourse as sophistical and to caution the reader, accordingly, against accepting his remarks at face value.

39. See *The Works of Aristotle*, ed. W. D. Ross, I (Oxford, 1928), *De Sophisticis Elenchis*, 165^a 21, 171^b 34; Buckley, p. 197, 197n.

Belial's address belongs primarily to *Dianoia*, not to *Ethos*. It is a demonstration of rhetorical skill rather than of moral intent. In such a speech one should not expect a revelation of his true character; and it is true that his actual works give little indication of his real nature as Milton has epitomized it. If his "thoughts" are "low" and "to vice industrious," he nonetheless draws many of his arguments from the commonplaces of nobility. If he is "timorous and slothful" to "Nobler deeds," he disguises the fact by appealing to a nobler heroism than that of action, the "better fortitude" of patient endurance: "To suffer as to do our strength is equal." If his actual ends are "ignoble ease and peaceful sloth" rather than true peace, he is too clever a speaker to say so; rhetorically it is peace, not idleness, that he proposes as final cause.

In this context Milton's moral commentary (so roundly condemned by Waldock as contradicting his "demonstration") is essential. Not only is it amply justified by epic practice and theory: it is absolutely necessary if the reader is to know the speaker's true *Ethos*—the real character, which the sophistical orator is more than likely to conceal. Belial's ethical traits, as Milton describes them, are thoroughly conventional. They are the familiar traits of the pleasure-addict, the voluptuary. (Belial had been traditionally associated, in fact, with modes of the *vita voluptuosa*, the life of pleasure; and Milton would subsequently exploit these associations in the council scene of *Paradise Regain'd*.) In the infernal council of *Paradise Lost* they are present, but consciously disguised. The "ignoble ease" and "peaceful sloth" that Milton attributes to him are only implicit in his discourse, never explicit. Both pertained conventionally to the "voluptuous life," just as the "open war" which Moloch advocates belongs to the active life. Equally conventional was the notion that the former was inferior to the latter; in comparison with the active life, the *vita voluptuosa* was not only ignoble, but vicious.

To counter Moloch's proposal, Belial could scarcely plead the superior merits of idleness, and an appeal to pleasure would have seemed ridiculous in the midst of Hell. He could, however, answer the call to action with an appeal to modes of life nobler and higher than activity. He could appeal to the blessings of the contemplative life (the *vita contemplativa*) and the ease that philosophy could bring to torment (*PL*, II, 146–48).

The relation between "demonstration" and "commentary" in these passages seemed to Waldock inconsistent and contradictory. Yet it is not (as Waldock believed) Milton's "exhibition" and "comment" that are at variance; it is Belial's Character and Thought. When he seeks to dissuade his companions from military action, he appeals to forms of *in*activity that could seriously be regarded as superior to anything that the active life could offer. The inaction that he *really* desires, however, is different; it belongs to an altogether diverse mode of life, the *vita voluptaria*.

Belial's oratory is, in short, very like his physical appearance, as the poet describes it:

> *A fairer person lost not Heav'n; he seem'd*
> *For dignity compos'd and high exploit:*
> *But all was false and hollow. . . .*

Nonetheless, Belial's "words could *please*"—and in this respect there *is* a close correlation between *Ethos* and *Dianoia*, just as there is in *Comus*. (The tempter in *Comus* displays the same rhetorical skill and an ethical significance that is remarkably similar.) The "pleasing" quality of Belial's oratory parallels his own character; it is appropriate to a speaker who exemplifies the life of ease and pleasure. The parallel will be still stronger if one accepts the view that he symbolizes not merely sensual pleasure, but *intellectual* hedonism as well—an "Intemperance" of the mind. His appeal to "thoughts that wander through eternity" might support this view. There is, moreover, a significant parallel in the type of eloquence that delights the fallen angels later in the same book. They too find ease and pleasure in contemplation, and they too experience the "pleasing sorcery" of "wandering" speculations on eternal matters—Providence, Foreknowledge, and Fate.

VI

Though *Dianoia* and *Ethos* are important considerations in the council-scene, the scene derives its primary justification from its relation to the plot. Its chief function is to initiate the principal action, the enterprise against man. Aristotle had maintained that actions should seem "probable" or "necessary"—the logical or plausible consequences of prior actions or of Character and Thought. Milton makes the decision to invade the newly-created world and expel or seduce its "puny in-inhabitants" seem "probable" by bringing the discussion of other alternatives to an impasse. The debate has demonstrated the futility of all previous proposals—Moloch's exhortation to "open war" against Heaven, Belial's counsel of peace, Mammon's scheme to establish an empire—and the speakers themselves are seriously divided by the conflict between their characteristic vices. Beëlzebub's proposal enables them to agree on a concerted policy. This is at once the "probable" or "necessary" outcome of both Character and Thought. Of Thought, because the progressive refutation of all previous proposals has left this "easier enterprise" the only practical alternative. Of Character, because the success of this scheme will give each of the speakers ample scope to indulge his own favorite vices on earth. (Significantly, Milton has already characterized the various demons proleptically in terms of their future operations in the fallen world. In Michael's survey of world-history their characteristic obsessions will appear, reflected and enlarged, in the vices of fallen man. For the *Ethos* of Moloch and Belial one need look little farther than the descendants of Cain, and Mammon's imperial ambitions find their earthly counterpart in Babylon.)

17. "Magnific Titles"

Satan and the Argument of Nobility

❦ In exhorting his followers to revolt, Milton's Lucifer opens his harangue with a favorite topic of Renaissance rhetoric—the appeal to nobility. Beginning his exordium with a conventional salutation, he immediately converts it into an instrument of rhetorical proof. To address his audience by their proper titles—"Thrones, Dominations, Princedoms, Virtues, Powers" (*Paradise Lost*, V, 772)—is not in itself remarkable. It is appropriate both to the speaker and the audience; it is a standard way of beginning a formal speech; it emphasizes the official character of his address; it courts the good will of his hearers by overt flattery. More noteworthy is what Satan does with these honorific terms in the further development of his speech. He takes them as a point of departure for sophistical argument and a characteristic appeal to pride. Arguing that these titles have been threatened by the recent edict establishing the Messiah's vicegerency, he treats them as evidence that the Son's monarchy violates the natural, inalienable rights of the angelic host:

> *If these magnific Titles yet remain*
> *Not meerly titular, since by Decree*

First published, in somewhat different form, in *Modern Language Review*, LXI (1966), 561–71, and here reprinted by permission of the Modern Humanities Research Association and of the editors.

> *Another now hath to himself ingross't*
> *All power, and us eclipst under the name*
> *Of King anointed . . . to th' abuse*
> *Of those Imperial Titles which assert*
> *Our being ordain'd to govern, not to serve.*

The word *assert* is significant in this context, for it implies logical proof. The "Imperial Titles" argue that their possessors are endowed with an innate right to sovereignty and dominion. To compel the angels to serve and obey contradicts their natural prerogatives and proper office.

Satan's speech belongs to deliberative oratory, since it attempts to exhort and "dehort"—to dissuade his followers from obeying God and Messiah and to persuade them to rebel. Like other deliberative orators, he bases his argument on aspects of felicity. For both Aristotle and Hobbes, nobility, glory, and honor are "constituent" parts of happiness,[1] and in developing these commonplaces Satan exploits several familiar types of logical or rhetorical arguments. As the titles themselves are really "added to the subject over and above the essence," he is employing a type of "consentany" argument, the argument from the "adjunct." In arguing from the name—maintaining that such titles as "Dominations, princedoms," entail the right "to govern," he is using a type of "derived argument," the argument from "notation." Finally, in denying the obligation "to serve" on the basis of his right "to govern," he employs a type of "dissentany argument," an argument from "adverses."[2]

Although Satan's argument *seems* reasonable, its conclusion is patently false, for it contradicts the Biblical conception of the angelic nature and office. As Milton points out in the *Christian Doctrine*, angels are "ministering spirits" (Hebrews 1:14) and "ministers of righteousness" (2 Corinthians 11:15); the Scriptures represent them as "standing dispersed around the throne of God in the capacity of ministering agents" (XV, 35, 101). They are, therefore, "ordain'd . . . to serve," and in denying this fact Satan is contradicting the traditional Christian view of their true function. Moreover, the argument he advances to establish this false conclusion involves an obvious fallacy. The angelic titles by no means contradict the obligation to serve God. Though they do imply command or presidency, this pertains only to authority over

1. See *Aristotle's Treatise on Rhetoric*, trans. Theodore Buckley (London, 1851), pp. 34, 279. Both Aristotle and Hobbes treat nobility primarily in terms of noble birth. Rhetorical proofs are either inartificial (such as divine and human testimony) or artificial (ethical, pathetic, and logical proof).

2. Milton, *Works* (Columbia Edition; New York, 1931–38), XI, 85 ff., 219 ff., 131 ff. Hereafter referred to by volume and page number only.

lesser angels or else, subsequently, over "nations, kingdoms, and particular districts" of the world (XV, 103 ff.). Satan is using the terms "govern" and "serve" in an *absolute* sense instead of in "a *qualified* sense" and thus commits the fallacies of *secundum quid* and *ignoratio elenchi*.[3] The fact that "Dominations" and "Thrones" may well have been "ordain'd to govern" inferior angels or parts of the world does not contradict the fact that they have also been "ordain'd" to "serve" God. Their government and service are directed to different "objects."

Furthermore, the titles themselves are contingent on obedience. In the feudal society of Heaven, the angels possess their degrees and ranks only on the condition of loyalty and fealty. As God created the "Spirits of Heav'n . . . in thir bright degrees,

> . . . *& to thir Glory nam'd*
> *Thrones, Dominations, Princedoms, Vertues, Powers . . .*
> (*Paradise Lost*, V, 834)

they hold their titles from Him. He has "created" them, and (as Abdiel points out), He can "uncreate" them, just as a monarch may create or degrade a peer. In this context the term "creation" has a double sense; it refers both to the angels themselves and to their titles of nobility.

Since Satan bases his argument on angelic titles, the question of their origin becomes highly important for his debate with Abdiel. Whereas the latter regards them as a derivative from God, Satan treats them as an inalienable birthright. The angels are "Ethereal Sons," the "birth mature Of this our native Heav'n" (V, 859–60). In this emphasis on "noble birth," he approaches the concept of nobility held by Aristotle and Hobbes.

In both of Milton's epics, such appeals to pride in titles as the basis of an *ad hominem* argument are a favorite device of the Archfiend, and his followers often adopt the same technique. Logically, this device exploits the commonplace of nobility. Rhetorically, it facilitates an easy transition from the exordium to the body of the speech. Sophistically, it serves Satan's purpose of seduction by arguing that nobility and merit depend primarily on rank and title rather than on obedience to God's will. Before examining other instances in demonic oratory, let us attempt to place it in its proper context, against the background of

3. See *The Works of Aristotle*, W. D. Ross, I (Oxford, 1928), *De Sophisticis Elenchis*, trans. Pickard-Cambridge, 168b, 166b, 167a. Fallacies "independent of language" include "the use of an expression absolutely or not absolutely but with some qualification of respect, or place, or time, or relation" and the fallacy "which depends upon ignorance of what 'refutation' is." Fallacies "that depend upon whether something is said in a certain respect only or said absolutely, are clear cases of *ignoratio elenchi* because the affirmation and the denial are not concerned with the same point." See also Miriam Joseph, *Shakespeare's Use of the Arts of Language* (New York, 1947), pp. 370–71.

Renaissance thought and the contrary example set by Milton's heroic archetype, the Son of God.

I

In appealing to title and birthright as arguments for rebellion, Satan is abusing a familiar *topos* of Renaissance rhetoric. As Kristeller has pointed out, a favorite theme of the humanists was "nobility, and as its chief cause they would favour merit more often than birth."[4] Dante had devoted a section of his *Convivio* to elucidating his *canzone* on this topic.[5] Chaucer's "loathly lady" had delivered a curtain-lecture on the subject in the Wife of Bath's Tale. Boccaccio's Sigismunda had harangued her father on this theme. Osorius had composed two complementary treatises on *Nobility* and *Christian Nobility*.[6] The same subject subsequently engaged Dryden in the preface to his *Fables*. Observing that the crone of the Wife of Bath's Tale "takes her 'Topiques from . . . the silly Pride of Ancestry without inherent Vertue, which is the true Nobility,'" he notes that Boccaccio's story treats "the same Argument of preferring Virtue to Nobility of Blood, and Titles. . . ." Arguing that "from Vertue first began The Diff'rence that distinguish'd Man from Man," Sigismunda declares that "he whose Mind is Vertuous, is alone of Noble Kind" and justifies her marriage to a lowly squire on the ground that

He claim'd no Titles from Descent of Blood,
But that which made him Noble, made him Good . . .

Guiscardo's "Merit" lies in "inward Vertue" rather then "external Port."[7]

In Milton's Messiah likewise, nobility derives primarily from merit rather than birthright. By birthright alone the Son excels all created beings, since he is second only to the Father; as God's "only Son" he is "by right endu'd With Regal Scepter" (V, 812). Yet he proves his title "Son of God" primarily through demonstrating his virtue. In offering his own life in order to redeem man, he is

. . . found
By Merit more then Birthright Son of God,
Found worthiest to be so by being Good,
Far more then Great or High. . . .

(III, 308)

4. Paul Oskar Kristeller, *Renaissance Thought, II: Papers on Humanism and the Arts* (New York, 1965), p. 15.

5. Trattato Quarto is a commentary on the *canzone* "Le dolci rime d'amor, ch'io solia."

6. *Hieronymi Osorii . . . de nobilitate civili, libri duo. Eiusdem de nobilitate Christiana libri tres* (Olyssipone, 1542).

7. *The Poems and Fables of John Dryden*, ed. James Kinsley (1958), pp. 1460, 1558.

Messiah reigns by "right of merit" (VI, 43), and in defeating the rebels single-handed he proves his superiority. Besides vindicating his own merit he proves the Father's right to the title "Almightie," which Satan had challenged as merely titular (VI, 294). In *Paradise Regain'd*, the ordeal in the desert is intended to test the "filial Vertue" of the "Son of God" and "shew him worthy of his birth divine And high prediction" (I, 141–42). The outcome demonstrates his right to bear the title of "Son of God":

> *. . . still expressing*
> *The Son of God, with Godlike force indu'd*
> *Against th' Attempter of thy Fathers Throne. . . .*
> (IV, 601)

After his fall Satan is more sparing in his use of the topic of nobility, nor do titles play quite so important a role in the development of the argument. For the most part, they serve as conventional salutations, emphasizing the formal character of his address and flattering his audience. Yet, in varying degrees, they usually strengthen and support his argument. As "testimony" to reinforce his point or intensify his appeal, they continue to serve as means of persuasion.

The titles he employs—"Princes, Potentates, Warriors, the Flowr of Heav'n" (I, 315)—to arouse his companions from the burning lake reinforce his exhortation to "awake" and "arise." Brief as it is, the speech makes two contrasting ethical and pathetic appeals—to pride and shame. It accomplishes its ends, moreover, largely through the contrast between the "magnific titles" of the salutation and the ironic questions whereby Satan goads his followers from their lethargy. By addressing them as "Warriors," he recalls them to a sense of military obligation; this appeal to duty and shame has its effect, for they feel "abasht," like soldiers caught sleeping on "watch." By qualifying the title "Flowr of Heav'n" with the observation that heaven is "now lost" to them "If such astonishment as this can seize eternal spirits," he not only heightens their sense of shame but also lays the foundation of his argument that unless they "arise" now they must "be for ever fall'n."

Satan opens his next formal address by hailing his followers as "Myriads of immortal Spirits" and "Powers Matchless, but with the Almighty" (I, 622). This is, under the circumstances, a peculiarly apt beginning, for Satan has just reviewed his troops, "summed" their "number," and gloried in their "strength" and "imbodied force." By greeting them now as "Myriads" and matchless "powers," he gives particular emphasis to two aspects of military strength—number and force. But these titles also provide a point of departure for his exhortation to renewed warfare against Heaven. He develops the motifs of angelic power, immortality, and spirituality to suggest the possibility of recovering Heaven:

> *For who can yet believe, though after loss,*
> *That all these puissant Legions, whose exile*
> *Hath emptied Heav'n, shall faile to re-ascend*
> *Self-rais'd, and repossess thir native seat?*
>
> (I, 631)

The term "Self-rais'd" links this argument with his earlier boast to Abdiel (V, 857 ff.) that the angels had been "self-begot" and "self-rais'd" by their "own quick'ning power." Once again Satan is insisting that the "puissance" is his "own." And once again he takes the celestial origin of the angels as a basis for argument. Through such phrases as "force of Gods," "host of Heav'n," "Sons of Heaven," and "Celestial Spirits" he builds up the argument that the fallen angels can and will escape from their "Bondage" in the "Infernal Pit."

By qualifying the title of "Powers"—adding that the angels are "Matchless, but with th' Almighty"—Satan makes an easy transition to the subject of their defeat and to justify his own "counsels" and actions as leader. The same reservation enables him to argue the advantages they can reap from their defeat. They have acquired a better knowledge of their own strength and that of the enemy, hitherto "conceal'd." Finally, this qualification lends persuasive force to his new strategy, his preference for fraud over force in the renewed warfare against God. Inherent in the opening lines of this speech are arguments that not only mitigate defeat, but also encourage his followers to resume the conflict, equipped with better military intelligence and a more practicable strategy.

In the opening speech of the infernal conclave, the terms of the salutation again hold the seeds of the argument. Once again Satan appeals to the power, immortality, and celestial origin of the angels as proof of better success in warfare. As "Deities" they must be immortal. As "Celestial" beings they belong, by nature and right, in Heaven. Hence in seeking to reclaim this "just inheritance" the fallen angels have good chance of success; they are "Surer to prosper than prosperity Could have assur'd us. . . ." Since "Celestial" and "Heav'n" are "conjugates in sense," in playing on these words Satan is employing the argument from "conjugates" and from "notation." The same is true of the terms "Powers," "vigour," and "vertues." Once again the titles he bestows on his audience have persuasive force; they are not simply the salutation common to most exordia, but a basis for exhortation as well:

> *Powers and Dominions, Deities of Heav'n,*
> *For since no deep within her gulf can hold*

Immortal vigor, though opprest and fall'n,
I give not Heav'n for lost. From this descent
Celestial Vertues rising, will appear
More glorious and more dread then from no fall. . . .
(II, 11)

Moloch subsequently employs a similar argument (II, 75 ff.), but without Satan's subtle use of the salutation for rhetorical proof. Beëlzebub, on the other hand, shares his master's rhetorical skill and exploits the same technique. Beginning with a formal salutation not unlike those of Satan and God the Father (V, 600 ff.),[8] he shifts ironically to an infernal title pointedly directed at the proposals already advanced for founding a "nether Empire":

Thrones and imperial Powers, off-spring of Heav'n,
Ethereal Vertues; or these Titles now
Must we renounce, and changing stile be call'd
Princes of Hell? for so the popular vote
Inclines, here to continue, and build up here
A growing Empire; . . .
(II, 310)

Dismissing this project as "vain" (God ordained Hell as a "dungeon" and will still extend "His Empire" over it as over Heaven), Beëlzebub opens the way for an alternative proposal—the enterprise against man.

II

Upon returning to Hell after his successful expedition to Eden, Satan again utilizes titles as a basis for argument. Yet there are several significant differences between this speech and most of the others we have examined. For one thing, it belongs to demonstrative rather than deliberative oratory. Satan is not exhorting his audience to undertake a particular course of action but seeking praise for his own exploit. He presents his formal report on the success of his expedition in such a way that it can hardly fail to earn "high applause" from his hearers. Secondly, showing his awareness of the ambiguity of the titles, he distinguishes between "possession" and "right." In this respect, his speech complements the conspiratorial address in Heaven, where his reference to ranks or titles that were "merely titular" implied a similar distinction between the mere "right" to titles and their actual possession. The

8. See also *Paradise Lost*, X, 34 ff., for another instance of the Father's adaptation of the salutation into a basis for argument. Kester Svendsen, "Epic Address and Reference and the Principle of Decorum in *Paradise Lost*," *PQ*, 28 (1949), 185–206, examines the forms of address in the poem from a different angle. See also Robert H. West, "The Terms of Angelic Rank in *Paradise Lost*," *Essays in Honor of Walter Clyde Curry* (Nashville, Tennessee, 1954), pp. 261–68.

threat he saw to the "possession" of such "magnific titles" subsequently became real when Messiah ejected the rebels from Heaven. After his expulsion Satan could employ these titles only in the sense of "right"; now, for the first time since his fall, he can use them in the sense of "possession" as well.

Though this exordium provides an effective point of departure for Satan's argument, it serves logically as a conclusion rather than a premise. The reason why the fallen angels now hold these titles in "possession" is that Satan has just conquered "a spacious World" for them to "possess, as Lords." The body of his speech is devoted to *how* he conquered it. That these titles now bear a fuller sense is the direct result of the devil's own exploits:

> *Thrones, Dominations, Princedoms, Vertues, Powers,*
> *For in possession such, not onely of right,*
> *I call ye and declare ye now, returnd*
> *Successful beyond hope, to lead ye forth*
> *Triumphant . . .: Now possess,*
> *As Lords, a spacious World, to our native Heaven*
> *Little inferiour, by my adventure hard*
> *With peril great atchiev'd.*
>
> (X, 460)

By relating his new conquest, Satan proves the statement with which he began—that the fallen angels now hold their titles "in possession" once more, not merely in "right."

III

A similar use of titles as a basis for argument occurs in the demonic councils of *Paradise Regain'd.* Taking as his point of departure the salutation "ancient Powers of Air and this wide world" (I, 44), Satan expatiates on the "many Ages" during which the demons "have possest, and rul'd . . . th' affairs of Earth" and the threat that the predicted "Woman's seed" offers to "all our power, . . . our freedom and our being In this fair Empire won of Earth and Air. . . ." Similarly, in a later council-scene, he calls the infernal powers by titles appropriate to their elemental domains—only to warn them that their jurisdictions are imperiled:

> *Princes, Heav'ns ancient Sons, Aethereal Thrones,*
> *Demonian Spirits now, from th' Element*
> *Each of his reign allotted, rightlier call'd,*
> *Powers of Fire, Air, Water, and Earth beneath,*
> *So may we hold our place and these mild seats*

Without new trouble; such an Enemy
Is ris'n to invade us, who no less
Threat'ns then our expulsion down to Hell; . . .
(II, 121)

In both of these councils, as in *Paradise Lost*, the terms of Satan's salutation have persuasive force, a direct bearing on the type of argument that follows.

IV

In his encounters with the gods of the Abyss and with Sin and Death, the devil employs the same device, converting the titles of his exordium into rhetorical proof. His speech to the deities of the void is a deliberative oration; he seeks to persuade them to give him the information he needs by pleading the "advantage" his mission will bring them. He bases his argument on the commonplace of regal power and imperial jurisdiction, promising to expel "All usurpation" from the new-created world and to re-erect there the "Standard . . . of *ancient Night*. . . ." Both in theme and diction this argument echoes the terms of his salutation:

Ye Powers
And Spirits of this nethermost Abyss,
Chaos *and* ancient Night. . . .
(II, 968)

In greeting Sin and Death "at the brink of *Chaos*" on his return-journey, Satan employs a demonstrative argument, praising them for erecting the triumphal bridge over the Abyss and rewarding them with vicegerency over his "new Kingdom" in the world. The relationship between their exploit and its reward is one of cause and effect and hinges on the concept of merit. It is because they have so "Amply . . . merited" of him that Satan appoints them his "Substitutes" and plenipotentiaries "on Earth." As in other instances, he lays the foundation of this argument in his salutation. Sin and Death have *proved* their worth and their right to the titles of son and daughter to God's antagonist:

Fair Daughter, and thou Son and Grandchild both,
High proof ye now have giv'n to be the Race
Of Satan (*for I glorie in the name,*
Antagonist of Heav'ns Almightie King). . . .
(X, 384)

The scene is a conscious parody of the exaltation of the Son of God in Book III, yet the parallel is more subtle than critics have usually recognized. In both cases it involves the relationship of title to merit and birthright. The Messiah demonstrates his worth—and his divine Sonship—by volunteering to die for man and thus proving that he is "By Merit more then Birthright Son of God." As the reward of his "Merits" he receives a universal kingdom as God's vicegerent. In this infernal counterpart of the scene in Heaven, Sin and Death likewise prove—by merit more than birthright—that they deserve the titles of son and daughter of the Adversary. As rewards they become vicegerents of the visible universe. Satan's exordium thus contains the seeds not only of his argument, but also of the parallel with the celestial council of Book III.

V

The validity and significance of titles of honor are primary considerations in Milton's argument of nobility. The lofty epithets Satan bestows on his legions have become empty and vain since their breach of fealty with Jehovah. In exploiting these titles as a basis of argument, he is reasoning from a false premise.

Milton's concern with the validity of titles is not limited, however, to the passages we have examined. It recurs throughout both epics, and it plays a prominent part in his prose works. Moreover, it has both moral and political implications. Though closely interlinked with the questions of authority and merit, it also serves as an index of meekness or ambition, humility or pride.

When Adam hails Eve as "Mother of all Mankind" (XI, 159), she answers "with sad demeanour meek" and confesses her own unworthiness:

> *Ill worthie I such title should belong*
> *To mee transgressour. . . .*

Her posterity, on the other hand, shows less reluctance to accepted unmerited titles. The giants of Cain's lineage achieve "Fame in the World, high titles, and rich prey" by "Subduing Nations" and performing "acts of prowess eminent . . . but of true vertu void" (XI, 785 ff.). Nimrod subjects his fellows to an "Empire tyrannous" in "despite of Heav'n, Or from Heav'n claiming second Sovrantie" (XII, 24 ff.). In thus arrogating "Dominion undeserv'd Over his brethren," he reveals his "proud ambitious heart" and assumes a title that belongs properly to God alone:

> *. . . Man over men*
> *He [Jehovah] made not Lord; such title to himself*
> *Reserving, human left from human free.*

The degenerate clergy unjustly "seek to avail themselves of names,/ Places and titles, and with these to joine/Secular power . . ." (XII, 515).

In *Paradise Regain'd* much of the debate concerns—directly or indirectly—the validity and precise significance of Jesus's title "Son of God." As Satan himself observes, the title is ambiguous. The "Sons of God both Angels are and Men" (IV, 197), and the tempter essays accordingly "to try whether in higher sort Then these thou bear'st that title. . . ." He attempts to "learn"

> *In what degree of meaning thou art call'd*
> *The Son of God, which bears no single sense;*
> *The Son of God I also am, or was . . .*
> *All men are Sons of God; yet thee I thought*
> *In some respect far higher so declar'd.*
>
> (IV, 515)

Though Satan's claim to this title ("And if I was, I am; relation stands") is no longer valid, he is nevertheless capable of perceiving its falsity when applied to Belial and his "lusty Crew, False titl'd Sons of God" (II, 178). Christ, in turn, denounces the claim of worldly conquerors to merit the titles of gods and sons of gods. Destroying the "flourishing works of peace," these "Worthies"

> *. . . swell with pride, and must be titl'd Gods,*
> *Great Benefactors of mankind, Deliverers,*
> *Worship't with Temple, Priest and Sacrifice;*
> *One is the Son of* Jove, *of* Mars *the other,*
> *Till Conqueror Death discover them scarce men . . .*
>
> (III, 74)

VI

Such attacks on the abuse of "magnific titles" by churchmen and rulers are even more pronounced in Milton's prose than in his epics, and analysis of the validity and significance of such titles is a significant aspect of his rhetorical procedure. In *Animadversions* he refutes his adversary's attempt to prove the "precedence" of bishops from "the title of eminence, *Angel*" (Revelation 2:1, 8, 12); by analyzing the title itself, Milton demonstrates that this "borrowed name, Angel . . . is to be understood as equally collective, and communicative to the whole preaching ministery of the place," rather than to a "Diocesan *Bishop*." A clergyman ought not to seek the title of "Lord," as the "due performance of his office would gaine him . . . the voluntary title of Father" (III, 154–5, 164). According to *The Reason of Church-Government*, St. Peter gave "the title of Clergy . . . to all Gods people";

when popes and prelates appropriated this "name to themselves and their Priests only," they usurped "the liberties and lawfull titles of Gods freeborn Church . . ." (III, 257–8).[9] In *Considerations Touching the Likeliest Means to Remove Hirelings out of the Church*, Milton bids the clergy to "lay down for shame that magnific title" of "embassadors of Jesus Christ," since they behave instead like his "tithe-gatherers" and "publicans" (VI, 91).

The political treatises emphasize the nature and limits of royal titles. In *The Tenure of Kings and Magistrates*, Milton argues that "the best foundation" of "hereditary title" is probably only "courtesie or convenience." But even if his title should be "of right hereditarie," a king can "forfet all his title and inheritance to the people" for his crimes. When a native prince breaks the law and "all the Covnants and Oaths that gave him title to his dignity, and were the bond and alliance between him and his people," he does not differ "from an outlandish King, or from an enemie" (V, 11, 20). *Eikonoklastes* challenges the king's "glorious title of the *Churches Defender*." Far from meriting the "title" of "*Father of his Countrey*," Charles I has been his country's "destroyer." As men are "by nature free," they are "born and created with a better title to thir freedom, then any King hath to his Crown" (V, 212, 254–5).[10]

In the *First Defense* Milton again scoffs at Charles's title of "Defender of the Faith" (VII, 41–3),[11] and refutes Salmasius's attempt to justify the king's "tyrannical power" by his title, "Lord." To Salmasius's argument that "in the statutes of the realm . . . the king is called 'our Lord the king' [*Rex Dominus noster*]," Milton replies that titles of honor do not constitute valid proof: "But what you know not is that many are called lords who are not lords; you know not how unfair it is to determine of the right and truth of things from titles of honor, not to say of flattery" (VII, 415). Though the "princes of the Gentiles exercise dominion" over their subjects and assume the specious titles of "Euergetae and benefactors," the "Christian king" must be "the

9. In *Of Prelacticall Episcopacy* Milton analyzes the "high titles" bestowed on Polycarp ("propheticall, Apostolicall", "Bishop of the Church of *Smirna*") to refute the argument that such titles refer to prelacy (III, 94–6). In *The Tenure* he accuses "a covetous and ambitious generation of Divines (for Divines they call themselves)" of "aspiring under another title [than episcopacy] to the same authority and usurpation over the consciences of all men" (V, 52–3).

10. Milton accuses Charles I of contesting with God "about that supreme title" of sovereign by laying "*restraints* . . . upon our consciences in things for which we were to answer to God onely and the Church" (V, 218).

11. Charles has as little right to this title as Salmasius to the self-assumed title "Defender of the King." They "deserve [their] titles both alike; for the king so defended the faith, and [Salmasius has] so defended him, that each of [them] seems rather to have ruined his case . . ."

people's servant." If he desires to be "lord and master [dominus] out and out, he cannot at the same time be Christian" (VII, 155–59).[12]

Milton likewise attacks the Spanish for abusing the argument based on title. In *A Declaration against Spain* he refutes their contention that "as the King of Spain hath assumed amongst his Titles, that of Rex Indiarum; so indeed all the Indies and Indian Sea, both North and South, are his proper Dominions . . ." (XIII, 551).

The Commonplace book also reveals Milton's interest in the validity of royal titles. According to one entry, "Augustus, the founder of the Empire, did not wish even to be called 'Lord'; for this is a title of God also" (XVIII, 218). Another quotes Angelo di Constanzo's opinion that by inflicting "an atrocious injury" on his vassal "the king loses the title of king and takes on the name of tyrant" (XVIII, 170–71). Such passages as these throw light on Milton's treatment of titles in both of his epics. If it is "unfair . . . to determine of the right and truth of things from titles of honor" or "flattery," if titles can be forfeited by breach of fealty, Satan is obviously using an "unfair" argument in maintaining that the angels' "Imperial Titles" are incompatible with the Messiah's dominion and that the latter violates their natural rights. Emphasis on the spuriousness of the titles of "benefactor" and "lord" when conferred on tyrants and "destroyers" recurs in Milton's prose and poetry alike. The realization that a true king—a Christian king—must be "the people's servant" characterizes the Messiah in *Paradise Regain'd* and *Paradise Lost.* It sets him apart from the Gentile princes, who "exercise dominion" over their peoples, and from Satan, who is the archetype of this pattern. Christ humbles himself to assume the "form of a servant" and thus exhibits the true norm of kingship. Satan, on the contrary, renounces his duties as a "ministering spirit" and "servant of God" in order to assume dominion over his fellows and over mankind. The one renounces titles; the other glories in them. The one, by his humility, demonstrates his merit and proves his right to the title of king; the other shows himself to be no true king, but a usurper and a tyrant.

VII

Though Milton is strongly critical of arguments based on titles, he sometimes employs them himself as means of rhetorical persuasion. *An Apology* concludes with an indirect appeal to the king to justify his title and prove himself "a true defender of the Faith" by reforming

12. To prove this point, Milton quotes Luke xxii, "Ye know that the princes of the Gentiles exercise dominion over them, and they that are great exercise authority upon them. But it shall not be so among you: but whosoever will be great among you, let him be your minister; and whosoever will be chief among you, let him be your servant."

the church (III, 365). In *Of Reformation* the author attacks the episcopacy for insulting the grave and worthy minister who is "a true Bishop of his fold" and for treating as "impure ethnicks, and lay dogs" the "people of *God* . . . dignify'd with so many glorious titles of Saints, and sons in the Gospel . . ." The final paragraphs contrast the "shameful end" of those who seek dignities and dominion in this world with the celestial titles that will be the reward of the faithful. The latter "shall receive, above the inferiour *Orders* of the *Blessed,* the *Regall* addition of *Principalities, Legions,* and *Thrones* into their glorious Titles . . ." (III, 18–19, 79). Like Satan, Milton realizes the rhetorical appeal of these angelic titles; but, unlike Satan, he represents them as strictly contingent on faithful service.

The Doctrine and Discipline of Divorce likewise employs the argument from title as a means of exhortation. Milton promises Parliament "a greater title . . . then is either in the power or in the policy of *Rome* to give her *Monarchs*; this glorious act will stile ye the defenders of Charity" (III, 377). In *The Tenure* he argues from the meaning of their titles that "the Peers and Barons of England had a legal right to judge the King: which was the cause most likely . . . that they were call'd his Peers, or equals . . ." Indeed, such titles as "Dukes, Earles, and Marqueses were at first not hereditary, not empty and vain titles, but names of trust and office, and with the office ceasing" (V, 25). They depend, in short, on merit rather than birthright. Similarly, in *The Readie and Easie Way,* Milton insists that "a free Parlament" will "deserve the true honor of that supreme title" only "if they preserve us a free people" (VI, 125). In a state letter he exhorts Louis XIV "by *that same goodly Ornament of your Title of Most Christian* [per illud *Christianismi* Tituli decus sanctissimum]" not to permit the persecution of the "Innocent Christians" in Piedmont nor to "suffer . . . your Titles . . . to be contaminated with this same Heaven-offending Scandal . . ." (XIII, 355–59).

Nevertheless, though Milton occasionally uses titles for rhetorical exhortation and persuasion, he usually treats them as pretentious vanities. In *The Readie and Easie Way* he asks why the nation should seek a change of government and "deliver themselves up to meer titles and vanities, to persons untri'd, unknown . . ." (VI, 364). In *A Second Defense* he praises Cromwell for scorning titles esteemed by the crowd but actually inadequate to express his true merits and deserts. All good men hail him as the greatest citizen, the leader of public counsel, the general of the bravest armies, the father of his country: "Other titles, though merited by you, your actions know not, endure not; and those proud ones, deemed great in vulgar opinion, they deservedly cast from them. For what is a title, but a certain definite mode of dignity? Your achievements surpass every degree even of admiration, and much more do they surpass every title;—they rise above the popular atmosphere of titles, as the tops of pyramids hide themselves in the clouds." Only "for the public benefit" has Cromwell assumed "something like a title, resembling most that of *pater patriae*, the father of your country"; he has despised "the name of king for majesty far more majestic" (VIII, 223–25).[13] According to the *History of Britain*, the failures of the ancient Britons were partly due to the lack of leaders "more then vulgar, . . . invincible against money, and vaine titles . . ." (X, 325). Finally, in the *Christian Doctrine* Milton points out that Christ had refused the "adulatory titles which were wont to be given to the Pharisees," including even the title "good" (Matthew xix. 17) (XIV, 233).

This highly critical attitude towards "magnific titles" characterizes Milton's use of the argument of nobility in both of his epics. In both poems the Messiah, as Milton's heroic archetype, proves himself a leader "more than vulgar" and "invincible against . . . vaine titles"—in *Paradise Lost* by renouncing his royal dignities, in *Paradise Regain'd* by refusing the "adulatory titles" and honors his tempter offers him. On the other hand, Satan as pseudo-hero and heroic *eidolon* not only desires dominion himself, but glories in the title of "Antagonist of Heav'n's Almighty King." Seducing his followers with titles once valid but now vain, he similarly beguiles Eve with the false title of "Goddess" and with false inferences from the more legitimate title of "Empress." Both in prose and poetry Milton makes extensive use of the argument based on title—but with a keen awareness of its dangers and a strongly critical attitude towards its validity.

13. Denouncing the abuse of "the title and surname of great" (IX, 185), Milton observes that "He alone deserves the appellation of great, who either achieves great things himself, or teaches how they might be achieved; or who describes with suitable dignity, the great achievements of others" (VIII, 95–97).

Part VI

❦

Satan's "Degradation"

❦

18. *Archangel to Devil*

The Background of Satan's Metamorphosis

❦ To many critics, Milton's "transformation scene"—the metamorphosis of the evil angels into serpents, in *Paradise Lost*, Book X—has seemed arbitrary and inconsistent, an unwarranted degradation of the heroic figures he had delineated in Books I and II. In Herford's opinion, the poet had reduced Satan to a serpent lest he be thought the hero of the poem.[1] For Waldock, the scene embodied the "technique of the comic cartoon . . . The method of the cartoon is to allow the villain of the piece to reach a pitch of high confidence and vainglory and then to dash him down. . . . To attempt to link such a scene as this with what happens in the first books of *Paradise Lost* is to try to bring incommensurables together. . . . The scene is amusing . . . but about Satan it proves literally nothing whatever."[2]

By thus isolating this episode from its literary and theological background, scholars have frequently underestimated Milton's debt to tradition, on the one hand, and the nature and significance of his innovations, on the other. Satan's metamorphosis was by no means an arbitrary invention on Milton's part. On the contrary, the convention

First published, in somewhat different form, in *Modern Language Quarterly*, XXI (1960), 321–35.

1. C. H. Herford, "Dante and Milton," *Bulletin of the John Rylands Library*, VIII (1924), 223.
2. A. J. A. Waldock, *Paradise Lost and Its Critics* (Cambridge, 1947), pp. 91–92.

of demonic disfigurement was an old one, and the belief that Lucifer and his companions forfeited their beauty with their allegiance—that their transition from angels to fiends entailed a corresponding debasement in form—had been a recurrent theme in medieval and Renaissance art and literature. The metamorphosis which Waldock and Herford found arbitrary was, in reality, based on a familiar convention.[3]

Nor was it "incommensurable" with Milton's initial representation of the fallen angels. Waldock mistook contrast for inconsistency. In emphasizing the contrast between Lucifer's pristine beauty and his ultimate hideousness, Milton was actually following an established tradition: the conventional degeneration from angel to devil. The alterations in Satan's appearance between Books I and IX conformed to a familiar pattern. They violated neither probability nor consistency.

The aesthetic value of this scene derived largely from two complementary factors: convention and surprise, or (as Tasso expressed it) verisimilitude and marvel. Satan's transformation gained additional force from its suddenness, credibility from the tradition behind it. Milton's most striking departure from convention resided, in fact, in the timing rather than in the nature of this metamorphosis. Unlike his precedessors, who had usually regarded Satan's disfigurement as simultaneous with his fall, Milton postponed this change until after the temptation and fall of man. Through this innovation he was able to present his devils initially in a heroic light. Satan himself, though shorn of "th' excess Of Glory," was no "Less than Arch Angel ruind," still endowed with much of his "Original brightness." His companions were likewise "Godlike shapes and forms Excelling human." This introductory portrait of the fallen angels as defeated heroes rather than as distorted fiends constituted a far greater variation on tradition than Milton's subsequent account of their transformation into serpents. The tradition of demonic transformation is far more extensive than scholars have hitherto recognized, and Milton's variations on this theme can be fully appreciated only against that background.

I

According to Neoplatonic theory, Lucifer's body lost its light and beauty after his rebellion and became dark, gross, ugly, and sensitive to pain. Psellus[4] devoted a chapter of his *Dialogus de Daemonum Energia* to the question "De angelici corporis a daemoniaco, splendorisque a solari differentia et discrimine," emphasizing the sharp distinction between the bodies of angels and demons—the former immaterial and

3. See Merritt Y. Hughes, "Myself Am Hell," *MP*, LIV (1956), 91–93, for parallels.
4. See Robert H. West, "Milton and Michael Psellus," *PQ*, XXVIII (1949), 477–89.

transparent, the latter opaque, material, vulnerable to fire and blows and sensitive to pain. Such was Lucifer's fate after his fall: "For since the angel whom Isaiah calls Lucifer [Isaiah xiv. 12] fell, he was deprived of that light with which he was created; and now he is dark and obscure and gloomy in appearance."[5]

Ralph Cudworth quoted Psellus' views in *The True Intellectual System of the Universe.*[6] St. Augustine, he observed, had defined "the difference betwixt the bodies of angels and devils in this manner: Daemones, antequam transgrederentur, coelestia corpora gerebant, quae conversa sint ex poena in aëream qualitatem, ut jam possint ab igne pati. . . ."[7]

Ficino maintained that, since the external form reflects the inner reality, good spirits possess beautiful shapes, while the bodies of evil demons are deformed.[8]

According to Boehme's *Mysterium Magnum*, Lucifer's fall consisted essentially in the obscuration of angelical by diabolical properties:

Thus this beautiful star did overshadow its light; and made its essence wholly astringent, rigorous and harsh; and its meekness and true angelic property was turned into an essence wholly austere, harsh, rigorous, and dark. (I, 50).

5. Migne, *Patrologia Graeca*, CXXII (Paris, 1864), cols, 838–39, 871 (Chapter 23: "Quomodo daemones percutiantur, deque daemoniaci a solido corpore differentia"). Cf. Ficino's translation of Psellus' *De Daemonibus*, printed with Iamblichus' *De Mysteriis Aegyptiorum, Chaldaeorum, Assyriorum* (Lugduni, 1577), cols. 335–36, 360–61.

6. Ralph Cudworth, *The True Intellectual System of the Universe* (London, 1845), III, 356–57. Cudworth also found support for this doctrine in Fulgentius' belief (*De Trinitate*, Book III) that angels "have ethereal or fiery bodies, but devils aerial" (p. 355) and in Jude vi ("the angels which kept not their first estate, but left their own habitation"). By sinning, the fallen angels lost "not only 'their dwelling-place' at large, those ethereal countries, and heavenly regions above, but also their proper dwelling-house, or immediate mansion; to wit their heavenly body. . . . But then again . . . that which was thus in part the natural result of their sin, was also, by the just judgment of God, converted into their punishment; for their ethereal bodies being thus changed into gross, aerial, feculent, and vaporous, themselves were immediately hereupon, as St. Peter in the parallel passage expresseth it [2 Peter ii.4), ταρταρωθέντες, 'cast down into Tartarus. . . .'" (p. 363).

7. *Ibid.*, pp. 353–54. See Augustine's *De Genesi ad Litteram*, Book III, Chapter 10 (*Patrologia Latina*, XXXIV [Paris, 1887]); cf. *Ioannis Wieri De Praestigiis Daemonum* (Basileae, 1577), col. 20: "Hi ergo spiritus antea divini, coelestes, puri, lucidi . . . angelicam essentiam non omnino perdiderunt: sed perditissimè, originali iusticia & lumine gratiae privati, vitiarunt, denigraruntque, ut iam aërei, mundani, obscuri, tenebricosi, & . . . immundi malique dicantur & sint. . . ."

8. *Plotini Opera Omnia . . . cum Marsilii Ficini Commentariis et ejusdem Interpretatione Castigata*, ed. Fridericus Creuzer (Oxford, 1835), I, 357. See also Huetius' *Origeniana* (*Patrologia Graeca*, XVII [Paris, 1857], col. 852): "Unde Porphyrius daemones, quorum animi sunt iniqui, corpora quoque dicit habere deformia: quorum vero probi sunt animi, corpora insuper esse formosa. Et Origines ex luce ordineque caelestium argumentatur, spiritus illis inesse Deo propinquiora [Ed. pr. propinquiores], lucidaeque intelligentiae compotes, atque una cum Apostolo Paulo spiritus a Deo longe degenerantes corporibus ex aëre caliginoso concretis includit. . . . Turpe vero corpus est animae incompositae signum, et in habitum vel affectum dissonum jam prolapsae. Postquam enim ob nequitiam

He was an angel, and hath belied his angelical form and obedience . . . in his centre he hath awakened the envious hateful forms and properties of the dark world, whence wrath and iniquity springeth. (I, 52)

His properties were as the venomous stings of serpents, which he put forth out of himself. When the love of God was withdrawn from him, he figured his image according to the property of the wrathful forms (wherein there are also evil beasts and worms, in the serpentine shape) . . . whence the combat arose, that the great prince Michael fought with him. . . . (I, 52)

Thus the light was extinct to him [Lucifer], for he made his angelicall essence . . . wholly rough, austere, cold, wrathful and fiery, in the dark wrathful property . . . and he became a devil; and was driven out of the angelical world. . . . (I, 117)[9]

Batman uppon Bartholome quoted St. Gregory the Great and St. John Damascene on Lucifer's transformation from angel to fiend:

The head of these evill spirites and leader, is *Lucifer*, the which as *Gregory* saith, hath that name, for he was made more cleere and bright then other Angells. For the first Angell was beautified as a precious stone: for whilest he was above all the companies of Angells, by comparison he was the more bright and cleere, then they. But he waxing proud against his Creator, lost light and cleerenesse and fairenesse: and as he was worthy he gate him a foule darke shape of Apostacie. Thereof speaketh *Damas. li. l. Chap. 18.* . . . He was of the creator made light, and by his owne will he became darknesse. . . .[10]

Vondel cited St. Bernard's comment on Lucifer's degeneration: "The source of all transgression is pride, which hath overcast Lucifer himself, shining most splendidly amongst the stars, with eternal darkness. Not only an Angel, but the chief among Angels, it hath changed into a Devil."[11]

Reginald Scot declared that "the shapes and various likenesses of Devils" correspond to "their various capacities in wickedness . . . resembling spiritually some horrid and ugly monsters, as their conspiracies against the power of God, were high and monstrous, when

daemones coelo sunt exturbati, crassiore quodam corpore circumceptos esse existimavit. Sic ille tom i. *in Joan.* num. 17: '*Ο καλούμενος δράκων ἄξιος γεγένηται ἀποπεσὼν της καθαρᾶς ζωῆς πρὸ πάντων ἐνδεθῆναι ὕλη καὶ σώματι.* Quod de diabolo statuit, de omnibus quoque daemonibus intelligendum est." Cf. Origen (*Patrologia Graeca*, XIV [Paris, 1862], col. 51).

9. Jacob Boehme, *Mysterium Magnum or an Explanation of the First Book of Moses Called Genesis*, trans. John Sparrow, ed. C. J. B. (London, 1924). Hughes (p. 93) has noted additional parallels in Boehme's *Description of the Three Principles of the Divine Essence*.

10. *Batman uppon Bartholome* (London, 1582), p. 10.

11. *Vondel's Lucifer*, trans. Leonard Charles Van Noppen (Greensboro, N.C., 1917), pp. 249–50. Wierus (col. 19) quoted a similar comment by Augustine (*Tract. in Joan. 42*): "Quaeris unde diabolus? Inde utique, unde & caeteri angeli. Sed caeteri angeli in sua obedientia perstiterunt, ille inobediendo & superbiendo lapsus est angelus, & factus est diabolus." Cf. Joseph Hall, *Works*, ed. Philip Wynter (Oxford, 1863), VII, 581–82: "The angels . . . long since, are ugly devils. . . ."

they fell from Heaven. . . ."[12] When conjured, they appear in shapes "answerable to the cause of their Fall, and the Dominions to which they belong" (p. 524).

[The] opinion of the antients is, That according to the division of the clean and unclean Beasts in the Law given unto *Moses*, the Shapes of Devils are disposed in the Infernal Kingdom: So that the most perverse and potent among the Devils represent the most ugly and mischievous among the Beasts, according to the following division; *viz.* such Devils as *Astaroth*, *Lucifer*, *Bardon*, *Pownok*, who incline men and instigate them to pride and presumptuousness, have the shapes of Horses, Lyons, Tygars, Wolves[.] Such as instigate to Lust and Covetousness have the forms of Hogs, Serpents, and other filthy reptiles or envious Beasts, as Dogs, Cats, Vultures, Snakes, &c. Such as incline to Murther, have the shapes of every Bird and Beast of prey. (p. 525).

Thomas Heywood[13] quoted Dante's description of Lucifer ("L'Imperador del Doloroso Regno," *Inferno*, Canto XXXIV, lines 28 ff.) to illustrate his hideousness after his fall:

> *Of the Rebellious,* Lucifer *is prime*
> *Captaine and King. . . .*
> *And as in his Creation he was fram'd*
> *More glorious far than others before-nam'd;*
> *More goodly featur'd, beautifull, and bright,*
> *And therefore had his name deriv'd from Light:*
> *So since his Fall, there's nothing we can stile*
> *So ougly foule, abominably vile;*
> *The putred Fountaine, and bitumenous Well,*
> *From whence all Vice and malefactures swell.*
> *Whose horrid shape, and qualities infest,*
> *Are by the Poet* Dantes *thus exprest. . . .*
>
> (p. 412)

Heywood further observed that, whereas the good angels "still take the shape of Man," the "bad Daemons"

> *In figures more contemptible appeare,*
> *One like a Wolfe, another like a Beare:*
> *Others resembling Dogs, Apes, Monkies, Cats,*
> *And sometimes Birds, as Crowes, Pies, Owles, and Bats.*
>
> (p. 580)

12. Reginald Scot, *Discoverie of Witchcraft*, ed. Brinsley Nicholson (London, 1886), p. 493.

13. Thomas Heywood, *The Hierarchie of the Blessed Angells,* [and] *the Fall of Lucifer with his Angels* (London, 1635), pp. 412–13. Heywood went on to explain Dante's description allegorically (pp. 413–14).

II

Aesthetic principles also influenced representations of Satan and his followers. The physical contrast between the good and evil angels symbolized the moral gulf between them. Valvasone called attention to this principle: "ed è permesso anco a' pittori di dipinger gli angeli buoni di corpo tutti risplendenti e belli, ed i cattivi, all' incontro, della più spaventevol forma che imaginar si sanno."[14] Vondel likewise recognized the importance of emphasizing the ethical distinction between good and evil spirits: "We should also make distinction between the two kinds of characters who contend on this stage; namely, the bad and the good Angels, each kind playing its own role, even as Cicero and our inborn sense of verisimilitude teach us to picture each character according to his rank and nature" (pp. 251–52).

In his dialogue *Il Figino, overo del fine della pittura,*[15] Comanini extolled Vida's[16] and Tasso's[17] grotesque descriptions of the devils and specifically commended Figino's contrasting portraits of Michael and Satan:

> . . . where (the better to express the greatness of Satanic pride) you [o Figino] portrayed him as a sinewy figure with ragged limbs, horrifying of aspect, black of visage, with hispid locks, with horns on his forehead, and with lower parts like those of a satyr. Contrariwise, in order to reveal the goodness and stalwart qualities of his antagonist Michael, you tempered your style in forming his image. His aspect is delicate, to be true; but all the same it breathes *un non sò che* of pride . . .; and though his limbs are beautiful, they are nonetheless robust.

Another significant influence on the development of this tradition was the Biblical account of the "war in heaven" (Revelation 12:7–9). Since this passage referred specifically to Satan as "dragon" and "serpent," Scripture itself seemed to testify to his monstrous appearance: "And the great dragon was cast out, that old serpent, called the Devil, and Satan, which deceiveth the whole world: he was cast out into the earth, and his angels were cast out with him."

Valvasone regarded this passage as authority for his own description of the rebel angels as monstrous beasts: "Hence I conclude that, desiring to speak poetically concerning the angels, I have spoken reasonably concerning them in terms of the images I have described. Moreover, for my descriptions I have the example and authority of St. John who calls Lucifer 'dragon' in his Apocalypse and attributes to him horn,

14. Erasmo di Valvasone, *L'Angeleida*, ed. G. Polidori (London, 1842), p. xxvi.

15. Gregorio Comanini, *Il Figino, overo del fine della pittura* (Mantova, 1591).

16. See Marcus Hieronymus Vida, *Christiados libri sex* (Cremonae, 1535), Book I, lines 139–55.

17. Torquato Tasso, *La Gerusalemme Liberata*, ed. Giovanni Leotta (Firenze, 1940), Canto IV, Stanzas 4–8.

crown, tail, and other things that belong properly to solid bodies." Vondel likewise cited this text as license for endowing the devils with animal forms: "St. John, in his Revelation, typifies the holy mysteries and the war in Heaven by the Dragon, whose tail drew after him a third part of the stars, supposed by the theologians to refer to the fallen Angels . . ." (p. 251). Moreover, illustrations of St. Michael's victory over the devil—a popular iconographical motif—often followed their Biblical source in portraying Satan as a dragon.

III

The contrast between the original beauty and subsequent hideousness of Lucifer and his angels was a familiar theme in medieval and Renaissance literature.[18] According to Guido delle Colonne, God punished Satan's transgression by turning him into a serpent or dragon:

> For the evil spirit is full of uncleanness and filth, and therefore God from the very beginning of his fall turned him into a brutish animal—that is, into a tortuous serpent; and because of his immense magnitude he is called a dragon. . . . This is that Leviathan who, having been made a serpent from the beginning of his ejection from Heaven, envied the glory of our first parents and dared to enter the Paradise of delight and . . ., by the vice of lying, influenced our parents with blind temptations. . . . Hence . . . it is certain that this Leviathan (i.e., the prince of devils cast out from the height of Heaven) either was turned bodily into a serpent himself or else entered the serpent. . . .[19]

Lydgate's *Pilgrimage of the Life of Man* reported that, though Lucifer was once "bryd ful cler and bryht, And passyngly ffayr unto the syght," now "he ys blak, and more horryble Than any deth, also mor terryble."[20] In Dante's opinion,

> *S' ei fu sì bel com' egli è ora brutto*
> *e contra il suo Fattore alzò le ciglia,*
> *ben dee da lui procedere ogni lutto.*
> (*Inferno*, Canto XXXIV, lines 34–36)

Richard Rolle declared that the devils became disfigured through sin:

> *But I wille shew yhow aparty*
> *Why þai er swa foul and grisly,*
> *For sum tyme þai war bright angels,*
> *Als þa er þat now in heven duels,*

18. Cf. the Old English Genesis, lines 67–71, 254–56. George Philip Krapp (ed.), *Junius Manuscript* (New York, 1937), pp. 4, 12.

19. *Lydgate's Troy-Book*, ed. Henry Bergen, Part IV, EETS, extra series, CXXVI (London, 1935), 141–42.

20. John Lydgate, *Pilgrimage of the Life of Man*, Part II, EETS, extra series, LXXXIII (London, 1901), 380.

Fra þat blisful place thurgh syn þai felle,
And bycome þan foule devels of helle,
And horribely defygurd, thurgh syn
Þat þai war wyth-fild and hardened þarin.
For warne syn war þai had ay bene
Bright aungels, als þai war first sene;
And now er þai made foule and ugly
Thurgh fylyng of þair syn anly,
Þan is syn mar foule and wlatsome,
Þan any devel þat out of helle may come. . . .[21]

IV

According to *Purity*, the rebel angels were transformed at the moment of their expulsion from heaven:

Þaȝ þe feloun were so fers for his fayre wedez
And his glorious glem þat glent so bryȝt,
As sone as Dryȝtynez dome drof to hymselven,
Þikke þowsandez þro þrwen þeroute,
Fellen fro þe fyrmament fendez ful blake,
[S]weved at þe fyrst swap as þe snaw þikke,
Hurled into helle-hole as þe hyve swarmez.[22]

Several mystery plays likewise represented the metamorphosis of the angels as contemporary with their fall. The York play, "The Creation, and the Fall of Lucifer," contains a stage direction to this effect:

Primus angelus deficiens, Lucifer.	*Each changes into*
Secundus angelus deficiens.	diabolus in inferno.[23]

After first boasting of his beauty as "Primus angelus deficiens," Lucifer reappeared as "deiabolus in inferno" (p. 5), lamenting his hideous change:

Whare es my kynde be-come, so cumly and clere,
Now I am laytheste, allas! Þat are was lighte.
My bryghtnes es blakkeste and blo nowe;
My bale es ay betande any brynande. . . .

(p. 5)

21. Richard Rolle de Hampole, *Pricke of Conscience*, ed. Richard Norris (Berlin, 1863), p. 64.

22. *Purity*, ed. Robert J. Menner, Yale Studies in English (New Haven, 1920), LXI, 10–11.

23. Lucy Toulmin Smith (ed.), *York Plays* (Oxford, 1885), p. 1.

In the *Ludus Coventriae*, Lucifer's transformation occurred at the moment of his banishment from Heaven:

> *At thy byddyng þi wyl I werke*
> *And pas fro joy to peyne smerte*
> *now I am a devyl ful derke*
> *Þat was An Aungell bryht.*[24]

In the Towneley play of "The Creation," the fallen rebels reproached Lucifer for the loss of their beauty and for his own transition from angel to fiend:

> *We, that were angels so fare,*
> *And sat so hie above the ayere,*
> *Now ar we waxen blak as any coyll,*
> *and ugly, tatyrd as a foyll.*
> *What alyd the, lucifer to fall?*
> *was thou not farist of angels all?*
> *thou art foull comyn from thi kyn;*
> *thou art fallen, that was the teynd,*
> *ffrom an angell to a feynd.*[25]

The apocryphal *Book of John the Evangelist* described Satan's metamorphosis as immediately prior to his fall: "And I asked of the Lord: When Satan fell, in what place dwelt he? And he answered me: My Father changed his appearance because of his pride, and the light was taken from him, and his face became like unto heated iron, and his face became wholly like that of a man: and he drew with his tail the third part of the angels of God, and was cast out from the seat of God and from the stewardship of the heavens."[26]

To the traditional Islamic doctrine that Iblis fell because he refused to revere the clay from which man was to be created, *The Gospel of Barnabas* added the following account of his transformation:

> They that loved God bowed themselves, but Satan, with them that were of his mind, said: "O Lord, we are spirit, and therefore it is not just that we should do reverence to this clay." Having said this, Satan became horrid and of fearsome look, and his followers became hideous; because for their rebellion God took away from them the beauty wherewith he had endued them in creating them. Whereat the holy angels, when, lifting their heads, they saw how terrible a monster Satan had become, and his followers, cast down their face to earth in fear.

24. *Ludus Coventriae*, ed. K. S. Block, EETS, extra series, CCX (London, 1922), 19.
25. *Towneley Plays*, ed. George England, EETS, extra series, LXXI (London, 1897), 5.
26. Montague Rhodes James (ed.), *Apocryphal New Testament* (Oxford, 1924), p. 189. In James's opinion (p. 187), the Latin text of this book can hardly be older than the twelfth century; the original version, however, may have belonged to the sixth or seventh century.

Then said Satan: "O Lord, thou hast unjustly made me hideous, but I am content thereat, because I desire to annul all that thou shalt do."[27]

V

Like their medieval predecessors, Renaissance writers and artists usually regarded Satan's metamorphosis as complete at the time of his fall or, at the latest, before his temptation of Eve. In Floris de Vriendt's painting "De Engelenval,"[28] Lucifer—expelled from Heaven by Michael and his angels—has been transformed into a seven-headed dragon. His companions, despite their human torsos, possess the heads, claws, and tails of beasts. In Andreini's *L'Adamo* the fallen rebels have already suffered their sea change before their initial appearance on earth to seduce man; in the very first act they lament their altered shape:

> *E'n vece d'aureo crine,*
> *E d'Angelico aspetto,*
> *Viperino è 'l capel, lo sguardo bieco,*
> *Apre il volto cruccioso un' aria fosca,*
> *Gravida di bestemmie è ogn' hor la bocca,*
> *E bestemmiante sbocca,*
> *Sulfureo nembo, schifa bava, e foco:*
> *Son d'aquila le man, di capra il piede,*
> *L'ali di vipistrello, e al fin l'albergo*
> *Un tartaro profondo, infausto, ed atro. . . .*[29]

In Vondel's version, Lucifer, smitten by Michael, was hurled from his chariot and transformed into a "hideous medley of seven beasts," symbolic of the seven deadly sins:

> *Gelyck de klaere dagh in naeren nacht verkeert,*
> *Wanneer de son verzinckt, vergeet met gout te brallen;*

27. Lonsdale and Laura Ragg (eds.), *Gospel of Barnabas* (Oxford, 1907), p. 81. The editors (pp. xlii–xliv) regard the text as a Venetian copy of a Tuscan original composed between A.D. 1300 and 1350. Cf. Mahomet Rabadan, *Mahometism Fully Explained*, trans. Joseph Morgan (London, 1723), I, 26: "The accursed Squadron, who before their Fall were so gloriously beautiful, were transformed into such hideously frightful and monstrous Appearances, and so much disfigured from what they once were, that Imagination itself can comprehend nothing which may be compared to have any Similitude, or bear any manner of Resemblance to them: So ugly were their Forms and Countenances, and so unaccountable the Alteration, that nothing can be thought on, which with any Likeness may be justly apply'd." Morgan's introduction (pp. vii–viii) declares that Rabadan's manuscript was written in 1603 in Spanish by "one of those seemingly converted *Moors*, called by the *Spaniards* CHRISTIANOS NUEVOS. . . ."

28. No. 112 in the Royal Museum, Antwerp.

29. Giovanni Battista Andreini, *L'Adamo Sacra Rapresentatione* (Milano, 1617), p. 15. Cf. the grotesque illustrations of the devils in the accompanying plates by Cesare Bassano. For an English translation, see Watson Kirkconnell, *Celestial Cycle* (Toronto, 1952), pp. 235–39.

Zoo wort zyn schoonheit oock, in 't zincken, onder 't vallen,
In een wanschapenheit verandert, al te vuil;
Dat helder aengezicht in eenen wreeden muil;
De tanden in gebit, gewet om stael te knaeuwen;
De voeten en de hant in vierderhande klaeuwen;
Dat glinstrend parlemoer in eene zwarte huit.
De rugh, vol borstlen, spreit twee draeckevleugels uit.
In 't kort, d'Aertsengel, wien noch flus alle Englen vieren,
Verwisselt zyn gedaente, en mengelt zeven dieren
Afgryslyck onder een, naer uiterlycken schyn:
Een' leeu, vol hoovaerdy, een vraetigh, gulzigh zwyn,
Een' traegen ezel, een rinoceros, van toren
Ontsteecken, eene sim, van achter en van voren
Al even schaemteloos, en geil en heet van aert,
Een' draeck, vol nyts, een' wolf en vrecken gierigaert.
Nu is die schoonheit maer een ondier, te verwenschen,
Te vloecken, zelf van Godt, van Geesten, en van menschen.
Dat ondier yst, indien 't de blicken op zich slaet,
En deckt met damp en mist ʒijn gruwelijck gelaet.[30]

His companions were similarly disfigured:

De monsters, in het licht geklautert, holp aen 't hollen,
En groeide in zulck een jaght. . . .

30. F. J. Poelhekke, *Vondel's Dichtjuweelen* (Leiden, 1907), pp. 513–14. Cf. *Vondel's Lucifer*, trans. Leonard Charles Van Noppen, pp. 419–20:

Even as bright day to gloomy night is changed,
Whene'er the sun forgets his golden glow,
So in his downward fall his beauty turned
To something monstrous and most horrible:
Into a brutish snout his face, that shone
So glorious; his teeth into large fangs,
Sharpened for gnawing steel; his hands and feet
Into four various claws; into a hide
Of black that shining skin of pearl; while from
His bristled back two dragon wings did sprout.
Alas! the proud Archangel, whom but now
All Angels honored here, hath changed his shape
Into a hideous medley of seven beasts,
As outwardly appears: A lion proud;
A greedy, gluttonous swine; a slothful ass;
A fierce rhinoceros, with rage inflamed;
An ape, in every part obscene and vile,
By nature lewd and most lascivious;
A dragon, full of envy; and a wolf
Of sordid avarice. His beauteous form
Is now a monster execrable, by God
And Spirit and man e'er to be cursed. That beast
Doth shrink to view its own deformity,
And veils with darkling mists its Gorgon face.

Wat green hier overal, waer't op een vlughten ging,
Een wilde woestheit, een gestaltverwisseling,
In leden en in leest! Men hoortze brullen, bassen.[31]

In Valvasone's *L'Angeleida*, the rebel angels had lost their pristine shapes before assembling for battle against the loyal spirits. Forfeiting their former beauty, they had assumed the forms of Harpies, Gorgons, Sphinxes, Hydras, Minotaurs, Centaurs, Chimeras, birds of ill-omen, satyrs, sea-beasts, and other monsters (pp. 37–39):

Puro candor di mattutin sereno
Allor che all' alba, il più temprato Maggio,
Amoroso piacer versa dal seno,
Non cominciò mai dì con sì bel raggio,
Ch' allo splendor, al candido che avieno
Gli angeli in sè, potesse far paraggio,
Allor che usciti dall' eccelsa mano
Di Dio, pargoleggiar nel ciel sovrano.

Ma poi che troppo in se medesmi intenti
Conobber mal la lor bellezza altera,
E non furo a sperar dubbiosi e lenti
Quel sommo onor che solo in Dio s'invera,
Tutte le membra lor, già sì lucenti,
Notte cosperse spaventosa e nera,
E mani e piè divini, ed ale e volti
Furon diversamente in bruti volti.

(pp. 36–37)

Lucifer had become a seven-headed monster with a hundred arms and a bull's tail—a hideous compound of Briareus (or Aegaeon)[32] and the dragon of the Apocalypse.[33]

Tra questi e quelli, empio gigante ed alto
Con cento braccia il crudo duce sorge;
Coperto il petto di ferrigno smalto,
Cinquanta scudi a sua difesa porge;
Arme cinquanta avventa al fiero assalto,

31. Cf. Van Noppen, p. 421:
What cries of pain now burst forth everywhere,
As from the fleeing hordes one hears, amid
This wild confusion and this change of form
In limbs and shapes, their roars and bellowings.

32. For this hundred-handed giant, who rebeled against Jupiter, see *Natalis Comitis Mythologiae* (Frankfurt, 1584), pp. 89–90.

33. Revelation 12:3: "a great red dragon, having seven heads and ten horns, and seven crowns upon his heads."

Ed in lui solo un gran misto si scorge
Di tutto il reo, di tutto il truce; e solo
Mostro è de' mostri del suo vario stuolo.

. . . .

Sovr' esso il nero e smisurato busto,
Sette teste il crudel corona d'auro,
Ma l'auro splende d'un colore adusto
Qual il volto miriam di fosco Mauro:
Gli cade poi dal deretan del fusto
Infin al suolo gran coda di tauro
Che 'l terzo dietro strascinando tragge
De' lumi ond' ardon le celesti spiagge.

Da' sette spechi delle bocche spira
Lezzo crudel che densa bava attosca:
Vibran quattordici occhi orribil ira
Dal fiero ciglio che lo sguardo imbosca:
Per le livide guance erra e s'aggira
Un sembiante sdegnoso, un' ira fosca
Che alberga in mezzo la Mestizia, e gli empie
Di serpentino crin l'orride tempie. (p. 42)

Valmarana's *Daemonomachia*, on the other hand, presented Lucifer's metamorphosis in two phases. While he was exhorting his troops before battle, horns burst suddenly from his forehead:

Erigit, haec fatus, bellantia signa superbus
Cornua, quae frontem tum primum visa minacem
Rumpere. . . .[34]

Afterwards, in the ensuing conflict with Michael, the two-edged sword of the Word of God destroyed his remaining beauty:

adversis radijs exarsit, & omnes
Exuit infelix formosae mentis honores
Lucifer, & quiquid [sic] *caelestibus hauserat oris,*
Angelicumque decus furiales vertit in artus:
Tum vero attonitus monstris, seque ipse per horrens . . .
Lucifer . . . solo iam nomine talis,
Evolat, oblitusque animi indignantia linquit
Sydera. . . . (pp. 28–39)

After his expulsion from Heaven, he had still to endure Nature's sarcastic comment on his altered appearance:

At qualis, quantusque venis? quam dispar ab illo,
Quem modo nutantes coeli timuere Tyrannum?

34. Odoricus Valmarana, *Primae Partis Daemonomachiae sive de bello intelligentiarum* (Bon., 1623), p. 25.

Quo decor egregius membris, suavesque colores
Totaque maiestas abijt? vigor igneus oris,
Ambrosijque nitor capitis, divesque thiaras
Quo abscessere loco? quidve est haec cornua fronti?
Formosos artus quis sic ferrugine pinxit?
Quis terror placido spoliavit lumine visus?

(p. 31)

VI

Despite minor variations as to the time and nature of Lucifer's metamorphosis, medieval and Renaissance writers and artists usually regarded his transformation as prior to, or simultaneous with, his fall. Paintings and literary versions of his rebellion and expulsion almost invariably depicted him as a deformed monster. Lorenzo Lotto's picture of "St. Michael Pursuing Lucifer" was one of the rare exceptions. Though falling headlong through space, Lucifer still retains his angelic form. "Contrary to the Renaissance tradition of representing Lucifer as a monster," declared Berenson, "Lotto shows him as an angel of great beauty."[35] Such an interpretation stands in striking contrast with the more conventional treatment of this subject by Raphael and Figino.

Milton's chief contribution to this tradition was an innovation in timing. Unlike his predecessors, who had conceived Satan's metamorphosis as simultaneous either with his revolt or with his fall, the author of *Paradise Lost* deferred the transformation of the rebel angels until after the temptation and fall of man.

This variation possessed several distinct advantages over the conventional chronology. In the first place, it reflected a shift in emphasis from Lucifer's rebellion in Heaven to his transgression in Eden. Though Christian tradition had usually interpreted the devil's deformity as a punishment for his initial revolt, Milton preferred to present it in a new light, as the penalty for an entirely different crime, the seduction of mankind. After all, he was writing not an *Angeleida*, but an *Adamo*. As his argument was not the angelic rebellion, but "Man's First Disobedience," it was both logical and appropriate that he should transfer Satan's metamorphosis from the revolt of the angels until after the fall of man. The former incident was only an episode rather than an integral part of the fable; the latter event marked the fulfillment of the epic action, the completion of the central event in *Paradise Lost*.

35. Bernard Berenson, *Lorenzo Lotto* (London, 1956), p. 133 and Plate 371. The painting is in the Palazzo Apostolico at Loreto.

Milton's altered chronology lent additional significance to Satan's serpentine form. In describing the rebel leader as a "monstrous Serpent" or dragon, Milton had, of course, the authority of Revelation 12:9 and 20:2 ("the dragon, that old serpent, which is the Devil, and Satan"), as well as the tradition represented by Guido delle Colonne and others.[36] In its new context, however, his shape possessed a special relevance to his felony in Eden. His punishment fitted his crime. As he was "punisht in the shape he sinn'd, According to his doom," his penalty recalled not only his transgression in Book IX, but also the divine verdict already pronounced on the serpent earlier in Book X. Since the nature, as well as the timing, of Satan's metamorphosis linked his disfigurement specifically with his primary action in the poem (the temptation of Eve), Milton had excellent reasons for depicting the fallen Archangel in serpentine form rather than in the more bizarre shapes described by Vida, Valvasone, and Vondel.

A second advantage of Milton's innovation in chronology was that it permitted him to reduce the infernal victory to its true dimensions—to reassert eternal Providence in spite of Hell's apparent triumph. The subject and genre of *Paradise Lost* made it virtually impossible to avoid conceding the devil a major, albeit temporary, victory. The Bible itself testified to the success of his strategy against Adam and Eve. On the other hand, his ultimate defeat by the Messiah necessarily lay outside the scope of the fable,[37] which covers a period of little more than a week. To have introduced Christ's future victories directly would have violated the unities of time and action;[38] they could only be indirectly foreshadowed or foretold. In order to mitigate the inevitable

36. See Huetius and Origen, *supra*. Cf. Wierus, col. 19: "Hic draco ille magnus, in terram proiectus cum suis angelis, serpens antiquus, qui vocatur Diabolus & Satanas, ut Ioannes ait, tortuosus serpens Esaiae." Richard Greenham (*Workes* [London, 1612], p. 845) observed that "The Divell is called *Daimôn* of his great knowledge and great experience . . .; for his forme and ugly shape, the Prince of darkenes; . . . for his hurting, a serpent: for his experience in hurting, an old serpent. . . ." In his poem "On the Morning of Christ's Nativity," Milton referred to Satan as "Th'old Dragon under ground," who "Swindges the scaly Horrour of his foulded tail."

Hughes (p. 93) has called attention to Origen's identification of Ophioneus ("the serpent deity, who—according to Pherecydes—led the Titans in an unsuccessful attack on Olympus" with the serpent who deceived Eve. Wierus (col. 19) makes the same identification: "Hunc [Diabolum] casum non solùm nostri & Hebraeorum Theologi docent: verùm etiam Assyrij, Arabes, Aegyptij & Graeci suis dogmatibus confirmant. . . . Pherecydes item daemonum lapsum describit: & Ophin, hoc est serpentem daemoniacum, rebellantis, & a divinae mentis placito deficientis exercitus caput & antesignanum fuisse tradit."

37. See also John Peter, *A Critique of Paradise Lost* (New York and London, 1960), p. 143.

38. For the principle of unity of action in the epic, see S. H. Butcher, *Aristotle's Theory of Poetry and Fine Art* (3rd ed.; London, 1902), pp. 35, 89–91. For unity of time in epic poetry, see R. A. Sayce, *The French Biblical Epic in the Seventeenth Century* (Oxford, 1955), p. 21; Ronsard, Chapelain, and several other critics and poets regarded a year as the maximum time limit for the epic action.

impression of demonic triumph, to invalidate Satan's temporary victory by exposing its ultimate futility, Milton resorted to literary artifice. Deferring Satan's transformation until the moment of success and thereby converting triumph to shame, he managed to divert emphasis from the devil's victory to the overruling power of Providence. The effectiveness of this scene depended largely on his mastery of timing.

Thirdly, the intrusion of divine judgment at this moment served to dissipate the illusion of heroism which still clung to the fallen Archangel. His degradation at the instant of declaring his success constituted a final, definitive verdict on his own merits and those of his enterprise. It unmasked his heroic pretense as vicious reality.

Fourthly, the episode acquired additional dramatic value through this sudden "reversal of intention." Aristotle had defined peripeteia as a "change by which the action veers round to its opposites" (Butcher, p. 41). This was one of the hallmarks of the "complex" type of plot (p. 39) which he preferred over the "simple" model (p. 45). The sudden reversal that reminded Waldock of the comic cartoon was actually a thoroughly respectable literary device. Behind it lay the authority of Aristotle and many of his Renaissance commentators.

The episode was a clear-cut example of "reversal of intention." Expecting applause, Satan received the opposite:

he stood, expecting
Thir universal shout and high applause
To fill his ear, when contrary he hears
On all sides, from innumerable tongues
A dismal universal hiss, the sound
Of public scorn. . . .

Thus was th' applause they meant,
Turn'd to exploding hiss, triumph to shame
Cast on themselves from their own mouths.
(lines 505–509, 545–47)

The scene met both of Aristotle's requirements for a peripeteia. It achieved surprise (Butcher, p. 43), and it avoided violating "our rule of probability or necessity" (p. 41). The element of surprise resulted largely from Milton's innovation in timing, probability from the long and well-established tradition of angelic metamorphosis.

Yet he had further enhanced its probability through adroit foreshadowing. The metamorphosis in Book X was not the first physical penalty that Satan and his peers had suffered for their sins. Even in the battle in Heaven, their bodies had grown "gross by sinning" (VI, 661) and vulnerable to pain (VI, 327). His expulsion from Heaven left him "chang'd in outward lustre" and with "th' excess of Glory obscur'd." Even though "his form had yet not lost All her Original brightness," it was nonetheless darkened. In Book IV, Zephon commented on his altered appearance:

> *Think not, revolted Spirit, thy shape the same,*
> *Or undiminisht brightness, to be known*
> *As when thou stood'st in Heav'n upright and pure;*
> *That Glory then, when thou no more wast good,*
> *Departed from thee, and thou resembl'st now*
> *Thy sin and place of doom obscure and foul.*
> (lines 835–40)

Gabriel likewise noted his "faded splendor wan." Satan's companions —"Thir Glory witherd"—suffered a similar diminution of luster.

Instead of completing Lucifer's metamorphosis at the time of his expulsion, Milton depicted his gradual degeneration in several stages: a grossness of texture as early as the angelic war; the partial obscuration of his brightness with his fall; and, finally, his transformation into a serpent at the conclusion of his enterprise against man.

19. "*Triumph to Shame*"

Satan's Humiliation and the Serpent's Doom

❦ The *crisis*[1] of *Paradise Lost* (if one uses the term strictly in its original sense) is literally the Son's sentence of *judgment* at the beginning of Book X. Containing *in potentia* the seeds of later developments presented indirectly through Michael's prophecies or directly through the fable, it foreshadows the contrary fates of man and devil. It looks forward not only to Adam's future redemption but also to the nature and mode of Satan's humiliation. The latter's transformation into a serpent and his compulsion to chew "bitter ashes" acquire verisimilitude and probability from the various details of the judgment already passed on the serpent as Satan's instrument. As Milton clearly informs us, Satan is "punisht . . . According to his doom"—an observation that links the scene of degradation with its antecedent, the scene of judgment:

> *Because thou hast done this, thou art accurst*
> *Above all Cattel, each Beast of the Field;*
> *Upon thy Belly groveling thou shalt goe,*
> *And dust shalt eat all the days of thy Life.*
> *Between Thee and the Woman I will put*
> *Enmitie, and between thine and her Seed;*
> *Her Seed shall bruise thy head, thou bruise his heel.*

First published, in somewhat different form, in (a) *Studies in Philology*, LIX (1962), 201–10; (b) *Journal of English and Germanic Philology*, LXIV, No. 1 (1965), 35–40.

1. See E. M. W. Tillyard, "The Crisis of *Paradise Lost*," *Studies in Milton* (London, 1951), pp. 8–52.

Although the curse applies literally to the serpent, its primary application is to Satan himself:

> *. . . yet God at last*
> *To Satan first in sin his doom appli'd,*
> *Though in mysterious terms, judg'd as then best:*

While the final clause of this "doom" must await the advent of Christ for fulfillment (XII, 383–433), the initial clauses are specifically "appli'd" to Satan in the transformation-scene of Book X, when ("punisht in the shape he sin'd") he falls "A monstrous Serpent on his Belly prone" and tastes "bitter Ashes," "soot and cinders." These details bear virtually the same relation to the curse on the serpent as does Michael's revelation to Adam in the final books of *Paradise Lost*. In both instances the ambiguity of the curse enables Milton to achieve surprise—the *maraviglia* that Tasso and other Italian critics regarded as the proper epic effect—without forfeiting probability. Just as the revelation of future redemption is based on the final clause of the curse,[2] the transformation-scene is founded, in large part, on the preceding clauses.

Since this scene is clearly an extension and application of the curse pronounced earlier in the same book, one may question the justice of Waldock's belief that it lacks a "valid development." Its "timing," moreover, is even more "masterly" than Waldock himself realized.[3] Milton introduces the metamorphosis at the very moment when Satan has openly defied the curse:

> *True is, mee also he hath judg'd, or rather*
> *Mee not, but the brute Serpent in whose shape*
> *Man I deceiv'd: that which to mee belongs,*
> *Is enmity, which he will put between*
> *Mee and Mankind; I am to bruise his heel;*
> *His Seed, when is not set, shall bruise my head:*
> *A World who would not purchase with a bruise,*
> *Or much more grievous pain?*

As Parish has observed, Satan realizes that the "sentence against the serpent . . . applies to himself (X, 332–45), but his report of this curse to his subordinates in Pandaemonium shows that his understanding is incomplete."[4] Despite his partial comprehension of the final cause of his "doom," he seems unaware that the *entire* curse is applicable to himself. The divine reaction to his boast is not only timely but also sing-

2. See John E. Parish, "Milton and God's Curse on the Serpent," *JEGP*, LVIII (1959), 241–47.
3. A. J. A. Waldock, *Paradise Lost and Its Critics* (Gloucester, Mass., 1959), pp. 91–92.
4. Parish, p. 243.

ularly pertinent. God enforces against him and his associates precisely those aspects of his sentence to which he had believed himself immune.

The theological basis of this scene is, then, the curse of Genesis 3:14, "upon thy belly shalt thou go, and dust shalt thou eat all the days of thy life." In this text, as interpreted by Reformation theologians, Milton found authority not only for applying the terms of the *entire* curse on the serpent to Satan, but also for his subtle exploitation of contrasting interpretations and for the primary emphasis of the scene— "triumph to shame," the deliberate humiliation of Satanic pride.

I

The punishment to which Satan and his companions are subjected acquires probability and verisimilitude from a theological tradition— that the curse of Genesis 3:14–15 applied literally to the serpent, but allegorically to Satan. According to John Diodati, the curse "is pronounced against the Serpent in a corporall sense, and against the Divell in a spirituall":

> The Serpent is condemned as a common enemy to all creatures, that he shal no more move with a body and head erected, nor walk openly and securely, as he did before; nor enjoy the good fruits of the earth, but shall hide himself in holes & caves, and lick the dust, and filth. The Devill receiveth either his first condemnation, or the confirmation of it: to be banished from heaven, driven under the earth, and into hell . . . deprived of all good, delight, and trust, loaden with confusion and despaire, and subject to have no other food, pastime nor entertainment, but in filthy, and wicked things, and actions.[5]

Peter Martyr Vermigli observes "how excellently the conditions of the serpent express the devil's nature and punishment": "The Devil was created upright by God, but he did not stand in the truth, and so he was cast down into the lowest places and the filthiest abodes of souls. For the Prince of this World is also called the Prince of Air and the Prince of Darkness, and is given up to the eternal fire. He delights in our vices, and indeed can almost be said to feed on them. Well, therefore, can it be said that he creeps on the earth like a serpent that has been cast down, as there is no hope that he will ever be lifted up again."[6]

According to Mercerus, the serpent was the type as well as the instrument of Satan, and the words of the curse applied "externally and

5. John Diodati, *Pious Annotations upon the Holy Bible* (London, 1643), p. 6. For Milton's knowledge of Diodati, Paraeus, Rivetus, and others, see Arnold Williams, "Milton and the Renaissance Commentaries on Genesis," *MP*, XXXVII (1940), 263–78; *idem*, "Renaissance Commentaries on 'Genesis' and Some Elements of the Theology of *Paradise Lost*," *PMLA*, LXVI (1941), 151–64.

6. *In primum librum Mosis, qui vulgo Genesis dicitur, commentarii . . . D. Petri Martyris Vermilii Florentini* (Tiguri, 1579), fol. 16.

literally" to the former as Satan's instrument, but "obscurely and mystically" to Satan himself, who was concealed in the serpent.[7] Paraeus maintains that the entire sentence is applicable to both Satan and the serpent. The words "upon thy belly shalt thou go and dust shalt thou eat all the days of thy life" are to be read, therefore, in a double sense. In their "higher sense" they refer to Satan.[8]

Similarly Rivetus observes that the curse may apply externally to the serpent, but allegorically (and principally) to Satan: "But . . . Satan is to be so understood in the serpent, and the punishments inflicted on Satan to be so announced in the penalties inflicted on the serpent, that one sense includes another. As is done in types . . ., the sense that concerns Satan is the principal sense, and the meaning chiefly intended by the Holy Spirit."[9]

This interpretation—enunciated by St. John Chrysostom[10] in his Seventeenth Homily on Genesis and elaborated by various Protestant theologians—is, in its essentials, the one Milton follows in *Paradise Lost*. While his description of the serpent's condition before the Fall makes it evident that the sentence of judgment applies literally to the beast, radically altering its posture and disposition, he places his primary emphasis on the extension of the curse to the devil.

Nevertheless, he also makes poetic capital of alternative interpretations. The force of the sudden reversal from "triumph to shame" lies not only in the fact that it is the probable or necessary consequence of the unfulfilled judgment, but also in the fact that it occurs unexpectedly.[11] The poetic value of the serpent's doom resides in its ambiguity, and Milton exploits its "mysterious terms" for the maximum of dramatic effect. Of the four members of the curse according to Paraeus ("1. Maledictio prae omnibus animalibus terrae. 2. reptatio super ventre. 3. pastus ex pulvere. 4. Inimicitiae cum homine serpenti lethales"),[12] Satan applies only the last to himself ("that which to mee belongs, Is enmity . . . between Mee and Mankind"). He is mistaken, of course, but his interpretation is identical with that held by many

7. *Joannis Merceri . . . In Genesin . . . Commentarius* (Genevae, 1598), p. 86.

8. *In Genesin Mosis Commentarius . . . Authore Davide Pareo* (Francofurti, 1609), cols. 567–72.

9. *Andreae Riveti . . . Theologicae & Scholasticae Exercitationes CXC. in Genesin* (Lugduni Batavorum, 1633), p. 172. Exercitatio XXXV ("An maledictio utrumque serpentem tam corporeum quam incorporeum feriat?"), pp. 171–76, also includes a discussion of the question "an gressus super ventre seu pectore sit serpenti naturalis, itemque an pulveris usus in cibo aut comestione fuerit serpentibus destinatus?" Rivetus observes that, whereas some theologians maintained that the serpent had possessed these characteristics before the Fall, others declared that it had originally walked erect and eaten herbs.

10. *Patrologia Graeca*, LIII, cols. 141–43. Both Pareus (col. 567) and Rivetus (p. 172) cite Chrysostom's interpretation.

11. Cf. Aristotle, *On the Art of Poetry*, trans. Ingram Bywater (Oxford, 1951), p. 45.

12. Pareus, col. 566.

Christian theologians. Several Protestant commentators take pains to refute this view. Mercerus notes that some divide "hanc sententiam ... ut pars in verum serpentem, pars in Satanam tantùm competat. Sanè non videntur illa primo loco posita, *Super pectus tuum ambulabis, & pulvere vesceris*, ullo modo Satanae convenire, sed serpenti duntaxat, ut eius natura ostendit. Rursum postremam illam partem, *& inimicitias ponam &c.* si de serpente ... intellexerimus, fraudabimus primos parentes & nos deinceps longè saluberrima promissione de Christo eos restituturos ... Atqui duas has huius sententiae in serpentem partes ita divellire, ut prior ad serpentem, posterior ad Satanam tantùm spectet, alienum videtur."[13] Paraeus observes that some recent commentators had divided these penalties, applying the first three to the actual serpent and the fourth to Satan alone.[14]

Satan's interpretation of the curse pronounced on the serpent is, then, no mere invention on Milton's part, but one of several alternative views conventional in Christian exegetical tradition, but specifically rejected by Paraeus, Rivetus, and Mercerus. The fact that he understands *part* of the sentence, recognizing in its final clause a reference to himself, throws into sharper relief his misinterpretation of its initial clauses. He underestimates the nature and extent of his punishment through regarding the first three penalties of his doom as exclusively applicable to the serpent, and he learns their true meaning only when they are actually enforced, miraculously, against himself. This reversal "contrary to expectation" is a Peripeteia accompanied by Recognition.

II

A further exploitation of exegetical tradition is evident in the particular values Milton stresses in this transformation-scene. If its theological basis is the allegorical curse against Satan, its keynote is humiliation. Applause is turned to the hiss of "public scorn," "triumph to shame." The illusory grove is designed "to work them furder woe or shame" (X, 555). Subsequently the devils are "yearly enjoin'd" to undergo this "annual humbling" in order "to dash thir pride" (X, 575–77). This emphasis on ignominy is likewise prominent in Christian exegetical tradition. According to St. John Chrysostom, "Est et hoc ineffabilis benignitatis Dei opus ... quia serpens quasi gladius quidam

13. Mercerus, p. 86.

14. Paraeus, col. 567. Cf. Rivetus, p. 172: "an hoc loco denunciata poena, vel serpentem solùm, vel Diabolum solùm, vel utrumque simul; vel partem comminationis, unum, partem aliam, alterum respexerit"; in support of the fourth opinion it could be argued that "nonnulla sunt quae ita ad serpentem verè referantur, ut Diabolo nullo modo quadrare possint, ut, quod *maledictus sit prae reliquis animalibus &c.* Alia etiam quae ita Satanam respiciunt," such as the war with the woman's seed.

diaboli servivit malitiae, perpetuam ipsi poenam infligit, ut per hoc quod sub sensum et sub aspectum cadit, intelligamus in quanta ignominia sit diabolus. Nam si is qui ut instrumentum ministravit, tantam expertus est indignationem, quale supplicium verisimile est suscepturum diabolum?"[15] Ignominy is the keynote of Mercerus' reading of Genesis 3:14,[16] and Rivetus interprets the same text as a reference to the devil's "supreme abjection and ignominy"—the fitting penalty for his pride and thirst for glory.[17]

By a skillful use of significant detail Milton constructs his transformation-scene out of a fusion of literal and allegorical interpretations

15. *Patrologia Graeca*, LIII, col. 141; cf. col. 143, "Et hoc quidem de visibili serpente: licet volenti postea considerare scriptorum seriem, et cognoscere si de sensibili serpente haec dicta sunt, multo magis accipienda esse de spirituali serpente. Etenim et illum pedibus nostris subjecit humiliatum, et id praestitit ut nos ejus capiti incumbamus."

16. Mercerus, p. 88: "Nunc verò in poenam peccati, & detestationem Satanae motoris serpentis hoc ipsi serpenti in ignominiam perpetuam cessit, ut super pectus ambularet & terra vesceretur . . ., ut quia velut sese erigere & attollere serpens aut in eo Satanas voluerat ad perdendum hominem, iam ita deinceps condemnetur ut sese attollere non possit, sed humi repat, per eam sese trahat, & non altiùs supra terram cibum quaerat aut sumat, sed ex terra ipsa supra quam non sese possit erigere. Cabalici hoc exponunt, quòd Satanas, de quo posteà in sensu mystico agemus, non posthac sit habiturus potestatem in animam, sed in corpus tantùm quod pulvis est."

17. Rivetus, p. 175: "Sed existimarem aliter esse Satanae applicanda comminationis verba, ut quae ad literam de serpente dicuntur & ei convenient, per quandam analogiam ita ad Satanam pertinerent, ut ipsius analogiae haberemus Scripturam interpretem. Nuper dicebamus gressum illum serpentis, & pulveris esum, aut per phrasim illam *lingere pulverem prono in terram capite*, summam abjectionem intelligi. Ut etiam Esai. 29. v. 4. post pronunciatam maledictionem contra Ariel *Humiliaberis* (inquit) *de terra loquêris, & de humo audietur eloquium tuum, & erit quasi Pythonis de terra vox tua, & de humo eloquium mussitabit.* Ubi est descriptio hominis victi, prostrati, extrema passi, aut extrema saltem metuentis. Qui enim in eo articulo sunt, neque hiscere audent coram hostibus, demisso vultu & strati humi. . . In his & similibus locutionibus habemus descriptionem summae miseriae & abjectionis. Satanam esse superbissimum spiritum, nemo qui artes ejus novit dubitare potest, & communis est omnium ferè Theologorum sententia, ob superbum indebitae gloriae & dignitatis appetitum, coelo fuisse deturbatum. . . . Nulla igitur potuit ipsi gravior infligi poena, quam si ignominia, subjectio, contemptus, & abjectio summa, quam anteà commeritus fuerat, & ex parte passus, confirmaretur & adaugeretur, adeò, ut praecisa ipsi omni spe veniae & restitutionis, pedibus etiam ipsorum hominum conculcaretur, & humi velut repens & pulverem lingens, victoriam infirmis hominibus quos se prostrasse putabat, concedere cogeretur. Tu ergo Satan, qui primos in coelo gradus & honores affectasti, qui homini gloriam quam amiseras invidisti, super pectus tuum gradieris & pulverem linges, id est victus & prostratus, subjicieris iis quos perdere voluisti, & in summam abjectionem & ignominiam detruderis illorum hominum more quorum victores colla premunt, & qui hostium à quibus sunt devicti pulverem pedum humi prostrati lingunt. Haec applicatio mirificè convenit cum sequentibus, de inimicitiis, & victoria seminis mulieris."

Cf. *ibid.*, p. 174: "Ex hac serpentis maledictione Proverbium ortum habet, *Lingua pulverem sicut serpentes*, Micheae 7. v. 17. de summa & extrema abjectione, & habitu eorum qui se victos fatentur, & à se verbera, plagas, aut gravem aliquam ignominiam supplices deprecantur, aut humillimum aliis & abjectissimum deferunt & profitentur obsequium. Hi enim abjiciunt se quam maximè possunt, ita ut humi strati terram toto corpore contingant. Sic Jesai. 49. v. 23. *Vultu in terram demisso adorabunt te, & pulverem pedum tuorum lingent.* Et Thren. 3. vers. 29. *Ponent in pulvere os suum, si fortè sit spes.*"

of the serpent's punishment. "Transform'd . . . suddenly into serpents, according to his doom giv'n in Paradise," Satan and his audience undergo *literally* the actual terms of the curse of Genesis 3:14. One clause of his sentence ("upon thy belly shalt thou go") receives concrete expression through his actual metamorphosis, when he falls "A monstrous Serpent on his Belly prone." In describing this transformation, however, Milton succeeds in giving poetic form to the *allegorical* interpretation of the curse—to the ignominy stressed by Mercerus and Rivetus. The "exploding hiss" the serpents utter, as a result of their metamorphosis, is also "the sound of public scorn," and as such it serves to crystallize the idea of shame. This detail, moreover, like the comparison of Satan to "Huge *Python*" (X, 531), recalls the text from Isaiah (29:4) quoted by Rivetus in his discussion of the curse, "erit quasi Pythonis de terra vox tua." Similarly, in the *Midrash Rabbah*, the serpent utters "cries" as the curse is enforced against him: "When the Holy One . . . said to him, *Upon Thy Belly Shalt Thou Go*, ministering angels descended and cut off his hands and feet, and his cries resounded from one end of the world to another. Thus the serpent comes to throw light upon the downfall of Babylonia and is itself illumined thereby, viz. *The cry thereof shall go like the serpent's* (Jer. xlvi, 22)."[18]

III

In applying to Satan the next clause of his doom ("and dust shalt thou eat"), Milton introduces a variation on Genesis 3:14, as well as on his own version of the curse earlier in Book X. His infernal serpents chew "cinders" and "ashes" and "soot" rather than "dust." Nevertheless, this detail should be regarded rather as an elaboration of the Biblical judgment than as a contradiction. According to one medieval commentator, the text ("Et terram comedes") could refer to either dust or ashes: "In hebreo habetur asphar . i . favillam vel pulverem"[19]—an explanation possibly influenced by the close similarity between the Hebrew words עָפָר (dust) and אֵפֶר (ashes).[20] The *Zohar* mentions a type of dust (*abaq*) which "was not ordinary dust, but ashes the residue of fire" and which "differs from dust proper in that it is sterile and unproductive."[21] The "Argument" to Book X of *Paradise Lost* declares that the devils ate dust as well as ashes; "deluded with a shew of the forbidden Tree springing up before them, they . . . chew dust and

18. *Midrash Rabbah*, trans. H. Freedman and Maurice Simon (London, 1939), I, 162.

19. *Textum Bibliae, cum Postilla Domini Hugonis Cardinalis* (Parisiis, 1530?).

20. See Samuel Lee (ed.), *A Lexicon, Hebrew, Chaldee, and English* (London, 1844), pp. 27, 49, 471.

21. *The Zohar*, trans. Harry Sperling and Maurice Simon (London, 1932), II, 151.

bitter ashes." "Dust and ashes" are similarly linked together in St. Augustine's account of the "apples of the country of Sodom."[22]

Milton's variation possesses two obvious advantages over the Biblical "dust." First, it enables him to exploit the legend of the Dead Sea apples and thus to represent the serpent's punishment[23] as a parody of the temptation of man. Secondly, the Biblical association of ashes and delusion (Isaiah 44:20, "He feedeth on ashes: a deceived heart hath turned him aside, that he cannot deliver his soul, nor say, Is there not a lie in my right hand?") lends further emphasis to the motif of illusion, a theme that was implicit in the "apples of Asphaltis" myth and that Milton himself develops in detail (X, 557, 563–64, 571).

A further debt to the exegetical tradition concerning Genesis 3:14 appears in the allegory of Sin and Death. While Satan and his peers are chewing cinders, his vicegerents are gorging themselves on "the draff and filth Which man's polluting Sin with taint hath shed" (X, 630 ff.). This diet recalls the type of food various commentators had attributed to Satan.[24] According to St. Gregory the Great, "Terram ... comedit, quia peccatores quaerit & depascitur, eisque ut cibo gaudet." In St. Jerome's opinion, "diabolum, qui priùs hominum mortibus pascebatur eos tantùm comedere, qui pulvis ac terra sunt, id est, homines terrenos." Others believed that "mysticè pulverem ei cibum esse, quia in coelis nulla ei haereditatis spes reliqua est, ut homini electo, sed de coelo praecipitatus damnatur, ut perpetuó humi in sordibus terrenis repat, cum impurus ille spiritus non modo ipse se inquinamentis mundi conspurcat & oblectat, ut sus in volutabro, sed & reprobos iisdem, secum immergit ac perdit." The filth of crimes and iniquities (Paraeus adds) is "suavissimus Satanae cibus," and he devours it "sicut immundus porcus pascitur excrementis."[25] Milton utilizes this traditional interpretation of the serpent's doom, but transfers it from Satan himself to his progeny.

IV

By these innovations on tradition Milton reconciles the conflicting demands of verisimilitude and the epic marvelous. The Biblical and exegetical tradition underlying the scene was twofold. It not only gave the poet authority for the Archangel's metamorphosis into a dragon but

22. St. Augustine, *The City of God*, trans. John Healey, ed. R. V. G. Tasker (London and New York, 1957), II, 324.

23. The verbal similarity between "Asphaltis" or "Lake Asphaltites" and the Hebrew word עָפָר in Genesis 3:14 may also have been a contributing factor to Milton's exploitation of the myth of the Dead Sea apples at this point.

24. Rivetus, p. 175, cites (but rejects) these opinions.

25. Paraeus, col. 572; cf. Diodati, p. 6, and Vermigli, fol. 16.

also linked Satan's doom with all of the principal clauses of the judgment pronounced on the serpent.

The innovations, on the other hand, consisted largely in timing and in embellishing the scene with details derived from classical sources. History contributed the Dead Sea apples to which Milton alludes in his reference to the fruit "which grew Neer that bituminous lake where *Sodom* flam'd." Mythology offered both a general analogy in the metamorphosis-tradition, where the wrong-doer is appropriately punished in a shape emblematic of his vice,[26] and a more specific parallel in the myth of Tantalus, who was likewise "deluded with a [false] shew" of fruit.[27]

In investigating the literary antecedents of this scene, scholars have stressed the tradition of the Dead Sea apples, described by Josephus, St. Augustine, and others.[28] Yet the implicit relationship with the Tantalus myth may be equally significant. Whereas the Dead Sea apples are not usually presented as an infernal torment, the fruit of the Tantalus legend, like that of Milton's epic, sprang from the soil of Hell. "Parcht with scalding thurst and hunger fierce," the devils of *Paradise Lost* suffer the same pangs as Tantalus. As in Tantalus' case, these torments of "famine" and thirst are intensified by the spectacle of delusive fruits (or, more specifically, apples) which tease the appetite, but leave it unsatiated. Finally, like Tantalus, they suffer a punishment that fits the nature of their crime. Having sinned by inciting others to partake of forbidden food, they are plagued with hunger in the midst of tempting "Frutage." The scene represents, therefore, a skillful fusion of mythology and natural history. In Milton's Hell the apples of the Tantalus myth are cross grafted with those of the Dead Sea and the tree of knowledge.

Though accounts varied as to the exact nature of Tantalus' crime and punishment, he was commonly supposed to have offended the gods by offering them human flesh to eat or, alternatively, by stealing their nectar and ambrosia and bestowing these on mortals. In return, he was punished in Hell by the spectacle of apples and water which eluded his

26. See Douglas Bush, *Mythology and the Renaissance Tradition in English Poetry* (new rev. ed., New York, 1963); Davis P. Harding, *Milton and the Renaissance Ovid* (Urbana, 1946); Erich Krause, *Die Mythen-Darstellungen in der venezianischen Ovidausgabe von 1497* (Würzburg, 1926). For further discussion of Satan's serpentine shape, see Merritt Y. Hughes, "Satan 'Now Dragon Grown' (*PL*, X, 529)," *Etudes anglaises*, XX (1967), 357–69; Irene Samuel, "The Valley of Serpents: *Inferno* XXIV–XXV and *Paradise Lost* 504–577," *PMLA*, LXXVIII (1963), 449–51; Mother Mary Christopher Pecheux, O.S.U., "'O Foul Descent!': Satan and the Serpent's Form," *SP*, LXII (1965), 188–96.

27. See "The Argument" to Book X of *Paradise Lost*.

28. See Kester Svendsen, *Milton and Science* (Cambridge, Mass., 1956), pp. 28–29; Josephus, *The Jewish War*, trans. H. St. J. Thackeray (London, 1928), 143–45. The scene also complements an earlier allusion to the Tantalus myth in Book II, where the water of Lethe "of it self . . . flies / All taste of living wight, as once it fled / The lip of *Tantalus*" (612–14).

grasp and taste and left him tormented by hunger and thirst. For the Renaissance, these aspects of the myth were familiar through classical sources—Homer, Pindar, Ovid, Propertius, Petronius, Seneca, and others—and through contemporary mythographies.[29]

The *Odyssey* describes Tantalus as "standing in a pool" with water "nigh unto his chin. . . . And trees, high and leafy, let stream their fruits above his head, pears, and pomegranates, and apple trees with their bright fruit, and sweet figs, and luxuriant olives. But as often as that old man would reach out toward these, to clutch them with his hands, the wind would toss them to the shadowy clouds."[30] The variety of fruits Homer describes is not characteristic of later versions of the myth. For Ovid, Propertius, and Seneca the fruits are "*poma*," and this conception is shared by many Renaissance scholars.[31] Thomas Wilson notes "the strange plague of Tantalus, who is reported to be in helle, havyng Water commyng still to his chinne, and yet never hable to drincke: and an Apple hangyng before his mouthe, and yet never hable to eate."[32] Cooper's *Thesaurus* and Elyot's *Bibliotheca* declare that "hee is in hell tormented in this wise: He standeth by a fayre river, having before him a tree laden with plesaunt Apples, and yet he is alwayes thirstie and hungrie: for as often as he stoupeth to drinke, or holdeth by his hands to gather the Apples, both the water and the tree doe withdraw them so from him, that hee cannot touch them."[33] According to Thomas, "Tantalus, . . . who for disclosing the secrets of the goddes, was tormented in hell with hunger & thirstines, not withstanding stood in a river up to the chin, and had goodly aples hanging over his nose continually."[34] The "Index of the Hardest Words" in Sylvester's translation of Du Bartas' *La Sepmaine* describes Tantalus as

29. *Paulys Real-encyclopaedia der classischen Altertumswissenschaft*, Neue Bearbeitung, ed. G. Wissowa, W. Kroll, and K. Mittelhaus (Stuttgart, 1932), *s.v. Tantalos; The Odes of Pindar*, trans. Sir John Sandys (London, 1915), pp. 7–9, 11. Cf. Carolus Stephanus, *Dictionarium Historicum Geographicum, Poeticum* (Oxonii, 1671), *s.v. Tantalus.* For Milton's knowledge of Renaissance dictionaries, see D. T. Starnes and E. W. Talbert, *Classical Myth and Legend in Renaissance Dictionaries* (Chapel Hill, 1955), pp. 226–339.

30. Homer, *The Odyssey*, trans. A. T. Murray (London, 1924), I, 429 (Book XI, ll. 582–92).

31. Cf. C. Stephanus, "poma fugacia captat Tantalus" (Ovid); "Pomaque quae nullo tempore tangat, habet" (Ovid, Amor. lib. 3. eleg. 6); "Tantaleo poterit tradere poma manu" (Propert. 2.1); "Perit unda in ore: poma destituunt famem" (Seneca in Herc Fur.); Ovid, *The Art of Love*, trans. J. H. Moxley (London, 1929), p. 117, "quod frustra captatis arbore pomis Garrulus in media Tantalus aret aqua"; J. P. Valerianus, *Hieroglyphicorum collectanea ex veteribus et neotericis descripta* (Lugduni, 1626), p. 366, "Nec bibit inter aquas, nec poma patentia carpit Tantalus" (Petronius).

32. Thomas Wilson, *The Arte of Rhetorique* (London, 1562), fol. 100.

33. Thomas Cooper, *Thesaurus Linguae Romanae & Britannicae* (Londini, 1584), *s.v. Tantalus*; Sir Thomas Elyot, *Bibliotheca Eliotae* (London, 1548), *s.v. Tantalus*; cf. *Natalis Comitis Mythologiae* (Genevae, 1641), pp. 624–29.

34. *Thomae Thomasii Dictionarium* (Cantabrigiae, 1596), *s.v. Tantalus.*

"a king of Phrigia, whome they fayned to stand in Hel up to the chin in water, & to have delicate Fruites dangling over his upper lipp, yet can touch neither: either to ease his hunger, or allay his thirst."[35] In Saltonstall's translation of Ovid's *Heroides*, Leander complains that

> *I catch at Apples which from me doe flie*
> *Like* Tantalus, *or the streame which glides by,*[36]

And Paris boasts to Helen of his family's superiority to the house of Atreus:

> *Nor yet our great Grandfather catcheth after*
> (*Like unto* Tantalus *in the* Stygian *water*)
> *Apples and water, which are both so nigh*
> *His lips, and yet from his touch'd lips doe flie.*[37]

Like Tantalus, the devils are punished both by elusive water and by delusive fruit, which exacerbate their hunger and thirst. Besides this similarity in their torments, there is a further parallel in the nature of their sin. Milton likens the "tasted fruit" to a "*Thyestean* banquet" —a comparison even more applicable to the feast Tantalus had spread before the gods. Similarly, with its "ambrosial smell" (IX, 852) and supposed properties of divinity, the forbidden fruit Satan offers Eve is comparable to the nectar and ambrosia Tantalus had stolen from the gods and given to men.[38]

Even more significant, however, is the parallel between the myth and the poem in their treatment of the crime-and-punishment relationship. The most striking feature of the "penance" imposed on the

35. Iosuah Sylvester, *Bartas: His Devine Weekes and Workes* (London, 1605), "A briefe explanation of most of the most-difficulties through the whole worke," *s.v. Tantalus.* The same explanation is reprinted in the 1641 edition.

36. Wye Saltonstall, *Ovids Heroicall Epistles. Englished by W.S.* (London, 1639), p. 137. Cf. *Pub. Ovidii Nasonis Heroides* (Venetiis, 1542), fol. lxx: "Velle quid est aliud fugientia prendere poma"—a passage which Ascensius, Ubertinus, and other commentators interpret as an allusion to the Tantalus myth: "sum, inquit, Tantalo similis: ille ut Homerus scribit poma capiti imminentia: & aquam abluentem conspicatur barbam. Et . . . siti fameque perpetua vexatur"; "Fugientia prendere poma more Tantali."

37. Saltonstall, p. 112. Cf. *Heroides* (1542), fol. lix: "Nec proavo stygia nostro captantur in unda Poma." The commentaries apply this passage to Tantalus: "Captantur in unda poma: ad Tantalum Pelopis patrem hoc refert: qui sitibundus in media aqua: exuriensque, cum ad verticem omnis generis poma habeat, nec bibere: ned famem sedare datum est"; "Inde Tantalus hac poena damnatus. apud inferos dicitur: ut nec undis: nec pomis tangentibus ora perfruatur."

38. See C. Stephanus "Alii, ut Tzetzes ac Didymus, putarunt hanc poenam irrogatam Tantalo, quia nectar & ambrosiam suius aequalibus impertiverit"; Spondanus (*Homeri . . . omnia*, p. 169), "Didymus noster & Tzetzes existimant Tantalum, qui in Deorum convivia admittebatur, aliquando Nectar & Ambrosiam ijs surripuisse, eamque coaetaneis suis impertivesse"; *The Odes of Pindar*, p. 11, "he stole from the gods the nectar and ambrosia, with which they had made him immortal, and gave them to the partners of his feast."

devils is its exaggerated resemblance to the crime in Eden. The instruments whereby Satan tempted Eve to transgress are, in turn, magnified and multiplied and converted into instruments of torture for the devil himself. Not only is Satan "punisht in the shape he sin'd," but the comparison between the forbidden tree and the delusive grove in Hell is emphasized repeatedly. The fruit is "like that . . . in Paradise, the bait of *Eve* / Us'd by the Tempter." For "one forbidden Tree" they imagine "a multitude / Now ris'n, to work them furder woe or shame." They fall "oft" into "the same illusion, not as Man . . . once lapst." Their humiliation is specifically designed "To dash thir pride, and joy for Man seduc'd," and they are "like in punishment, / As in thir crime."

Several Renaissance writers find an analogous relationship between Tantalus' punishment and his crime. Spondanus declares that Tantalus was afflicted with perpetual hunger and thirst because of the cruel and inhuman feast he had prepared.[39] Carolus Stephanus observes that Tantalus was punished with a perpetual desire for food because he had contaminated the food of the gods.[40] Holyoke emphasizes the parallel between the "loathsome" feast Tantalus had offered the gods and the equally "distastefull" banquet they gave him in return: ". . . on a time hee entertaining some gods, to make triall of their Divinity, killed and dressed, and served up his sonne *Pelops* at the feast, which fact the Gods after they had descried, they so abhorred; that for the loathsome banquet he made them, they made him one as distastefull, for hee was set in water to the chin, and apples bobbed him on the lips, yet had he no power to stoope to the one to quench his thirst, nor to reach up to the other to satisfie his hungry appetite."[41]

Tantalus and Satan are alike punished with delusion for assaying to delude others. For tempting others, both are tempted with illusory fruit. Tantalus had sought "to make triall" of the gods' divinity; Satan had tempted Eve. The mythical king and the Biblical devil are both "like in punishment, / As in thir crime."

39. *Homeri quae exstant omnia* (Basileae, 1606), p. 169: "Quidam dicunt eum aliquando Deos hospitios excepisse, Pelopemque filium, vel quod Deorum providentiam experiri vellet . . . : vel quod inde epulas lautiores arbitraretur, cum filium sibi omnium rerum charissimum Dijs epulandum traderet, in convivio exhibuisse. Quod Dij cum intellexissent . . . Tantalum ad inferos detruserunt, & propter tam cruentum & inhumanum convivium, ibi eum perpetuo famis & sitis tormento addixerunt."

40. Stephanus, *Dictionarium*: "Fuerunt qui dixerint Deos aliquando in hospitio ab hoc fuisse acceptos, qui cum lautum convivium illis parasset, Pelopem filium caesum inter caeteras epulas apposuit. . . . Verum quia Deorum epula humana caede contaminasset, perpetuo epularum desiderio ad inferos addictus est, qui tamen praesentes lautissimo regioque apparatu semper habet epulas, neque ullo pacto illas potest attingere, quamvis insatiabili fame excruciaretur."

41. Francis Holyoke, *Dictionarium Etymologicum Propriorum Nominum* (London, 1633), *s.v. Tantalus.*

In fusing the legend of the Dead Sea apples with the Tantalus myth, Milton had been anticipated to some extent by Edward Browne. In his *Sacred Poems, or Briefe Meditations*, Browne associates "drunken Tantalus" with the glutton plagued by the Dead Sea apples among the damned in Hell:

> *See drunken Tantalus doth rore for thirst,*
> *Yet to his chin in water so accurst*
> *He lies and howles, and cannot get a tast*
> *And dying lives, yet's dying life doth last.*
> *See how the Glutton cryes, and longs for meate,*
> *Yet* Sodom's *Apples he doth daily eate.*
> *It seems they doe not fill his hungry maw.*[42]

Unfortunately, Browne's lines are so ambiguous that it is uncertain whether he is actually identifying "drunken Tantalus" with "the Glutton" or presenting him as a separate personification of Drunkenness. If one can accept the former alternative, then the passage is remarkable for equating the elusive fruit of the Tantalus legend specifically with the Dead Sea apples. But even in the light of the second alternative, the verses are still significant. Like *Paradise Lost*, they transplant the Dead Sea apples from Palestine to the soil of Hell. Like *Paradise Lost*, they represent perpetual hunger in the sight of food as one of the torments of the damned. Finally, like *Paradise Lost*—but unlike most versions of the Tantalus myth—they depict the actual eating of the delusive fruit. Traditionally Tantalus does not succeed in even clutching—much less in eating—the illusory apples. In Browne's poem, however, as in *Paradise Lost*, the fruit is seized and devoured, but does not satisfy hunger.

The striking parody of the temptation of man which Milton achieves through this skillful fusion of the Tantalus myth and the Dead Sea apples accentuates the contrast (already enunciated in Book III) between God's punishment of the fallen angels and His merciful treatment of fallen man. Whereas man had been deceived by one tree, the devils are deluded by a multitude. Whereas man fell once through the deceptive fruit, the devils fall "oft" into the "same illusion." Whereas man is to find grace, the devils are condemned to perpetual remorse—a penance whose etymological sense is implicit in the central action of this scene; the fallen angels must "*chew*" their bitter ashes over and over again "with hatefulest disrelish." As in the case of the Hell Hounds who "gnaw" Sin's entrails in Book II, Milton's symbolism reflects the literal meaning of "remorse."

42. Edward Browne, *Sacred Poems, or Briefe Meditations* (London, 1641), p. 14.

By means of this parody Milton gives further development and emphasis to the motif of the reversal from "triumph to shame." In Book IX the serpent and the forbidden fruit were the instruments whereby Satan had achieved a world conquest; in Book X they become the instruments of his punishment. Ironically his humiliation consists in a magnified, but distorted, re-enactment of his victory. The apple of which he had boasted (X, 487) serves to aggravate his penance.

In thus utilizing a show of the forbidden fruit as an instrument of divine punishment, Milton could also draw on the current association of the apple with divine wrath. According to Bythner's *Clavis Linguae Sanctae*, the English and German words for this fruit echo a Hebrew phrase signifying the wrath of God:

Allusivè sed appositè tamen potest huc referri Anglic. *an apple*, & German. *ein apfell, pomum*, quod pomum sit quasi אַף־אֵל *ira Dei*, habito scil. respectu ad primi peccati memoriam, juxta illud: *Adam primus homo damnavit secula pomo.*[43]

As an instrument of divine wrath the delusive "Frutage" is less violent than thunder, but more telling, as it is directed against the devils' most vulnerable spot—their pride.

V

"Satan does not degenerate . . . ; *he is degraded.*" At most Waldock's observation is a half-truth. If Satan seems debased because he alters his tactics and discards violence for guile, the primary responsibility rests with Milton's Biblical sources. In presenting his shift from force to fraud, the poet was following scriptural tradition.

Though this change in tactics involved a comparable shift in epic prototypes—a partial substitution of the Ulysses-pattern for that of Achilles or Turnus—it did not violate heroic decorum or the conventional *ethos* of an epic hero. The heroic idol is just as specious in the fallen commander who glories in his strength as in the cunning dissembler who prosecutes his enterprise by guile. In either case the defeated Archangel embodies only the "semblance" rather than the "substance" of heroism.

In terms of this false ideal Satan remains superficially heroic throughout the poem; he does not degenerate. Yet by Christian standards his apparent heroism is at best a "splendid vice," and at worst brutishness. In terms of Christian morality he not only remains falsely heroic throughout the narrative, but also inevitably deteriorates ethically. In the course of the fable he rededicates himself to evil in a series of positive moral decisions, and thus forges himself the invisible chains that fetter

43. Victorinus Bythner, *Clavis Linguae Sanctae* (Cantabrigiae, 1648), p. 5; cf. Genesis 3:18.

his will and bind him (without hope of escape) to Hell. Through frequent reiteration the evil qualities he has displayed earlier, in the angelic revolt and immediately after his fall—pride, ambition, disobedience, envy, malice, revenge—become moral habits. They reshape, redefine—and deform—his character.

Behind these renewed affirmations of an evil purpose lie ethical presuppositions that Milton shared with Aristotle—the conception of virtues and vices as habits strengthened by repetition, and the interpretation of character in terms of moral purpose and decision (*proairesis*).[44]

The pattern for the Archangel's progressive degeneration is firmly established at the very beginning of the poem. In his first address he refuses to "repent" or to "sue for grace." In his second speech he explicitly commits himself to "ill" as the "contrary" of God's will:

> *If then his Providence*
> *Out of our evil seek to bring forth good,*
> *Our labor must be to pervert that end,*
> *And out of good still to find means of evil. . . .*

This is the primary ethical intent underlying his epic enterprise—the destruction of man in order to "spite" the Creator—and the moral purpose it involves is substantially the same as that he enunciates later in his soliloquy on Mount Niphates: "Evil be thou my Good. . . ." Notwithstanding this similarity, several critics still cling tenaciously to the opinion that the former speeches are "heroic" and the latter "degraded."

The soliloquy culminates in Satan's fresh dedication to evil, after considering (for the first time) the alternative possibility of repentance. Earlier he had categorically ruled out this possibility, and now he considers it only to reject it. The speech concludes with an act of *proairesis* that reaffirms his original intent. On Niphates he reveals essentially the same moral purpose as beside the burning lake.

A similar rededication to evil distinguishes two of his later soliloquies. His first glimpse of Adam and Eve awakens milder thoughts. Still later, even at the very instant of beginning the temptation, the sight of his victim's beauty temporarily diverts him from his purpose, allaying his hatred and arousing "wonder," "pleasure," and even a suggestion of "love." Momentarily it bereaves "his fierceness of the fierce intent it brought" and leaves him "stupidly good," "abstracted . . . from his

44. Cf. Aristotle, *Nicomachean Ethics*, trans. W. D. Ross (London, 1954), p. 29, ". . . by doing the acts that we do in our transactions with other men we become just or unjust . . . brave or cowardly. . . . Thus, in one word, states of character arise out of like activities." For Milton's conception of *proairesis*, see John F. Huntley, "*Proairesis, Synteresis*, and the Ethical Orientation of Milton's *Of Education*," *PQ*, (1964), 40–46.

own evil." On both occasions, however, these milder sentiments only temporarily distract him from his "fierce intent," and in rejecting them he strengthens his former purpose and hardens his heart and will. Confronted by moral alternatives, he makes the same decisions as earlier—and entrenches himself still more deeply in crime.

Milton delineates the Satanic *ethos*, then, primarily in terms of a sequence of moral choices. Each of these confirms the devil's overruling purpose and brings him a step nearer to its "probable" result—the temptation of Eve. The "heroic energy" that has impressed many critics as the salient aspect of his character, results in large part from a combination of several factors. First, the plot itself has been conceived and constructed in terms of Satan's enterprise—its inception, its execution, and its punishment. Secondly, the enterprise itself has been presented as the object of Satan's moral purpose, the "probable" and "necessary" consequence of his character. Thirdly, at most of the crucial points in the development of the fable, he voluntarily reaffirms his original intent. His character and action throughout the plot are dominated by revenge, and this intent he pursues as inexorably as Achilles, with a constancy and an energy that in other contexts might indeed be heroic.

A similar development marks his resort to fraud and his choice of the serpent as the most appropriate instrument for his purpose. Compelled at various points in the fable and episodes to disguise his intent, his identity, or his tactics, he displays relatively early in the poem the qualities of character, thought, or action that subsequently dominate his "fraudulent" temptation of Eve. In portraying them so soon in the narrative Milton was preparing the foundations for Satan's subsequent actions, endeavoring to make the devil's behavior in the crucial scene appear plausible and necessary, the "probable" consequence of his character and thought.

Although Satan's resort to guile is consistent with a hero of the Ulysses type, it nevertheless represents a deterioration in character from a Christian viewpoint. In electing to pursue his enterprise by fraud rather than by force, Satan sinks from bad to worse—from crimes of violence to crimes of malice. Primarily it is in this sense that he can be said to "degenerate." Yet it is not until the transformation-scene that he tastes (*literally* tastes) the inevitable penalty. Then for the first time he is indeed "degraded."

VI

Satan's degradation is not an afterthought. In the structure of the fable it occupies a position only slightly less significant than the scenes of temptation and judgment. Nor is it inconsistent with the heroic idol;

the illusion and the exposure are complementary, not contradictory. As with Spenser's Duessa, falsehood impersonating truth and vice masquerading as virtue must be stripped. Satan's ultimate exposure was inevitable. After postponing his metamorphosis (conventionally associated with the angelic war) and investing him with the arms, the character, and indeed the very role of an epic hero, Milton was virtually compelled to "degrade" him.

The quasi-heroic scenes of the early books and the comic metamorphosis of Book X are actually as inseparable as the two faces of a single folio. One is the reverse of the other, but they are still two aspects of the same thing. Milton could scarcely have given us the "heroic" Archangel of Books I and II unless he had deferred Satan's transformation until a later point in the narrative. If we accept the portrait in the early books we must also accept the transformation-scene, for both are made possible only by Milton's innovation in timing. We cannot have our cake, and eat it too.

Both, finally, are Milton's own inventions, and as such they testify to his skill as poet or "maker." The brevity of his Biblical sources and the complexity of exegetical tradition alike afforded him opportunity to "invent," freedom to exercise his own originality. This, in the context of Renaissance poetic theory, was what it meant for a poet to imitate and to "feign."

The pseudo-heroic archangel of the early books and the "ridiculous" devil of the transformation-scene represent (in part at least) the poet's response to problems posed by neo-Aristotelian criticism—the problem of achieving gravity, elevation, and variety within the epic genre; the problem of maintaining consistency and verisimilitude in character; the problem of making an evil *persona* both "appropriate" and "good." It is scarcely surprising, therefore, that Milton's "anti-hero" seems a many faceted figure. Tragic, heroic, comic—he is all of these, and contemporary criticism can ignore his diversity only at its own peril. Moreover, all three of these aspects were, in varying degrees, conventional. Medieval and Renaissance drama had not infrequently degraded the devil to a comic buffoon, the butt of slapstick jokes or the dupe of ingenious conjurors. Yet an "archangel ruined" is nonetheless a tragic personage, and more than one Renaissance tragedy had introduced him as such, either as antagonist or protagonist. Renaissance epic, in turn, had portrayed him occasionally in heroic terms as a warrior, the valiant and redoubtable adversary of Michael.

For Milton neither the tragic nor the heroic vision was complete. Only the comic mode could expose the vanities of the builders of Babel, the abstruse absurdities of the astronomers, or the futility of Satan's ambitious conspiracies. To emphasize the deformity of sin, the ugliness of vice, the poet resorted (as Renaissance theory directed him) to the Ridiculous. Though the comic elements in his epic are not obtrusive, he exploited them deliberatively—even "methodically"—as a form of moral judgment, a device for introducing the divine estimate of character and action.

The comic technique underlying the transformation-scene is all the more effective because Milton uses it so sparingly. Though he could have presented Satan in a comic light throughout the poem, he did not (fortunately) choose to do so. A consistently ridiculous devil would not only have violated epic decorum, but also have spoiled the comic impact of the metamorphosis. As it stands, the scene is a superb example of consistency in *ethos* and variation in style. It complements, even as it destroys, the product of Milton's calculated irony—his portrait of the pseudo-hero, his Satanic *eidolon*.[45]

45. Although the authority for Satan's form as serpent or dragon is Biblical, Milton may also have encountered the classical tradition that associated the serpent specifically with the hero. In his *Life of Cleomenes* Plutarch observed that "the men of old time associated the snake most of all beasts with heroes." Photius, in turn, explained that speckled snakes were called heroes (*s.v.* ἥρος ποικίλος). If Milton was aware of this tradition, he would have relished the additional irony it lent to his heroic *eidolon*. (See Jane Harrison, *Prolegomena to Greek Religion* [3rd ed.; New York, 1959), pp. 325 ff., for a discussion of this tradition.)

❦

Appendixes

Index

❦

Appendix I

Renaissance Definitions of the Hero

❦ Renaissance definitions of the hero emphasize his merit—the magnitude of his deeds and virtues and his excellence in warfare or in the arts and sciences. According to Robertus Stephanus, *Thesaurus Linguae Latinae* (Basileae, 1586), *s.v. Heros*, "Heroes dicuntur ij qui quum sint homines, rebus tamen gestis eam opinionem apud vulgus emeruerunt, ut inter divos relati creduntur. Proinde heroes in quavis arte & scientia dici possunt, qui in ea plurimum excellerunt." Ambrosius Calepinus, *Dictionarium undecim linguarum* (Basileae, 1598), *s.v. Heros*, defines the hero as "*A passing excellent man in vertue and noblenesse, half a god.*" "Dicti autem sunt à veteribus heroës viri nobiles & illustres, qui mortales quum essent, rerum tamen à se gestarum magnitudine, quàm proximè ad deos immortales accesserunt, eamque apud vulgus opinionem meruerunt, ut post mortem in deorum numerum credantur relati, quales ij fuerunt, de quibus fabulatur antiquitas altero parente Deo, altero mortali prognatos esse." Lucian had defined the hero as one "qui neque homo est, neque deus, & simul utrumque est." Servius had explained the term as meaning "vir fortis, semideus, plus ab homine habens. . . ." (Stephanus, *loc. cit.*)

Various etymologies were suggested for the word. According to Calepinus, "Sunt enim qui heroëm dictum putent ἀπὸ τοῦ ἐροῦ τῆς ἀρετῆς: hoc est, ab amore virtutis. . . . Augustinus . . . ἀπὸ τῆς ἥρας: hoc est, à Junone, primumque nescio quem ejus filium Heroëm appellatum. Hoc videlicet mysticum significante fabula, quod aër Junoni deputetur, ubi volunt cum daemonibus Heroas habitare. Quo nomine appellant alicujus meriti animas defunctorum." Augustine applies the term *hero* to aerial souls ("animas aërias") between the sphere of the moon and the region of storms and winds. (Calepinus, *loc. cit.*) According to Stephanus, "Gaza putat deductum esse ab ἔρω. Plures tamen ab ἥρα, id est Junone."

Hesychius (*s.v.* ἥρως) explains the term as meaning "mighty, strong, noble, venerable" (δυνατός, ἰσχυρός, γενναῖος, σεμνός); see Jane Harrison, *Prolegomena to the Study of Greek Religion*, (3rd ed.; New York, 1959), p. 333. According to the *Etymologicon Magnum*, ed. Marcus Musurus (Venetiis, 1499), *s.v.* Ἥρωες, heroes were the "ancient, first-born men," "men who were demigods" (ἡμίθεοι ἄνδρες). The *Etymologicon* lists the conventional etymologies—from the earth, from love, from discourse—and records the tradition that heroes sprang from the union of gods and mortals.

Thomas Cooper, *Thesaurus Linguae Romanae & Britannicae* (Londini, 1578), *s.v. Heros*, defines the hero as "He that for the love of vertue sustayneth great labours and travailes, or he that doth things for excellencie above man's condition. A passing excellent man in vertue and noblenesse. halfe a god." As examples, he cites Virgil's "magnanimi heroes" and Statius' "semidei heroes." Cf. *Heroicus*, "Noble or pertaining to noble men" and *Herois*, "A passing noble woman."

The *Lexicon Latinograecum Vetus*, ed. Henry Estienne (*Glossario duo*, *s.l.*, 1573) equates the heroes with lares; *s.v. Lares familiares* (Ἥρωες κάτοικίδιοι).

A more extensive definition appears in Henry Estienne's own *Thesaurus Graecae Linguae* (*s.l.*, 1572) *s.v.* Ἥρως: "Heros, Semideus. Qui ex deo & homine natus credebatur, aut reliquos homines virtute sua ita superabat ut ad deos proximè accedere vinderetur, ob eamque post mortem in divorum numerum referretur: tanto homine praestantior quanto deus daemone. . . . Zenon apud Laertium lib. 7, heroas vocat solutas corporibus animas sapientum: & Pythagoras apud eundem totum aera censet plenum esse animis, eosque & daemonas & heroas existimari." According to Philo's *De mundo*, "Alias animas constitutionem diviniorem sortitas, ab omni terrestri situ cogitatione abhorrere: at quae sint earum purissimae, eas verò opinio est excelsissimo in loco apud aetherem ipsum stationem habere. quas qui in Graecia philosophari instituerunt, heroas & daemonas apellavere." Estienne cites a variety of etymologies for the term—from *love*, *speech*, *earth*, *air*, and *Juno*: "Caeterùm quod ad etymon attinet, Plato in Cratylo ab ἔρως derivat, (quoniam heroes ex diis deabusve mortalium amore captis nati putabantur, aut vicissim ex mortalibus deum itidem amore captis) vel ab *εἴρειν* hoc est *λέγειν*, quoniam *σοφοὶ ἦσαν καὶ ῥήτορες καὶ δεινοὶ καὶ διαλεκτικοί, ἐρωτᾶν ἱκανοὶ ὄντες.* Alii derivare maluerunt ab *ἔρα* id est terra, quòd partim è terrenis & mortalibus hominibus orti essent. Alii ab *ἀήρ*, quoniam (ut Hesiodus habet) *ἠέρα ἑστάμενοι πάντη φοιτῶσιν ἐπ' αἶαν.* Augustinus ab *ἥρα*, id est Juno, quòd ei aer deputetur, in quo inter lunae gyrum & nimborum ac ventorum cacumina, aeriae istae animae, lares, genii, heroesque isti, hoc est alicuius meriti defunctae animae, degere creduntur."

Charles Estienne's *Dictionarium Historicum Geographicum, Poeticum*, Editio Novissima, ed. Nicolas Lloyd (Oxonii, 1671), *s.v. Heroes* defines the term conventionally as noble and illustrious mortals who had merited deification, according to popular opinion: "*Heroes*, dicti sunt à veteribus viri nobiles, & illustres, qui mortales cum essent, rerum tamen à se gestarum magnitudine, quam proximè ad deos immortales accesserunt, eamque apud vulgus opinionem emeruerunt, ut post mortem in Deorum numerum credantur relati, quales fuerunt semidei illi, de quibus fabulatur antiquitas, quos altero parente Deo, altero mortali, prognatos credebant." He derives the word from Greek words for *earth*, *air*, *speech*, *Juno*, *love*, etc. According to Servius, "Heroas quidam à terra dictos volunt, quod terra *ἥρα* [*ἔρα*] dicta sit, unde initio nati creduntur homines, qui nomen à matre traxerunt." Martianus Capella assigns them a position between the mountains and the middle air and gives the same etymology: "A medietate aeris, usque in montium, terraeque confinia, hemithei heroesque versantur, qui ex eo quod Heram (*lege* Eran) terram veteres dixerunt, Heroes nuncupati." Plato's *Cratylus* derives them from love (*ἀπὸ τοῦ ἔρωτος*), "ab *amore*, quòd videlicet Heroes vel ex amore eorum erga mulieres humanas, vel amore virorum erga Deas sunt geniti." But Plato also derived the word from the verb *to speak* (*ἀπὸ τοῦ εἴρειν*), "*dicere*; Antiqua enim, ut ait Atticorum lingua *ἥρωες* ii, qui dicendi, seu interrogandi facultate valerent, appellati sunt. Itaque Oratorum, quod addit, & Sophistarum genus, est Heroica natio." St. Augustine and Isidore cite the etymology from Hera (Juno), "nempe quia aer est dicatus Junoni, ac *heroes* putantur post obitum in aere cum daemonibus habitare." Hence Philo, in his *De mundo*, writes that the Greeks used the terms *heroes* and *daemons* for the beings that Moses called *angels*, "qui inter Deum & Homines medium locum obtinent, sc. inter Coelum & Terram." Thales applied the term *heroes* to "hominum animas jam separatas corporibus."

Charles Estienne is, however, skeptical of all these Greek etymologies and prefers a derivation from "Chaldean" (i.e., Aramaic): "Atque haec ostendunt, ut se torserint Graeci in hujus vocis etymo. Sed verisimile est id vocabulum originem potius Chaldaeis debere. Nam his חורן dicuntur *nobiles, liberi candidati* ἥρωες, uti docet Fabricius in Dictionario Syro-Chaldaico."

Tasso's prose works offer several definitions of the hero and his divine paternity. According to the dialogue *Il Messagiero*, the tutelary deity (or angel) who endowed the hero with superlative gifts of nature is metaphorically called his father: "As he grows in age and reveals his valor, he is called *hero* and regarded as superior to other men. Hence he is believed to be rather the son of some god than of a man; for the special providence that this god had exercised in his birth merits the name of father or protector. Hence Homer assigns certain gods to his chief heroes—Achilles, Agamemnon, Ulysses—as companions in danger. The word *hero* derives from the Greek word for *love*, because the love between God and man is the cause of his birth." (Tasso, *Prose*, ed. Francesco Flora, Milan, 1935, pp. 60–62.)

Another dialogue *Il Cataneo* likewise raises the question of definition. Are heroes 1) "sons of the gods," 2) "souls separated from the body and become demons, as the Platonists affirm," 3) "rhetoricians and eloquent speakers"? None of these conventional definitions pleases Cataneo. Heroes are "those who resemble Codrus, who was willing to die for his country and acquired immortal fame" and men like "Brasidas, Miltiades, Cimon, Themistocles, Alexander, Mutius, Horace, Epaminondas, Agesilaos, Pyrrhus, Camillus, Scipio, and Caesar, whose virtue seems to far surpass the human condition." Yet the name also belongs to the "martyrs of Christ." If the word "derives from *love*, it fits them better than any others, for no love was so ardent as that which impelled them to death." Hence charity is a virtue proper to heroes; it is "eroica senza fallo; ma d'altri eroi, ed in altro modo più maraviglioso e divino, che non conobbero le nazioni gentili." (Tasso, *Prose*, ed. Flora, pp. 196–97.)

Tasso's derivation of the word *hero* from love and the conception of the hero as "rhetorician" both stem from Plato's *Cratylus* (*Plato*, trans. H. N. Fowler [Loeb Classical Library; London and New York, 1926], VI, 57): "for the name [ἥρως] has been but slightly changed and indicates their origin from love (ἔρως). [They] were all born because a god fell in love with a mortal woman, or a mortal man with a goddess. . . . And either this is the reason why they are called heroes, or it is because they were wise and clever orators and dialecticians, able to ask questions (ἐρωτᾶν), for εἴρειν is the same as λέγειν (speak). Therefore, when their name is spoken in the Attic dialect (*ΗΕΡΟΣ*), . . . the heroes turn out to be orators and askers of questions, so that the heroic race proves to be a race of orators and sophists."

The association of *heros* and *eros* also recurs in Bruno's *De gli eroici furori*. Frances A. Yates, *Giordano Bruno and the Hermetic Tradition* (Chicago, 1964), pp. 279–82, interprets these *furores* in terms of the "supreme Hermetic experience" which renders the soul "divine and heroic"; they are "the *furor* of Venus interpreted as the means whereby man becomes the *magnum miraculum* of the *Asclepius*, having miraculous powers and living in consort with the race of demons to which he himself belongs in his origin."

Appendix II

Heroes and Daemons

❦ In the Pythagorean and Neo-Platonic traditions, the relative position of *heroes* and *daemons* shows marked variations. In the *Golden Verses of Pythagoras*,[1] the heroes are second to the gods in importance and precede the daemons. Cf. John Hall's translation, in *Hierocles upon the Golden Verses of Pythagoras* (London, 1657), fol. a 4:

> *Worship th' immortall Gods, as by the Law*
> *They are establish'd . . .: let the illustrious race*
> *Of Heroes be ador'd in th' second place.*
> *Then the terrestriall Princes* [daimonas], *whose decrees*
> *Claim thy observance. . . .*

According to Hierocles' commentary (p. 9), "these Poems assigne the first place to the IMMORTALL GODS, the middle to the ILLUSTRIOUS HEROES, and the last to the GODS OF THE EARTH. . . ." Heroes "are plac'd in the middle station of rationall Substances, filling the whole Orbe of Beings, next and immediately under the immortal Gods; but preceding humane nature, and so knitting together the extreams of the highest and lowest Substances":

> The middle sort both in essence and quality are those *Illustrious Heroes*. These ever contemplate the Creatour, and are glorious in a life resembling his, but not

1. For Milton's knowledge of Hierocles, see *Works* (Columbia Edition; New York, 1931–38), XVIII, 307.

so perfectly and immutably. For, being united unto God in a middle nature, and seated in a posture uncapable of evil, they turne and move towards him by different waies and motions, contracting and dividing the united theory of the principall [substances] making the last of that intuition to initiate them into a knowledge of those mysteries. Now these are very rationally said to be Illustrious *Heroes*, as being alwaies good, alwaies cover'd with splendor, and uncapable either of evil or forgetfulnesse. Now those are *Heroes* that are favorits [of God] passionately devoted and enjoying a friendly conversation with him. These raise and retrieve us from the sordidnesse of humane life, and introduce us into divine policy. And these are commonly called good Spirits, as being skilfull and understanding the Divine Laws, and so we call them Angells [or *Embassadors*] as convaying unto us the rules of living happily, But we frequently making use of a Triple notion, divide the generality of the second station into three kindes; & that which is immediately substituted to the Heavenly [*Substances*] we call Angells, but that which descends to the more Terrestriall, *Heroes*: for those which are seated the middle of either extreams, we call *Spirits*, as *Plato* frequently instances; but some comprehend the whole middle Orb in one of the terms we have specifi'd, calling them all Angells, or Spirits, or Heroes; & that for the Reasons we have instanc't before. Now we have been told, that *Illustrious Hero's* doth inclusively comprehend all that order, as Ectypes of the first generation, as flame witnesses fire, and the Son resembles his Father. . . . (pp. 20–24)

Hierocles draws a distinction between the ethereal *daemons* of the second sphere and earthly *daemons* or "Terrestriall Princes":

Those souls of men that are beautifi'd with truth and virtue, are here call'd *Δαίμονας* [*Spirits* or Princes] as knowing and Masters of Science; & so distinguishing them from those *demones* that are situated in the second sphere of Essences, he calls them TERRESTRIALL, as enabled to govern upon earth, to *inform* or assist humane bodies, and remain upon the earth . . .: for the first [species] is Heavenly, the second Aethereall: now consequently all men being Terrestriall, as being of the third series of rationalls, they are not all knowing, nor all wise, & therefore he very pertinently call'd wise men, TERRESTRIALL PRINCES. (pp. 24–25)

Hierocles' distinction between "terrestriall" daemons and daemons of the "second sphere" represents an attempt to bring the *Golden Verses* into line with the conventional belief concerning the relative rank of heroes and daemons. As Miss Harrison has observed (*Prolegomena*, p. 349), "As early as Hesiod, theology attempted some differentiation between heroes and daemons; daemons being accounted divine in some higher sense." Plutarch's *De Defectu Oraculorum* (*Moralia*, trans. F. C. Babbitt [Loeb Classical Library; London and Cambridge, Mass., 1936], V, 415) summarizes the traditional order: "Hesiod was the first to set forth clearly and distinctly four classes of rational beings: gods, [daemons], heroes, in this order, and, last of all, men; and as a sequence to this, apparently, he postulates his transmutation, the golden race passing selectively into many good divinities, and the demigods into heroes." Others "postulate a transmutation for bodies and souls alike; . . . from men into heroes and from heroes into [daemons] the better souls obtain their transmutation." Plato's *Laws*, trans. R. G. Bury, ([Loeb Classical Library; London and New York, 1926], I, 297–99) assigns divine honors in the following order: 1) "the Olympians and the gods who keep the State," 2) "the gods of the underworld," 3) the daemons, and 4) the heroes. In Hesiod's *Works and Days*, trans. Hugh G. Evelyn-White ([Loeb Classical Library; London and New York, 1929], pp. 11–15) the men of the golden age become *daemons*, "pure spirits dwelling on the dearth, and . . . kindly, delivering from harm, and guardians of mortal men. . . ." The generation of the silver age become "blessed spirits of the underworld." After the men of the bronze age (who "loved the lamentable works of Ares and deeds of violence") followed a fourth generation, "which was nobler and more righteous, a god-like race of hero-men who are called demigods" and fought at Thebes or Troy:

> ἀνδρῶν ἡρώων θεῖον γένος, οἳ καλέονται
> ἡμίθεοι. . . .

Iamblichus, like most Neo-Platonists, ranks the *daemons* above the *heroes*. Cf. *Iamblichi Chalcidensis . . . de mysteriis*, trans. Thomas Gale (Oxonii, 1678), pp. 8 ff. In his spiritual hierarchy the gods precede the daemons, and these are followed, in order, by heroes and souls (p. 9). For differences in their natures, powers, and operations, see pp. 39 ff. For the different apparitions of the orders in this hierarchy—gods, archangels, angels, daemons, archontes, heroes, and souls—see pp. 41 ff. Gale's note calls attention to the conception of heroes as "animas à corpore separatas" and observes that Thales, Pythagoras, Plato, and the Stoics held the same opinion (p. 189).

Appendix III

Mazzoni on the Nature of the Hero

❦ Renaissance theory and practice comprehended a wide variety of diverse and sometimes contradictory conceptions of the hero. In particular, the idealized figure of Platonic and Aristotelian tradition seemed incompatible with the spotted or even vicious character of the usual epic protagonist. In Plato's opinion, Homer had flagrantly dishonored the heroes and gods by investing them with human frailties. Jacopo Mazzoni,[1] in his *Della Difesa della Comedia di Dante*, Part I (Cesena, 1687), pp. 23 ff., describes this as an error in poetic imitation. Since poetry is imitation, it is an "essential error" for a poet to represent an object as other than it really is:

Stabiliscasi dunque per ferma, e risoluta conclusione, che il genere della Poesia sia l'imitatione, e conseguentemente, ch' ogni specie di poesia faccia Idoli, & Imagini nel modo che si è gia insegnato. E perche la drittura della imitatione, . . . coll' autorità di Platone, consiste nel rappresentare le cose appunto, come sono, però segue che fallo essentiale in Poetica sia il rappresentarle diversamente e con dissimilitudine. Il qual fallo fù nomato da Proclo nel principio delle quist. Poetic. μιμῆσθαι ἀνομίως, cioè *imitare dissimilmente*. E per questo parve, che Platone stimasse nel 2. della Republi. c' Homero peccasse essentialmente nella imitatione, rappresentandoci molti brutissimi vitij de' Dei, e de gli Heroi, dovendo fare egli tutto il contrario, s' havea da rappresentare colla sua dritta

1. For Milton's knowledge of Mazzoni and Tasso, see *Tractate of Education*; Langdon, *op. cit.*; and my "Milton and Mazzoni," *Huntington Library Quarterly*, XXIII (1960), 207 ff.

imitatione la natura Divina, e l'Heroica. È dunque errore essentiale. *Quando quis* (dice Platone) *verbis nudis fingit, quales Dij, & Heroes sint, instar pictoris nulla ex parte similia figurantis ad ea quae imitari conatur*. . . . E Proclo nel principio delle quist. Poet. havendo dimostrato, che li Poeti hanno usata imitatione dissimile nell' esprimere la natura de' Dei, e degli Heroi, soggiunge . . . *Bisogna, che l'Imitatore tribuisca concetti proprij alle attioni, e che l'imagini di quelli sieno fatte con molto consiglio, e sieno scelti quei nomi, che sono più convenienti a concetti.*

Nevertheless, Mazzoni draws a sharp distinction between philosophical and poetic conceptions of the hero. The former is a purified soul, the latter a soldier notable primarily for military fortitude (Part I, pp. 399 ff.):

. . . la virtù Heroica si può prendere in due modi, cioè, o secondo il senso Philosophico, o secondo il senso Poetico. È la virtu Heroica secondo il senso Philosophico, quella che ha tutte le qualita descritte da Aristotele nel settimo dell' Ethica, e da Plotino nell' Eneiade prima, il quale nomina la virtù Heroica; virtù d'animo purgato, e da Macrobio nel sogno di Scipione. E perche parve agli antichi, che questa virtù fosse di tanta perfettione, di quanta non potesse in alcun modo esser capace l'anima rinchiusa nell' invoglio delle membra terrene, però si lasciarono volontieri molti di loro indurre a credere, ch' ella havesse il suo vero soggetto nell' anime separate da questo corpo, e dimoranti sotto il Concavo della Luna. E per questo S. Agostino parlando dell' Heroe ha cosi detto. *Nomen Heroum à Iunone dicitur tractum, quia graecè Iuno Hera appellatur. Et ideo nescio quis filius eius secundum Graecorum fabulas, Heros fuit nuncupatus, hoc videlicet mysticum significante fabula, quod aer Iunoni deputetur, ubi volunt cum Daemonibus Heroas habitare*. E altrove pur nelli medesimi libri. *Inter Lunae girum nimborum, ac ventorum cacumina aereas esse animas: sed eas non oculis videri, & vocari Heroas, & Lares, & Genios*. Mercurio Trismegisto anchora ha nel Pimandro scritto, che gli Heroi habitano la purissima parte dell' aere, dove non arrivano le nebbie, Al qual parere si sottoscrive Iamblico ne' Misterij degli Eggittij. Tale è dunque il sentimento della voce Heroe nelle schole de' Philosophi, e specialmente Platonici.

In the poetic sense, however, heroic virtue consists entirely in military fortitude:

Ma secondo il senso Poetico non contiene la virtù Heroica altro, che la fortezza militare, e massimamente de que' Soldati, che nelle prime guerre fatte da Greci, o fra loro, o con Barbari, si scopriro più di tutti gli altri valorosi. E per questo Philostrato nel libro, ch' egli inscrisse *Heroica*, trattando a punto di quelli, che veramente Heroi sono stati nomati, ha fatta solamente mentione di quelle persone principali, che si trovano alla guerra Troiana. Hora simili persone furo scelte per conveniente soggetto del Poema Heroico, di che si fa piena fede Horatio in que' versi,

Res gestae, Regumque, Ducumque, & tristia bella
Quo scribi possent numero, monstravit Homerus.

E poi in un certo modo fu anchora communicata da' Poeti la voce d'Heroe a gli altri valorosi soldati, che non furo tanto antichi, di modo che li Poeti, c'hanno di quelli poetato, sono stati reputati degni del nome di Poeta Heroico.

The proper subject for the heroic poem is, then, "the noble actions of valiant soldiers. The reason is that the ancients believed that military fortitude was the only virtue, or at least superior to the others." Hence the Greeks referred to fortitude as ἀρετή, and the Latins called it *Virtus*. "[A]ppo li Poeti sono Heroi nomati quelli, c'hanno la fortezza militare."

This characteristic (Mazzoni continues) was regarded by poets as so essential to the heroic nature that they ascribed it not only to living men but even to the souls of the dead. The ancients tended to regard the spirits of the heroes as irascible and malevolent rather than as benevolent (pp. 402 ff.):

Questa vera, e sola proprieta de gli Heroi, secondo l' opinione de' Poeti, fu da' medesimi stimata tanto essentiale alla natura Heroica, che non ne vollero ancho privare l'anime separate da questo corpo, havendo essi in molti luochi de' suoi Poemi mostrato, che l'anime de gli Heroi ritenevano quella medesima fierezza, e superbia militare, nella quale s'erano habituate in questa vita. E per questo pare, che l'anime de gli Heroi fosseno piu tosto collocate da' Gentili nell' ordine de' Genij, de' malefici, che in quello de' benefici. . . . [L]a Virtù heroica, secondo l'opinione de' Poeti . . . non era altro, che una fortezza, o per parlare più propriamente, una bravura militare, la quale per se sola e, scompagnata dalla prudenza, è più tosto atta, a nuocere, & a distruggere, che a giovare, & a conservare la generatione humana. E mi pare c'Horatio descrivene interamente la natura di questa fortezza heroica in que' versi.

Scriptor, honoratum si forte reponis Achillem,
Impiger, iracundus, inexorabilis, acer,
Iura neget sibi nata, nihil non arroget armis.

Per questo dunque finsero anchora li Poeti, che per gli habiti contratti in questa vita, l'Anime degli Heroi ritenesseno dopo la separatione dal corpo la medesima inclinatione, e prontezza ad uccidere, & a distruggere gli huomini, c'havevano mentre ch'erano rinchiuse in questo corpo. E però furo da Poeti collocate nell' ordine, del quale fecero Capo Vegiove [il capo delli Dei cattivi], e passò poi questa opinione nella credenza di molti nobili Scrittori Gentili. Pausania . . . cosi scrive. *Heroum autem, & Deorum in homines irae praeter hoc Cleomenis, alia etiam reperiuntur exempla. Siquidem & Protesilaus, cui honores ad Eleusinem habentur, heros nihilo Argo clarior, per seipsum Persen Artabacten graviter est ultus: neque unquam Megarenses posteaquam sacrosanctum agrum colere ausi sunt, Deorum qui Eleusine coluntur, iram lenire potuerunt.*

After noting other examples in Pausanias and Philostratus of the ire displayed by the spirits of dead heroes, Mazzoni quotes the Scholiast on Aristophanes' *Birds* ("*Gli Heroi sono iracondi, e duri a quelli che egli accostano*") and Athenaeus' opinion that heroes appeared in the guise of "*Demoni iracondi, e nocivi*":

E stimano, che gli Heroi fosseno gravi, e crudeli ne'castighi, e più tosto di notte, che di giorno. Adunque perche paresseno cattivi non per propria natura: ma per l'ebrieta, li dipinsero colle coppe grandi in mano.

Suidas had similarly observed that "*gli Heroi sono più pronti a far male, che bene.*" The ancients believed that "the souls of dead heroes were disposed rather to harm than to benefit men."

In Mazzoni's opinion, the major genres were directed towards different classes of society—tragedy to "princes, magistrates, and powerful men," comedy to persons of "stato basso, e mezano." But the heroic poem was primarily "directed towards soldiers" (pp. 65 ff.):

accioche per mezzo delle virtuose attioni de gli Heroi rappresentate in quello, essi fossero, come da pungente stimolo di gloria punti ad imitarle.

Heroic poetry thus served the state as an instrument of military instruction and persuasion:

E perche bisognava anchora, che la facolta civile pensasse alla eruditione militare, accioche nelle occasioni delle guerre fosse la Repub. atta a potersi difendere, pero parmi, che si possa probabilmente pensare, che a questo fine la medesima facolta civile facesse nascere il Poema Heroico, nel quale s'haveesse [*sic*] a celebrare la soprana fortezza de gli Heroi, e specialmente di quelli, che sprezzaro generosamente la morte a pro della Patria, a fine che rimarando li nostri soldati simili essempi, fossero conseguentemente più pronti a sprezzare li pericoli della morte, per salute e per augumento del publico bene.

Index

Q

R

S